Global Awareness

Global Awareness

Thinking Systematically about the World

Robert P. Clark

ROWMAN & LITTLEFIELD PUBLISHERS, INC.
Lanham • Boulder • New York • Oxford

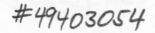

ROWMAN & LITTLEFIELD PUBLISHERS, INC.

Published in the United States of America
by Rowman & Littlefield Publishers, Inc.
A Member of the Rowman & Littlefield Publishing Group
4720 Boston Way, Lanham, Maryland 20706
www.rowmanlittlefield.com

PO Box 317, Oxford, OX2 9RU, United Kingdom

British Library Cataloguing in Publication Information Available

Library of Congress Cataloging-in-Publication Data
Clark, Robert P., 1940–
 Global awareness : thinking systematically about the world / Robert P.
Clark.
    p. cm.
Includes bibliographical references and index.
 ISBN 0-7425-1592-3 (cloth : alk. paper)—ISBN 0-7425-1593-1 (pbk.:
alk. paper)
 1. Globalization. I. Title.
 JZ1318.C59 2002
 363.7'009'051—dc21

2002004593

Printed in the United States of America

♾™ The paper used in this publication meets the minimum requirements of
American National Standard for Information Sciences—Permanence of Paper
for Printed Library Materials, ANSI/NISO Z39.48-1992.

This book is dedicated to Gizelle Mirentzu Fournier and Genevieve Lorraine Fournier, my connections to the future.

Vilma Iraheta wanted to send something special to El Salvador for her father's birthday. So she flipped on the computer in her suburban Maryland home and typed *elsalvadorpizza.com*.

Click, click, click, and her order was placed. On Wednesday, a Pizza Hut employee on a motorcycle roared up to her father's home 1,900 miles away in El Salvador with two Giant Pizzas—from Vilma in Washington, with love.

"The Internet is beautiful," declared Iraheta, a D.C. corrections employee.

—Mary Beth Sheridan, "Sending Back More than Love and Money: Internet Lets Immigrants Shop Abroad," *Washington Post,* December 23, 2001

Contents

List of Figures		xi
Preface		xiii
Chapter One	Thinking about the World as a Single Place	1
Case Study One	*Thinking about the AIDS Pandemic*	23
Chapter Two	Global Awareness	36
Case Study Two	*Making Connections in the News: Endangered Species and Endangered Languages*	61
Chapter Three	Systems	70
Case Study Three	*What Determines the Price of Gasoline? The Global Energy System*	93
Chapter Four	Changing Systems	107
Case Study Four	*The Lake Victoria Disaster*	129
Chapter Five	Global Systems	137
Case Study Five	*Global Systems and September 11, 2001*	161
Chapter Six	Invisible Systems	174
Case Study Six	*Mexican Strawberries and Michigan Schoolchildren*	197
Chapter Seven	Globalization and Nation-State Politics	204

Case Study Seven   *American Labor Unions and the Cargo*
                     Container Revolution   235

Appendix One   A Glossary of Selected Terms   249

Appendix Two   Global Systems and the Structure of Cyberspace 255

Index   271

About the Author   285

Figures

CS 1.1	Trends in AIDS Cases and Deaths, 1981–2000	33
2.1	How the Internet Works	50
2.2	Causal Relationships during Phases of Demographic Expansion and Decline	51
2.3	The Biosphere	52
2.4	Contrasts between the Industrial/Mechanical Worldview and the Holistic/Systems Worldview	56
3.1	Elements of a Generic System	82
CS 3.1	Gasoline Pipelines in the United States	98
CS 3.2	Crude Oil Prices, 1860–1999	100
4.1	The Natural Growth of Complex Systems	119
4.2	Four Possible Scenarios as a Growing System Nears Its Limits	125
5.1	A Fundamental Dilemma: A Positive Feedback Loop with No Easy (or Cheap) Exit	145
7.1	Distribution of World Domestic Product, 1989 (Percent of Total to Quintiles of Population Ranked by Income)	206
7.2	Distribution of Population by Average Income, per Person, 1993	206
7.3	America's "Four-Party System"	213

Preface

This book is intended to raise the reader's awareness and understanding of global trends, forces, and events by showing him or her how to think about the world in systems terms. It is based on my experiences in teaching "global awareness" to university undergraduates for more than a decade. Through this book, I hope to share with others what I have learned about understanding globalization and its effects on our lives.

Sometime in the last quarter of the twentieth century, the Global System Paradigm began to emerge as an alternative way to interpret and explain world events. While numerous books and articles have examined globalization from almost every conceivable angle, these studies have for the most part not been grounded in the paradigm as a way of looking at the world. Thus, despite the flurry of interest in things global, the paradigm itself has not been easily accessible to university students and others seeking a better grasp of globalization. This book is offered as an attempt to make this paradigm more familiar, understandable, and accessible to the nonexpert.

1

Thinking about the World as a Single Place

KEY IDEAS IN THIS CHAPTER

In this book, **globalization** is defined as the process by which more and more people come to **experience the world as a single place.** This momentous transformation requires that we be able to **think globally,** that is, think about our world as a single, integrated entity. Thinking this way is not as easy as it sounds. To help us, we must call on a number of perspectives, approaches, or ways of thinking.

To be useful to us, a way of thinking must do the following:

- **Identify** the **important agents, actors, or units of analysis.**
- **Describe** the **important dynamics** or the ways these actors change over time.
- **Analyze** these changes, that is, identify their **causes and consequences.**

In this chapter, I discuss these perspectives or approaches:

- **Sociology: Globalization and Culture**
- **Economics: Globalization and the Multinational Corporation**
- **Biology: Globalization and the Biosphere**
- **History: Globalization and World Systems**
- **Futurism: Globalization and the World to Come**
- **Biography: Globalization in the Lives of Individuals**

Let us begin our study of how to think about globalization by considering for a moment a situation confronting a seventy-six-year-old doctor in rural China named Gao Yaojie.[1] Once one of her region's leading gynecologists, Dr. Gao has been called out of retirement to help younger physicians diagnose and treat the epidemic spread of the AIDS virus, HIV. Unlike the case in many other parts of the world where AIDS is found, in rural China the virus spreads through the practice of selling blood to illegal and unscrupulous blood collectors known locally as "blood heads." Some of the towns in Dr. Gao's area have the highest localized HIV infection rates in the world, in some cases reaching 20 percent.

We can certainly sympathize with Dr. Gao's plight, but what does it have to do with us? How are we to understand the complex connections between the deaths of Dr. Gao's patients and our lives? Dr. Gao is certainly confronting the consequences of global forces at work, and so we are all connected to her and her patients in some way. But what does it mean to say that we are "connected" to AIDS victims in China? In this book, the word *connections* will describe cause-and-effect relationships, but how can we know what the causal relationships are between each of us and Dr. Gao's patients? How can we grasp something so enormous and complex as the forces and institutions that connect us to these distant people? How, in other words, can we improve our ability to think about the world as a single place?

WHAT IS GLOBALIZATION?

Global forces play a critical role in our lives many times each day, often without our being aware of it. Global networks of production, distribution, consumption, and waste disposal are indispensable to the maintenance of the material quality of our lives. Global systems make it possible for populations, food, manufactured products, cultural objects, information, and many other things to move around the world in unprecedented volume and at unprecedented speeds. Global systems bring us fresh blueberries in New England in January and make tilapia (a fish native to East Africa) the "catch of the day" (actually taken from a fish farm in Central America) at an Italian restaurant in a Washington, D.C., suburb. Global communications media offer us video coverage in real time of the aerial bombardment of Baghdad and personal contacts around the world via the Internet. Global manufacturing facilities produce Christmas ornaments in China and athletic shoes in Vietnam. Global systems spread hepatitis from fieldworkers in Mexico to schoolchildren in Michigan and combine AIDS and tuberculosis in a dual epidemic across vast stretches of Africa and Asia. Global organizations include the 180 or so nation-state governments, the communications systems that carry information around the world, the several tens of thousands of multinational corporations that constitute the global economy, and the 4,800 international nongovernmental organizations registered with the Union of International Associations in Geneva, as well as about 600 transnational social movement organizations.[2]

Precisely because of its enormous range, scope, and complexity, globalization often seems far beyond our powers of perception, description, comprehension, and analysis. We need some new intellectual tools to help us think about such things. To provide you with some of these tools is the purpose of this book.

There are almost as many ways to define *globalization* as there are people who write about it. Roland Robertson, a professor of sociology at the University of Pittsburgh, has defined it as the process by which we come to *experience, or become aware of, the world as a single place.*[3] In other words, for Robertson globalization is a process by which we come to think about the world as a whole. Robertson's definition forces us to develop our ability to think about something that is almost incomprehensible: the world in its totality.[4]

Although we may think we have grasped such an enormous concept at the level of general principles, comprehension often eludes us when we read about people like Dr. Gao who are grappling with the impact of global forces in their daily lives. The case study that follows this chapter returns to this subject to illustrate how people think about a particular global phenomenon, the AIDS pandemic. In this chapter, we shall meet some people who have written about globalization and learn more about their perspectives and how they think about the world as a single place. We shall then be better prepared to consider the perspective advanced in this book beginning in chapter 2.

Let us begin by recognizing that the world cannot be experienced directly as a single place. By *directly* I mean empirically or through direct observation. We are confined within a sensory "prison" that permits us to experience directly only that extremely tiny portion of our world that is near to us in time and space. The world is simply too complex, too big (or, at times, too small), or too far away to be thought of holistically. Our world is too distant in the past to be grasped in its entirety, too far into the future to be predictable. Thus, if we are to think about the world as a single place, it will have to be done indirectly. Because our own senses are inadequate for such a task, we will have to acquire the mental tools necessary to experience the world indirectly. Our kit will include verbal tools such as metaphors and similes, visual tools like graphs and maps, and imagination tools like analogues and paradigms.

To be useful to us, these mental tools must help us accomplish three tasks. First, the perspective must identify the key actors or agents at work in the world. These are the *units of analysis* for that approach. Who, or what, is doing the things that matter in globalization, and how can we find and observe them? Second, how does the perspective describe the way the world changes? In each case, the portion of the world that interests us is the part that is changing in some way. We need to be able to identify these changes and describe them. These changes form the *pattern of world dynamics.* Finally, each perspective must be able to treat the world analytically, by which I mean how the perspective explains the *causes and consequences of change* in the world. The approach must be able to explain to us how we are connected to events distant from us in time and space. To experience the world as a single place means that we must know and understand how changes in a far-off locale, or actions taken by people we do not know, have consequences for us.

In this chapter, I outline six perspectives on globalization and discuss what each tells us about the world as a single place. I identify for each perspective its key actors, agents, or units of analysis; its important dynamics; and its analytical conclusions. The approaches discussed here do not constitute a complete list of ways to think about the world. The pressures of space have limited me to only a few of the most frequently encountered ones. By the same token, what follows is not an exhaustive review of each perspective in its entirety. Such a review would require a book by itself. Rather, I focus on an author, a group of authors, or a book or two as illustrative of the central themes one finds in each perspective. Each of these perspectives is popular and has many followers. Each can shed light on globalization. After this review, we will be in a better position to understand the perspective I call *global awareness* and to appreciate how it helps us think about the world as a single place.

SOCIOLOGY: GLOBALIZATION AND CULTURE

We begin our review with sociology and culture to emphasize that globalization is about more than economics (the next approach to be discussed) or nation-state politics (the subject of chapter 7). These latter two perspectives are, of course, important, and I will devote appropriate space to both of them. But as Robertson reminds us, economic and political transactions and relationships are all filtered through, and significantly shaped by, cultural codes.[5] The ways in which people identify themselves, relate to others, embrace or reject values, and ascribe meaning to objects are all of supreme importance. And this is especially true as people struggle to experience the world as a single place.

How and why culture matters in relation to globalization depend to a large degree on how we define our terms.[6] Robertson, for example, defines *culture* as "that which individuals, groups and societies produce and acquire in order to function effectively."[7] Some of the most important features of this produced and acquired set of ideas, he says, involve identity (how one thinks of him- or herself), differentiation (how one thinks of others), and representation (how one portrays him- or herself and others). Globalization affects these aspects of our lives by increasing their complexity. As we more frequently and more profoundly experience the world as a single place, we know (and know more about) more and more people who differ from us in some significant way(s). As Robertson puts it,

> In a world which is increasingly compressed . . . and in which its . . . nationally constituted societies and the inter-state system are increasingly subject to the . . . constraints of multiculturality or . . . polyethnicity, the conditions of and for the identification of individual and collective selves and of individual and collective others are becoming ever more complex.[8]

John Tomlinson, a scholar at the Nottingham Trent University in the United Kingdom, has written an important study of the ways in which culture and globalization affect each other.[9] Tomlinson defines *culture* as "the order of life in which human beings construct meaning through practices of symbolic representation."[10] He defines *globalization* as "complex connectivity. . . . the rapidly developing and ever-densening network of interconnections and interdependences that characterize modern social life."[11] His book explores how culture thus defined changes complex connectivity and how globalization thus defined changes the way(s) people construct meaning. Tomlinson's book describes a wide variety of such interconnections; I can do no more here than cite a few illustrative examples. On the one hand, globalization affects culture through the process of deterritorialization or by separating our experiences from the locale in which they occur. People become disconnected from specific locales as they acquire an increasing ability to experience people and events at a distance. On the other hand, culture affects globalization by causing people to become more reflexive, to reflect more on the nature of their experiences and relationships. By encouraging us to be more reflexive, culture heightens our consciousness of distant events and people and alerts us to adjust to incoming information about our own behavior and its consequences. In these and many other ways, cultural change and globalization interact with each other as a sort of grand positive feedback loop. With each cycle of change, each dimension pushes the other to new levels.

Another way in which the concept of culture shapes our ability to think about the world is through the comparative study of civilizations. According to one leading proponent of this approach, Matthew Melko, the term *culture* describes how people live in relation to one another.[12] Civilizations, then, are large and complex cultures that differ from simple cultures in that they have greater control of their environments, they are technologically advanced, and they produce an economic surplus, which frees some members from subsistence labor. Endowed with this surplus, civilizations can invest in such cultural features as cities and writing.

Civilizations change over time. Sometimes they are tightly integrated; at other times, they are more loosely connected. Sometimes they are at peace with their neighbors; at other times, war prevails. Civilizations expand to absorb and incorporate other cultures, religions, languages, and so forth. But no civilization ever expands indefinitely. Thus, there will always be (more or less) discernible boundary lines between civilizations; and outside observers will be able to study their interactions. In sum, civilizations change, and they change fast enough to be thought of chronologically; that is, they have a history. Finally, as if anticipating the central argument of this book, Melko observes that civilizations are composed of multiple integrated systems, each of which is composed of subsystems. These systems can also be thought of as being composed of patterns, which "are the arrangements that give the parts a relationship to one another and to the civilization as a whole."[13]

Whatever the definition sociologists choose, eventually they confront the question of global (or globalizing) culture. Is there emerging a single set of values that eventually all people on Earth will embrace, or is the contrary more likely: is the world becoming even more fragmented culturally as it becomes more of a single place?[14] If there is a consensus among sociologists that answers this complex question, it probably is rather mixed. If by a global culture one means a single, homogeneous set of values that everyone on Earth endorses, then the answer is probably no; if one means that there is emerging an integrated network of communications media over which cultural values are transmitted, then the answer is probably yes. If one is concerned about the emerging dominance of a single set of cultural objects (McDonalds, Coca-Cola, Disney), then the evidence seems to suggest that these objects are all received differently in different cultures and are integrated into different cultures to a different degree and with different local meanings. On the other hand, it is also clear that globalization serves to commodify cultural objects (that is, turn them into commercial objects for sale) almost universally. Finally, if one is worried about the increasing homogenization of cultural markers such as language and religion, then the evidence is mixed. It does seem that the globalization of culture is causing the loss of linguistic diversity (see case study 2); but other cultural markers such as religious faith and ethnonationalism seem clearly to be increasing in diversity and fragmentation as globalization proceeds.

ECONOMICS: GLOBALIZATION AND THE MULTINATIONAL CORPORATION

The domain of the discipline of economics is vast. As it pertains to globalization, economics includes the large-scale production, distribution, and consumption of goods and services. A partial listing of what this encompasses might include the following:

- The factors of production. Traditionally, these are land and natural resources (including energy supplies), labor, and capital (including both financial capital and technology). In an increasingly globalized marketplace, however, knowledge or information becomes a critical factor of production in its own right. Because all factors of production are scarce (that is, there is never enough to satisfy all demands simultaneously), there must be some way to allocate them to specific purposes.
- The organization of these factors of production, especially the privately owned firm or enterprise. Some economists speak of the mode of production as "an abstraction which refers to the main social forces (especially classes) which organize and control the generation and distribution of the economic surplus in a given society or group of societies."[15] One of the paramount goals of any mode of production is to increase the productivity of the enterprise or of one of the factors of production, especially labor.
- The coordination or connection of the factors of production by means of institutions (markets) and technologies (transport, communications).

- The ownership of the factors of production by the private firm, enterprise, or corporation. Of special importance to this discussion is the multinational corporation or enterprise.
- The regulation, coordination, control, and in some cases ownership of these factors by the state. The subdiscipline that studies this field is known as political economy. The branch that includes global economics is called international political economy.
- The dominant ideas or ideology that guide people in their management of all of the above. In today's globally integrated economy, the dominant ideology has three important dimensions:
- Privatization and consumer sovereignty: a belief that the free (more or less) or lightly regulated market is the most efficient way to allocate resources and a transfer of ownership of the factors of production from the state to private firms.
- Commodification: the transfer of material objects and human relationships into the market where they take on economic value, acquire a price, can be bought and sold, and have their value determined by the law of supply and demand.
- Transnationalization: the erasure of nation-state boundaries as barriers to economic transactions; the firm comes to be the equal of the state as the principal actor, agent, or unit of analysis in the economic system. Many scholars now assert that globalization has weakened the state to such a degree that the firm is now the preeminent actor in the world economy. The "new diplomacy" that emerges involves firm-to-firm interactions as well as state-to-firm and the more traditional state-to-state modes.[16]

The subdiscipline of international political economy (IPE) focuses our attention on the interplay between politics and economics, or between the state and the market, in the allocation of scarce resources.[17] Scholars in this field may disagree about the relative importance of domestic and international forces or about the comparative power of states and social forces (firms, interest groups, and so forth). But they agree that economic outcomes (what is produced and what is consumed, by whom, and with what consequences) are the product of the interactions of both sets of actors or agents.

There are three competing views of IPE. The *liberal* view holds that the individual is the most important actor or unit of analysis.[18] When individual producers and consumers are free to interact in an open marketplace, unfettered by state regulations or imperfect information, the outcome will always be the most efficient possible allocation of scarce resources. The *realist* view holds that the state (or the nation-state) is the most important actor or unit of analysis. Individuals interact in the market but only under rules set down by the state. The state's goal is to maximize its own power in the international arena. Economic decisions are subordinated to that goal. In an earlier time, such views were known as mercantilism. Today, these ideas are espoused by advocates of state-driven industrial or trade policies. Finally, the *Marxist* view holds that the most important actor in economics is the social/economic class. The economy is divided into those who sell labor and those who buy it; and the latter use the state and the market as devices to ensure their victory in the competition between these two classes. In the context of globalization, Marxists see the world system as the appropriate unit of analysis.

No matter what perspective of IPE one might adopt, the *multinational corporation* (MNC) is still an important (some might say, *the* important) actor or unit of analysis. The MNC is an enterprise that controls assets, including factories, mines, plantations, sales offices, marketing outlets, and so forth, in two or more countries. It will also probably offer goods or services in many different countries, derive a considerable portion of its revenues from overseas operations, have employees and stockholders from many different countries, and conduct abroad a wide range of manufacturing, research, and development activities.[19] MNCs are among the most significant of the global networks operating today. One count, in 1995, identified about 40,000 MNCs with about 250,000 foreign affiliates.[20] These corporate entities accounted for 70–80 percent of all international trade. The 350 largest MNCs in the world account for more than one-quarter of the world's production of goods and services. The largest MNCs have annual gross sales larger than the gross domestic products of all but a few of the world's largest countries.

Many IPE scholars contend that the rising power of MNCs has caused a parallel decline in the power of the state. At least three trends associated with globalization are put forward to explain this causal relationship. First, globalization has occasioned a retreat of the state from the regulation and coordination of the economy that were characteristic of the era of the welfare state, and MNCs have exploited this retreat to expand into the power vacuum left behind. Second, states have entered into a number of international agreements (such as the North American Free Trade Agreement) through which they commit themselves to removing the barriers to the movement of goods, services, and many of the factors of production. By renouncing state power in this arena, national governments lose much of their ability to control MNC behavior. Finally, globalization makes it easier for MNCs to relocate their production facilities in search of cheaper factors of production, especially labor. The result has been what IPE scholars call "footloose industries," firms that can move out of a country if the state tries to regulate them too closely.

Many of these themes are brought together in a 1994 book by Richard J. Barnet and John Cavanagh entitled *Global Dreams*.[21] The book's central argument is that

the emerging global order is spearheaded by a few hundred corporate giants, many of them bigger than most sovereign nations. . . . By acquiring earth-spanning technologies, by developing products that can be produced anywhere and sold everywhere, by spreading credit around the world, and by connecting global channels of communication that can penetrate any village or neighborhood, these institutions . . . are becoming the world empires of the twenty-first century.[22]

To illustrate their argument, Barnet and Cavanagh focus their attention on four interlocking global domains: culture (films, music, publishing), commercial transactions (shopping malls, global products), the workplace, and money. Their unit of analysis is the multinational corporation, several specific examples of which they discuss in lengthy case studies: Sony, Philip Morris, Ford, Citicorp, and others.

It is important to note that while Barnet and Cavanagh are sharply critical of the damage done to the world by globalization in general and by MNCs in particular, they do not blame the leaders of these firms for being particularly greedy or uncaring. They emphasize that the firms they studied are a positive social force in many ways. They make products that millions of people want, they are environmentally conscious, they treat their employees well, and their leaders possess a global vision that surpasses that of most people. But in the larger sense the impact of these MNCs is pernicious politically, economically, socially, and environmentally. Moreover, their leaders seem unaware of these negative consequences and feel no responsibility to prevent or remedy them. Most worrisome of all, Barnet and Cavanagh assert, the power and reach of multinational corporations have expanded because the power of other countervailing institutions has been weakened by globalizing technologies and institutions. That is, MNCs have become the new world empire because other institutions—cultures, social structures, and the state—have become so weakened. It is as if the forces of globalization have created a power vacuum into which the MNC has flowed.

BIOLOGY: GLOBALIZATION AND THE BIOSPHERE

Biologists view the world as a grand environmental setting within which many different living organisms interact (or have interacted in the past) with each other and with parts of the nonliving world (energy, for example, or elements such as nitrogen or carbon). These organisms range in size over nearly two dozen orders of magnitude, from the microscopic (viruses, bacteria) to the huge (elephants, whales). For biologists, the central actor or unit of analysis varies, depending on the classification scheme one selects. Some researchers might study, for example, the flow of essential elements such as carbon and nitrogen through living systems. Others might look at entities smaller than the organism: genes, cells, or tissue. Still others might examine individual organisms, populations of similar organisms, or species (a category of organism that is self-reproducing but cannot breed with members of other species), perhaps classified according to the function each performs in its respective system. Finally, biologists can study ecological systems (large sets of interacting organisms) and the largest of such systems, called biomes (such as tropical rain forests, deserts, or temperate-zone grasslands).[23]

Ecology is the subdiscipline of biology that seems best suited to helping us think about the world as a single place.[24] Ecology (the term was coined by the biologist Ernst Haeckel in 1866) is the study of how living organisms interact within large and complex systems known as ecosystems. System connections (that is, how system components cause each other to change) are the principal unit of analysis. "Ecolacy" is the mastery of these connections, just as literacy is the mastery of words and numeracy is the mastery of numbers.[25]

Ecosystems can be studied on different scales. The Earth can be examined as a single global ecosystem that contains all its living organisms, the Earth itself, and the atmosphere surrounding the planet. Other ecosystems may be much smaller, such as a freshwater pond. Energy and nutrients pass through the ecosystem to sustain its internal dynamics or patterns of change. In particular, energy passes through the ecosystem by a network of feeding relationships called a food chain or food web. Organisms feed on each other in a hierarchy wherein each depends on the next lowest member of the hierarchy for its food. To be of use to the feeder, the energy must be wrested from the source before it becomes waste matter (that is, before the source has finished with it). Sometimes this process is violent, as when a predator kills and eats its prey; sometimes it is less so, as when farmers harvest a crop of grain or livestock managers butcher their herds for human consumption.[26]

Even though an ecosystem may have endured for millennia, and even though it may look strong and robust, such systems are apt to be very fragile because they depend on a very delicate balance of interacting organisms that may have evolved over a very long time. (In case study 4 I will examine the catastrophe that has befallen one such ecosystem, that surrounding Lake Victoria in East Africa.) Even the slightest disturbance, such as the removal of a key species, may plunge the ecosystem into instability and even possibly collapse.

Ecosystems are frequently studied as if they were self-regulating. That is, the organisms within a given ecosystem interact with each other via feedback mechanisms to ensure that the larger system remains stable. Material substances such as nitrogen and carbon are recycled through the system and used over and over again. Energy is received from the sun and processed through the system to power the actions of the component organisms. But is it possible to think of the Earth as a single, huge self-regulating system? Many ecologists think so. Some of them have begun to study the Earth as more than just a large self-regulating system. They see the Earth as an organism in its own right. They refer to this organism as Gaia, after the ancient Greek goddess of the Earth. Even among global ecologists this idea remains very controversial. Tyler Volk, for example, asserts that although the Earth may be a self-regulating system, it cannot be thought of as a single organism (except metaphorically).[27] Organisms, he writes, are subject to the forces of evolution by natural selection, and these forces apply only where there is competition for scarce resources. Because there is only one Earth, it has no competitors and thus does not evolve in the same way organisms do. But the idea of Gaia can still stimulate us to think about the world as a single biological place.

In an earlier book I argue that competition among sets of organisms, called life systems, has had a powerful influence on the shape of globalization ever since the invention of agriculture some ten millennia ago.[28] The central concept here is *coevolution,* the mutual adjustment of species to each other across many generations. Driven by the competition for scarce resources, especially energy, humans and the plants and animals they domesticated for food gradually formed interconnected systems. The invention of agriculture brought humans into contact with previously unknown microorganisms as well as dense populations of their fellow humans. The result was the introduction of diseases into the package. We call the resulting system a *coevolved life system.* At some point in the distant past, there were many such systems in the world, each with its distinctive array of plants, animals, and diseases. Over time, globalization brought them into contact with each other. The various processes of competition, cooperation, conflict, absorption, and so forth gradually reduced this diversity, and there has emerged a *global coevolved life system* that now dominates the biosphere.

For some observers, energy flow is the key to understanding self-regulating systems. While all other resources are recycled repeatedly through systems, energy is what Earth system scientists call throughput. Energy reaches the Earth from the sun and is absorbed by photosynthesizing plants to produce plant tissue. The energy is then consumed by herbivores, carnivores, and eventually human beings and then dissipated away from Earth in the form of heat. Because there is no way to keep energy from dissipating, all Earth systems depend on their ability to wrest energy from neighboring systems, use it efficiently, and dissipate its waste product. To a great degree, industrial society has depended on the energy that reached the Earth several hundred million years ago and was stored in the fossilized tissue of plants and animals before being dug up and burned in the form of petroleum, coal, and natural gas.

According to Vaclav Smil, civilization can be thought of as a set of technologies and institutions whose purposes are threefold.[29] The first is to capture energy from terrestrial sources (for example, food or fossil fuel); the second, to transform it to serve its larger purposes (for example, build monuments or mobilize an army); and the third, to dissipate the remaining waste products to some distant reservoir, which ecologists call a sink. To accomplish these goals, humans have for millennia intervened extensively in the natural biogeochemical cycles that move nitrogen, carbon, sulfur, and other elements through the biosphere. Many of the emerging global environmental concerns, such as global warming and acid rain, have their roots at least partly in this human intervention. The increase in the human population and in the per capita consumption by the members of that population will inescapably occasion even greater interventions in the coming decades.

Ecology forces us to think of the world as a single living system confined within limits.[30] These limits are set by space, matter, and energy. The population of a given organism that can be supported by a given ecosystem for a given span of time with a given set of conditions is known as the system's carrying capacity. Human ingenuity (expressed through technology and social organization) can stretch these limits, as we have been doing for about 10,000 years through agriculture. But ecologists insist that we cannot go beyond these limits. Eventually all ecosystems grow to reach their limits and then must restrain their growth, either peacefully and harmoniously or violently and with considerable upheaval. When an ecosystem's carrying capacity is exceeded, the population it is sustaining must be reduced, by either emigration, lowered reproduction, or increased deaths (or some combination of all three). The Earth's carrying capacity for its human population is not fixed, however. How many people the Earth can support depends to a great extent on how we define the material quality of our lives: how much we wish to consume, with what degree of equality of distribution, and so forth.[31]

HISTORY: GLOBALIZATION AND WORLD SYSTEMS

Using the recorded past as a way to think about the world plunges us into a debate among world historians about whether there can ever be a "science of history" or a "theoretical history."[32] Our understanding of the natural world is codified in the laws that describe universal and permanent phenomena, such as the atomic structure of matter. But are such laws possible in the written records of the past? How are laws of history possible if historians are describing what they believe to be unique events? A science requires a body of laws based on observed patterns that we believe will be repeated. How can history provide us with such laws if every civilization, every ruler, every invention, and every social movement is unique, one of a kind? If history never "repeats itself," how can its laws be identified? Before we consider one representative historical approach to globalization, let me note why many historians believe that such laws can be identified.

"History" is not some amorphous set of unconnected events that somehow "just happen." History (that is, the systematic recording of salient phenomena from the past) is the work of identifiable entities or great systems known variously as civilizations, cultures, states, firms, armies, and so forth. Historians may disagree about the number and boundaries of these entities, but history requires actors or agents just as other perspectives such as sociology or economics do.[33] Moreover, the variations in the behaviors of these entities are usually a matter of a (more or less) public record (although that record must frequently be supplemented with evidence gleaned from less obvious and less public sources). The disagreements among world historians are not so much about the "facts" of the past (for example, that much of the twentieth century was taken up with extremely violent and bloody conflicts between armies representing nation-states with vastly differing ideologies and interests) as they are about the meaning of such facts. The real challenge in the historical perspective is to select accurate and valid metaphors or analogies that will connect something with which we are familiar (for example, the life cycle of a human being, from conception to death) to something far beyond our direct experience (for example, the "life cycle" of a nation-state). In this, world historians must take care to choose metaphors and other organizing concepts that exhibit valid and insightful similarities with the world actors.

One particular area of contention involves the application of the so-called organismic analogy to actors in history. Is it justified to apply concepts from one field (biology, in this case) to a second field (the historical behavior of large entities such as civilizations)? Obviously civilizations are not organisms, but perhaps some systems principles apply to both. The founder of general systems theory, Ludwig von Bertalanffy, certainly thought so, as he wrote:

> The fact that simple growth laws apply to social entities such as manufacturing companies, to urbanization, division of labor, etc., proves that in these respects the "organismic analogy" is correct. In spite of the historians' protests, the application of theoretical models, in particular, the model of dynamic, open and adaptive systems, to the historical process certainly makes sense. This does not imply "biologism," i.e., reduction of social to biological concepts, but indicates system principles applying in both fields.[34]

One approach that has much to offer us is called the *history of world-systems*.[35] "World-systems" are, in the words of Christopher Chase-Dunn and Thomas Hall, "intersocietal networks that are systemic."[36] By *networks* Chase-Dunn and Hall mean patterns of interactions (for example, trade or warfare) among social units; by *systemic* they mean that these interactions exhibit patterns (that is, they resemble one another across space and time). If observers can identify the patterns and understand their causes and consequences, then they can begin to understand why these networks behave the way they do.

Perhaps most important for our purposes, the world-system is

> a new level of social organization—a global hierarchical division of labor that includes households, neighborhoods, communities, firms, regions, states, the world market, and the interstate system of competing states. . . . [T]he most important unit of analysis for the study of social change is not societies or states but the entire world-system.[37]

Since about 1500, the world-system has been structured around a *core* of powerful and wealthy states, a *periphery* of poor and weak states and societies, a *semiperiphery* of societies and states that lie somewhere in between core and periphery (both geographically and in terms of development), and an *external area* that has no interaction at all with the world-system (an area obviously shrinking rapidly before the pressures of globalization). The systemic logic or pattern of such a system is that the core exploits the periphery to advance the well-being of the former, while the semiperiphery contains those societies and states in transition from the latter status to the former.

Many of the leading historians who study world systems believe that the single world system we know today began in Europe in about 1500 and spread out to incorporate all the various regional and local systems. In his provocative and stimulating book, *ReORIENT: Global Economy in the Asian Age,* Andre Gunder Frank vigorously refutes this notion.[38] In this book, Frank challenges what he considers the Eurocentric perspective on the patterns of global economic change between 1500 and 1800. Received wisdom about this important period in world history holds that "the West" (European states, especially Britain, and their overseas empires) rose to world dominance because of some exceptional internal property (for example, the Protestant ethic or the invention of capitalism). Such a property gave them a huge advantage over the weak and stagnant countries of "the East," the Asian economies (principally China and India) that were mired in backward and traditional institutions and cultural values. The rise of "the West" produced the single integrated world economy we know today by incorporating the rest of the world into this system of European creation.

Frank challenges this thesis at every point. There was in 1500, he asserts, already a single global economy with a worldwide division of labor and multilateral trade. This economy had its own systemic character and dynamic, whose roots in Afro-Eurasia reached back several millennia. If there was a dominant member of this world economy, it was Asia in general and China in particular. Europe was a marginal partner in this system for 300 years. It was not until after 1800 that European states and firms began to emerge as the dominant actors in this world system. For three centuries, Europeans were able to do little more than ride along as minor players in the global economy, and they were able to do this only by drawing on the enormous resources of precious metals (gold and silver) they withdrew from the Americas and transferred to Asia to pay for Asian goods. If "the West" "rose" to dominate the world system, it was not because of any exceptional internal quality its peoples possessed but, rather, because of the nature of the already existing world system and its dynamics. The driving forces in this world system were all economic. Europe, Asia, Africa, and the Americas were all linked by commodity trade, and their internal dynamics were shaped by the way this trade changed what economists call "factor prices," primarily the costs of wage labor.

One of Frank's goals in writing *ReORIENT* was to contribute to what he calls "horizontally integrative macrohistory." Too much history, he asserts, consists of "microhistory," that is, merely stories of events in specific places disconnected from any larger pattern, meaning, or context. The challenge for macrohistorians is to identify recurring patterns or similarities (that is, significant changes that occur in several different places at about the same time) that indicate similar causal forces at work. In this endeavor, Frank clearly advocates holistic or systemic models and their relevant metaphors. As he puts it,

> Since the whole is more than the sum of its parts, each part is not only influenced by other parts, but also by what happens in the whole world (system). There is no

way we can understand and account for what happened in Europe or the Americas without taking account of what happened in Asia and Africa—and vice versa— nor what happened anywhere without identifying the influences that emanated from everywhere, that is from the structure and dynamics of the whole world (system) itself. In a word, we need a holistic analysis to explain any part of the system.[39]

We will encounter these ideas frequently throughout this book as we develop the Global System Paradigm as a way to think about the world.

Finally, many historians of globalization see clear differences between "world history" and "global history."[40] World history is usually written from the perspective of one of the participants (for example, Britain in the Industrial Revolution), whereas (ideally) global history is written as if the events are seen from space. Their subject matter differs as well. World history seems all-inclusive. The word *world* derives from a Middle English word meaning roughly "manage," and thus its historical discipline takes for its realm of concern virtually all of human existence. Global history, on the other hand, focuses on those processes that have brought about globalization and traces them as far back in the past as seems necessary (for example, the technologies that made possible the tapping of fossil fuel) or on those processes that are best studied on a global level (for example, large-scale migration).

FUTURISM: GLOBALIZATION AND THE WORLD TO COME

The past offers one valuable window into the world as a single place; the future provides another. Unlike the past, however, the future has no single discipline or perspective devoted to its study. In any university, we know to go to the Department of History to find people who study the past, but it is usually much more difficult to find those who study the future systematically. Nevertheless, I believe that futurism is a provocative perspective that suggests novel ways of thinking about the world.

There is considerable debate about whether or not the future really exists and, if it does, where one could find it. Let us leave aside the realm of science fiction, where time travelers are able actually to experience the future "before it happens," and concentrate on those visions in which the future is somehow knowable because it is connected to the past and the present. Some scholars see time in much the same way as biologists see living organisms. If biologists know the genetic material of an organism and the conditions in which it lives (its nutrition, for example), and they know the laws that govern its development, they can predict how the mature organism will look and behave. In much the same way, some scholars argue, the future somehow "grows" out of conditions in the past and the present. There is a direct and almost physical connection between past and future. If one perceives the present and the past correctly, and if one also knows the laws that govern development or growth, then one can forecast fairly accurately what the future will be like.

A second perspective argues that the future exists as numerous images in the mind of each person. These images (which come from what our paradigm tells us about the future) shape the goals toward which that person strives. The striving behavior of countless millions of uncoordinated individuals when accumulated in some manner produces a new present, whereupon the whole process repeats itself in an infinite number of iterations. In this way, the future is what systems thinkers call an emergent property of a culture because it emerges out of the interactions of the members of that culture. If feedback (a systems term to be explored in the next two chapters) is information about the past that shapes our behavior, then *feed-forward* is information about the future that does the same thing.

Box 1.1.   Twelve Techniques for Predicting the Future

1. Social physics: the search for the underlying social laws that postulate the basic regularities of human behavior, regardless of individual intent or volition or the behavior of specific individuals. Usually this presumes a closed system or at least one in which all relevant variables are known.
2. Trends and forecasts: extrapolation from time-series data, either as straight-line projections, cyclical trends, or some other alternative projection based on upper and lower limits.
3. Structural certainties: events legally prescribed and traditionally reinforced. These are events not derived from time-series data but, rather, are based on custom or law.
4. Operational code: "rules of the game." These may not be realized by the actors or participants themselves but may be inferred by outside observers.
5. Structural requisites, an idea borrowed from biology and medicine: a system has certain requirements, and to fulfill these requirements, certain structures (such as institutions) must fulfill certain functions. The future of the system requires that such structures perform their assigned functions.
6. The overriding problem: the search for one dimension of behavior so important that all others are subordinated to it and its development.
7. Sequential development or organic growth: all organic systems develop through identifiable stages (for example, infancy, adolescence, maturity, etc.), and these can be applied analogously to larger social systems as well.
8. Accounting schemes or an inventory of factors that affect an individual's future: these can range from factors that exhibit a high degree of stability (constant) to those that are wholly fortuitous or unpredictable (random).

9. The writing of alternative futures, as in science fiction: these are apt to be the work of singularly gifted individuals, but they may be used to stimulate systematic thinking about possible alternatives.

10. Consensus techniques, such as the Delphi technique: a panel of experts is asked to predict the timing or the probability of certain events (such as particular inventions), and then these predictions are refined through some kind of interaction among the panel members.

11. Simulations, contingency planning, gaming, brainstorming, and other collective thinking exercises that stimulate novel thought processes.

12. Incrementalism: this form of decision making makes no attempt at long-range prediction. Instead, decision makers simply choose their next step from a list of available next options that differ only marginally or incrementally from the status quo.

Source: Daniel Bell, "Twelve Modes of Prediction," and T. J. Gordon, "Current Methods of Futures Research," both in *Political Science and the Study of the Future,* ed. Albert Somit (Hinsdale, Ill.: Dryden Press, 1974), 40–67, 89–113.

Regardless of where we think the future is and how we can know it, futurism contributes something very important to thinking globally. There are a dozen or so formal techniques for thinking about the future, and virtually all of them depend on our understanding of cause and effect. (See box 1.1.) That is, we believe that each time a given event occurs, it changes the probability of all possible events occurring in the future. The huge majority of such changes in probability are so minor that we can treat them as insignificant. However, some changes will not be trivial. If we can identify the key events in the past and the present, and if we can understand how they change future probabilities, then we can forecast the future with greater accuracy. Thus, virtually every technique for knowing the future requires that we understand clearly the past and the present. In this way, futurism imposes on us a certain discipline and rigor that we find extremely helpful in thinking about the world as a single place.

We shall examine here two examples of futurism that illuminate globalization. The first is by the science writer and computer scientist Ray Kurzweill, entitled *The Age of Spiritual Machines.*[41] Kurzweill's central theme is that the relentless increase in computer speed and capacity through the coming decades will dramatically alter the relationship between human beings and technology. By the year 2020, more or less, computer capacity will exceed human intelligence, and shortly thereafter it will be possible to buy for $1,000 or less a machine with greater thinking capacity than a human. The exponential growth in computing power, which actually dates back to the beginning of the twentieth century, will not only continue but actually accelerate in the coming decades. The steadily rising curve in computing power will feed on itself in a classic example of a positive feedback loop. The human brain and the computer will meld in some sort of hybrid superintelligent techno-organism that will cause us to reconsider the true meaning of "human." Nanotechnology (the ability to manufacture extremely tiny objects) will make it possible to make computers the size of molecules and to insert them into living organisms to create combinations as yet unimagined. As more and more of these hybrid techno-organisms join together across greater and greater distances, global neural networks become possible. If "thinking about the world as a single place" is essentially a cognitive problem, these global thinking networks should help us do it better. Most significantly for us, however, these far-flung neural networks open the possibility of a global consciousness or a global entity capable of thinking about itself—truly global awareness.

Kurzweill helps us think about the world by showing how changes in information technology are erasing the boundary between human beings and technology, thus leading to a global consciousness. Another author, the French chemist Joël de Rosnay, goes one step further. In his book, entitled *The Symbiotic Man,* he argues that technology is erasing boundaries among humans, technology, *and* the biosphere, thus producing a global techno-organism that he calls the "cybiont."[42] De Rosnay asserts that

> human beings, their societies, their machines (mechanical or electrical), and their coevolving infrastructures and infostructures, connected by communications networks and regulatory loops, now form a series of indissociable nested systems, a new global living organism: the cybiont. . . . a planetary macroorganism currently in evolution. A hybrid biological, mechanical, and electronic superorganism that includes humans, machines, networks, and societies. In this book, it appears under several designations: living planetary macrocell, social ecosystem, and macroscopic living being.[43]

De Rosnay supports his vision of the planetary future with a review of much the same material on the evolution of information technology that one reads in Kurzweill, but de Rosnay adds important insights from chaos and complexity theory and from the biological concept of coevolution. Thus, the emergence of the cybiont is a consequence of more than simply more computing capacity. For de Rosnay, the cybiont is emerging from the coevolution of humans, other organisms, and technologies to form a macroorganism that will eventually be planetary or global in scope, a sort of "Gaia plus computers," as it were.

BIOGRAPHY: GLOBALIZATION IN THE LIVES OF INDIVIDUALS

All of the preceding perspectives are examples of academic disciplines, intellectual traditions, or ways of thinking that direct our attention to abstractions. In these approaches, actors are not specific, real human beings but, rather, classes or categories of people who are given certain properties or characteristics by the authors. These approaches all have their merits, but another good way to think about globalization is to focus on specific real people as they go about the tasks and challenges of their daily lives. Journalists are very adept at describing such people and the challenges they face. I shall refer to this perspective as personal anecdotes or biographies. Because this approach is explicitly less concerned with the techniques of study and more concerned with the details of the life of a real person, there is no need to precede this review with a discussion of the methodologies involved.

The first example I have is by an author who is not only a journalist but a playwright as well. In her book *Money Makes the World Go Around*,[44] Barbara Garson takes us on a tour of the global financial system by tracking the movement of her own money through two different channels. As described in the first half of the book, Garson deposited a portion of the advance of the book's royalties in a small community bank in upstate New York about an hour and a half drive from New York City. Because deposits like these are fungible (that is, they can be converted easily and immediately into other financial instruments), Garson found that from this point on her specific money could not be tracked. It was immediately absorbed into that huge flow of global money that washes across the world's financial network more or less continuously. However, she could follow transactions that contained a part of her deposit, and they took her on a journey around the world. From her original bank, the funds traveled (electronically, as is always the case) to a large bank in New York City, which then used them (among other things) to underwrite a letter of credit for a seafood importer in Brooklyn. With this letter of credit, the importer arranged to pay for a shipment of shrimp from Thailand, so Garson set out to meet the people there whose lives had been touched by her money. Her journey took her to Thailand, Malaysia, and Singapore. In the course of her travels, she met Chinese labor contractors, illegal immigrants from Burma and Indonesia, Texas oil refinery engineers, and many other people involved in spending a small portion of her deposit.

The rest of the advance Garson invested in an aggressive mutual fund with headquarters in New York City. As a shareholder of this fund, Garson was able to watch from a close-in vantage point as the fund used her (and many other people's) money to turn a profit without adding much value to the overall economy. The fund's directors accomplished this feat by buying manufacturing firms in financial trouble, restructuring them (a euphemism for firing most of their workers), and selling them to holding companies that simply wanted to move the plants overseas. Garson was able to follow a small portion of her money through a mutual fund to a small plant in Portland, Tennessee, which manufactured lawn furniture. After the fund bought (and then sold) the parent company (Sunbeam), the plant was moved to Mexico just as that country was experiencing the collapse of its currency. In this way, Garson was able to see how her tiny investment had contributed to huge gains for some investors but the impoverishment of workers in both Tennessee and Mexico.

In a second example, *Mollie's Job*,[45] journalist William Adler followed not money but a specific job as it moved from Paterson, New Jersey, to Simpson

County, Mississippi, and then to Matamoros, Mexico. The job in question involved the operation of a machine to wind copper wire into coils to be installed
in ballasts, the electronic component that regulates the flow of electric current in
florescent light fixtures. The three people who held this job (all, not incidentally,
women of color) were Mollie James (in New Jersey—hence the book's title),
Dorothy Carter (in Mississippi), and Balbina Duque (in Mexico). At the beginning
of the story, the job was one of a thousand or so in a plant in Paterson owned and
operated by Universal Manufacturing, a firm founded by a Paterson native. One
of the employees of this plant was Mollie James, a young African American
woman who used the job to lift herself out of the poverty into which she was
born in rural Virginia. After World War II, rising wages and an aggressive (and corrupt) union led to excessively high labor costs, so the company relocated the
plant to Mississippi. Here, another African American woman, Dorothy Carter, a
native of a small town in Mississippi, held the job and enjoyed the rising standard
of living it afforded her and her family. Following the death of the founder of the
company, however, the plant was sold to a series of conglomerates and holding
companies, finally ending up the property of MagneTek. This latter company immediately closed the Mississippi plant and moved it (and Mollie's/Dorothy's job)
to Matamoros to join the thousands of American firms located along the
U.S.–Mexico border. At this point, a young Mexican woman, Balbina Duque,
came to hold the job, and the rest of the book describes what it is like for her and
many tens of thousands of other Mexican women to work for multinational corporations on assembly lines near the border.

From Garson's and Adler's accounts, we learn much about how globalization
affects specific real people. There are both winners and losers in these stories
(more, it seems, of the latter than of the former). But a central theme of both
books is that most of these people were completely unaware of the ways in
which the transactions of the global economy affected them and were certainly
unable to defend themselves against the negative impact of these forces. These
books describe in rich detail a number of very powerful invisible systems, a
theme to which we shall return in chapters 6 and 7.

Each of the approaches we have discussed offers us something important in our
effort to think about the world as a single place. The disciplines of sociology and
economics describe for us some of the cultural and financial resources at stake
as globalization determines its winners and losers. The discipline of biology reminds us that we are not alone on this planet, and our ability to think about the
world must include some appreciation of the biosphere as well. The history of
world systems calls to our attention the underlying systems that have been the
principal actors in globalization for hundreds if not thousands of years. Futurism
alerts us to the forces that are creating some sort of global entity capable of self-
awareness and perhaps even self-reproduction. And journalism, biography, and
personal anecdotes help us remember that beneath all the abstractions of global

systems there are real people struggling to cope in their daily lives with the costs of globalization. Let us now move on to see if we can combine these features into a new paradigm that will improve our global awareness.

NOTES

1. Elisabeth Rosenthal, "In Rural China, a Steep Price of Poverty: Dying of AIDS," *New York Times,* October 28, 2000.

2. George Lopez, Jackie Smith, and Ron Pagnucco, "The Global Tide," *The Bulletin of Atomic Scientists* (July–August 1995): 33–39.

3. Roland Robertson, "Globalization Theory and Civilizational Analysis," *Comparative Civilizations Review* 17 (1987): 20–30. Roland Robertson, *Globalization: Social Theory and Global Culture* (London: SAGE, 1992), chapter 3.

4. Kenneth E. Boulding, *The World as a Total System* (Beverly Hills: SAGE, 1985).

5. Robertson, *Globalization,* 4.

6. For a sample of the various definitions of *culture* used by sociologists when they discuss globalization, see Mike Featherstone, ed., *Global Culture: Nationalism, Globalization and Modernity* (London: SAGE, 1990).

7. Robertson, *Globalization,* 40.

8. Robertson, *Globalization,* 98.

9. John Tomlinson, *Globalization and Culture* (Chicago: University of Chicago Press, 1999), 19.

10. Tomlinson, *Globalization and Culture,* 19.

11. Tomlinson, *Globalization and Culture,* 2.

12. Matthew Melko, "The Nature of Civilizations," in *Civilizations and World Systems: Studying World-Historical Change,* ed. Stephen K. Sanderson (Walnut Creek, Calif.: AltaMira Press, 1995), chapter 1.

13. Melko, "The Nature of Civilizations," 30.

14. Arjun Appadurai, "Disjuncture and Difference in the Global Cultural Economy," in *Global Culture: Nationalism, Globalization and Modernity,* ed. Mike Featherstone (London: SAGE, 1990), 295–310. Robertson, *Globalization,* chapters 1, 6, 8. Tomlinson, *Globalization and Culture,* chapters 1–3.

15. Stephen Gill and David Law, *The Global Political Economy: Perspectives, Problems and Policies* (Baltimore: Johns Hopkins University Press, 1988), 56.

16. Susan Strange, "States, Firms and Diplomacy," in *International Political Economy: Perspectives on Global Power and Wealth,* 3d ed., ed. Jeffrey A. Frieden and David A. Lake (New York: St. Martin's Press, 1995), chapter 4.

17. Gill and Law, *The Global Political Economy.* Jeffrey A. Frieden and David A. Lake, eds., *International Political Economy: Perspectives on Global Power and Wealth* (New York: St. Martin's Press, 1995).

18. Note that the word *liberal* here means something different from the way it is used in contemporary U.S. political language. The *liberal* in international political economy is one who advocates free trade and free markets, policies that are usually espoused by "conservatives" in U.S. politics today.

19. Maryann K. Cusimano, Mark Hensman, and Leslie Rodrigues, "Private-Sector Transsovereign Actors—MNCs and NGOs," in *Beyond Sovereignty: Issues for a Global Agenda,* ed. Maryann K. Cusimano (Boston: Bedford/St. Martin's Press, 2000), 267–68.

20. Joshua Karliner, *The Corporate Planet: Ecology and Politics in the Age of Globalization* (San Francisco: Sierra Club Books, 1997), 5.

21. Richard J. Barnet and John Cavanagh, *Global Dreams: Imperial Corporations and the New World Order* (New York: Simon and Schuster, 1994).

22. Barnet and Cavanagh, *Global Dreams,* 14.

23. Tyler Volk, *Gaia's Body: Toward a Physiology of Earth* (New York: Springer-Verlag, 1998), chapter 4.

24. Much of the following is derived from Sally Morgan, *Ecology and the Environment: The Cycles of Life* (New York: Oxford University Press, 1995).

25. Garrett Hardin, *Living within Limits: Ecology, Economics, and Population Taboos* (New York: Oxford University Press, 1993), 14–16.

26. Volk, *Gaia's Body,* 242.

27. Volk, *Gaia's Body,* chapter 3.

28. Robert P. Clark, *Global Life Systems: Population, Food, and Disease in the Process of Globalization* (Boulder: Rowman and Littlefield, 2001).

29. Vaclav Smil, *Cycles of Life: Civilization and the Biosphere* (New York: Scientific American Library, 1997).

30. Hardin, *Living within Limits.*

31. Joel E. Cohen, *How Many People Can the Earth Support?* (New York: Norton, 1995).

32. Michael Geyer and Charles Bright, "World History in a Global Age," *American Historical Review* (October 1995): 1034–60. Ludwig von Bertalanffy, *General System Theory: Foundations, Development, Applications* (New York: George Braziller, 1968), 109–19, 197–203.

33. Stephen K. Sanderson, ed., *Civilizations and World Systems: Studying World-Historical Change* (Walnut Creek, Calif.: AltaMira Press, 1995).

34. Von Bertalanffy, *General System Theory,* 118.

35. The literature on world systems is enormous. The reader is referred to the extensive bibliography at the end of Christopher Chase-Dunn and Thomas D. Hall, *Rise and Demise: Comparing World-Systems* (Boulder: Westview Press, 1997), 276–306.

36. Chase-Dunn and Hall, *Rise and Demise,* 4.

37. Chase-Dunn and Hall, *Rise and Demise,* 1.

38. Andre Gunder Frank, *ReORIENT: Global Economy in the Asian Age* (Berkeley: University of California Press, 1998).

39. Frank, *ReORIENT,* 37.

40. Bruce Mazlish, "An Introduction to Global History," in *Conceptualizing Global History,* ed. Bruce Mazlish and Ralph Buultjens (Boulder: Westview Press, 1993), 1–24. Bruce Mazlish, "Comparing Global History to World History," *Journal of Interdisciplinary History* 28, no. 3 (winter 1998): 385–95.

41. Ray Kurzweill, *The Age of Spiritual Machines: When Computers Exceed Human Intelligence* (New York: Viking, 1999).

42. Joël de Rosnay, *The Symbiotic Man: A New Understanding of the Organization of Life and a Vision of the Future,* trans. Phyllis Aronoff, Rémy Charet, Howard Scott, and Wanda Romer Taylor (New York: McGraw Hill, 2000).

43. De Rosnay, *The Symbiotic Man,* 255, 284.

44. Barbara Garson, *Money Makes the World Go Around: One Investor Tracks Her Cash through the Global Economy, from Brooklyn to Bangkok and Back* (New York: Viking, 2001).

45. William M. Adler, *Mollie's Job: A Story of Life and Work on the Global Assembly Line* (New York: Scribner, 2000).

Case Study 1

Thinking about the AIDS Pandemic

KEY IDEAS IN THIS CASE STUDY

Since its appearance in the early 1980s, the **AIDS pandemic** (an epidemic of worldwide proportions) has become one of the most dramatic examples of a harmful global system. Before the disease runs its course, which may take several more decades, it will prove to be one of the three or four most devastating contagious diseases ever to afflict humankind.

This case study illustrates how various approaches or perspectives can be used to explain this aspect of globalization: where AIDS came from, why and how it spreads, and what its consequences have been and are likely to be. The case study is organized into the following sections:

- **Sociology: AIDS as a Cultural Phenomenon**
- **Economics: Can Anyone Profit from AIDS?**
- **Biology: How HIV Spreads**
- **History: AIDS, the Bubonic Plague, and World Systems**
- **Futurism: The Future of AIDS**
- **Biography: AIDS in the Life of the Individual**

Early in July 1981, the *New York Times* ran its first article on the mysterious new disease that had surfaced in New York and San Francisco over the previous three or four years.[1] The disease seemed to afflict gay men, primarily by attacking their immune systems and making them susceptible to other diseases, especially tuberculosis and several rare types of cancer. Early in 1982, the U.S. Public Health Service identified sexual transmission as the route by which the disease spread, but health officials also noted the appearance of the disease among drug users, recipients of blood transfusions, and infants born to infected mothers. Apparently blood was also a route of transmission, and heterosexual contact could also spread the disease. That same year, the Centers for Disease Control and Prevention (CDC) named the disease AIDS, for "acquired immune deficiency syndrome." In 1983, separate groups of researchers in the United States and France isolated the virus that causes the disease and gave it a name too: HIV, for "human immunodeficiency virus."

Other diseases in history may have killed a greater proportion of the population: the bubonic plague in Europe and Asia in the fourteenth century, smallpox in the Americas after 1492, or the influenza pandemic of 1918–1920. But AIDS seems destined to claim the record for inflicting the greatest absolute number of deaths in a single pandemic wave. As of December 31, 1999, according to the United Nations AIDS Surveillance Project, a total of 18.8 million people had died of the AIDS epidemic since its beginning in 1981–1982.[2] About 2.8 million of those deaths occurred in 1999. The rising rate of new infections was even more disturbing. At the end of 1999, some 34.3 million people were living with the virus that causes AIDS, HIV. An estimated 5.4 million of those infections began in 1999. As the disease passed its twenty-year mark in mid-2001, it was thought to have infected almost 60 million people, of whom about 22 million have already died. Inasmuch as medical research has yet to identify a cure for the disease, virtually all of those currently infected will die from AIDS-related causes. Moreover, about 16,000 new cases of HIV infection occur each day.

There is still considerable controversy about where the AIDS virus came from and how it got into the human population; but we do know quite a bit about the factors that promoted (and continue to promote) its rapid spread. Some of these factors are inherent in the nature of AIDS and the way its virus is spread; we will learn more about these factors when we discuss the biological perspective below. However, many factors that have promoted the AIDS pandemic are closely related to globalization. For example, the increased export of animals from tropical rain forests to zoos and medical research facilities in Europe and North America has increased the handling of monkeys and chimpanzees, thought by many to be the reservoir species for the AIDS virus. The increase in vaccination programs in the developing world has raised considerably the number of syringes available to the general population, and the rise of the drug culture in Europe and North America and of global narcotics trafficking has promoted the sharing of needles. The rapid growth of Africa's population and its urbanization have brought prostitutes and their clients into much denser concentrations while at the same time opening up vast stretches of previously untouched rain forest to human habitation. The increase in commercial air travel has facilitated the long-distance movement of large populations at unprecedented speeds. For example, it has been determined that the disease was introduced into North America by an airline employee who flew frequently between San Francisco and European cities. Finally, the increasing openness of gay culture in North American and European cities greatly facilitated the spread of the disease within this specific population. Thus, as more people came to experience the world as a single place via the AIDS pandemic, they discovered that there were harmful consequences of globalization; and this harm was not distributed equally across the population.

SOCIOLOGY: AIDS AS A CULTURAL PHENOMENON

In Spain in the early 1970s, the military dictatorship of Francisco Franco was still in power, and his authoritarian regime enforced a set of conservative cultural values, especially regarding the rights of women generally and sexual activity in particular. Married women were not allowed to vote, to own property or bequeath it to heirs, or even to be away from home overnight without their husbands' consent. To speak of birth control technologies was taboo, and the law prohibited the sale of condoms without a doctor's prescription. By the late 1980s, only a decade and a half later, a remarkable change had occurred. The government had launched a massive publicity campaign to encourage the country's youth to practice safe sex, and the leading character in this campaign was a cartoon figure of a talking condom, complete with arms, legs, and face. This character appeared on television, in magazines and newspapers, and on billboards all over the country to advise the nation's youth to use condoms "just in case" of AIDS. In only fifteen years, the use of a condom had gone from being a criminal act to being an accepted part of the country's popular culture. Many things had happened during these intervening years: Spain became a constitutional democracy in 1978 and joined the European Union in 1983. But the most significant development was the AIDS epidemic. The Spanish case offers only one small example of how AIDS and culture have mutually influenced each other in the course of the globalization of the disease.

In an article that first appeared in 1990, a sociologist from Toronto's York University, John O'Neill, appeals to scholars in his discipline to take on the challenge of transforming AIDS into a *virus sociologicus*. The sociology profession, he asserts, "cannot remain ideologically ignorant of virology." The "global panic" caused by AIDS, he says, was not just a biological event but a cultural one as well, for it forced all social scientists to reevaluate "our moral values regarding trust and community."[3]

Recall from chapter 1 that sociologists may define *culture* as the way people construct meaning. One of the fundamental assumptions sociologists make about our world is that we construct our reality socially, that is, through experiences that are mediated through human interaction. There is very little, if any, "reality" "out there" except what we create. This assumption applies to what we know about the world, and it applies to what we do *not* know as well.

This latter dimension, what people did not know, is what worried O'Neill about the AIDS global panic. Despite nearly a decade of intensive scientific research and massive publicity campaigns aimed at raising public consciousness about the AIDS threat, most people continued to manifest what O'Neill terms "socially structured carnal ignorance."[4] That is, most people continued to be ignorant of what AIDS is, where it comes from, how it spreads, and so forth. Most importantly, according to O'Neill, this ignorance was the product of certain social structures. Many of the reasons for our ignorance stem from the asymptomatic nature of the infection itself. That is, people infected with HIV usually do not know it for a long time, sometimes for years, because it does not manifest itself via symptoms right away. Thus, carriers and potential victims engage in behavior that puts them at risk without being aware of doing so. This problem makes the disease bad enough; but, O'Neill warns, the problem was made much worse because, as he puts it, "there exists an enormous bias in the social sciences against the study of the ways in which our ignorance, misinformation and deception is [sic] socially structured."[5]

The AIDS panic that gripped the world in the 1990s threatened to produce two crises. One was a crisis of legitimation of the sexual cultural values that had emerged from the 1960s onward. On the one hand, those who had been most committed to sexual freedom would now reject its principles; on the other, many people would be tempted to turn against the gay community and thus undermine the regime of civil liberties that protects their individual rights. The second crisis was to contribute to a further weakening of mass public confidence in the state in particular and in industrial society generally. (I say a "further weakening" because the AIDS pandemic was merely one of a number of sensational failures in the technology of industrial society during the 1970s and 1980s. Others included the nuclear power plant accidents at Chernobyl and Three Mile Island and the *Exxon Valdez* oil tanker spill.) The state had been seen as the guarantor of a healthy world. If an accident were to occur, the state would make things right again. Neither of these things happened with regard to AIDS, and the global panic that ensued chipped away a little bit more of an already eroding public confidence in the effectiveness of the democratic, industrial state.

ECONOMICS: CAN ANYONE PROFIT FROM AIDS?

It may seem perverse to suggest that an economic perspective can illuminate something as profoundly devastating to humanity as the AIDS pandemic. Yet diseases do not arise and propagate in an economic vacuum. Diseases require medical responses, including hospitalization, the work of health care professionals, and the dispensing of medicines to alleviate suffering. And in the world of global capitalism and multinational corporations, many people see these responses as subject to the law of supply and demand just as much as any other product or service offered on the market.[6]

AIDS is a disease for which neither a cure nor a vaccine has been discovered as of this writing (late 2001). However, several drugs have been developed that can counteract the damaging effects of the disease by strengthening the patient's immune system or by suppressing the production of enzymes that the virus needs to reproduce. The first AIDS drug, called AZT, was introduced in 1987 by the drug firm Burroughs Wellcome (bought by Glaxo in 1995 to create Glaxo Wellcome). AZT slows the spread of the disease, but 16,000 victims in the United States and ten times that number in Africa still died the first year it was available. In 1996, after a decade and a half of research, large pharmaceutical firms began to place on the market several much-improved drugs that have had a dramatic effect in reducing the death rate from AIDS. In 1999, for example, only 10,100 victims died from AIDS-related causes in the United States. The problem with these drugs is that they must be taken in a complicated three-drug cocktail. An example of one such cocktail might consist of two Videx capsules at 7.00 a.m. followed at 7.30 a.m. by one Zerit capsule and five Viracept tablets, with the entire regimen repeated twelve hours later.

Because this cocktail cannot cure AIDS but only suppress its more deadly consequences, once begun it must be continued for the rest of the patient's life. The administration of such a regimen obviously depends on a dense and sophisticated network of health professionals, educators, and distributors. The drugs alone cost between $15,000 and $20,000 per patient per year in the United States, which places it far out of reach of virtually all the AIDS victims in the developing world. The African nation of Zimbabwe, for example, has about 1.5 million people infected with HIV. To treat this population with these drugs would cost about $18 billion per year, which is nearly three times the gross national product of the country. To treat Uganda's estimated 930,000 HIV-infected people would cost $11.2 billion, or 172 percent of its GNP.

Medicine is a huge global enterprise. World pharmaceutical sales in 2000 were slightly more than $373 billion. About 40 percent of this revenue was generated by markets in North America; Africa, the region hardest hit by AIDS, accounted for only about $4.7 billion or about 1.3 percent of the total sales. World pharmaceutical production is dominated by a comparative handful of large multinational corporations. The six largest pharmaceutical firms in 1999 had total sales of $116.5 billion and employed more than 322,000 workers. Three of these firms were American: Merck (1999 sales of $32.7 billion), Bristol-Myers Squibb ($20.2 billion), and Pfizer (recently merged with Warner-Lambert; $29.1 billion for the merged firm). One firm was British: Glaxo Wellcome (merged with SmithKline Beecham; $13.7 billion); one was German: Boehringer Ingelheim ($5.4 billion); and one was Swiss: Roche ($18.4 billion).

These firms collectively are responsible for having developed virtually all of the drugs available for use against AIDS. Their legal right to market these drugs without competition is protected by national patents. However, laboratories in developing countries such as India and Brazil have the ability to produce identical drugs known as "generics" and to sell them for a tiny fraction of the price charged to customers in industrialized countries. The firms owning the patents oppose such a move because it threatens to reduce their profits. While firms such as Merck see little market for their products in countries like Zimbabwe or South Africa, they do not want the generics on the market in the developing world for fear they will drive down the price in the United States and Europe. Meanwhile, millions of AIDS victims suffer and die in the developing countries.

Numerous factors complicate the distribution of anti-AIDS drugs in the developing world. We can begin with patent protection. In 1993, at the urging of U.S. pharmaceutical firms, the administration of President Bill Clinton pressed for the incorporation of worldwide protection of patent rights in the global trade regime then emerging. When the World Trade Organization (WTO) came into existence on January 1, 1995, its rules incorporated an agreement known as Trade Related Aspects of Intellectual Property Rights (TRIPS). In brief, TRIPS provides that any member state of the WTO agrees to respect the exclusive marketing rights of patent holders in any other member state. The pharmaceutical firms argue that they need to be free to charge the market price for these drugs because they need to be able to recoup the enormous sums they have invested in research and development of new drugs. However, in the twelve months ending November 2000, after reinvesting some $21 billion in research and development, America's ten largest drug makers still had $100 billion more in sales than their manufacturing costs. The rate of return on assets for the drug industry is the highest of any manufacturing sector in the U.S. economy.

Another complicating factor involves the absorptive capacity and the competing needs of developing countries. Most poor countries lack the network of health care professionals, clinics, distribution systems, educational programs, and so forth that would be needed to administer such a complicated public health program. One proposed AIDS countermeasure would involve bringing large numbers of doctors from African countries to the United States to equip them to administer the AIDS cocktails, but that would leave their countries dangerously short of scarce medical personnel in the interim. Then there is the question of competing needs. The World Health Organization has shown that the spending of $10,000 on health care in the Third World would save about 9,900 dehydrated children, *or* several hundred tuberculosis patients, *or* one AIDS victim. Finally, there is debate over competing strategies to counteract the disease. Advocates of prevention assert that for comparative handfuls of money they can supply enough condoms to stop the spread of AIDS in its tracks. Treatment advocates resist arguments based on prevention, arguing that once we begin to weigh treatment against prevention, prevention will always seem more cost effective, so the already infected victims will simply be left to die unattended and in agony.[7]

In 2001, several developments appeared to offer some hope that the conflict between the needs of AIDS victims in developing countries and the profit motive of the giant pharmaceutical firms might be resolved. Several of the large drug makers offered their products at reduced prices to certain selected national markets in Africa. One of the largest pharmaceutical firms, Merck, promised to give AIDS sufferers in Botswana free drugs for five years. Another large firm, the Swiss-based Roche, agreed to cut the price of its AIDS drug by some 70 percent in Brazil, in return for which Brazil agreed not to break the patent and produce the drug locally.[8] And an extra $100 million was given to Botswana by Merck and the Bill and Melinda Gates Foundation to be spent on training nurses, education, more condoms, and increasing the number of hospital beds.[9] Finally, the United States withdrew its patent complaint in the WTO against the Brazilian government over its plan to allow government-run laboratories to manufacture generic versions of any foreign drug patented before 1996. This case was widely regarded as signaling the acceptance by the United States of the determination of governments in developing countries to make AIDS medicines available to their people regardless of the patent protection these drugs enjoy within the WTO.[10]

BIOLOGY: HOW HIV SPREADS

HIV has much in common with viruses in general.[11] Viruses are among the tiniest of all organisms, some 100 to 300 times smaller than bacteria, capable of being seen only with the aid of an electron microscope. They are also among the most ancient of all organisms. Some viruses evolved using as their reservoir hosts lines of reptiles that extend back in time several hundred million years at the least. Viruses have carved out their niche in the biosphere by virtue of their simplicity, but they achieve this simplicity by relying entirely on the cells of the host organism (humans in the case of HIV) to perform the basic functions of life: energy capture, metabolism, and reproduction. Outside a host cell, a virus is little more than a tiny fragment of DNA (or RNA) surrounded by a thin protein membrane. However, each virus cell has on its outer covering tiny receptors capable of identifying the markers on the outside of susceptible or vulnerable cells of the host's body. These receptors attach themselves to these markers and penetrate the outer covering of the host cell, allowing the virus to use the host cell's energy and reproductive mechanism to make millions of copies of itself. When these copies become numerous enough, they overwhelm the host's immune system and the host (as we humans would put it) "gets sick."

But HIV is also different from most other viruses in ways that make it extremely difficult to combat. For one thing, HIV is a retrovirus, which means that its genetic material is contained in RNA instead of DNA.[12] When the virus attaches itself to a cell of the host's body, it inserts its RNA into the host cell. The viral RNA is then converted into DNA so that it can be spliced into the DNA of the host cell. This extra step (converting RNA into DNA) offers an additional opportunity for the introduction of errors in the copying process. Because of this, HIV mutates within the host's body much more rapidly and much more frequently than other viruses do. Not only does this enable the virus to hide undetected for longer periods, but it also means that HIV can evolve resistance to drugs at a much faster pace.

In addition, HIV chooses to do its damage at an especially critical site in the body: the immune system. HIV cells target primarily immune system cells such as the white blood cells that stimulate the production of antibodies and the killer T cells that destroy infected cells at other places in the body. Because HIV uses the cells of the host's immune system to reproduce, most of the damage done by AIDS occurs because the host's immune system is weakened. Without this front line of defense, the host falls prey to illnesses that would not affect a person whose immune system was strong and intact. Much of the mortality inflicted by AIDS in developing countries, especially in Asia, is due not to AIDS itself but to tuberculosis, which invades the body of an AIDS carrier much more easily than the body of a person whose immune system is intact.

Finally, because it is in large part a sexually transmitted disease (STD), AIDS can survive in very small populations. Contagious "crowding" diseases like measles require a fairly large population of potential hosts because the transmission of the microorganisms is a difficult process at best. STDs do not require such a large population, however, because the people who carry them are in much more intimate contact with potential hosts than are people in the general population. Moreover, the carriers of the disease are "asymptomatic," meaning that they may not exhibit symptoms of the disease for a very long time after they have become infected. Often they may not even be aware that they are carrying the disease until after they have infected others. A study by the CDC released in 2001 reveals that about four out of ten people in the United States infected with HIV do not learn of their condition for a decade after they acquire the virus.[13] During this long period, the virus can inflict considerable damage on the victim's immune system, and the carrier can unknowingly spread the virus to many other people.

HISTORY: AIDS, THE BUBONIC PLAGUE, AND WORLD SYSTEMS

The AIDS pandemic is not the first instance in which global systems have been associated with a widespread epidemic. Beginning with the first recorded urban plague, in Athens in 430 B.C.E., long-distance trade and migration brought about the movement of viruses and bacteria from their natural reservoirs to vulnerable human populations. World systems analysis can help us understand the AIDS pandemic by comparing our current plight to one of the earliest of these global epidemics: the spread of the bubonic plague through Asia and Europe in the fourteenth century.[14]

The bubonic plague is a bacterial epidemic caused by the bacillus *Yersinia pestis*. The bacillus resides in populations of small burrowing or ground-dwelling animals such as rats, marmots, and prairie dogs. These animals live in the wild in areas known as "natural plague reservoirs." So long as the bacillus is confined to the animals that live in these reservoirs, they are of little concern to human populations. The bacillus cannot travel unaided, and the carrier species move relatively little unless they are disturbed by natural upheavals such as earthquakes or by intruding human populations during war, migration, or the preparation of land for farming. However, the rats or other carriers carry in their hair or fur tiny fleas, called rat fleas, that feed off the blood of their host. These fleas can carry in their guts several hundred thousand bacilli of *Y. pestis*. When the carrying animal dies, the fleas jump to another carrier. As they feed on their new host, they regurgitate some of the bacilli into the blood stream of the host. Once inside the body, the bacilli migrate to the portion of the lymphatic system closest to the point of entry: the groin or the armpits and neck. There they cause the swelling of painful lumps, called "buboes" (from the Greek word for groin, *boubon*), that disfigure the body and drain infected liquid. Other symptoms include high fever, delirium, and vomiting. For the last 100 years or so, treatment by antibiotics has usually been sufficient to save most of the victims, but in the Middle Ages the horrendous effects of the disease and its extremely high rate of mortality caused people to shun its carriers as pariahs.

For probably thousands if not tens of thousands of years, this "unholy trinity" of bacteria, fleas, and rats lived undisturbed in their natural reservoirs, primarily in South and Southeast Asia. In 542 C.E., the plague burst out of Asia and entered Europe to cause what is referred to as the "plague of Justinian" after the Byzantine emperor during whose reign the attack occurred. For the next 700 years there were no recorded instances of the plague; but in the mid–thirteenth century Mongol troops invaded the Himalayan foothills in the border region between China, Burma, and India. When they returned to China, they brought the plague with them to ravage Asian and European populations for the next 400 years.

The specific mechanisms by which the plague spread were war and long-distance commerce. The disease first devastated China, reducing its population in half, from about 123 million in 1200 to 65 million in 1393. The disease then slowly crept westward, carried by the camel caravans of merchants along the Silk Road. This complex network of trade routes had connected China to Europe since before the time of Christ. Now, in addition to silk, spices, and other exotic goods, the camels, horses, and donkeys of the caravans also brought rats, fleas, and *Y. pestis*.

By 1346, the plague had arrived with Mongol soldiers at the Black Sea port of Kaffa (now called Feodosiya). Kaffa was at the time operated as a trading center by merchants from Genoa. As part of their siege tactics, the Mongols used catapults to hurl over the city walls the cadavers of their troops who had been killed by the plague, a macabre early form of germ warfare. When the Genoans fled the city and headed back to Italy by ship, they unknowingly carried with them the rats and fleas that brought the plague to Europe once again. By October 1347 the disease reached the Sicilian port of Messina, and by December it was on the European mainland. While there would be surges and declines of the disease, Europe would not be truly free of the plague for at least three centuries. The initial wave, which lasted until 1350, has gone down in history as the Black Death. It was responsible for killing about one-third of the European population of about 60 million.

FUTURISM: THE FUTURE OF AIDS

Predicting how AIDS will behave over the next several decades is crucial to understanding the fate that awaits countries like India or China or entire continents like Africa. But predicting the future of AIDS is a highly complex process that challenges even the most gifted and best equipped epidemiologists.[15] Because the virus is spread primarily by sexual activity, and because this activity is both highly variable across populations and supremely sensitive and private, reliable data are very hard to obtain. But there is a more fundamental problem than this, and it is the great uncertainty over the correct paradigm to use to describe the changes that will occur in the HIV virus over time.

Like all viruses, HIV confronts evolutionary pressures to adapt to its environment (that is, the human immune system). Some strains of HIV will be selected over others because of their genetic fitness. Two models of disease evolution are available to help us predict how AIDS will evolve. Many epidemiologists believe that diseases facing the pressures of natural selection will become less virulent (capable of making a person sick) over time. They believe that a virus like HIV faces a dilemma. If it is too virulent and either kills its victims quickly or renders them so immobilized that the disease cannot be transmitted to other potential victims, then the disease commits "suicide" figuratively speaking. On the other hand, if the disease weakens too much, then it will cease to cause the behaviors that help it to move from host to host (coughing, vomiting, diarrhea, and so forth). Thus, the pattern of evolving disease virulence shows a high peak early in an epidemic's history, followed by a decline in virulence to a moderate level, where the disease seems to remain more or less stable. It neither disappears nor grows worse; it simply adapts to the biological characteristics of its hosts, on whom it depends for survival and reproduction.

This model is certainly not universally embraced, however. One leading critic of this paradigm, the epidemiologist Paul Ewald, argues that there is no inherent reason why a disease must evolve toward a less virulent form.[16] Many other factors affect the ease or difficulty of transmission of a virus from one person to another. Because HIV carriers remain asymptomatic for up to a decade, and the HIV virus is transmitted by the direct mingling of body fluids through sexual activity, pregnancy, or sharing of contaminated needles, the virus can be transmitted from person to person almost regardless of its level of virulence. If Ewald is correct, then HIV will not adapt by becoming less virulent, and the future of the AIDS pandemic looks grim indeed.

It is still too early, however, to be able to say definitively which model will apply to AIDS. In the mid-1990s, observers were hopeful that the disease was moderating because the infection and death rates were declining in cities in North America and Europe. However, the number of AIDS cases and deaths in the United States stopped declining in mid-1998 and remained stable through mid-2000.[17] (See figure CS 1.1.) Clearly we are still in the middle of a disease pattern that has yet to resolve itself.

Figure CS 1.1   Trends in AIDS Cases and Deaths, 1981–2000

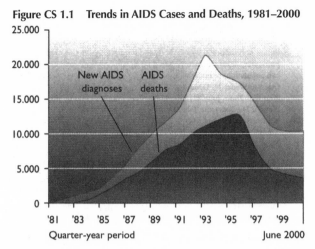

Source: Susan Okie, "Sharp Drop in AIDS Toll May Be Over," *Washington Post,* August 14, 2001; © 2001, *The Washington Post.* Reprinted with permission.

BIOGRAPHY: AIDS IN THE LIFE OF THE INDIVIDUAL

Every issue of the British weekly news magazine *The Economist* carries the obituary of someone whose recent death is of importance to those who follow contemporary world affairs. Usually the person selected is someone prominent in politics, economics, the arts, technology, science, or so forth. The deceased whose obituary appeared in the magazine's issue of July 28, 2001, was none of these.[18] Instead, he was an average man, "ordinary" in the words of the obituary: Paul Omukuba of Nairobi, Kenya. He worked before his death as a waiter in a club in Nairobi and then as a store clerk at a Kenyan coffee farm. His death left behind a widow and two small children.

Even the cause of Paul's death, AIDS and related infections including tuberculosis, was rather unexceptional. About 6,575 Africans die of AIDS every day, about 700 of them in Kenya. Nor was Paul noteworthy because of the reason he contracted AIDS. He was, in the words of a Red Cross nurse who counseled and cared for him, a "typical Kenyan man," with many girlfriends with whom he engaged in unprotected sex, and he never thought AIDS would happen to him.

What was remarkable about Paul Omukuba was the public recognition given to the cause of his death. According to *The Economist,* funerals and death notices are important public events throughout Africa, and no less so in Kenya. Families typically take out large announcements in local newspapers to announce the death of a loved one, with a photograph of the deceased, a list of accomplishments, and so forth. If the cause of death is AIDS, however, there are no such notices. Death from AIDS remains a taboo subject, as does the disease itself. And therein lies part of the reason why AIDS continues to ravage Africa and why Paul Omukuba's death was so important. As *The Economist* puts it,

> HIV has been able to spread so catastrophically in Africa because almost no one talks about it. Sex and AIDS are a subject for jokes, not for serious discussion or classroom education. Kenya's President Daniel arap Moi declared AIDS a national disaster in 1999, but he regularly reminds women to obey men, and has blamed women for the spread of the disease. He cannot bring himself to urge the use of condoms, but instead suggested recently that the way to fight AIDS was for everyone to abstain from sex for two years. . . . All this has produced a climate in which basic sex and health education are ignored, and young people are not told honestly that unprotected sex spreads the HIV infection.[19]

Paul Omukuba's loved ones resolved not to let the cause of his death go unremarked and unnoticed. Their obituary notice in the Nairobi *Daily Nation* was decorated with two red ribbons to show he died of AIDS. At his funeral his relatives and friends also wore red ribbons. Perhaps most significantly, Paul's sister brought his infection to the attention of family elders, who decided that because his widow was also HIV-positive, she should not be given in marriage to a new husband (as traditional practices would have directed). Instead, she should remain unmarried so that at least one life may be saved from the epidemic sweeping Africa. These measures may appear small to the outside world, but they doubtless required considerable social courage. But the hope of Paul Omukuba's family is that their actions will embolden others to speak out as well, so that Kenyans can begin to come to grips with the disease that is devastating their country.

NOTES

1. This article is described in a twentieth-anniversary article written by the physician who wrote the original article. See Lawrence K. Altman, "The Cause of the Outbreak Is Unknown," *New York Times,* July 3, 2001.

2. These data can be found at www.unaids.org.

3. John O'Neill, "AIDS as a Globalizing Panic," in *Global Culture: Nationalism, Globalization and Modernity,* ed. Mike Featherstone (London: SAGE, 1990), 329.

4. O'Neill, "AIDS as a Globalizing Panic," 330.

5. O'Neill, "AIDS as a Globalizing Panic," 331.

6. Much of this section is drawn from Barton Gellman, "An Unequal Calculus of Life and Death"; Barton Gellman, "A Turning Point that Left Millions Behind"; and Bill Brubaker, "The Limits of $100 Million." This three-part series, entitled "Death Watch: AIDS, Drugs and Africa," appeared in the *Washington Post* on December 27, 28, and 29, 2000.

7. Stephanie Flanders, "In the Shadow of AIDS, a World of Other Problems," *New York Times,* June 24, 2001.

8. Jennifer L. Rich, "Roche Reaches Accord on Drug with Brazil," *New York Times,* September 1, 2001.

9. "AIDS in Botswana: A New Approach," *The Economist*, August 11, 2001: 36–37.

10. Barbara Crossette, "U.S. Drops Case Over AIDS Drugs in Brazil," *New York Times*, June 26, 2001.

11. Ann Guidici Fettner, *The Science of Viruses* (New York: William Morrow, 1990).

12. Denise Grady, "Scientists Shifting Strategies in Quest for an AIDS Vaccine," *New York Times*, June 5, 2001.

13. David Brown, "4 of 10 People with HIV Get Late Diagnosis," *Washington Post*, August 15, 2001.

14. This section is based on my discussion of the biology of the Silk Road in Robert P. Clark, *Global Life Systems: Population, Food, and Disease in the Process of Globalization* (Boulder: Rowman & Littlefield, 2001), chapter 6. See the notes of this chapter for further sources.

15. Roy M. Anderson and Robert M. May, "Understanding the AIDS Pandemic," *Scientific American* (May 1992): 58–66.

16. Paul Ewald, *Evolution of Infectious Diseases* (Oxford: Oxford University Press, 1994), especially chapter 1.

17. Susan Okie, "Sharp Drop in AIDS Toll May Be Over," *Washington Post*, August 14, 2001.

18. "Obituary: Paul Livingstone Tito Omukuba," *The Economist*, July 28, 2001: 79. See also "AIDS in Nigeria: Silent Leaders Help the Virus to Spread," *The Economist*, June 30, 2001: 41–42; and Henri E. Cauvin, "To Fight AIDS, Swaziland's King Orders Girls to Avoid Sex for 5 Years," *New York Times*, September 29, 2001.

19. "Obituary," 79.

2

Global Awareness

KEY IDEAS IN THIS CHAPTER

Global awareness requires that we be able to **think about the world as a single place.** For this we need to acquire a new **paradigm** or set of ideas that enable us to make sense of the world. As more and more people begin to experience the world as a single place, a **paradigm shift** is occurring.

The approach introduced here is called the **Global System Paradigm.** This perspective involves the application of systems theory to an understanding of global events and trends.

The Global System Paradigm helps us experience the world as a single place by

- showing us how to look for **common properties** or features in different systems and to understand thereby how one system resembles another;
- providing us with a **holistic worldview** that allows us to see how parts of a system are connected and how systems are connected with each other; and
- showing how we are all **connected to unseen others** who are distant in time and space—the paradigm helps us do this by making invisible systems visible to us.

In the 1970s, environmentalists sought to rally their followers with the slogan "Think Globally, Act Locally." As it happens, "thinking globally" is much more difficult than "acting locally." As Richard Barnet and John Cavanagh point out, "We are all participants in one way or another in an unprecedented political and economic happening, but we cannot make sense of it. We know that we are supposed to think globally, but it is hard to wrap the mind even around a city block, much less a planet."[1] And it is not just economists and political scientists who feel frustrated. Several years ago, historians Michael Geyer and Charles

Bright alerted us to the challenge of writing "world history in a global age" in these terms:

> Lacking an imagination capable of articulating an integrated world of multiple modernities, globality is enveloped in an eerie silence, which, however, cannot mask its powerful effects; and contestations over the terms of globalization, lacking a language that can accommodate, even facilitate, difference, turns into implacably hostile rejections of otherness. A reversal of this silence entails, above all, thinking and narrating the history of *this* existing world and how it has come about. This project must proceed with an understanding that, unlike the systems builders of the European past, who visualized the world and thought world history long before they could possibly experience the world as a whole, we contemporaries of the late twentieth century experience the world long before we know how to think it.[2]

Even Earth system scientists have great difficulty understanding how the world works. With global warming becoming a growing concern among activists and policy makers, climatologists have struggled to develop world climate computer models that can account for observed changes in the Earth's surface temperature. While they know some ingredients of such a model fairly accurately (such as the role of greenhouse gases or deep ocean currents), other factors (such as particles suspended in the atmosphere or cloud cover) remain unfathomed mysteries.[3]

As we have already seen, in this book *globalization* means the process by which more and more people come to experience the world as a single place. The aim of the book is to help you acquire the language and other mental tools necessary to think about our world this way.

HOW WE MAKE SENSE OF THE WORLD: PARADIGMS AND PARADIGM SHIFTS

One of the founders of the world systems approach, Jay Forrester, once observed that "everyone uses models all the time." "Every person," he writes,

> in his private life and in his community life uses models for decision making. The mental image of the world around one, carried in each individual's head, is a model. One does not have a family, a business, a city, a government, or a country in his head. He has only selected concepts and relationships which he uses to represent the real system. . . . All of our decisions are taken on the basis of models. All of our laws are passed on the basis of models. All executive actions are taken on the basis of models. The question is not whether to use or ignore models. The question is only a choice between alternative models.[4]

In this passage, Forrester is describing one way to make sense of the world. Models are a way of improving our understanding of something distant, complex, or unfamiliar by comparing it with something else that is near, simple, or familiar to us.[5] This book is based on the idea that we can improve our ability to make sense of the very complex process known as globalization by means of intellectual tools such as models, visualizations, metaphors, and analogies. Forrester's approach would have us do so by improving the model(s) or mental image(s) we use to understand the process. In this book we will refer to these models and images as a *paradigm*.

What is a paradigm? Originally, the word was used in the study of languages to refer to a set of all the possible forms of a word that contain a particular element, but gradually the word came to mean a pattern or example. With the publication of *The Structure of Scientific Revolutions* in 1962,[6] the physicist and historian Thomas Kuhn broadened the word's meaning to mean not just a hypothesis, proposition, or belief "but a whole set of shared premises and values that determines the nature of scientific inquiry."[7] Some people use the word to refer to a model or pattern, but it is more than that. A model or pattern is meant to be copied, but a paradigm is more "like an accepted judicial decision in the common law, . . . an object for further articulation and specification under new and more stringent conditions."[8] Kuhn also popularized the term *paradigm shift* to refer to the process by which large numbers of scientists changed their shared premises and values. Since Kuhn's book, we have broadened the word *paradigm* to refer to a person's overall perspective or worldview and the term *paradigm shift* to refer to wholesale transformations of perspective or worldview by large populations.

A paradigm is an essential component of our thought processes inasmuch as it shapes the way we interact with virtually everything in our environment. A paradigm is a mental framework that informs our understanding of cause and effect. If something changes around us, our paradigm helps us explain why the change occurred and what is likely to happen next. When we act in a certain way, we do so with the understanding—supplied by our paradigm—that certain events will follow. Our paradigm helps us identify ourselves and others, predict what we and others around us will do, and explain why we and they did it. In short, our paradigm is central to our attempts to make sense of a world that otherwise might appear random and without meaning. There is a danger in failing to recognize the crucial role of paradigms in how we think about our world, as was pointed out by a group of global modelers some two decades ago:

> Paradigms are unquestioned and nearly subconscious beliefs that serve to screen, order, and classify incoming impressions and thus to shape subsequent mental models. For instance, if one has a paradigmatic belief that humans are aggressive, selfish, and competitive, one sees and remembers greedy behaviour on the part of oneself and others, and one tends to forget or even *not to notice* altruistic, loving, cooperative behaviour. Paradigms are thus self-fulfilling hypotheses as long as they are at least partly congruent with the real world. Only when massive evidence contradicts them are they shifted or changed.[9]

Paradigms play a central role in social interaction as well. Kuhn makes the paradigm an essential feature of what he calls "normal science," that is, what the great majority of the members of a given scientific community (for example, bio-chemists) do in the course of their professional lives.[10] Adoption of the reigning paradigm is required for a novice to enter the field. The professional paradigm is a shared commitment to the same rules and standards of scientific practice, and it determines the problems to be solved and the facts relevant to finding their so-lution. Without a paradigm to guide them, members of any profession are apt to be engaged in the purely random gathering of facts. Acceptance of a paradigm frees a group of like-minded individuals from having to create their field anew everyday, but it also constrains the members of this group and prevents them from undertaking investigations based on alternative paradigms. Some critics of Kuhn have blasted him for seeming to endorse this authoritarian nature of science as a mode of thought and inquiry.

This book proposes a new paradigm for understanding and explaining glob-alization. Many of the elements of this paradigm will be familiar to the reader, but their combination in a package of concepts may strike the reader as un-usual. What this book asks of you, then, is the adoption of a new paradigm for experiencing the world as a single place. This process may not be easy.

Kuhn emphasizes that the choice of a new paradigm to replace an existing one is a long process that may involve considerable stress for the participants. To be accepted, an alternative paradigm must seem better than the existing one for defining the problems to be solved, explaining unexplained phenomena, identifying the criteria for evaluating solutions, and predicting the future. How-ever, warns Kuhn, no alternative paradigm will be able to solve all the problems to which it is applied. To a considerable degree, a new paradigm emerges as preferable because of certain aesthetic reasons: it simply looks more elegant, more efficient, or more precise.[11] The advocates of a new paradigm may hope to persuade others by putting forward fact-based arguments, but these will sel-dom convince all their opponents. As Kuhn puts it, "The competition between paradigms is not the sort of battle that can be resolved by proofs."[12] Moreover, because a paradigm is a coherent package of interconnected ideas, it must be adopted as a whole rather than piecemeal. Again, Kuhn warns, "The transition between competing paradigms cannot be made a step at a time, forced by logic and neutral experience. Like the gestalt switch, it must occur all at once (though not necessarily in an instant) or not at all."[13] For these reasons, a paradigm shift usually occurs not by mass conversion of the members of a profession but by the gradual replacement of the group's older members by younger ones who enter the field already committed to the new paradigm.

Kuhn makes it clear that most people will resist adopting a new paradigm, likely expending considerable psychic energy in doing so. "The transfer of al-legiance from paradigm to paradigm is a conversion experience that cannot be forced," he writes.[14] But why should this be so? At the level of the individual, the problem is one of identity. To a certain degree, all of us shape our vision of our own identities around a paradigm's central premises and values; to cast off that paradigm and embrace a new one means a change in identity as well. To many, such a change may be as traumatic as, say, adopting a new religion or national citizenship. At the level of institutions, more material interests are at stake. Budgets and personnel decisions are made on the basis of a paradigm's description of problems to be solved and how solutions are to be sought. To introduce a challenging paradigm means the reallocation of funds and bureaucratic power. Those already entrenched will resist efforts by the advocates of the new paradigm to unseat them and reallocate resources.

Thinking about the world as a single place has undergone paradigm shifts in the past and will doubtless do so again in the years to come.[15] In 1492, for example, when Columbus and his crew arrived in the Western Hemisphere, they believed that they had landed on an island off the coast of Asia. Their global paradigm based on the work (including maps) of Claudius Ptolemy in the second century C.E. contained only three continents: Europe, Africa, and Asia. The passage westward from Europe to Asia crossed open ocean. There was no landmass between Europe and Asia. Columbus himself went to his grave believing that his expeditions had taken him to Asia, and for nearly three centuries this paradigm would inspire cartographers to draw the Americas as simply an extension of Asia. It was not until 1778 when the English explorer James Cook sailed into the Bering Sea that the world understood that North America and Asia were two separate masses of land. (It bears mentioning, though, that North America and Asia are separate only when the planet is relatively warm and sea levels are high. In the distant past when the Earth's temperature dropped and the sea levels receded, the Bering land bridge reappeared and the two continents were indeed one. Perhaps Columbus was right after all!)

Another important global paradigm shift took place during the first two-thirds of the twentieth century. Until 1912, the prevailing paradigm of Earth system scientists was that the continents were immovable and that their present locations are where they had always been. In that year, a German geophysicist and meteorologist named Alfred Wegener proposed the theory that the continents had at one time been joined in a supercontinent that he named Pangaea. Lacking any detailed knowledge of the ocean floor or other aspects of the planet's crust, Wegener was unable to explain how such a monumental event as the separation of the continents had taken place, and he was criticized and ridiculed by geophysicists and geologists. We have known since the 1950s and 1960s, however, that Wegener is correct. The continents are not immobile but, rather, float on top of huge tectonic plates and are being separated by a process known as seafloor spreading at the rate of perhaps an inch each year.

Let us now turn to the task at hand: fashioning a paradigm to understand globalization. Our definition of *globalization*—the process by which people come to experience the world as a single place—has been provided by Roland Robertson.[16] Robertson has been quick to point out that with this definition he did not intend to suggest that the world is moving toward an integrated, unified, homogeneous culture or that a single cohesive system is being crystallized out of this process. He does argue that a global culture is emerging, not in the sense of a set

of normatively binding values or ideas, but simply as a consciousness or awareness of the increasing interdependence of all of us across the entire world—"the
penetration of local life by globally diffused ideas," as he puts it.[17]

Our challenge, then, is to devise a paradigm that enables us to understand
globalization and the many ways it affects us daily—in other words, to think
about the world as a single place. Several problems complicate our search. First,
as noted in chapter 1, we cannot possibly experience the world as a single
place by means of direct observation. In fact, our direct experiences will be limited to an extremely small portion of our world. We must rely on a paradigm
that enables us to find meaning in our experiences of the world as a whole; and
this can only be done indirectly.[18] Second, in this endeavor we are not free
agents. We cannot invent just any paradigm; we have to devise our perspective
from the intellectual tool kit that prevails in society generally. A global awareness paradigm cannot be isolated from any larger intellectual perspective but,
rather, must be grounded in such a perspective.

We are discovering that the entire world is an extremely difficult object to think
about, and the leading ways of thinking that we have inherited do not lend themselves to thinking about such an object. Most of the time, when we think analytically about something we proceed by comparing it with something else: for example, General Motors is larger than the economy of Costa Rica, the Internet is a
faster means of communication than the Pony Express, and so forth. But the
world is unique, in a class by itself. If we choose the world as our unit of analysis, then we have nothing with which to compare it, and that makes thinking
about it much more difficult.[19] Moreover, as traditionally practiced, the scientific
method does not lend itself to the study of extremely complex systems because
such inquiry requires that we introduce change one variable at a time to see what
the effects will be. As Robert Jervis has pointed out, with complex systems we
cannot change just one thing.[20] By their very nature, systems are entities in which
changes occur at multiple points, often without our intending these changes or
even perceiving or understanding them. Thus, the empirical testing of explana-
tory propositions (one of the key features of the scientific method) becomes virtually impossible for anything as large and as complicated as the global system.

For the last three centuries or so, people living in the Western intellectual tra-
dition have viewed their world through the prism known as secular, rational humanism.[21] This mode of thought reached its fullest expression in the Enlightenment of the eighteenth century.[22] Its central premises are the orderly nature of
the Universe, the existence of laws that govern that Universe, the perfectibility
of humans and of our social order (the idea of progress), and the central role of
reason (exemplified in science) in discovering these laws and achieving that
state of perfection. An important corollary of these ideas is the notion of predictability. If we can know the laws governing the Universe, and if we can acquire sufficient information to apply these laws, then we can in principle predict
(and, by implication, control) the future. And last, the preferred way to learn
these laws and acquire this information was by breaking complex problems into

small pieces and studying them in great detail. If possible, the pieces should be isolated from all confounding outside influences, a strategy known as "holding all other factors constant."

Since the beginning of the nineteenth century other paradigms have emerged in Western thought to challenge most if not all of these assumptions. In the nineteenth century, Romanticism argued that the Enlightenment's emphasis on reason distances us from understanding how our emotions shape our behavior. In the early twentieth century, nationalism arose to exalt ethnic ties even though in most cases there was little empirical evidence of the existence of these ties. And in the last half of the twentieth century, postmodernism asserted that there is no single truth, no idea that can be found to be valid universally and eternally. Moreover, texts seldom if ever really mean what their authors say they mean; true meaning has to be inferred by means of especially insightful interpretation by outsiders.

But of all these problems with the Enlightenment, the one that most obscured our attempts to think about the world as a single place is the reductionism and fragmentation implied in the linear paradigm known as the scientific method. Beginning in the latter quarter of the nineteenth century, the compartmentalization of knowledge into professional specialties began to be reproduced in the very structure of the contemporary university in its departments, faculties, and degree programs. Professional associations, doctoral education, and specialized journals and other media of communication aggravated the problem. Scholars trained in one highly specialized field could not understand the vocabulary or appreciate the significance of the issues of other fields; and their professional advancement often depended on a degree of specialization and concentration that cut them off from collaboration with researchers in other disciplines.

It is indeed ironic that as the domains of politics, economics, demographics, information, epidemiology, and many others are becoming global in scope, the domains of knowledge about these trends remain fragmented, partial, and isolated. Fortunately, a new paradigm has emerged that offers another possibility, a way to think about problems or issues holistically. This new paradigm, which will be described shortly, combines ideas from a number of intellectual perspectives. Some of these ideas, such as general systems theory, have been around for half a century; others, such as chaos theory or the science of complex adaptive systems, for only about half that long.

The debate between environmentalists and ecologists about the role of humans in the natural world illustrates how these worldviews affect how we approach solving problems in the real world. During the first half of the twentieth century, many biologists held the view that nature, if left alone, would inexorably progress from "lower" to "higher" forms of organization. Plants and animals were seen as fusing together into a biosphere possessing a coherence and inner harmony that some would liken metaphorically to the soul of a human being. Many later environmentalists would hold onto these beliefs, but by the mid-1970s ecologists had begun to see the natural world in a new light. Instead

Box 2.1. Alternative Paradigms in the New Millennium

	Existing Paradigm (Linear, Near Equilibrium)	Emerging Paradigm (Nonlinear, Far from Equilibrium)
Dominant institutions are	the nation-state; the industrial production system	numerous; the nation-state and industrial production system are only two among many
Nation-states are	sovereign and autonomous; primary actors in international system	only partially autonomous; only one among many international actors
Industrial production is	concentrated in a few countries (international division of labor)	spread throughout entire world (global manufacturing system)
Connecting systems	function slowly, inefficiently; changes are transmitted with significant delays	function efficiently, with great speed; changes are transmitted extremely quickly
Factors of production	cannot be moved easily or cheaply	can be (and are) moved easily and cheaply
Changes are	• linear and slow; there is time to adjust • isolated and affect only their immediate surroundings	• exponential and rapid; there is little time to adjust ("overshoot") • highly interconnected and potentially, if not actually, global in scope
System relationships are	simple, linear, largely known, and relatively easy to observe and understand	complex, nonlinear, largely unknown, and mostly beyond our observation and understanding
Consequences of decisions	can be accurately predicted into the medium and long term	cannot be accurately predicted beyond the near term
Failures of large systems will	be relatively rare, isolated, and easily absorbed	increase sharply, with a corresponding rise in social and environmental costs

of harmony and cooperation, they saw ecosystems that were not progressing toward anything in particular but simply competing for scarce resources using any and all strategies at their disposal. Whereas environmentalists (mostly non-scientists) pursued public policies toward land and resource use that were reformist and fundamentally moralistic, ecologists (mostly scientists) stressed our lack of knowledge about how ecosystems fit together and our inability to do much to raise natural systems to some "higher" or "better" purpose. This is certainly not the place to attempt to resolve this debate or the larger debate of which it forms a part. Secular rational humanism, postmodernist chaos theory, and the other paradigms will continue to do battle for the foreseeable future. But whatever perspective we fashion to experience the world as a single place will probably embrace elements of these competing worldviews.

The principal features of the two alternative paradigms—the *existing paradigm (linear, near equilibrium)* and the *emerging paradigm (nonlinear, far from equilibrium)*—are outlined in box 2.1. Perhaps the best way to describe systems that are nonlinear and far from equilibrium is by comparing their properties with those of linear systems that are near equilibrium.[23] Whereas change in linear systems is slow, smooth, and regular, the dynamics of nonlinear systems exhibit patterns that appear to be irregular and unpredictable. Whereas linear systems are only slightly changed by slight perturbations in their environments, nonlinear systems exhibit the tendency to change dramatically and fundamentally in similar circumstances. Whereas linear systems seem to have very few transactions with the outside world, nonlinear systems are very open to their environments, and high levels of flows or transactions with the environment are the rule. And of greatest significance to the policy sciences, whereas linear systems appear to be predictable and controllable, nonlinear systems are clearly unpredictable and therefore substantially beyond the control of policy makers. Of course, policy makers continue to strive to get nonlinear systems under control, but they seldom succeed and, in fact, may make things worse by provoking the system into what is called counterintuitive behavior (that is, a system outcome that is exactly the opposite of what the policy makers expected and intended).

THE GLOBAL SYSTEM PARADIGM

The paradigm we will use to make sense of globalization, to think about the world as a single place, is called the Global System Paradigm (GSP). The GSP comprises four elements:

- An ability to *perceive the world as a single place*. Robertson's definition of *globalization* focuses on both systemic connections and human awareness of those connections. As he puts it, "Globalization as a concept refers both to the compression of the world and the intensification of consciousness of the world as a whole."[24]

- An understanding of *how the component parts of our world interact* to produce change. Garret Hardin refers to this dimension of thought as *ecolacy,*
  by which he means "the mastery of connections."[25] In this, he is applying the
  term *ecology,* a word coined by the nineteenth-century German biologist
  Ernst Haeckel to refer to the science of connections in the natural world.
- A focus on the *system and its interconnections* as the principal actor or
  agent in the world and thus the *unit of analysis* as we try to make sense
  of the world.
- The internalization of this awareness so profoundly that we come to accept it without consciously evaluating it against other competing alternative perspectives. This is what Michael Polanyi has referred to as *tacit
  knowledge,*[26] that is, knowledge so deeply internalized that we are not
  aware of it. For a growing number of people, globalization has become
  virtually invisible because they no longer regard such experiences as un-
  usual or out of the ordinary.

The GSP is the product of decades of intellectual struggle to understand and
portray an increasingly complex and challenging world. In chapter 3, we shall
encounter some of the ideas that form the bases of general systems theory,
which is the cornerstone on which the GSP rests. Here I discuss some of the
ways in which this paradigm emerged out of the interactions of personal and
professional agendas and international institutions during the 1970s and 1980s.

If one can identify a birthplace of the GSP, it would be the Massachusetts Institute of Technology (MIT) in Cambridge, Massachusetts. In 1957, supported
by a grant from the Ford Foundation, a group of MIT scholars led by Jay Forrester began work on a methodology known as "industrial dynamics" as a way
to understand and design corporate policy.[27] From that early work emerged the
key ideas about the structure of systems and their dynamic behavior. The importance of feedback loops is a central feature of this approach. In 1968, the
group formalized its model through Forrester's book *Principles of Systems,*[28]
and the next year, the group extended the approach to the growth and stagna-
tion of cities, which resulted in *Urban Dynamics.*[29]

Meanwhile, in April 1968, a group of thirty individuals from ten countries
gathered in Rome at the invitation of Aurelio Peccei, an Italian industrial man-
ager and economist. These individuals—scientists, educators, economists, and
others—were assembled by Peccei to discuss (as they put it) "the present and
future predicament of mankind." Out of this meeting grew the Club of Rome, a
group of private citizens (now numbering about 100) formed to advance the
understanding of what they call the *world problematique,* a set of interlocking
global problems involving poverty, population, food, energy, pollution, changing values, and others.[30] Although the club's members represent many diverse
cultures and ideological beliefs, they are united in their view that the world
problematique presents civilization with its greatest challenge to date. The
problems are themselves so complex, and are so interwoven, that they defy

analysis and solution by traditional methodologies. Our inability to resolve these problems has stemmed, the club believes, from humankind's propensity to study "single items of the problematique without understanding that the whole is more than the sum of its parts, that change in one element means change in the others."[31]

To attack the world problematique, the club launched its Project on the Predicament of Mankind. Phase 1 of the project emerged out of meetings held in summer 1970 in Berne, Switzerland, and Cambridge, Massachusetts. At the time, the group was searching for ways to effect the transition (inevitable, in its view) from industrial growth to equilibrium. The group solicited a presentation from Forrester on his model of world system dynamics. The working document that formed the core of Forrester's presentation was the basis for *World Dynamics,* published originally in 1971. Impressed by Forrester's model, the Club of Rome established an international research program at MIT headed by Dennis Meadows, with financial support from the Volkswagen Foundation. The team set out to apply Forrester's model to real world data from five key sectors that ultimately limit growth: population, agricultural production, natural resources, industrial production, and pollution.

The Club of Rome project led to the publication of a number of influential and highly controversial books on global system dynamics, including *The Limits to Growth* (1972), *Mankind at the Turning Point* (1974), and *Beyond the Limits* (1992).[32] *The Limits to Growth* was particularly controversial; it was translated into twenty-eight languages and sold nine million copies. Each of these studies has a distinctive approach. For example, *The Limits to Growth* attempts to deal with the world as a single system, whereas *Mankind at the Turning Point* divides the world into ten regions, each with its own culture, traditions, and development trajectory.[33] But gradually, over the span of about a decade, a consensus emerged as to the following:

1. There is no known reason why basic needs cannot be supplied for all the world's people into the foreseeable future. These needs are not being met now because of social and political structures, values, norms, and worldviews, not because of absolute physical scarcities.
2. Population and physical capital cannot grow forever on a finite planet.
3. There is no reliable and complete information about the degree to which the Earth can meet the needs of further population growth. There is a great deal of partial information, which optimists interpret optimistically and pessimists, pessimistically.
4. Continuing current policies through the next few decades will not lead to a desirable future. It will produce an increasing gap between the rich and the poor, problems with resource availability and environmental destruction, and worsening economic conditions for most people.
5. The interdependencies among peoples and nations over time and space are greater than is commonly imagined. Actions taken at one time and on

one part of the globe have far-reaching consequences that are impossible to predict intuitively and probably also impossible to predict (totally, precisely, maybe at all) with computer models.

6. Because of these interdependencies, single, simple measures intended to reach narrowly defined goals are likely to be counterproductive.

7. Cooperative approaches to achieving individual or national goals often turn out to be more beneficial in the long run to all parties than competitive approaches.[34]

The use of computer models to examine global systems attracted considerable attention around the world. Seven months after the publication of *The Limits to Growth*, representatives of a dozen scientific organizations met in London to create the International Institute for Applied Systems Analysis. The representatives' objectives were to promote international collaboration on these issues and encourage the application of systems analysis to the solution of problems of global importance.[35] By the early 1980s eight such global computer models had been developed at universities and other research institutions in the United States, the United Kingdom, Germany, Argentina, the Netherlands, Japan, and the then–Soviet Union.[36] Another twenty or so projects were actively under development. Although the developers of these projects represented many diverse political and cultural points of view, they were labeled by critics as the purveyors of "gloom and doom."[37] It is true that one of the components of the systems approach is its focus on limits. Ecologists in particular are sensitive to the fact that no system can expand forever. Eventually, all growing systems must reach their limits and begin to reduce their own growth, or they must experience such reductions involuntarily.

From the beginning the critics of *The Limits to Growth* have been numerous and passionate.[38] Criticisms have been leveled at virtually every aspect of *The Limits to Growth*, from the incomplete inventory of factors in its model to the incorrect assumptions it makes about the availability of natural resources. Advocates of continued growth were quick to point out the numerous instances in which a computer model's forecast of some crisis or shortage of some critical input (fossil fuel energy was frequently cited) was proven to be wrong. Supporters of the systems approach replied that a single incorrect forecast does not necessarily invalidate the overall approach. They also concentrated on making their models more accurate, comprehensive, and realistic. But they also noted that in a counterintuitive way the forecasts' "errors" are proof that the approach works. If people changed their private behavior (consumption patterns) or their public policies (taxation, subsidies) in response to a forecast problem, and thereby averted the problem, then the forecast had done its job even at the cost of being thought wrong.

In the meantime, while the MIT group and the Club of Rome were pursuing their research agendas, other scientists and government agencies were promoting the international coordination of data gathering that would begin to illuminate our understanding of the world as a single integrated system.[39] It took the emerging prospect of irreversible climate change to spur scientific cooperation that crossed disciplinary as well as national boundaries. In the mid-1950s, scientists began to be aware of the dramatic increase of carbon dioxide in the atmosphere, and oceanographers and atmospheric scientists began to coordinate their efforts to increase their understanding of global weather patterns. The competition between the United States and the Soviet Union to be the first in space raised considerable interest in planetary science (as well as producing dramatic photographs of the Earth as a single place). In 1958, the International Geophysical Year Project brought together Earth scientists for the first time in a coordinated effort to gather data on the planet as a whole. This was followed by the International Biological Project, which ended in 1974 after bringing together ecologists and physiologists to investigate how living organisms and their environments fit together in ecosystems.

Since the late 1970s, many international scientific bodies have been created to encourage the collaborative effort to solve the problems associated with global environmental change. The most ambitious and inclusive of these bodies is the International Geosphere Biosphere Program (IGBP), established jointly by the U.N. Economic and Social Council, the U.N. Environment Program, and the World Meteorological Organization. Some of the more specialized organizations, such as the Arctic Climate System Study, focus on a particular region of the Earth, whereas others, such as the World Ocean Circulation Experiment, concentrate on a particular global subsystem. One particularly important group is the World Climate Research Program, which has established a program to develop a model to make long-term forecasts of the climatic phenomenon called "El Niño." To ensure that economic, political, and social factors are not left out of the equation, the International Social Science Council established the Human Dimension of Global Environmental Change Program, based on and linked to the IGBP. The near-term objective of these various bodies is to develop computer models of global change that can help us improve our ability to predict the consequences of our policies and actions. But in a more long-term perspective, these organizations serve to bring together scientists and policy makers from many different disciplines and many different countries and to encourage them to think in systems terms about problems that affect the world as a single place.

HOW DOES THE GLOBAL SYSTEM
PARADIGM HELP US MAKE SENSE OF THE WORLD?

Because it is not easy to think about the world as a single place, we need to invent or adapt tools to help us do so. Various kinds of tools appear frequently throughout this book. For example, we need an inventory to help us gather and organize descriptive information about the world's various systems and subsystems. For this purpose, I offer the *Global Systematique*. (See box 2.2.) The title of

Box 2.2.   The Global Systematique

The Global Systematique is a set of interconnected systems that are global in scope. The systematique consists of the following systems:

1. Two nonhuman domains
   - The physical system (nonliving), including subsurface features, material deposits, land masses, water, atmosphere, and solar energy.
   - The physical system (living but not human), including plants and animals.

2. Six human domains
   - The technology system or all those things that humans use to mediate their relationships with the nonhuman domains and with each other, including energy, food, transportation, communications, weapons, shelter, and so forth.
   - The social system or how human populations organize themselves to conduct interpersonal and intergroup relations, including demographics, migration, class structure, affinity groups, families, kin groups, tribes, racial and ethnic ties, habitats, and so forth.
   - The cultural system, including values and attitudes, religion, language, thought systems, science, nationalism, and so forth.
   - The economic system or how people organize themselves for production, including markets, price mechanisms, resource allocation devices, the factory system, property and ownership, labor, the concept of the firm, and so forth.
   - The political system or how people organize themselves to resolve public conflicts, solve public problems, and exercise public power, including states, constitutions, laws and enforcement, bureaucracies, parties, and so forth.
   - The paradigm system or the set of images, metaphors, models, and so forth that we use to make sense of our world or explain how things work.

3. One linking or connecting domain. This domain contains the networks or linking systems, or the components that connect all or some of the above, including communications technology, education, history (versions of the past), and prediction (visions of the future or "feed-forward").

Source: Inspired by Kenneth E. Boulding, *The World as a Total System* (Beverly Hills: SAGE, 1985).

this inventory follows the example of the Club of Rome in labeling its set of *interconnected problems* a "problematique." This inventory lists a set of *interconnected systems* of global scope, hence the term *systematique*. To some degree the inventory is rather arbitrary, as any set of categories like this must be. The inventory seeks to be inclusive even at the risk of designing categories that may be overlapping. It consists of nine domains or subsystems. Two of these embrace the nonhuman part of the world: nonliving physical systems and living systems other than human. There are six human domains, five of which are fairly straightforward: technology, social systems, economic systems, cultures, and politics. The sixth human domain treats our dominant paradigms separately from other cultural phenomena in recognition of the great importance of paradigms in shaping the way we experience the world as a single place. Finally, a ninth domain treats connections separately from technology, culture, or economics, in recognition of the key role of linkages or connecting tissue in globalization.

Verbal tools like the global systematique inventory may be adequate for describing the component parts of systems. But to depict how these parts are interconnected—to describe causal relationships, flows, or transactions—we need tools that are more visual. Systemic relationships are inherently difficult to envision, so we must develop or adapt graphics that help us "see" them more clearly.

For example, figure 2.1 depicts how the Internet works. This graphic is fairly simple because the flow of Internet traffic is depicted as moving only in one direction. There are no feedback loops to complicate matters. When we move to somewhat more complicated systems, in which changes in system parts feed back into each other, the graphics become considerably more complex. Figure 2.2, for example, shows the complex interactions between and among changes

Figure 2.1   How the Internet Works

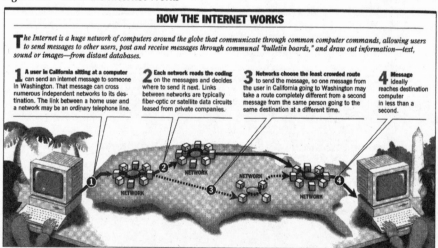

Source: David S. Hilzenrath, "Mixed Returns on the Net," *Washington Post*, November 10, 1996; © 1996, *The Washington Post*. Reprinted with permission.

Figure 2.2   Causal Relationships during Phases of Demographic Expansion and Decline

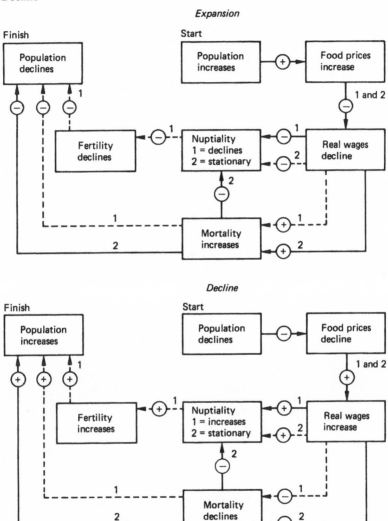

Arrows indicate the presumed direction of causality.
+ and — symbols indicate positive and negative effects
on the next step. Dotted lines indicate a weaker
relationship than do solid lines. The role of fertility
is strong for path 1 and weak for path 2.

Source: Massimo Livi-Bacci, *A Concise History of World Population,* 2d ed., trans. Carl Ipsen (Malden, Mass.: Blackwell Publishers, 1997), 84, figure 3.1. Adapted from E. A. Wrigley and R. Schofield, *The Population History of England 1861–1871* (London: Edward Arnold Publishers, 1981), 408. Used by permission.

in population, fertility rates, food prices, wage levels, and other factors. The plus and minus signs indicate the direction in which each change causes changes in the next part of the system. We can even use graphics to depict component part relationships in extremely large systems. Figure 2.3 depicts one of the largest possible systems in which we live, the Earth's biosphere and its various components. The purpose of such a picture is to show, first, the relationships and interconnections between and among the various parts of the biosphere and, second, the fact that the Earth is a closed system, with the crucial exception of energy.

Figure 2.3.   The Biosphere

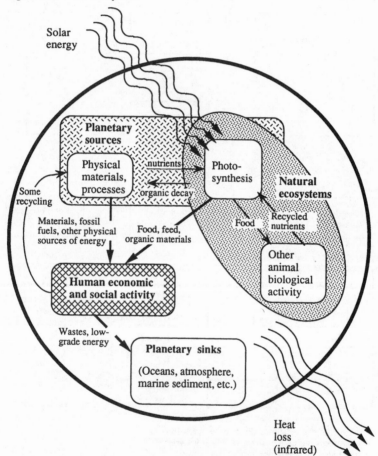

Note: The biosphere is essentially a closed system. Only solar energy enters, and heat leaves. All other system components—nutrients and other physical resources—are recycled many times through the biosphere's subsystems. Human activity uses the available energy and recycled materials and generates wastes, which are deposited in planetary sinks.

Source: A. J. McMichael, *Planetary Overload: Global Environmental Change and the Health of the Human Species* (Cambridge: Cambridge University Press, 1993), 41, figure 2.1. Reprinted with the permission of Cambridge University Press.

In chapter 1 I examined the globalization of culture and inquire whether there is emerging a single set of values embraced by the majority of the world's people. Whether or not such a culture is coming into being, many observers of globalization believe that even in highly industrialized countries most people do not experience the world as a single place in their daily lives. Even though they may receive information about the world via the news or entertainment media, and even though they may consume products made by a global labor force, they still do not understand or appreciate the holistic or integrated nature of the world in which we all live. John Tomlinson believes that even though people may be cognitively connected to the world as a whole, they are affectively or emotionally disconnected for two reasons.[40] First, people see no way for them to exert any influence over distant events or trends; Tomlinson refers to this as "experiential distance." Second, people see no connection between what happens abroad and their daily lives. They do not appreciate how they are connected to sweatshop labor in Southeast Asia or the rise of AIDS in Africa. What do all these things have to do with them? To offset these barriers to global awareness, I offer the Global System Paradigm.

In the next chapter, we will see that all systems, however they are constructed and wherever we find them, possess certain *common properties or features*.[41] These properties are what set systems apart from other parts of our world that are "not systems." Some systems thinkers refer to these common properties as "invariances." (See box 2.3.) The founder of general systems theory, Ludwig von Bertalanffy, claims that these invariances are "isomorphic laws," that is, laws that "hold for certain classes or subclasses of 'systems,' irrespective of the nature of the entities involved": "There appear to exist," he writes, "general system laws which apply to any system of a certain type, irrespective of the particular properties of the system and of the elements involved."[42] These common properties or features usually do not appear very much alike when we see them displayed by systems as different as, say, the human circulatory system and the world's fossil fuel energy system, but the similarities are there all the same. What is invariant across systems is the degree and form of their organization, that is, how the component parts are arranged and how they interact with each other.

If we know what to look for, we can use this knowledge about the common properties of systems to understand how events and forces in our world are related even if they do not appear to be related on the surface. For example, in the case study following this chapter, you will read about two newspaper articles that appeared on the front page of the *New York Times* on the same day. These articles appear to have nothing in common, but in fact the trends they describe are just different examples of a single important consequence of globalization: pressures for homogenization. Once we understand how global systems work, we will see more clearly how our lives are affected many times each day by globalization.

The advantages of general systems thinking become apparent whenever we meet a novel problem or question. If a specialist in a particular field, say,

Box 2.3. Examples of the Invariances Exhibited by Systems

According to Anatol Rapoport, all systems possess the following three
properties:

- *Continuity (maintenance) of identity.* By this, Rapoport means that
  the patterns of the relationships between and among the component
  parts of a system persist even though the parts themselves may
  change. For example, even though the cells of a person's body
  change over time, the person's identity remains the same; and even
  though the members of a football team change, the team's identity
  remains unchanged.
- *Organization (the structured flow of information).* Systems are not
  disordered or random collections of parts. Rather, they are structured
  or organized so that information flows between and among the parts.
  Information means the reduction of disorder, so organization is defined by the flow of information. The quantity of information flow is
  roughly analogous to the quantity of organization.
- *Goal directedness.* If we ask, "Why does a system do x?" there are
  two ways to approach the answer. If we answer in terms of objective
  or purpose ("The system does x in order to achieve y"), we have used
  an answer based on the rational calculation of an end or a purpose.
  If we answer in terms of processes internal to the system ("The system did x because its component parts interacted in such a way as to
  produce that behavior"), then we have used a systemic or dynamic
  answer. To attribute a goal to a large sociotechnical system requires
  that we treat the system as a rational being, but, Rapoport says, this
  is warranted if it is based on logical inferences drawn from the observation of human behavior.

Source: Anatol Rapoport, *General Systems Theory: Essential Concepts and Applications* (Tunbridge
Wells, U.K.: Abacus Press, 1986).

economics, confronts a problem from a quite different field, say, biology, he
or she will first have to master the vocabulary and concepts of biology before making advances toward understanding and solving the problem. The
general systems thinker, however, can begin to grasp the problem from biology right away because he or she can apply the important fundamental
principles of system operations to the issue or question at hand.[43] In this
way, the GSP equips us to *grasp quickly the nature of a particular global
problem,* for example, the AIDS pandemic, even if we do not know much
about AIDS per se.

The GSP leads us to look at problems *holistically* or in their entirety.[44] Consider the AIDS pandemic we have examined from many different perspectives in case study 1. Like any pandemic, AIDS can be defined as a problem at seven levels of living systems: the pathology of individual cells, the failure of entire organs, the death of a single human being, the death of so many human beings that an entire social group is destroyed, a challenge for the public health services of a country, the weakening of society generally across an area the size of, say, southern Africa, and a challenge for the health services of international organizations such as the World Health Organization. The GSP enables us to look at the AIDS crisis at all seven levels and to understand how each level fits into the larger global epidemic pattern.

Ever since the Scientific Revolution that began in Europe in the seventeenth century, people (at least those living in Western cultures) have been taught to solve problems by breaking them down into their component parts and then examining the parts. It was believed that once we understood the functioning of each part, we would then understand the entire phenomenon under examination. The GSP, in contrast, teaches us to try to grasp the system holistically, that is, as a whole or in its entirety. Anatol Rapoport refers to this mode of thinking as *pattern recognition* or simply *recognition*.[45] The holistic or pattern recognition approach to thinking is an essential part of everyday life. Recognition of patterns enables one to identify a friend one has not seen in years even though virtually all the cells in his or her body have changed since one last saw him or her. One is able to recognize one's friend as the same person not by recognizing the component parts of his or her body but by observing how they are related, how they fit together. This is what we mean by *holism*. The GSP teaches us to focus on the patterns of connections and interactions between and among the parts, not on the parts themselves.

But the most significant gift we get from the GSP is the way it changes our worldview. The Scientific and Industrial Revolutions of the seventeenth, eighteenth, and nineteenth centuries left humankind with a worldview that drew its inspiration from the machine as metaphor. Ervin Laszlo contrasts this industrial or mechanistic worldview with the holistic perspective of the systems paradigm.[46] Figure 2.4 summarizes some of the principal differences between the two worldviews. I believe that the holistic/systems worldview offers us by far the greater power to understand the processes of globalization.

This transformation of our worldview has a moral or ethical component as well. The GSP raises our awareness of how we are connected to other people distant from us in both time and space. The GSP sharpens our understanding of how we are connected to past generations, how their sacrifices made our lives better today, and how we are connected to future generations, what we owe the future. Armed with this new paradigm, we should better appreciate what connects us to the people (often in the developing world) on whose labor we depend for the consumer goods we enjoy. And of course the GSP will also make us more aware of how our fortunes are connected to the well-being of the natural world that surrounds us.

Figure 2.4   Contrasts between the Industrial/Mechanical Worldview and the Holistic/Systems Worldview

The Industrial/Mechanical Worldview	The Holistic/Systems Worldview
• Nature is a giant machine composed of replaceable parts. • Objects are perceived as separate from their environment. People are separate from each other and from their environment. • All things are seen as distinct, material entities. • The accumulation of material goods is the central ethos. • Material growth is the leading measure of social and economic success. • Humans are the dominant species on Earth and deserve to have their needs ranked first.	• Nature is an organism made up of irreplaceable parts and characterized primarily by energy flows. • All objects, including people, are properly seen as integrated into larger entities, called systems (or communities). • Matter can also be seen as the configuration of energy that flows and interacts. • Living in balance with the needs of the larger system is the central ethos. • Cooperation among interactive parts is the leading measure of social and economic success. • Human beings are only one among many species, all of which have a legitimate claim on the Earth's resources.

Source: Adapted from Ervin Laszlo, *The Systems View of the World: A Holistic Vision for Our Time* (Cresskill, N.J.: Hampton Press, 1996), 10–13.

The British author Geoff Mulgan has written extensively about what he thinks is the most important issue facing an increasingly interconnected world: the tension between the personal freedom we derive from living in a prosperous democratic society and the constraints we experience from living in a world in which we are increasingly dependent on the actions of others.[47] The title of his book, *Connexity,* refers to "the age of connections," wherein we are increasingly affected by distant events. The process by which this connection occurs is called "disintermediation," the removal of intermediaries between ourselves and the distant others on whom we rely. On the one hand, "connexity" increases our personal freedom by increasing our range of choices in life. On the other, we confront daily the limits and constraints placed on us by the very systems that bring us these enhanced alternatives.

In an earlier era, the resolution of a similar dilemma lay in the notion of consent. That is, individual freedom was reconciled with the constraints of having to share society with others by virtue of each person's free acceptance of, and consent to, these constraints. Hence, Thomas Jefferson's phrase in the Declaration of Independence: "Government derives its just powers from the consent of the governed." Today, however, consent seems to have lost its legitimacy, its power to command our allegiance, for the simple reason that we find ourselves enmeshed in countless global systems without being aware of it, without ever having been asked to consent to such connections.

For Mulgan, then, the solution to this dilemma lies in the principle of reciprocity. He sees reciprocity as more than an economic principle (the law of supply and demand) and more than a political principle (consent of the governed). It is a profoundly moral injunction to act toward others as we expect them to act toward us, based, as he puts it, "on our innate sociability and our instinctive dispositions to act ethically."[48] Mulgan believes that the age of connections holds as much promise for good as it does threat of ill. While others may decry the disconnectedness of our contemporary society, Mulgan thinks that connexity engenders greater "moral fluency," that is, an enhanced sensitivity to a moral code that forces each of us to act ethically toward countless unseen others who may be living on the other side of the world. As he puts it, "A more connected world should be a more moral one."[49]

The problem, however, is that reciprocity depends on trust, and trust depends on our being aware of or conscious of the existence of these unseen others. We are more apt to act ethically toward others if we can read the social environment sufficiently to be able to trust people far away, of whom we will never even be aware, much less meet face to face. The phrase political scientists use to describe this is "social capital." But this social capital requires an awareness of connections. Unfortunately, globalization weakens this awareness by exposing us to the effects of distant, unseen systems. Mulgan is well aware of this problem: "Means have become divorced from ends. Capital markets separate owners from any knowledge or responsibility for the uses made of their capital; buyers are detached from any awareness of where their products come from; currency traders gamble with other people's money without any personal responsibility for their actions."[50]

Globalization weakens our sense of moral imperative, or obligation to act ethically toward others, by making it easier to exit from relationships, by commodifying relationships, by facilitating anonymity, and by shielding us from personal responsibility. It is my hope that the GSP can counteract these forces by helping us see invisible systems, fix personal responsibility, and increase our empathy, our ability to feel what others are experiencing.

The word *liberal* has its roots in a Latin word, *liberalis,* meaning "of, or pertaining to, a free person." Thus, it is commonly understood that we teach and study the liberal arts to liberate us, to free us from the chains of falsehood and ignorance. But I never understood the nature of the "prison" from which we are trying to free ourselves until I read the following by Albert Einstein: "The individual feels the nothingness of human desires and aims and the sublimity and marvelous order which reveal themselves both in nature and in the world of thought. *He looks upon individual existence as a sort of prison and wants to experience the universe as a single significant whole.*"[51]

The essence of the human condition, then, is a fundamental connectedness with other parts of the world. The goal of our emerging paradigm must be to

try to free ourselves from the falsehood of individual disconnectedness, from
the myth that we are separate and discrete beings entitled to conduct our life
without an awareness of how we are affected by other parts of our world and
without due regard for how we, in turn, affect them. In searching for these connections, we must be aware of the fragmenting impact of contemporary life. We
must understand that such fragmentation is a social and intellectual artifact that
is not inherent in the nature of knowledge. We must also appreciate that its effects are potentially extremely harmful to us as individuals and to society as a
whole. We must acquire the tools necessary to overcome this fragmentation so
that we can begin to introduce some identity, meaning, and coherence into our
lives. The remainder of this book will be devoted to exploring how the Global
System Paradigm will help us achieve this goal.

NOTES

1. Richard J. Barnet and John Cavanagh, *Global Dreams: Imperial Corporations and the New World Order* (New York: Simon and Schuster, 1994), 13.
2. Michael Geyer and Charles Bright, "World History in a Global Age," *American Historical Review* (October 1995): 1058.
3. Andrew C. Revkin, "The Devil Is in the Details: Efforts to Predict Effects of Global Warming Hinge on Gaps in Climate Models," *New York Times,* July 3, 2001.
4. Jay W. Forrester, *World Dynamics,* 2d ed. (Cambridge, Mass.: Wright-Allen Press, 1973), 14.
5. Gerald M. Weinberg, *An Introduction to General Systems Thinking* (New York: Wiley, 1975), 28.
6. Thomas S. Kuhn, *The Structure of Scientific Revolutions,* 3d ed. (Chicago: University of Chicago Press, 1996 [1962]). This book would be on most lists of the 100 most influential books of the twentieth century. To date it has sold over one million copies in twenty languages.
7. Mark Davidson, *Uncommon Sense: The Life and Thought of Ludwig von Berta-lanffy (1901–1972), Father of General Systems Theory* (Los Angeles: J. P. Tarcher, 1983), 100.
8. Kuhn, *The Structure of Scientific Revolutions,* 23.
9. Donella Meadows, John Richardson, and Gerhart Bruckmann, *Groping in the Dark: The First Decade of Global Modeling* (New York: John Wiley and Sons, 1982), 8.
10. Kuhn, *The Structure of Scientific Revolutions,* 10–17.
11. Kuhn, *The Structure of Scientific Revolutions,* 151–53.
12. Kuhn, *The Structure of Scientific Revolutions,* 148.
13. Kuhn, *The Structure of Scientific Revolutions,* 150.
14. Kuhn, *The Structure of Scientific Revolutions,* 151.
15. The following two cases are described in Robert Clark, *The Global Imperative: An Interpretive History of the Spread of Humankind* (Boulder: Westview Press, 1997), 80–83, 21–22.
16. Roland Robertson, "Globalization Theory and Civilizational Analysis," *Comparative Civilizations Review* 17 (1987): 20–30. Roland Robertson, *Globalization: Social Theory and Global Culture* (London: Sage, 1992), especially chapters 3, 8.

17. Robertson, "Globalization Theory and Civilizational Analysis," 26.

18. Robertson, *Globalization,* 50–57.

19. Tyler Volk, *Gaia's Body: Toward a Physiology of Earth* (New York: Springer-Verlag, 1998), 50–51.

20. Robert Jervis, *System Effects: Complexity in Political and Social Life* (Princeton: Princeton University Press, 1997), 73–91.

21. Dennis Farney, "Chaos Theory Seeps into Ecology Debate, Stirring up a Tempest," *The Wall Street Journal* (Europe), July 12, 1994.

22. Edward O. Wilson, *Consilience: The Unity of Knowledge* (New York: Knopf, 1998), chapter 3.

23. L. Douglas Kiel, "Nonequilibrium Theory and Its Implications for Public Administration," *Public Administration Review* 49, no. 6 (November–December 1989): 544–51. L. Douglas Kiel, "The Nonlinear Paradigm: Advancing Paradigmatic Progress in the Policy Sciences," *Systems Research* 9, no. 2 (1992): 27–42.

24. Robertson, *Globalization,* 8.

25. Garret Hardin, *Living within Limits: Ecology, Economics, and Population Taboos* (New York: Oxford University Press, 1993), 14–16.

26. Michael Polanyi, *The Tacit Dimension* (New York: Doubleday, 1966).

27. Forrester, *World Dynamics,* ix–x.

28. Jay W. Forrester, *Principles of Systems* (Cambridge, Mass.: Wright-Allen Press), 1968.

29. Jay W. Forrester, *Urban Dynamics* (Cambridge: MIT Press, 1969).

30. For current information about the Club of Rome, consult the organization's Web site at www.clubofrome.org.

31. Donella H. Meadows, Dennis L. Meadows, Jørgen Randers, and William W. Behrens III, *The Limits to Growth* (New York: Signet Books, 1972), xi.

32. Meadows et al., *The Limits to Growth.* Mihajlo Mesarovic and Eduard Pestel, *Mankind at the Turning Point: The Second Report to the Club of Rome* (New York: Dutton, 1974). Donella H. Meadows, Dennis L. Meadows, and Jørgen Randers, *Beyond the Limits: Confronting Global Collapse, Envisioning a Sustainable Future* (Post Mills, Vt.: Chelsea Green Publishing Co., 1992).

33. Mesarovic and Pestel, *Mankind at the Turning Point,* 55.

34. This is a partial list. For a complete list, see Meadows, Richardson, and Bruckmann, *Groping in the Dark,* 15–16.

35. Meadows, Richardson, and Bruckmann, *Groping in the Dark,* 1.

36. Meadows, Richardson, and Bruckmann, *Groping in the Dark,* 20–21. Donella H. Meadows, "Whole Earth Models and Systems," *The CoEvolution Quarterly* (summer 1982): 98–108.

37. "Environmental Scares: Plenty of Gloom," *The Economist,* December 20, 1997: 19–21.

38. One of the earliest critiques, and still one of the best, is by H. S. D. Cole, Christopher Freeman, Marie Jahoda, and K. L. R. Pavitt, eds., *Models of Doom: A Critique of* The Limits to Growth (New York: Universe Books, 1973).

39. "A Problem as Big as a Planet," *The Economist,* November 4, 1994: 83–85.

40. John Tomlinson, *Globalization and Culture* (Chicago: University of Chicago Press, 1999), 171–80.

41. Ervin Laszlo, *The Systems View of the World: A Holistic Vision for Our Time* (Cresskill, N.J.: Hampton Press, 1996), chapter 2.

42. Ludwig von Bartalanffy, *General System Theory: Foundations, Development, Applications* (New York: George Braziller, 1968), 37.

43. Weinberg, *An Introduction to General Systems Thinking*, 43–47.

44. For another example of this kind of analysis, see James Grier Miller and Jessie Louise Miller, "Systems Science: An Emerging Interdisciplinary Field," *The Center Magazine* (September–October 1981): 44–45.

45. Anatol Rapoport, *General System Theory: Essential Concepts and Applications* (Tunbridge Wells, U.K.: Abacus Press, 1986), chapter 1.

46. Laszlo, *The Systems View of the World*, 10–13.

47. Geoff Mulgan, *Connexity: How to Live in a Connected World* (Boston: Harvard Business School Press, 1997).

48. Mulgan, *Connexity*, 14.

49. Mulgan, *Connexity*, 124.

50. Mulgan, *Connexity*, 14.

51. Albert Einstein, "Religion and Science," in *The World as I See It*, trans. Alan Harris (New York: Citadel Press, 1993), 26, emphasis added.

Case Study 2

Making Connections
in the News: Endangered Species
and Endangered Languages

KEY IDEAS IN THIS CASE STUDY

One of the strengths of the Global System Paradigm (GSP) is that it enables us to **make connections** among otherwise seemingly unrelated events, trends, and other aspects of global affairs. The GSP helps us do this by **identifying common properties** of events or trends. By applying the GSP in our reading of the daily news, we are made more aware of the connections among unrelated events. This case study illustrates this process with a number of examples drawn from **newspaper articles** that appeared on the same day, sometimes in the same newspaper, often in adjacent positions on the same page:

- April 8, 1998: endangered species and endangered languages
- June 23, 2000: immigrant smuggling and money laundering
- May 5, 2000: computer viruses and tuberculosis
- September 1, 1996: wolves in India and alligators in Florida
- August 7, 1999: male strippers in Mexico and a Taiwanese rock star in China

Chapter 2 showed you several ways in which the Global System Paradigm (GSP) improves our ability to think about the world as a single place. One of those strengths is how the paradigm helps us see parallels among dissimilar events or trends, to identify the common or similar properties that connect distant phenomena that would otherwise seem quite unrelated. If we learn to apply the GSP as we read the news, for example, we are sensitized to look for such similarities. Moreover, the systems paradigm helps us organize the information we receive so as to make sense of it. Because systems everywhere exhibit the same general properties (identified as invariances in chapter 2), once we know that two events represent system behavior we can compare them directly. This case study presents pairs of news articles drawn from the *New York Times* and/or the *Washington Post* on each of five days over the past several years. In each example, I shall show not only that the articles are related but that they actually illustrate the same dimension or aspect of globalization.

◆ ◆ ◆

On *April 8, 1998,* the front page of the *New York Times* carried two adjacent articles. One deals with a just-released report by a Switzerland-based environmental organization, the World Conservation Union (WCU), that revealed that at least one of every eight plant species in the world was in danger of extinction.[1] The report, based on more than two decades of research by conservationists and botanists around the world, added some 34,000 species of plant life to the WCU's list of imperiled organisms. These new findings covered the entire range of plant life, from cereal grains and trees to flowering plants and fruits. Of the some 270,000 known species of plants, about 12.5 percent are now described as "endangered," meaning that they are likely to become extinct if the causes of the endangerment continue. The two principal causes cited in the report are the destruction of large areas of wild countryside by agriculture, logging, or development and the invasions of alien species that grow without control when introduced into a new habitat and crowd out the native species. With 4,669 of its 16,108 native plant species cited as endangered (nearly one in three), the United States leads the world in the total number of plants at risk. Other countries reporting high percentages were Australia, Turkey, Spain, and Jamaica.

The second article deals with the accelerating decline and threatened disappearance of most of the languages spoken by North American Indian peoples.[2] Despite some five centuries of population decline and cultural assimilation, 211 of the approximately 300 native languages spoken in North America in 1492 are still spoken today. But these languages are suffering their sharpest decline in recorded history. Of the 175 native languages still spoken in the United States, only twenty are still spoken by mothers to babies. Some thirty languages are spoken by parents and grandparents, seventy are spoken only by grandparents, and fifty-five more are spoken by ten tribal members or fewer. This trend is not confined to North America. About one-half of the world's 6,000 languages are expected to disappear over the next century. The chief reason, both in North America and globally, is the increased mobility of languages and of people. Non-Indian languages intrude more pervasively into the Indian world via radio, television, music, and film; Indians migrate out of their native lands in search of jobs, education, and increased income. Tribal leaders are attempting to save their languages by using the media of global communications, especially television and the Internet, but these are difficult strategies because they rely on adults learning the language. Meanwhile, fewer and fewer children learn the language in the home. In California, for example, of the eighty languages spoken before Europeans arrived, only fifty survive today, and not a single one of these is spoken by children.

From these articles we learn that globalization tends to reduce diversity (both biological and cultural) and promote homogenization. Globalization has this consequence because it identifies certain components—for example, plant species and languages—that contribute to the efficiency or productivity of large-scale systems and encourages these few at the expense of the marginalized species and languages that are not favored and thus are left behind.

Two adjacent articles in the *New York Times* on *June 23, 2000,* report the death of fifty-eight illegal Chinese immigrants in a cargo container in England and summarize an analysis of illegal money laundering prepared by the Financial Action Task Force, an advisory body to the Group of 7. The first article, from Dover, England, reports that the Dutch driver of the truck in which the Chinese immigrants died was charged by a local court with manslaughter.[3] The fifty-eight deceased Chinese were part of a group of sixty who were making their way from Fujian Province in southern China in search of work and a better way of life. Because immigration by unskilled workers into Britain is virtually impossible, and entry by skilled workers is only slightly easier, these Chinese along with many hundreds of other immigrants from all over Asia had to resort to illegal concealment in order to complete the trip. Although no one was able to say for sure, authorities in Britain speculated that the Chinese had entered Europe from the east and made their way to Germany and then to Belgium. At the Belgian port of Zeebrugge, the sixty Chinese were loaded aboard a cargo container carried by truck that was then sealed from the outside as is common practice for freight shipments. Without ventilation and in unseasonable heat, after the five-hour ferry ride to Dover nearly all the Chinese had died. Four days after their bodies were discovered, no one had come forward to identify the deceased or claim their bodies, probably because their family members were also in Britain illegally.

The second article deals with a report from a special task force created by the world's leading industrial nations, called the Group of 7 or simply G-7, to study illegal money laundering across national boundaries.[4] The term *laundering* refers to the transfer of illegally obtained money through false bank accounts so that it can enter the world's financial stream without revealing its source. The report identifies some fifteen countries as potential havens for deposit and laundering of illegally obtained sums of money. The study, the result of more than a decade of investigation, was issued after U.S. and European banking officials became concerned that bank secrecy laws and lax regulation had contributed to the economic crises in Asia, Latin America, and Russia in the late 1990s. The report names fifteen countries as being especially vulnerable to this problem, including large and influential countries such as Israel, the Philippines, and

Russia and tiny island nations such as the Bahamas, Dominica, and St. Kitts and Nevis. The purpose of the report was not to impose criminal sanctions but, rather, to warn banks and brokerage houses to scrutinize carefully all financial transactions with customers in those countries as possibly linked to criminal syndicates or other high-risk activities. The U.S. and European governments decided to bring pressure to bear on laundering centers because the volume of financial transactions by drug cartels, criminal organizations, and corrupt officials has exploded to some $600 billion each year. The ease of moving huge sums of money rapidly around the world without oversight has contributed to the instability in world financial markets since 1998.

From these articles, we see that globalization is synonymous with the long-distance movement of both human beings and money in unprecedented volume and at unprecedented speed. In both cases, it is extremely difficult for government authorities to maintain proper surveillance over the modes of transport, and the consequence has been the increased use of these modes by criminal organizations to carry out their illicit trafficking. In all cases, innocent people are hurt, and in many instances deaths result from this trafficking.

On *May 5, 2000,* two articles in the *Washington Post* discussed the "Love Bug" computer virus as it spread across the world via the Internet and a report calling for stiffer restrictions on immigrants to stop the spread of tuberculosis in America. The "Love Bug" was a computer virus disguised as a love letter that infected millions of computers around the world in early May 2000.[5] The virus was contained in a program disguised as an e-mail message whose subject line was "I Love You." Enticed by this message label, millions of unsuspecting computer users had opened the message's attachment, whereupon the virus (more technically it was a "worm" because it was transmitted as an attachment to another message) invaded their computers' hard drives and began to wreak havoc. The program deleted computer files and rearranged the computers' connection to Internet Explorer, but most of its damage was done by its self-replicating feature. The virus sent copies of itself to every address in the infected computer's e-mail address directory. The virus also contained a code that attempted to steal the computer's stored passwords and send them back to the originator of the virus, to enable that person to gain access to the infected computer once it was restored to working order. The e-mail message apparently originated in the Philippines, swept across Asia and Europe, and then reached the United States. It attacked 80 percent of the computers in Sweden, 70 percent in Germany, and more than one-third in Great Britain. It clogged computer systems from Belgium's banking network, to the British Parliament, to the Ford Motor Company and the Pentagon. The Centers for Disease Control and Prevention in Atlanta and the Food and Drug Administration in Washington were cut off, as was the International Monetary Fund headquarters in Washington. One computer security expert joked that it was not necessary to be a computer geek to know that something was wrong with the message. "We should know by now," he said, "that if someone you don't know well tells you 'I love you,' you should worry about whether he could give you a virus."

The second article describes a proposed plan for eliminating tuberculosis in the United States by, among other measures, requiring immigrants from certain countries to undergo TB skin tests.[6] Those testing positive for the disease would have to be treated before they could receive a permanent visa, the highly prized "green card." The report, issued by the Institute of Medicine of the National Academy of Sciences, reflects the increasing fear by public health officials that the growing tuberculosis pandemic will reach the United States via immigration. Today TB infection rates are at a historic low point in the United States, but just the opposite is true worldwide. TB kills between two and three million people each year around the world, and in many parts of the world (such as Russia) the emergence of antibiotic-resistant forms of the disease is threatening to make eradication much more difficult. TB is transmitted from person to person via droplets contained in coughed or sneezed vapor. It is especially acute in densely concentrated populations and among people whose immune systems have been weakened by malnutrition, exhaustion, or AIDS. In 1999, 43 percent of the 17,500 new cases of active TB reported in the United States occurred in people born elsewhere, a proportion up from 27 percent in 1992. Cases tend to be concentrated in cities and states with large immigrant populations. The current immigration requirement is for a chest X-ray; the proposal is to add the skin test as a requirement for people seeking permanent visas if they come from countries where more than 35 percent of the population is infected. The 35 percent figure represents the infection rate worldwide. The proposal estimates that about one-quarter of a million visa applicants would be affected.

From these articles we learn that globalization has made it easier for microbes to cross national boundaries, and this is true metaphorically as well. It is significant that years ago computer experts chose to refer to malicious electronic codes as "viruses" because these electronic messages replicate themselves in exactly the same way as their biological namesakes. That is, both biological and electronic viruses reproduce by gaining entry to the victim's internal components (cells, storage) and using the information stored there to make copies of themselves. They then propagate throughout the system by infecting more victims. Industrialized states try to protect themselves by erecting barriers to the movement of computer viruses and epidemics and by frequent testing of both people and electronic messages.

On *September 1, 1996,* the *New York Times* carried an article on the growing threat posed to villagers in India from attacks by wolves, and the *Washington Post* reported on the growing incidence of alligator attacks in new suburban developments in Florida. The *Times* article begins by relating the tragic case of a four-year-old child who was seized by a 100-pound wolf and carried away from his village in India.[7] When authorities found the boy three days later, all that remained was his head. The attack was one of a number inflicted by a pack of wolves that had been roaming the surrounding area, driven to killing small children by hunger or "something else that has upset the natural instinct of wolves to avoid humans." Wolves were once the scourge of ancient India, and even as recently as 1878, British officials recorded 624 human killings by wolves in this area. But until these recent attacks, rural India had not experienced this sort of threat for more than a century. Now, in a series of attacks that began in April 1996, thirty-three children had been carried off and killed by wolves, and twenty others had been seriously maimed, all in the same stretch of the Ganges River basin about 350 miles from New Delhi. These new attacks sparked hysteria among many of the region's nine million inhabitants. Rumors placed the blame not on wolves but on werewolves, while others blamed Pakistani soldiers dressed as wolves even though Pakistan is about 1,000 miles to the west. At least twenty people had been killed by villagers because it was thought that they were somehow responsible for the attacks. Many eyewitnesses refused to accept the idea that wolves were responsible and insisted that the attackers were human—or at least adopted human form. Mr. Ram Lakhan Singh, the animal conservationist chosen to lead the effort to kill wolves suspected of attacking humans, believed that hunger was the most likely cause of the attacks. In the early 1970s, India set aside several tens of thousands of square miles for wild animal sanctuaries, where the wolf population has soared. But as the human population also increased exponentially, their habitats have pressed against the wolf sanctuaries. Singh believed that the killings were simply the result of interspecies competition for an increasingly scarce food supply. If wolves and humans are to coexist peacefully, the wolf population will have to be reduced and confined to sanctuaries where their population and food supply are in balance.

On the same day, the *Washington Post* reported on the growing threat posed by wild alligators to the suburban population of Florida.[8] The article tells of an attack against a seven-year-old child who fell from his bicycle into a swamp in Everglades National Park. Fortunately, he escaped—but with serious injuries. But the incidence of alligator attacks against humans has been rising sharply. With 800 to 1,000 people moving into Florida every day, large tracts of swamp and wetlands are being replaced by homes, office buildings, schools, and shopping malls. Ordinarily alligators are shy animals that prefer to avoid human beings, but the expansion of the suburban population brings more and more people into their habitat each day. In 1995, state officials received about 15,000 calls from residents wanting alligators removed from their neighborhoods. Despite the fact that the alligator is protected by state law, the state killed some 4,000 animals and permitted the destruction of some 7,200 more on private or public lands. The alligator was placed on the endangered species list in 1967 in an effort to stem the rapid decline of its population. Although it is no longer endangered, the gator is still protected from indiscriminate hunting. The state tightly controls commercial alligator farming and prohibits unauthorized killing, although courts have allowed it for self-defense. Alligators normally prefer to eat small animals such as fish and birds, but they will attack cows and deer—and humans—if provoked and hungry enough. A representative of the Florida Game and Fresh Water Fish Commission summed up the problem by observing that "people and alligators can exist with each other, but there has to be mutual respect."

These articles help us understand that globalization is accompanied by the growth of the human population and by the spread of that population into areas previously dominated by other large meat-eating animals. As these two populations come into contact, they will naturally compete with each other for the available food supply and will then attack each other when that competition breeds aggression. In both India and Florida, humans have been hunting and killing their competitors for centuries. Now the expansion of the human population has provoked a similar response from wolves and alligators.

Finally we have two reports from *August 7, 1999.* In one the *Washington Post* reported on the growing popularity of male strip shows in Mexico City.[9] The hugely controversial show called "For Women Only" is seen as challenging Mexico's culture of machismo as well as the traditional social values of home and family promoted by the Catholic Church. But for thousands of women, the show represents neither cultural nor political rebellion but, rather, is simply a sexually exciting spectacular that has never been available to them before. In Mexico's male-dominated culture, clubs for men only are taken for granted, and mistresses are the norm, even for prominent politicians. Feminism has yet to take root as a mass movement. Yet when ten of Mexico's male soap opera and film stars decided to imitate the 1997 British film *The Full Monty* and create their own touring strip show, the response from women across the country and across the socioeconomic spectrum was wildly enthusiastic. In towns across Mexico, the performers had to post guards between the stage and the audience to keep admiring women from assaulting them. Catholic priests placed radio and newspaper advertisements to order women to seek repentance through confession the day after attending the shows. State legislators passed resolutions condemning the show even before it arrived in their region. All of which simply guaranteed that each show would sell out. In its first three months, the show drew nearly 200,000 women. Tickets sold for between $15 and $70 per show. It would be an error to see "For Women Only" as simply a challenge to Mexico's sexual mores. In fact, the show is part of a fundamental social and cultural revolution in the role and status of women in Mexico generally. From the home to the national legislature, women are asserting their right to equality, and if that includes the right to see male strippers, they say, the men of the country will just have to get used to it.

In the second article, the *New York Times* reported on the explosive popularity of a sexy Taiwanese rock star, Ah-Mei, in China's capital of Beijing.[10] In mid-1999, in the midst of a crisis between China and Taiwan over who should exercise sovereignty over the island nation off China's coast, Ah-Mei (referred to as the Madonna of Taiwan) attracted 45,000 screaming fans to Beijing's biggest stadium. Ticket scalpers were charging $250 per ticket for her show, nearly five times the average monthly wage in Beijing. Some 2,000 armed police patrolled the stadium to keep fans from rushing the stage, while the stadium's electronic scoreboard flashed admonitions to "observe discipline, maintain order." Despite Ah-Mei being Taiwanese, no one in the capital city seemed perturbed in the least by her performance. And to put it mildly, Ah-Mei certainly challenged traditional Chinese views on the nature of appropriate entertainment. She was scantily clad, she was sexy and suggestive on stage, and she was the number one rock star in China. Politics and political leaders seem increasingly irrelevant to China's youth, as Ah-Mei's presence in Beijing attests. "She is the coolest," said one young female admirer in the audience, "[and] I don't care where she's from." In cultural terms, Ah-Mei's performance reveals how far Taiwanese popular culture has infiltrated mainland China in the past decade and a half. The two most popular television shows in China are both from Taiwan, and Taiwanese teahouses have become popular hangouts in Beijing.

These articles remind us that globalization moves much more than consumer goods across national boundaries. Entertainers and entertainment styles and values also move with ease from country to country. Some of this entertainment moves by recorded music, film, or television; some of it is carried by consumer goods to which it is attached, such as clothing or food. But much of it is carried by the performers themselves as they perform live. When these performers arrive, they are eagerly, even wildly, embraced by some (women and youth in these examples), while others are repelled by what they offer. But if a country is to participate in globalization, its people have to take its products more or less as a package. They will have difficulty enjoying the benefits of global trade, for example, without having to endure threats to their traditional values and ways of life.

NOTES

1. William K. Stevens, "One in Every 8 Plant Species Is Imperiled, a Survey Finds," *New York Times,* April 8, 1998.

2. James Brooke, "Indians Striving to Save Their Languages," *New York Times,* April 8, 1998.

3. Roger Cohen, "Britain Charges Dutch Truck Driver in Migrants' Deaths," *New York Times,* June 23, 2000.

4. Joseph Kahn, "15 Countries Named as Potential Money-Laundering Havens," *New York Times,* June 23, 2000.

5. John Schwartz and David A. Vise, "'Love' Virus Assaults World Computers," *Washington Post,* May 5, 2000.

6. Susan Okie, "TB Tests of Immigrants Urged," *Washington Post,* May 5, 2000.

7. John F. Burns, "In India, Attacks by Wolves Spark Old Fears and Hatreds," *New York Times,* September 1, 1996.

8. "In Florida, Alligators Slither up against Development," *Washington Post,* September 1, 1996.

9. Molly Moore, "Way, Way South of the Border," *Washington Post,* August 7, 1999.

10. Seth Faison, "What Crisis? A Taiwan Temptress Seduces China," *New York Times,* August 7, 1999.

3

Systems

KEY IDEAS IN THIS CHAPTER

The intellectual foundations of systems thinking include **cybernetics, information theory, biology,** and **complexity theory** or the theory of complex adaptive systems.

A system is a collection of highly interconnected component parts, including **inputs, conversion processes, outputs,** and **feedback.**

Systems exist to **transport matter, energy,** and **information** from where they exist to where they are needed and to **change their form** so that we can use them.

Entropy, information, and **time** are three concepts essential to understanding why systems make us pay a price for their services.

"As any poet knows," writes Gerald Weinberg, *"a system is a way of looking at the world."*[1] I believe that the systems approach introduced in chapter 2 is a powerful tool we can use to experience, or to think about, the world as a single place. Although we usually are unaware of doing so, we use systems thinking frequently in our daily lives. We are using the systems approach whenever we define an object in our world in terms of something larger and more inclusive, explain a change in one thing as the consequence of a change in something else, ask for someone's "input" to a decision, or emphasize the importance of "feedback" as a way of improving our performance.

The power of systems thinking has to date not been fully exploited to increase our understanding of globalization, and some observers might say with good reason. To some, the systems perspective may appear unnecessarily daunting or intimidating. In its more technical form, the systems approach can be heavily quantitative and formula based, which may make it inaccessible to the general public. The paradigm's complex, computer-mediated methodology requires substantial investment to learn its basic structure. The approach has a special vocabulary, which, while precise and meaningful to experts, can be unfamiliar and daunting to the public. And in the eyes of many critics, the approach has an ideological cast to it and is used to argue for a particular policy stance regarding economic or demographic growth.

Notwithstanding these objections, I believe that the systems perspective has much to offer to help us experience the world as a single place. I do not try to apply systems thinking to every phenomenon in our universe, from the behavior of subatomic particles to the structure of galaxies; nor do I find it necessary to embrace every proposition advanced by every systems thinker. Rather, I seek to use the systems paradigm as a way to visualize the invisible and to understand the enigmatic in globalization. I use systems thinking as a lens through which I can focus my attention on the distant and complex structures that make globalization happen and give it its shape. For me, systems thinking has heuristic value, meaning that it helps us solve problems or answer research questions by suggesting connections and relationships that may not be immediately obvious.

THE FOUNDATIONS OF SYSTEMS THINKING

During the sixteenth and seventeenth centuries, the Scientific Revolution fostered the analytical method of experimentation and problem solving. To discover the nature of a certain segment of our world, investigators took it apart to observe its components one element at a time. To solve a problem, they divided it into its constituent elements, identified the source of the problem, and then reassembled the parts. Without question these techniques succeeded in producing the brilliant achievements of modern science and technology. But they also prevented people from seeing complex systems as integrated wholes. In the twentieth century, holistic thinking emerged in Europe and North America as an alternative perspective or worldview. We call such a worldview the systems paradigm.

Like any complex worldview, the systems perspective is the product of a vast number of intellectual achievements. The founder of general systems theory, Ludwig von Bertalanffy, traces systems thinking back to a seventeenth-century German philosopher and mathematician, Gottfried Wilhelm Leibniz,[2] whereas others see the origins of the systems approach as far back as Aristotle. I cannot review here in even summary form all of these achievements. Instead I focus on four fields of research that have been important to the development of systems thinking in the last 100 years: *cybernetics* (the science of self-guiding entities), *information theory* (the mathematical theory of communication), *biology* (the science of living systems), and the sciences of *complexity* (or complex adaptive systems).[3]

Cybernetics

The systems paradigm has its roots in both the Industrial Revolution of the nineteenth century and the Information Revolution of the twentieth.[4] One of the central ideas of systems thinking is the concept of feedback or information that systems use to alter their behavior (to be discussed shortly). The first significant writing on feedback mechanisms is that of the British scientist James Clerk Maxwell in a paper published in 1868.[5] At the time, Maxwell referred to the mechanism as a "governor," a term that derives from the Latin word *gubernare,* which in turn derives from the Greek word *kybernan,* meaning "to steer" or "to guide."

Half a century later, scientists at the Massachusetts Institute of Technology (MIT) began the work that would produce cybernetics. In the 1930s, Vannevar Bush built one of the earliest computers, called the differential analyzer, which enabled researchers to simulate the behavior of dynamic systems, and Harold Hazen published some of the first scholarly articles on the feedback control of systems. In the 1940s, Gordon Brown created the Servomechanisms Laboratory to study feedback systems and their behavior, and Norbert Wiener coined the term *cybernetics* to describe the scientific study of the methods of control and communication common to machines and living organisms.[6] Today the prefix *cyber-* has entered many of the world's languages as a way of denoting systems that span the globe carried on electronic networks. This work laid the foundation for the research of Jay Forrester, Dennis Meadows, and others in the 1960s and 1970s that produced the world systems model and led to the Global System Paradigm discussed in chapter 2.

The invention of the computer was critical to the vision of systems that guides us today. The first electronic computer was the Electronic Numerical Integrator and Computer (ENIAC), built at the University of Pennsylvania in the early 1940s. ENIAC was sponsored by the U.S. Army to calculate the trajectories of artillery shells. (Prior to ENIAC, this job was done by hand by hundreds of young women who were referred to as "computers," from which the machine eventually got its name.) Although ENIAC was far superior to any other calculating technology available at the time, it still had its limitations, chief of which was that it was not programmable. To prepare the machine for a specific kind of computation, technicians had to rewire it to change the physical connections between jacks and plugs. By mid-1944, the creators of ENIAC, J. Presper Eckert and John H. Mauchly, and their associates had begun to think about ENIAC's successor machine, called the Electronic Discrete Variable Automatic Computer (EDVAC). A consultant to their team was a mathematician from Princeton University's Institute for Advanced Study, a Hungarian émigré named John Von Neumann. In June 1945, while working on the Manhattan Project at Los Alamos, New Mexico, Von Neumann completed a 101-page document titled "First Draft of a Report on the EDVAC" in which he laid out the first vision of a programmable computer. His inspiration was the human brain and how its neurons resemble electronic circuitry. The programmable computer would have to have the capacity for receiving and producing information (what we call "input" and "output" today), but most importantly it would have to possess a memory capable of deciding what to do with the information (what we call below the system's "conversion processes"). In endowing the computer with an operational system that resembles that of the human brain, Von Neumann and the other creators of EDVAC gave us a technological metaphor for thinking about complex systems of all kinds.[7]

Information Theory

Claude Shannon is considered the founder of the science of electronic communications.[8] Shannon was born in Michigan in 1916. He completed his undergraduate education at the University of Michigan in 1936, at the age of twenty, and studied electrical engineering and mathematics at MIT, where he received both his master's and his doctorate in 1940 at age twenty-four. In 1941, Shannon went to work at the Bell Telephone Laboratories, where he worked on the problem of how to communicate information most efficiently. At the time, switching circuits of increasing complexity were replacing human operators, and Bell Labs scientists were trying to improve their system's ability to transmit information without corrupting it into noise. Shannon's work on this problem led him to formulate a theory of information, which appeared in 1948 in a two-part article in the *Bell System Technical Journal* entitled "A Mathematical Theory of Communication."[9] In 1958, Shannon moved to MIT, where he remained until his retirement two decades later. He died in 2001.

Today we are so accustomed to Shannon's way of describing information that we take it completely for granted, but at the time it was a revolutionary concept. In essence, Shannon identified the fundamental property of information as its *binary condition*; that is, it exists in either one or the other of (but no more than) two conditions. Thus, all information can be represented by choosing one of two alternatives: yes or no, on or off, plus or minus, positive or negative. All possible alternatives can then be represented by the numerical values "0" or "1." Such a system lends itself to being transmitted electronically because electric current is also binary. A switch is either opened and the current flows or it is closed and the current is off. From this understanding, Shannon derived the concept of the *binary digit* (either 0 or 1) as the basic accounting unit of information. *Binary digit* was shortened to *bit,* and the accounting nomenclature of the computer age was born. (Shannon credits J. W. Tukey with having suggested the word *bit.*) The only remaining task was to develop codes or vocabularies that could translate any kind of information into long strings of 0s and 1s.

The bit is the smallest unit of computerized data. Binary digits make it possible to translate numbers based on units of ten (0 through 9) into numbers based on units of two (0 and 1). Thus, for example, 0 = 0 and 1 = 1, but 2 = 10, 3 = 11, 4 = 100, 5 = 101, 6 = 110, 7 = 111, 8 = 1000, 9 = 1001, 10 = 1010, and so on. A set of bits that represent a single value or character is called a "byte." There are usually eight bits in a byte, but there may be more. The size of a message is equal to the number of bytes needed to encode it. Thus, one million bytes are called a megabyte, one billion are a gigabyte, one trillion are a terabyte, and so forth.

We measure the world's production of information in terms of millions of terabytes or "exabytes." In 1999, the world produced an estimated 2.1 million terabytes (or 2.1 exabytes) of more or less permanently stored information. This information was stored in four media: paper, film, optical disks, and magnetic disks. By far the greatest amount (1.69 million terabytes) was stored on magnetic devices (computer disks, tapes, and so forth). Film (cinema, photographs, x-rays) was the next-largest storage medium at 0.42 million terabytes. Paper storage (books, newspapers, office documents) accounted for much less (only 240 terabytes), while optical disks accounted for very little (only 80 terabytes). We also created quite a bit of ephemeral information, not stored anywhere but allowed to disappear as soon as it was used. About 610 billion e-mail messages represent some 11 terabytes, but telephone messages far exceeded this at about 576,000 terabytes.[10]

Biology

According to Stuart Kauffman, biologists have not entirely ignored the self-organizing properties of complex systems, but they have tended to explain the existence of complexity in living systems almost exclusively in terms of the Darwinian paradigm of evolution by natural selection.[11] There are a few exceptions to the rule, however, and they have played a critical role in improving our understanding of the place of systems in our lives.

First and foremost of these is the founder of general systems theory, Ludwig von Bertalanffy, who was born in Vienna, Austria, in 1901.[12] He received his doctorate in biology in 1926 from the University of Vienna, where he was much influenced by the neopositivist school of philosophy. By the 1930s he was widely regarded as one of Europe's leading biologists. Even in his early works he was much preoccupied with the search for the organizing principles of living organisms at different levels of size and complexity, a search that required that he confront each organism as a whole or system. After World War II, he and his wife and son emigrated, first to Switzerland, then to Britain, and eventually to North America. By the early 1950s he found himself at the Ford Foundation's Center for Advanced Study in the Behavioral Sciences in Palo Alto, California. There he met some of the leading figures in the systems approach, including the sociologist Kenneth Boulding, the mathematician Anatol Rapoport, and the physiologist Ralph Gerard. Together with these scholars, Bertalanffy founded the Society for General Systems Research, which became one of the focal points for research in the field. For the next two decades, he held a number of distinguished research and teaching appointments in the United States and Canada. His final academic appointment was at the State University of New York at Buffalo, where he died at the age of seventy. By the end of his life, he was world famous as one of the leading scientific thinkers of the twentieth century, having written half a dozen groundbreaking books in the field of systems theory and its applications.

In the 1990s, many important contributions to systems thinking were made by biologists. One of the leaders in this advance has been Stuart Kauffman, of the Santa Fe Institute (see below).[13] One of Kauffman's leading ideas involves what he and others call *self-organizing complexity,* the ability of random and unorganized particles of matter to fashion themselves into a coherent system without conscious direction from outside ("order out of chaos," as it would appear).[14] It is thought that such complex self-organizing occurs when a random event intrudes into a collection of component parts that have reached a certain critical level. The point at which a "heap" of unorganized particles makes a transition to an organized system is referred to as a *bifurcation point.* By describing the transition this way, Kauffman asserts that the emergent system has many possible "futures" or future states, and the "choice" of one over the others is largely a matter of chance. Kauffman hypotheses that life itself is an emergent property of a spontaneously self-organizing system, but the obstacles to testing such a hypothesis are daunting.

Many scholars are reluctant to accept the idea of self-organizing complexity. The idea seems to refute the notion, so important to many fields of inquiry, that a system tends to move toward a single state that is best for it and attempts to remain at or near that state once it has been achieved. Many economists in particular are more comfortable dealing with a market system that is moving toward a single equilibrium,[15] whereas complex systems experiencing positive feedback may face a choice from among multiple equilibrium points. Thus, markets may confront several possible states of equilibrium, and there is no way of determining the superiority of one over the others. We will revisit some of Kauffman's theories in the next chapter, on system dynamics.

Complexity Theory

In the last three decades of the twentieth century, a new paradigm emerged to help us think about complex systems.[16] This perspective is still so new that it carries many names, including chaos science, chaos theory, adaptive systems, complex systems, deterministic chaos, nonlinear dynamic systems, and self-organizing systems. Complexity theory emerged first among physicists but spread to other fields in which conventional linear theories seemed inadequate, including biology, epidemiology, and economics. Many complexity scientists, especially those from the physical sciences and mathematics, see chaos as reality itself. The Santa Fe Institute in New Mexico is one of several organizations at the center of this community of scholars. Others, particularly management consultants and social scientists (with the exception of some economists), see chaos theory primarily as a metaphor or a vocabulary that helps us think and talk about complex systems. In the early 1990s, complexity science attracted much attention, but when it failed to generate much practical knowledge, interest waned.[17] In particular, critics point to the failure of complexity theorists to discover a unified theory of complex systems that explains the behavior of all such systems at any level.[18] Nevertheless, as a paradigm, complexity theory has contributed much to raising our awareness of the role of complex systems in our life.

Contemporary complexity thinkers trace their intellectual lineage back to the French physicist and mathematician Jules Henri Poincaré (1854–1912), to whom is attributed the discovery of one of the paradigm's central tenets: *sensitive dependence on initial conditions*. This proposition holds that in complex systems, tiny, even imperceptible, variations in inputs can lead to enormous (and unpredictable) changes in outputs.

Given the central importance of this idea to the entire paradigm, it is not surprising that the theory reemerged in its contemporary form from efforts to improve weather forecasting. In 1963, a meteorologist from MIT named Edward Lorenz was attempting to develop a computer program that could predict changes in weather patterns from a relatively small set of nonlinear equations. He discovered that repeated computer runs of the same equations using successive iterations of what appeared to be the same initial data produced dramatically different outcomes. When he investigated further, he found that in fact the initial data sets were not identical; they only appeared to be because the computer had not carried out the calculations to absolute or 100 percent accuracy. Because the computer rounded off the results of the calculations in each successive run, extremely tiny differences had crept into the equations, imperceptible to a human observer but sufficient to alter fundamentally the outcome of the calculations. Lorenz had discovered *deterministic chaos,* meaning that complex systems operating on the basis of known and well-understood rules (determinism) would still yield surprising and unpredictable results (chaos).

At first glance, these two ideas—determinism and chaos—would appear to be mutually contradictory. After all, if we know the laws governing a physical system, we should be able to predict its behavior. Yet we have integrated these contradictory ideas into our culture through the concept of chance, luck, or fate. As David Ruelle has written, "*Chance* and *determinism* are reconciled by long-term unpredictability. . . . *A very small cause, which escapes us, determines a considerable effect which we cannot ignore, and we then say that this effect is due to chance.*"[19]

The complex adaptive systems paradigm helped consolidate the systems approach by linking together in a single body of ideas a number of important properties of systems.[20] For example, the apparently chaotic behavior of a system derives not only from the diversity of its component parts but from the interconnectedness of these parts. Indeed, simple components obeying simple rules of behavior can, if they are connected in a nonlinear way, produce extremely complex systems. Such systems exhibit emergent behavior, wherein the collection of parts works together to produce the system's behavior. These systems consist of a network of "agents" that act independently of one another without any guidance or central control. The human brain and its 100 billion neurons are frequently cited as an example of such a system, wherein a huge number of independently acting elements can still produce a coherent, highly complex system. Although they are without central coordination, these elements are capable of cooperating in communities to produce complex behavioral patterns that no single component could achieve on its own.

Self-organizing systems are capable of learning through feedback. Not only do they adjust or adapt to feedback at a given moment; they are also capable of incorporating such learning into the very structures and operations of the systems so they can repeat the process again and again under varying circumstances. Again with the human brain as a model, self-organizing systems are capable of constantly rearranging themselves as the effects of previous experiences are processed through the system. Self-management and learning through feedback allow these systems to adapt by internal specialization. Self-organizing systems possess many different kinds of components. This diversity allows the system to respond to a constantly changing environment by internal specialization and rearrangement. Because internal components that are no longer useful can be discarded and new ones can be added, the system need never become locked into obsolete behavioral responses to changes in the environment.

Nonlinear systems are those in which the component parts interact such that the behavior of one component affects a second and the behavior of the second is fed back to affect the first. The effects of this feedback are multiplicative. This is in contrast to linear systems, wherein one component affects a second but the second does not affect the first. The consequences of linearity are simply additive. Thus, the behavior of complex systems cannot be predicted using linear cause-and-effect paradigms. Specific outcome events are unpredictable. Because complex systems exhibit a sensitive dependence on initial conditions, a rational response to complex system behavior would include flexible adaptation to unexpected change and the development of feedback signals to encourage the free flow of information in real time.

THE STRUCTURE AND FUNCTIONING OF SYSTEMS

System has been defined in many ways.[21] But most definitions contain the following ingredients:[22]

- A system is a grouping or collection of *component parts*. All systems that are of interest to students of globalization will involve, at a minimum, human beings and technologies interacting. Such systems are referred to as *sociotechnical systems*.[23] Other elements of our world may be involved, including other living organisms, raw materials, energy, and so forth. Usually human beings are involved in any given system only partially and only insofar as they are acting out *social roles* (for example, professor and students in the classroom "system").

- These component parts are *highly interconnected*. Here I use the term *interconnected* to refer to a causal relationship. That is, two parts are interconnected when a *change in one produces a change in the other*. Some systems thinkers place the greatest emphasis on the idea of interaction. Von Bertalanffy has defined a system as any entity maintained by the mutual interaction of its parts, and Anatol Rapoport has written that a system is a whole that functions as a whole by virtue of the interaction of its parts.[24]

- Systems thinkers usually see the component parts as "operating together for a *common purpose*."[25] This aspect of systems thinking is controversial, but it will be helpful to keep in mind that by *purpose* we do not necessarily mean that the system was designed by some external intelligence "in order to" accomplish that end. *Purpose* in this sense may mean simply the end product(s) of the system's actions. Most systems thinkers believe that a system has "goals" that differ from the goals of its component parts. If the system is an organization that includes human beings (as is the case with all the systems we are considering here), then it is common to refer to its goals as somehow different from the personal goals of each individual member. Such would be the case for organizations like corporations or sports teams.[26] For some scientists, to suppose that systems have "goals" suffers from the so-called teleological fallacy (the idea that the Universe is moving toward a particular end state). But systems thinkers such as von Bertalanffy have maintained that "[system] behavior directed toward a . . . final state . . . is not something off limits for natural science. . . . Rather it is . . . behavior which can be well defined in scientific terms and for which necessary conditions and possible mechanisms can be indicated."[27]

- *How the parts are interconnected is more important* than the parts themselves. To use systems thinking to improve our ability to understand globalization, we must focus most of our attention on the way(s) the parts interact with one another. Indeed, von Bertalanffy asserts that the principal virtue of systems thinking is its ability to understand phenomena that are "not understandable by investigation of their respective parts in isolation."[28] In the next chapter, we shall see that a change in a system usually is the result not of changes in the individual component parts, but of changes in the relationships among the parts.[29] Unfortunately, the parts are much easier to detect and describe than the interactions between and among them are.

- Many of the important properties of systems derive not from the component parts, but from the way they interact. We say that these properties "emerge" from the system's behavior, and so they are referred to as *emergent properties*.[30] The biologist Stuart Kauffman believes that life itself is an emergent property. Indeed, the notion of emergent properties enables us to explain how life began through the spontaneous self-organization of substances that were not themselves living.[31]

- Without knowing what to look for or how to interpret what we see, we may not be able to deduce a system's emergent properties simply by knowing what its components are. For example, suppose a person who had never seen an airplane and did not know the concept of "powered flight" was ushered into an airplane hangar and shown the component parts of a Boeing 747 laid out on the floor. Without knowing that these parts constitute a system and without knowing what that system can do, the person would not be able to describe how the parts could be assembled to fly. Some systems thinkers warn against believing that the emergent properties are "inside" the system, for the existence of such properties is thought to depend on observations made from outside the system.[32] The fact that systems display emergent properties is one of the reasons why awareness of a system is often *knowledge dependent,* meaning that we are not aware of a system's existence unless we know what to look for.

- A system is separated from its surroundings by a *boundary,* a line that tells us where the system ends and the environment begins. These boundaries may be *physical,* such as the skin on the human body; *conceptual,* such as the social roles people assume under differing circumstances; or *metaphorical,* meaning that we use the concept to make it easier to think about systems as isolated from the rest of the world.[33] Boundaries reflect to some degree the perceptions and interests of the observer. We read occasionally that "everything is connected to everything else," which may be literally true. But many connections are so tiny that we can treat them as if they were virtually nonexistent. If we really tried to identify and analyze all of a system's connections, then there would only be one enormous system—the Universe. In deciding what belongs inside the system, we make judgments based on our assessment of important cause-and-effect relationships. That is, we determine which causal relationships we must understand in order to comprehend the behavior of the system as a whole. Ideally, we will draw the boundary so that it encompasses the smallest number of interacting parts that we need to observe to understand the dynamic behavior of the system but wide enough to include all relevant factors.[34]

- In theory, a system may be *closed* to the outside world, with a boundary that allows nothing to enter or leave. Such a system, if it did exist, would be of little interest to us. All living systems (and, therefore, all global systems) are *open* to their environments.[35] That is, they are constantly exchanging matter, energy, and information with the rest of the world. Indeed, that is what makes them interesting and important. Thus, a system's boundary must be partially porous or open, allowing some things to pass through but blocking or impeding the flow of others. Moreover, all open systems are, by definition, *dynamic*; that is, they experience change. Dynamic systems may achieve and maintain a certain *steady state*—but only by importing key resources from their environment and exporting waste. The laws of closed systems do not apply to open systems, "which maintain themselves through constant commerce with their environment, i.e., a continuous inflow and outflow of energy through permeable boundaries."[36] Growth of a complex system may require hundreds of inputs, but

at any given moment a small number, perhaps only one, will be truly critical. The availability of this input (or these inputs) will constrain the system's growth. The limiting input may constitute only a small part of the
system. What matters is the role the input plays in the system's activity.[37]

- Systems change in order to adapt to changes in their environments. The
idea of *system adaptation* is not as straightforward as it might appear at
first glance.[38] What systems actually do in order to adapt to changes in
their environments is to a large degree a function of the timescale involved. If an organism engaged in some behavior (say, a chicken pecking
at grains of corn on the ground) changes that behavior in response to immediate or proximate changes (say, grains newly thrown), then we say
such change is "instinctual." That is, the organism was already genetically
programmed to adapt this way. If the chicken's beak changes shape over
very long spans of time to adapt to changes in the shape or availability of
grains, then we refer to such change as "evolutionary." If the chicken
learns that it can acquire more grains by pecking at a button in an experi-
mental cage, then we call such adaptation "learned behavior." Students of
globalization will be most interested in this third kind of adaptation, behavioral changes that occur in the midrange of timescales. The other two
forms of adaptation—instinctual and evolutionary—are virtually beyond
our control, and organizational policies will seldom be aimed at these
kinds of system changes.

- Systems are arranged in the world in some sort of *hierarchical order,* with
"lower" level systems encompassed within "higher" level systems that are
larger and more complex. Systems thinkers often try to classify systems
according to some hierarchic principle. (See box 3.1 for an example.) For
example, Ervin Laszlo distinguishes three levels of system organization:
suborganic (the basic building blocks of the physical world, beginning
with subatomic particles), organic (living organisms, ranging from the microscopic to the enormous), and supraorganic (groups of organisms, such
as herds of animals, fields of plants, or human collectivities).[39] Von Bertalanffy has put forward a classification scheme with nine levels, ranging
from "static structures" like crystals to "symbolic systems" that incorporate
language, mathematics, and so forth.[40] Kauffman has asserted that our
biosphere is packed with living systems (he calls them "autonomous
agents" because of their ability to transform matter and energy without
external assistance) arranged hierarchically. Single-celled organisms are
at the base of the hierarchy, but the peak may extend as high as (or even
beyond) the blue whale or a stand of aspen trees.[41] Some systems thinkers
use the term *holarchy* to refer to "any whole and its parts. These parts, in
turn, are wholes in themselves with their own parts, and so on. Thus a holarchy can be considered as the nested system of wholes and parts over
numerous levels."[42] As more research in systems accumulates, we now
understand that typologies based on hierarchic levels are largely arbitrary

and that in the real world the dividing lines between systems are never pure and precise.

- Complex systems *do not need centralized control* in order to function. Systems scientists have discovered numerous instances in which individual component parts, without any outside coordination or direction and following a few simple rules involving behavior and communication with their nearest neighbors, can evolve surprisingly complex, coordinated collective behavior patterns. From cells in our body, to ants forming bridges with their own bodies, to plants and animals in complex ecosystems, individuals can congregate into complex wholes on their own, without guidance from a central controller.[43] We shall return to this property of complex systems later in this book, when we examine the challenge we are presented with when we try to track and regulate invisible systems.

Box 3.1   An Example of a Classification of Systems Arranged in Hierarchical Order

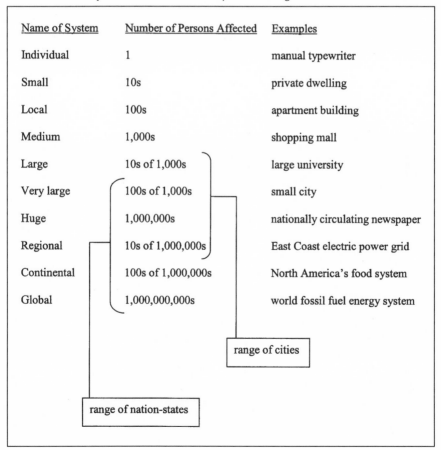

Name of System	Number of Persons Affected	Examples
Individual	1	manual typewriter
Small	10s	private dwelling
Local	100s	apartment building
Medium	1,000s	shopping mall
Large	10s of 1,000s	large university
Very large	100s of 1,000s	small city
Huge	1,000,000s	nationally circulating newspaper
Regional	10s of 1,000,000s	East Coast electric power grid
Continental	100s of 1,000,000s	North America's food system
Global	1,000,000,000s	world fossil fuel energy system

range of cities

range of nation-states

Figure 3.1   Elements of a Generic System

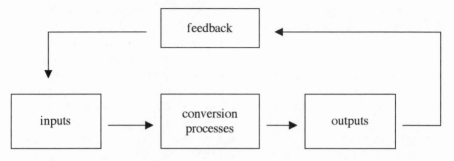

Real world systems come in such variety that they defy easy generalization. No matter how systems are classified, however, a generic system always contains the following four features (see figure 3.1):

- *Inputs:* the matter, energy, and information that enter the system.
- *Conversion processes:* the processes by which matter, energy, and information are transformed. Such transformations generally involve (a) the rearrangement of the inputs to alter their form and (b) the movement of the transformed material from one place to another. These actions require the expenditure of substantial amounts of energy, which we can regard as one of the costs of systems.
- *Outputs:* the transformed matter, energy, and information as they emerge from the conversion processes.
- *Feedback:* information about a system's action(s) that is returned to the system to alter or influence future action(s).

These four components interact as a cycle. That is, they function in sequence to achieve their goal and return to the first stage to repeat their functions. The object of such a cycle is the throughput and transformation of matter, energy, and information. The cyclical nature of systems is important because without returning to the initial stage, the system would not be in a position to continue to perform work. When we say that systems work in cycles, we do not mean that the four stages are repeated without changes. All the systems of interest to us change constantly, often in quite surprising ways. Indeed, it is the change in a system that attracts our attention to it in the first place and makes us want to know more about it.[44]

The idea of feedback is crucial to our understanding of what a system is and how it differs from things that are not systems.[45] We may on occasion observe an object whose current behavior (what we label "outputs") has no influence over its future behavior. Such an object does not observe and react to its own performance and thus cannot correct mistakes, seek goals, or generate growth. An example of such an object would be a watch lying untouched on a table. Although such an object contains interacting component parts, by itself it is not a system because it is unaware of the fact that it is showing the wrong time, and it has no way to correct itself if it begins to do so. But if the watch is picked up by its owner and adjusted to reflect the correct time, it becomes part of a system.

As figure 3.1 suggests, feedback can be portrayed as information flowing through a system in a circular pattern that we refer to as a *feedback loop*. A feedback loop is a path that connects information about the current state or condition of a system to a decision about some future state or condition. Jay Forrester asserts that the feedback loop is the basic unit of which systems are composed.[46] Our simple model of a system shows only a single feedback loop, but in the real world complex systems contain many feedback loops. The connections among these many loops make the behavior of the system even more complex and difficult to understand and explain.

Feedback loops are of two kinds. A negative feedback loop signals the system to reduce or reverse its performance, damp down its actions, and return to some kind of equilibrium. Some systems analysts refer to this as "goal seeking" because they presume that such systems have as their goal their own equilibrium. A thermostat in a room is frequently used as an example of such a feedback device. As the room becomes warmer or colder (that is, as the room temperature climbs or drops further and further beyond the levels established as desirable), the thermostat signals the heating/cooling system to operate to restore the desirable temperature. Political and social systems exhibit many kinds of negative feedback loops, including the U.S. constitutional structure known as checks and balances and the familiar feature of international politics known as the balance of power.[47]

In contrast, a positive feedback loop signals the system to continue or increase its previous actions. Such feedback is said to be "growth generating" because the effect is to cause the system to expand. Investors receiving a favorable report on their investments will be more likely to increase such investments in the future, helping to drive up the price of the stocks in question. As a factory increases its production of a given item, it experiences economies of scale that in turn make the item cheaper and increase its share of the market. Incremental peace processes are based on the assumption that success in small steps builds mutual trust and confidence between the parties in conflict and thus facilitates further steps to resolve conflicts.

Observers sometimes associate certain feedback types with stability or instability. Actually, negative and positive feedback loops can be either stabilizing or destabilizing, depending on the context. If a negative feedback loop functions correctly, its system tends to exhibit stability. If negative feedback fails to restore the system to its goal condition, however, the system may fluctuate wildly and become unstable. Systems with positive feedback loops tend to exhibit growth, which some may interpret as instability depending on the values of those affected by the system. To complicate matters further, many real world systems possess both negative and positive feedback devices whose operations tend to offset each other.[48]

In the next chapter, I examine why systems tend to grow, how they grow, and the corrective mechanisms that operate to prevent growth from going on without limits. We shall see that of crucial importance is the ability of the system to sense and respond to feedback signals without time delays.[49]

WHY DO SYSTEMS EXIST?

Systems thinkers point out that living systems at all orders of magnitude and complexity, from single cells to international organizations, exhibit similarities of structure and operation.[50] Why should this be so? The answer lies in the tasks or challenges that all living entities confront if they are to avoid decay and death. Stripped to their essentials, these tasks are the following:

- Take in matter and energy, which virtually always requires moving these resources from where they exist to where they are needed.
- Convert matter and energy from the form in which they occur naturally to the form in which they can be utilized.
- Store matter and energy in anticipation of some future time when their supply will be inadequate.
- Export the used matter and energy, in the form of products or waste, to the environment (usually to other systems).
- Maintain all of the components in the proper relationships to each other, which usually calls for internal dividers and an external container, called a boundary.
- Receive, process, and transmit information that provides feedback about system performance as well as produce output signals to other entities (systems) with which it shares the environment.
- Reproduce.

In other words, living systems exist because the matter, energy, and information they need are not where the system needs them and are not in the form in which they are needed. Thus, systems exist to transport matter, energy, and information from where they exist to where the system needs them to be and to change them into a form that the system can use.

In his book *The Energy of Life*,[51] the biologist Guy Brown describes this process for the human body at the cellular level. Brown likens the cell to "a vast, teeming metropolis" of almost unimaginable complexity. Within this metropolis, hundreds of thousands of different molecule-sized "machines" are working at a frantic pace, doing tens of thousands of different sorts of tasks. Many of these molecules are packed inside tiny bags within the cell, each separated from the others by a membrane, and the entire cell is further separated from its environment by a membrane as well. The bags within each cell are connected by tiny channels or tunnels that Brown calls metabolic pathways. These pathways are actually networks of enzymes that move molecules by changing their form so that they can be passed along to the next enzyme in the sequence.

The power stations of the cell are some 1,000 mitochondria where the energy supplies are received and transformed into fuel for the cell's functions. But in order for the mitochondria to do their job, other molecules must assist. Within Brown's teeming metropolis are two principal kinds of molecular machines: the enzymes and the transporters. There may be up to 10,000 different types of these machines in each cell, and they may be present in numbers ranging from 10 to 100 million, depending on what they have to do and how quickly the cell needs them to do their tasks. The enzymes convert one kind of molecule to another type of molecule by chopping pieces off, adding pieces on, or taking pieces from one molecule and adding them to another. The transporters carry a molecule from one bag to another across the membranes of the cell. They also function to transport molecules from the cell's environment (the body's blood supply) across the cellular membrane to within the cell. The transporters perform this function by binding to particular molecules and then changing their shape so that these molecules can be released to pass through the membrane. Each enzyme and each transporter performs only one task, but they all perform it over and over again about 1,000 times per second.

Metabolic pathways exist to move molecules from the blood to inside the cell, to move the molecules through the cell until they are converted as end products (such as carbon dioxide or water), and to then carry them outside the cell where they are taken away by the blood. There are three different types of such pathways to transport the three different types of products: mass transfer pathways to move bits of molecules, energy transfer pathways to move energy, and signal transfer pathways to transport information.

ENTROPY, INFORMATION, AND TIME

Systems exist to perform an essential service, but this service is not performed for free. Systems make us pay a price for moving matter, energy, and information and for transforming them so they can be used again and again. Some 150 years ago, scientists studying thermodynamics (the science of heat, its generation and movement) identified *entropy* as an inescapable consequence of the operation of "heat engines" (the name given at the time to steam engines).[52] In 1871, British scientist James Clerk Maxwell invented his famous "demon," a tiny imaginary being who could see and control individual molecules in such a way as to derive work from a system without entropy. But subsequent generations of physicists have demonstrated that even Maxwell's "demon" would have to bear some cost in lost energy, and most now believe that entropy is the inevitable product of any system as it performs work.[53] How systems deal with the consequences of entropy has much to do with how they affect us and our world.

To perform work, systems must acquire the three components of our world: matter (the substance or substances of which physical objects are composed), energy (the property of matter that enables it to perform work), and information (from the Latin, *informare,* meaning "to give form to"). Although energy can be neither created nor destroyed, its form is changed as the system performs work. For example, in the eighteenth century, the steam engines built by Thomas Newcomen and James Watt transformed chemical energy into kinetic energy by burning coal, boiling water to create steam, and using the expansion and contraction of the steam to raise and lower a piston attached to a moving beam. Every time such a transformation occurs, some energy is "lost" to us forever. Metaphorically speaking, such lost energy is the "price" systems charge us for their work. Of course, from nature's perspective the energy is not lost because it still exists somewhere in the Universe. To be precise, we would say that the energy has been *rendered unavailable for future work.* Thus, entropy is defined as the measure of the amount of energy rendered unavailable when a system performs work; but from our perspective for all intents and purposes the energy I use to power my car or heat my home has been lost forever.

Open systems counteract the effects of entropy by importing more free energy from the environment and exporting waste to the environment.[54] Physicists and biologists have coined the term *ectropy* (i.e., the opposite of entropy) to refer to the ability of living systems "to use the environmental substances, rich in easily released energy, to maintain . . . a given level of entropy and even to lower it."[55] The ability of a system to persist counter to entropy appears to violate the laws of thermodynamics, but such is not the case.[56] To survive, grow, and become more complex, open systems must have found a way to import free energy from elsewhere in the Universe.[57] And as there exists in the Universe an enormous quantity of free energy, we are often led to believe that the growth and complexity of the systems we enjoy are available "for free." This is a dangerous misperception, for global systems must always be "paid for" in energy terms. Every time work is performed, the entropy of the Universe grows larger. How systems manage to spread these costs and what this has to do with globalization is discussed in chapter 4.

The concept of entropy was originally intended to apply to the energy dynamics of physical and biological systems. However, in the 1940s, beginning with the work of Claude Shannon discussed earlier, scientists began to understand that there is a profound connection among thermodynamic entropy (the decay of physical systems), information entropy (the deterioration of meaning in communication systems), and organizational entropy (the increased disorder of a sociotechnical system).[58] All three kinds of systems require a steady infusion of matter, energy, and information to persist counter to entropy. It is true that early systems thinkers like von Bertalanffy drew a distinction between open systems, through which matter and energy flow, and feedback or cybernetic systems, which receive only information.[59] Today we understand, however, that for the systems paradigm to illuminate global events, it must encompass the flow of all three resources.

Systems depend on the flow of information just as they depend on the processing of matter and energy. Information is what a system's component parts do "to give form to" some particularly important aspect of system functioning. Information is transmitted via the process of *communication,* a process that requires a sender and a receiver, a set of symbols (an alphabet) available to both, and a channel over which signals can be sent. The sender transmits information by constructing a message from the available alphabet, encoding that message, and transporting the symbols so that the receiver can decode them and understand the message.

The value of information derives from its role in the *reduction of uncertainty.* The amount of information included in a message is a function of the amount of uncertainty the receiver experiences regarding its content. If the receiver already knows the contents of the message, its information content is virtually zero. If the contents come as a complete surprise to the receiver, we say its information content is very high. Just as a system needs a constant infusion of free energy to maintain itself counter to physical entropy, so also does it need constantly to import information to reduce disorder, disorganization, and uncertainty.

But there is always a price to pay. Indeed, David Ruelle links a system's complexity with the information it contains. *"An entity is complex,"* he writes, *"if it embodies information that is hard to get."*[60] Although he does not define *hard to get* precisely, it obviously has something to do with the cost of obtaining the information necessary to "give form to" a given system (for example, the DNA in a cell in the human body).

In the mid–twentieth century, Shannon, Norbert Wiener, and others advanced the proposition that entropy is an inescapable consequence of information generation and transmission.[61] That is, entropy affects not only the energy available for use after a system performs work but its information level and clarity as well. Wiener has demonstrated that the clarity and structure of information depend on energy availability because information is always transported by some physical process. Thus, as the energy of a system inevitably decreases, to be replaced by heat or waste (or entropy), the information contained within the system tends just as inevitably to become disorganized or random (known as "noise"). Thus, we encounter the fundamental dilemma presented by information theory: information is essential to reduce uncertainty, but its transmission and receipt at the same time increase uncertainty as well. In commonsense terms, the more we know, the more uncertainty we experience. These changes are the fundamental costs of a system performing work. In a closed system, information entropy increases to a maximum just as thermodynamic entropy does. In the near term, open systems disguise such costs by shifting them from one system to another (a process involving "dissipative structures," to be discussed in chapter 4), but eventually the bill must be paid in full by someone or some system.

Earlier we encountered the issue of defining a system by drawing its physical or conceptual boundary so as to include some things and exclude others. Another way of asking what to include in a system and what to leave out involves the length of the time horizon we define for the system.[62] How far back in time can we reasonably stretch the system's "past," and how far ahead in time can we project its "future"? Cultural differences play a role here, for a person's cultural view of the passage of time affects the way he or she selects the time interval that defines the "life" of the system. Different intellectual traditions see the passage of time differently, and these differences influence how their adherents describe the properties of the systems they study.

Scientists have debated the nature and direction of time for hundreds of years.[63] For most of us, it seems self-evident that time has a direction. Hot water cools, and eggs can be scrambled; but these processes never reverse themselves without substantial physical intervention from outside. On the other hand, scientists operating from the paradigm of Newtonian mechanics assume that time is reversible and uniform, so they tend to disregard its effects in studying system dynamics. Albert Einstein once wrote to a friend that "for us convinced physicists, the distinction between past, present and future is an illusion, although a persistent one." Or, as Stephen Hawking puts it in one of his famous articles, "Physics is time symmetric," which is his way of stating that the laws of physics are indifferent to the direction of time.

There is a contrary view, of course, but it appears now to be the minority opinion. Biologists and ecologists, for instance, favor a more evolutionary concept of time, which means that the passage of time produces system changes that are irreversible. Systems studied by these scientists tend to show marked evolutionary change across broad sweeps of time. The leading spokesperson for this perspective is Ilya Prigogine, who asserts that although the behavior of individual molecules may indeed be time symmetric, this is of little relevance. What matters are the properties of the larger system of which these molecules form a part. If such a system is unstable (as are all the systems in which we are interested in this book), then time irreversibility is a statistical property of the overall entity. From this vantage point, the behavior of individual particles is not fundamental. Rather, the average, statistical properties of the whole system are fundamental, and these are decidedly not time symmetric.

These conflicts continue to rage. Among other points of dispute is the question of how one can make a transition from time-irrelevant behavior at the particle level to time-irreversible behavior at the system level. Important as they are, these debates will not detain us here, for there is a much more pressing issue concerning time and system behavior. I refer to the issue of intergenerational obligations and responsibilities. If we do not take seriously the time horizon over which our system is to operate, we risk creating a system whose actions have serious and negative consequences for future generations. Our decisions about the system's time horizon have inescapable moral and ethical consequences and implications. As Lewis Perelman puts it, "When we define the temporal horizons of a system, we get no disagreement from either the dead or the unborn":

> When all temporal boundaries are arbitrary, one can draw them as close to one's immediate interests as desired. The problems of the past are dead, and the problems of the future can take care of themselves. We have a kind of intergenerational libertarianism at work. Once the entropic concept of irrevocability is discarded, all generations are created equal; each has an equal right and responsibility to maximize its own welfare.[64]

There is much more we need to consider about the appropriate time horizon for global systems, but I shall postpone a complete discussion until the next chapter, when we examine system dynamics or how and why systems change over time.

NOTES

1. Gerald M. Weinberg, *An Introduction to General Systems Thinking* (New York: Wiley, 1975), 52.

2. Ludwig von Bertalanffy, *General System Theory: Foundations, Development, Applications* (New York: George Braziller, 1968), 10.

3. Joël de Rosnay, *The Symbiotic Man: A New Understanding of the Organization of Life and a Vision of the Future* (New York: McGraw-Hill, 2000), chapter 1. From a methodological standpoint, the invention of the computer was also important because it gave researchers the technology they needed to visualize and simulate highly complex systems, many of which are invisible.

4. Jay W. Forrester, *World Dynamics,* 2d ed. (Cambridge, Mass.: Wright-Allen Press, 1973), 13.

5. Norbert Wiener, *Cybernetics, or Control and Communication in the Animal and the Machine* (New York: Wiley, 1948), 19.

6. Wiener, *Cybernetics.*

7. T. A. Heppenheimer, "How Von Neumann Showed the Way," *Invention and Technology* (fall 1990): 8–16.

8. Charles A. Gimon, "Heroes of Cyberspace: Claude Shannon," INFO NATION Web site, at www.skypoint.com.

9. Shannon's papers are reprinted in Claude E. Shannon and Warren Weaver, *The Mathematical Theory of Communication* (Urbana: University of Illinois Press, 1998).

10. "Byte Counters," *The Economist,* October 21, 2000.

11. Stuart A. Kauffman, *The Origins of Order: Self-Organization and Selection in Evolution* (New York: Oxford University Press, 1993), xiii.

12. Mark Davidson, *Uncommon Sense: The Life and Thought of Ludwig von Bertalanffy (1901–1972), Father of General Systems Theory* (Los Angeles: J. P. Tarcher, 1983), chapter 2.

13. Stuart A. Kauffman has written three major books applying complexity science to such challenging questions as the origin of life: *The Origins of Order: Self-Organization*

and Selection in Evolution, At Home in the Universe: The Search for the Laws of Self-Organization and Complexity (New York: Oxford University Press, 1995), and *Investigations* (New York: Oxford University Press, 2000).

14. Stuart A. Kauffman, "Antichaos and Adaptation," *Scientific American* 265, no. 2 (August 1991): 78–84.

15. "Market equilibrium" is the state or condition of the market at which supply and demand are perfectly balanced. It represents the most efficient possible allocation of goods in the market because no other state can do a better job of producing the well-being of the market's participants. Conventional welfare economics assumes that there is only one such possible state or condition. All others are defective or imperfect by definition. Complexity theorists challenge this assumption.

16. The literature on chaos theory is enormous. The reader is invited to begin with two of the earliest works in this field: James Gleick, *Chaos* (New York: Viking, 1987); and Heinz Pagels, *The Dreams of Reason: The Computer and the Rise of the Sciences of Complexity* (New York: Bantam, 1988).

17. "Making the Complex Simple," *The Economist,* January 27, 2001: 79–80.

18. John Horgan, "From Complexity to Perplexity," *Scientific American* 272, no. 6 (June 1995): 104–9.

19. David Ruelle, *Chance and Chaos* (Princeton: Princeton University Press, 1991), 48.

20. These properties are derived from a paper entitled "Introduction to the Chaos Network Conference: Questions and Answers about Chaos in Organizations," written by Glenda Eoyang, June 26, 1993, and distributed to participants in the Third Annual Chaos Network Conference, St. Paul, Minnesota, in September 1993. See also David H. Freeman, "Is Management Still a Science?" *Harvard Business Review* (November–December 1992): 26–38.

21. See, for example, Robert Jervis, *System Effects: Complexity in Political and Social Life* (Princeton: Princeton University Press, 1997), chapters 1–2.

22. Obviously these four component parts can be subdivided into many subsystems and processes. For one approach, which identifies nineteen critical subsystems of all living systems, see James Grier Miller and Jessie Louise Miller, "Systems Science: An Emerging Interdisciplinary Field," *The Center Magazine* (September–October 1981): 44–55.

23. F. E. Emery and E. L. Trist, "Socio-Technical Systems," in *Systems Thinking: Selected Readings,* ed. F. E. Emery (Baltimore: Penguin, 1971), chapter 14.

24. Davidson, *Uncommon Sense,* 25–26.

25. Jay W. Forrester, *Principles of Systems* (Cambridge: MIT Press, 1968), 1-1.

26. D. Katz and R. L. Kahn, "Common Characteristics of Open Systems," in *Systems Thinking: Selected Readings,* ed. F. E. Emery (Baltimore: Penguin, 1971), 88–89.

27. Von Bertalanffy, *General System Theory,* 46.

28. Von Bertalanffy, *General System Theory,* 37.

29. Ervin Laszlo, *The Systems View of the World: A Holistic Vision for Our Time* (Cresskill, N.J.: Hampton Press, 1996), 6–7.

30. Von Bertalanffy, *General System Theory,* chapter 3.

31. Kauffman, *The Origins of Order,* 21–22.

32. Weinberg, *An Introduction to General Systems Thinking,* 60.

33. Weinberg, *An Introduction to General Systems Thinking,* 144.

34. Forrester, *Principles of Systems,* 4-2. Davidson, *Uncommon Sense,* 33–34.

35. Von Bertalanffy, *General System Theory,* 39–41.

36. Katz and Kahn, "Common Characteristics of Open Systems," 91.

37. Donella H. Meadows, "Whole Earth Models and Systems," *The CoEvolution Quarterly* (summer 1982): 102.

38. G. Sommerhoff, "The Abstract Characteristics of Living Systems," in *Systems Thinking: Selected Readings,* ed. F. E. Emery (Baltimore: Penguin, 1971), 177–82.

39. Laszlo, *The Systems View of the World,* chapter 3.

40. Von Bertalanffy, *General System Theory,* 28–29, table 1.2.

41. Kauffman, *Investigations,* 120–21.

42. Tyler Volk, *Gaia's Body: Toward a Physiology of Earth* (New York: Springer-Verlag, 1998), 32–33.

43. George Johnson, "Mindless Creatures, Acting 'Mindfully,'" *New York Times,* March 23, 1999.

44. Some scholars refer to these cycles as thermodynamic cycles because they result in the processing, transport, and transformation of energy. See Kauffman, *Investigations,* 53–73.

45. Forrester, *Principles of Systems,* 1-5. For an early statement on feedback, see Wiener, *Cybernetics,* chapter 4.

46. Forrester, *Principles of Systems,* 2-39; Forrester, *World Dynamics,* 17.

47. Jervis, *System Effects,* chapter 4.

48. Jay W. Forrester, "System Dynamics—Future Opportunities," in *System Dynamics, Studies in the Management Sciences,* vol. 14, ed. A. A. Legasto Jr., J. W. Forrester, and J. M. Lyneis (Amsterdam: North-Holland Publishing Co., 1980), 12–14.

49. Forrester, *Principles of Systems,* 2-25–2-39.

50. Miller and Miller, "Systems Science," 44.

51. Guy Brown, *The Energy of Life: The Science of What Makes Our Minds and Bodies Work* (New York: Free Press, 1999), chapter 2.

52. Professor Chris Hillman, a mathematics professor at the University of Washington, maintains a Web site dedicated completely to the exchange of information about entropy, especially in information. See "Entropy on the World Wide Web," at math.washington.edu/~hillman/entropy.html.

53. Ruelle, *Chance and Chaos,* chapter 17. See also "The Cost of Forgetting," *The Economist,* December 13, 1997: 73–75.

54. Ludwig von Bertalanffy, "The Theory of Open Systems in Physics and Biology," *Science* 111 (1950): 23–29, reprinted in F. E. Emery, ed., *Systems Thinking: Selected Readings* (Baltimore: Penguin, 1971), chapter 4. Some theorists refer to the free energy used to power system work as "negative entropy" or "neg-entropy." See Katz and Kahn, "Common Characteristics of Open Systems," 94–95.

55. V. I. Kremyanskiy, "Certain Peculiarities of Organisms as a 'System' from the Point of View of Physics, Cybernetics, and Biology," in *Systems Thinking: Selected Readings,* ed. F. E. Emery (Baltimore: Penguin, 1971), 142.

56. Mary Lukas, "The World According to Ilya Prigogine," *Quest* 4, no. 10 (December 1980): 15–18, 86–88.

57. Von Bertalanffy, *General System Theory,* 97–98, 124–31.

58. Anatol Rapoport, *General System Theory: Essential Concepts and Applications* (Tunbridge Wells, U.K.: Abacus Press, 1986), chapter 4. Von Bertalanffy, *General System Theory,* 41–44.

59. Von Bertalanffy, *General System Theory,* 149–50.

60. Ruelle, *Chance and Chaos,* 136.

61. Wiener, *Cybernetics,* 70–72.

62. Lewis J. Perelman, "Time in System Dynamics," in *System Dynamics, Studies in the Management Sciences,* vol. 14, ed. A. A. Legasto Jr., J. W. Forrester, and J. M. Lyneis (Amsterdam: North-Holland Publishing Co., 1980), 75–89.

63. The following is drawn from Tony Rothman, "Irreversible Differences," *The Sciences* (July–August 1997): 26–31.

64. Perelman, "Time in System Dynamics," 83, 79.

Case Study 3

What Determines the Price of Gasoline? The Global Energy System

KEY IDEAS IN THIS CASE STUDY

Energy is one of the key sectors of any industrialized economy, and any marked change in the price of energy has an impact on economic growth and stability. For the first century of the Age of Oil, from 1860 to the early 1970s, Americans were shielded from the consequences of their dependence on the enormous and complex system that provides them with the precious substance that powers their society: petroleum. The American motorist gets the fuel for his or her automobile at the end of a long, complex, and often invisible system called the global energy system. Although we may sense very acutely the impact of price changes of gasoline at the pump, for most of us it is virtually impossible to identify the causes of such changes.

- The **global energy system** is so long and complex that it takes about six weeks for energy to travel from where it leaves the ground to where one puts it in the fuel tank of one's car.
- Gasoline prices are very sensitive to the price of the raw material from which the fuel is made: crude (unrefined) petroleum. Between 1860 and 1973, the price of petroleum declined gradually, but after 1973 a **new pricing arrangement** was introduced that is much more sensitive to both market forces and political pressures.
- As with any scarce and precious substance, gasoline prices are influenced by both **supply and demand factors.** Identifying these factors and weighing their importance are not easy for the nonexpert. The Global System Paradigm can help us identify some of these important factors.

In spring and summer 2000 and again in 2001, motorists in the highly industrialized countries in Europe and North America were profoundly upset at what they perceived to be sudden, unexpected, and unwarranted increases in the prices they paid for gasoline. In the first quarter of 2000, for example, crude oil prices increased by about one-third, and the price of gasoline at the pump rose in the Washington, D.C., area from $0.98 to $1.54 per gallon. Because energy is one of the key sectors of any industrialized economy, any marked increase in the price of energy has an impact on economic growth and stability. In the case of gasoline, price increases affect virtually everything, from home pizza deliveries to national defense.[1]

For the first century of the Age of Oil, from 1860 to the early 1970s, Americans were shielded from the consequences of their dependence on the enormous and complex system that provides them with the precious substance that powers their society: petroleum. This dependence began to be painfully obvious after the first "oil shock," in 1973. Today, American motorists get the fuel for their automobiles at the end of a long, complex, and often invisible system called the global energy system. They may see immediately the price changes of gasoline at the pump, but it is virtually impossible for them to identify what caused such changes. This case study seeks to identify these causal factors by describing the global system for extracting crude oil, refining it into gasoline, and delivering that gasoline to nearby locations where we can buy it.

THE GLOBAL ENERGY SYSTEM

In virtually every respect, our Earth is a closed system. Every substance on which we depend—carbon, nitrogen, hydrogen, and so forth—exists on the Earth in a finite quantity and is recycled endlessly through numerous complex systemic processes to provide the bases for civilization, indeed, for life itself.[2] Everything, that is, except for energy. Unlike all the other resources on which we rely, energy flows into, through, and eventually out of the biosphere, radiated out into the cold emptiness of space from where it came. During its brief time on Earth, however, energy plays a critical role in maintaining our lives and, today, our way of life. This is possible because of an extraordinary global energy system that links people, energy-bearing resources, institutions, and technologies to move energy from where it exists to where we need it and to transform it from its natural state into the fuel of highly industrialized society.

Energy is not a "thing"; energy is a property of matter that enables that matter to perform work. The word *work* in this context is only vaguely related to the social or economic meaning of the term. Rather, we mean, as John Peet explains, that "energy has the ability to cause changes in the physical or chemical nature, structure, or location of matter or things. . . . Energy is not a thing that can be seen or touched; it is a concept used to explain changes in the state of matter under certain circumstances."[3] For this reason, when we talk about "extracting," "transporting," or "consuming" energy, we are really talking about extracting, transporting, or consuming the particular matter–energy combination or configuration that gives the matter economic, social, or cultural value. The energy system I describe here is in reality a system for the transformation of matter to wrest from it economically valuable energy.

Virtually all the energy we use comes to us initially in the solar energy created by enormous thermonuclear reactions in the Sun and radiated constantly and in massive quantities from that star out into space. Much of this energy arrives on Earth a short time (i.e., from a few hours to a few years) before we use it. Ecologists refer to this as energy flows, but I call it *real-time energy* to suggest that we use it more or less immediately after its arrival.[4] Some of this energy can be stored for brief periods in the tissue of plants and animals, but even this portion must be used relatively quickly.

Some of this real-time energy makes its way into our world via the carbon cycle. Photons of light striking the leaves of photosynthesizing plants trigger the process by which plant tissue is created using the carbon dioxide in the atmosphere or dissolved in water. This process is very inefficient. Over the course of a year less than one-half of a percent of the incoming solar radiation is converted into plant tissue.[5] Carbon is the crucial element in these processes. It is able to bond with very many other elements, especially hydrogen, to form numerous long chains known as hydrocarbons or carbohydrates. Its connections to other elements are stable yet capable of fostering reactions. Carbon must be cycled rapidly through the biosphere because although it is essential to life, it is extremely rare outside living matter.[6]

Some of the carbon remains in the plant tissue in the form of carbohydrates, and some of the energy received by the plants is bound up in these carbohydrates. Some of this energy is then passed on to herbivores when they consume the plants, and then to carnivores when they eat the herbivores, and so on through the so-called food chain or food web. At each stage when energy is passed from one organism to another, there are huge inefficiencies. Each organism takes most of the energy for its own metabolic requirements, and much of the remainder is "wasted" in the form of heat.

Another portion of real-time energy enters our world through its influence on weather patterns. Solar energy heats the Earth's atmosphere, water, and land to different degrees, and the natural system's attempts to redress the imbalance produce wind, moving water (ocean currents), and so forth. Until the late eighteenth or early nineteenth century, human civilization depended almost entirely on real-time energy, and the process of globalization went forward entirely dependent on human and animal muscle power, wind, and moving water.

There is another source of energy, however, and its exploitation has proven to be crucial to industrial civilization and to globalization as we know it. Beginning about 360 million years ago and lasting some 70 million years (a period known as the Carboniferous Period), lush forests and tropical swamps covered much of the Earth. The climate promoted the growth of vegetation and marine organisms. Upon death, much of this biomass sank to the bottoms of lakes and decayed so that this portion of the Earth's energy-bearing carbon supply was not recycled back through the living biosphere. Instead, it was covered over by countless deposits of sediment and then by geologic faults as the Earth's crust moved and shifted. After tens of millions of years of being subjected to enormous heat and pressure, this biomass became fossilized. This fossilized carbon accounts for approximately 22 percent of the planet's entire carbon pool, estimated at about 49,000 metric gigatons (1 metric gigaton equals one billion metric tons). I refer to the energy contained in the fossilized carbon pool as *stored energy,* although more conventionally it is called energy stocks.

Depending on how long it lay in these deposits and other factors, some of this biomass became fossilized in solid form (coal), some as liquid (petroleum), and some as gas (natural gas). The portion that fossilized in liquid form has a lower density than salt water, so it tends to flow upward in the Earth's crust as it floats on top of the brine that saturates the tiny pores that make up the crust's subsurface. Some of the world's oil succeeded in reaching the surface, where for centuries people collected it and used it for lighting oil lamps or for medicinal purposes. Frequently, however, as the oil rose, it encountered impermeable layers of shale or dense rock where it became trapped in petroleum reservoirs. These deposits lie far beneath the surface and can be reached only by drilling holes and inserting pipes. Unfortunately, these deposits are distributed in a highly uneven way across the Earth, and the only way they can be exploited usefully is by means of a global petroleum system.

There are differences of opinion (even among experts) about how much oil there is in the world and how long it will last at current or predicted rates of use. The consensus is that today proven or known oil reserves equal about one trillion barrels (a barrel of oil contains 42 gallons), but this number fluctuates and rose steadily over the decade of the 1990s as new discoveries exceeded withdrawals.[7] About one-fourth of these known reserves were discovered during the five-year period between 1985 and 1990. Estimated reserves (deposits thought to exist but not actually discovered) are between 300 billion and one trillion barrels.

One reason why oil is such a politically sensitive resource is that it is distributed around the world in a highly unequal manner. About one-seventh of the world's known reserves are in the Western Hemisphere, and about one-fifth are in Eurasia and Africa outside the Middle East. The remaining deposits, amounting to about 65–67 percent of the total, are in the Middle East, more than one-quarter in Saudi Arabia alone.

The global energy system extracts from the Earth about 65–70 million barrels of oil each day or roughly 25 billion barrels per year. Such a rate of production could be sustained for only forty more years without new reserves being discovered and exploited, although the years of reserves remaining differ widely from country to country. The reserves of Saudi Arabia, for example, will last for another eighty-one years, whereas those of the United States, for only another decade.[8]

The global fuel system is so long and complex that it takes about six weeks for energy to travel from where it leaves the ground to where one puts it in the fuel tank of one's car. Most of the oil in "old" fields (that is, discovered and developed before the 1990s) was found and extracted using fairly simple technologies: seismic devices to detect and measure the sound waves created by small explosions, drills that traveled vertically, and simple pumps not unlike large water pumps. Today, however, the extraction of oil involves advanced information technologies (computer simulations, satellite imagery) to find the oil and complex drilling techniques capable of drilling multiple lateral or horizontal wells from single wellheads that sit on relatively small pads on the surface or on floating platforms.[9] New drilling technologies are making it possible to probe farther and farther beneath the surface to bring up oil previously thought to be out of reach. In 1978, the deepest oil well offshore was about 1,000 feet. By 1998, an offshore well had been sunk more than 3,000 feet, and exploration in the Gulf of Mexico was predicted to soar as many new fields were brought into production.[10]

To be of value to civilization, crude oil must be moved from where it comes out of the ground to where the motorist needs his or her refined product. About one-third of the oil extracted each year (about eight billion barrels) moves across international boundaries to get from production site to the consumer. For example, even though the United States is the world's second-largest producer of oil, the nation uses so much energy that it still must import more than one-half of the oil it consumes, and virtually all of this oil is carried most of the way by oil tankers. Some of the largest of these ships may be 400 meters long and weigh nearly one million deadweight tons.[11] Some 800 tankers are on the high seas each day just to service the energy needs of the United States alone. Some of these tankers belong to independent shipping firms, but others (representing about 30 percent of global capacity) are the property of the oil companies themselves.[12] For example, Mobil (before its merger with Exxon) operated ten very large crude carriers with a capacity of two million barrels each and twelve smaller crude oil carriers with a capacity of 600,000 to one million barrels each.[13]

The world's oil industry is concentrated in a relatively small number of huge global corporations. A wave of mergers since 1998 has reduced their number to six: Exxon-Mobil, with annual revenues in 2000 of more than $200 billion; Royal Dutch/Shell, $150 billion; British Petroleum–Amoco, $150 billion; Total-FinaElf, slightly more than $100 billion; Chevron-Texaco, slightly less than $100 billion; and ConocoPhillips, slightly more than $50 billion.[14] A group of smaller firms, such as Atlantic Richfield, has revenues in the $15 billion to $18 billion range. The production of these major oil companies is supplemented by a fairly large number of much smaller firms. Although small, these latter companies are important because they are located in countries whose reserves are critical to world fossil fuel production. One of these is Russia, the world's second leading exporter of crude oil, where more than half a dozen companies compete for market share. Most of them earn annual revenues under $2 billion.[15]

Figure CS 3.1   Gasoline Pipelines in the United States

Note: Waterways (most of which are in the eastern part of the country) are indicated by thick black lines. Pipelines are indicated by thinner black lines, and stars represent refinery locations.
Source: Association of Oil Pipe Lines, at www.aopl.org. Used by permission.

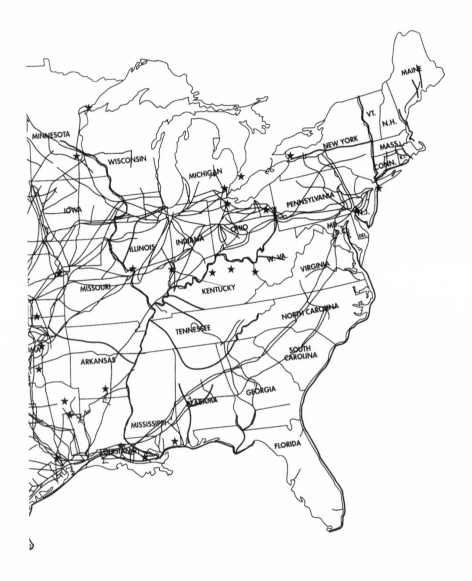

Crude oil bound for the eastern United States enters the country through ports on the Gulf of Mexico. Most comes into the port of Houston, Texas, to be refined into many different products, ranging from diesel and jet fuel to automobile gasoline, paint thinner, cleaning fluid, plastics, chemical feed stocks, and many others.[16] From refineries near Houston or Baton Rouge, Louisiana, the oil products enter a part of the vast network of pipelines that extends over 200,000 miles. (See figure CS 3.1.) For example, the pipeline that supplies the motorists in my neighborhood in Fairfax, Virginia, extends from Houston to the port of New York. At a speed of 3 to 8 miles per hour, the gasoline or other fuel takes fourteen to twenty-two days to make the complete trip to New York. The main pipeline is about one meter (36 inches) in diameter and is buried underground for most of the distance. As the refined product nears its destination, it is brought up to the surface to be stored in tank farms. From here, tank trucks carry the gasoline to one of the 176,000 retail gasoline stations throughout the United States.

THE GASOLINE PRICING SYSTEM: SUPPLY AND DEMAND

Gasoline accounts for about 17 percent of all energy consumed in the United States. The principal use for gasoline is to fuel automobiles and light trucks as well as boats, recreational vehicles, and various pieces of farm equipment. Gasoline prices are very sensitive to the price of the raw material from which it is made: crude (unrefined) petroleum. Between 1860 and 1973, the price of petroleum declined, rapidly at first and then more gradually, as can be seen in figure CS 3.2.[17] Measured in constant 1997 dollars, the price of a barrel of Texas crude at the wellhead declined from an average of about $20 around 1900 to

Figure CS 3.2.   Crude Oil Prices, 1860–1999

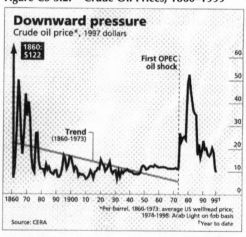

Source: "Cheap Oil: The Next Shock?" *The Economist*, March 6, 1999: 23; © 1999, the Economist Newspaper Group, Inc. Reprinted with permission. Further reproduction prohibited.

less than $10 in 1973. Then the first of the great oil shocks changed fundamentally the world's energy system, and a new pricing arrangement was introduced that is much more sensitive to both market forces and political pressures.

The price of gasoline at the pump is such a critical part of our consumer economy that numerous analysts are hard at work to tell us the reasons for increases and decreases and to predict where prices are headed over the near term. For example, in late August 1990, in the wake of Iraq's invasion of Kuwait, which led to the Gulf War, *Washington Post* reporter Mark Potts undertook to explain to his readers "how a complex chain of events determines the cost of gasoline."[18] Of the $1.28 average price of a gallon of gas, about 44.5 percent (57 cents) went for crude oil costs and profits, 23.4 percent (30 cents) went for refining and distribution costs and profits, 14.8 percent (19 cents) went for state sales and excise taxes, 7 percent (9 cents) was accounted for by federal taxes, and 10.2 percent (13 cents) accounted for dealer markup. More recently, the website "How Stuff Works" explained "where your money goes" when you fill the tank of your car.[19] In April 2001 the average retail price of a gallon of regular gasoline was $1.55. Approximately 37 percent of this amount (about 57 cents) went to the crude oil suppliers and the tanker companies that transported it to the refineries. The costs of refining and transporting the refined product to local outlets, and profits going to these firms, added another 32 percent (about 49.6 cents). Federal, state, local, and city taxes added another 27 percent (about 41.8 cents). (While many American motorists complain about these taxes, American gasoline is among the most lightly taxed in the world. In Britain, for example, a gallon of gas cost $4.71 in September 2000, with $3.40 going to taxes.) Finally, the local retailer adds about 5 percent to cover operating costs and provide a few cents of profit per gallon.

The relative importance of each of these components fluctuates primarily in response to changing prices of crude oil. According to the Energy Information Administration of the U.S. Department of Energy, in 1999 the average price of a barrel of crude oil was $17.51, and crude accounted for 37 percent of the retail price of gasoline: $1.22 per gallon. The other components accounted for the following: taxes, 36 percent; refining costs and profits, 13 percent; and distribution and marketing costs and profits, 14 percent. In 2000, in contrast, when the price of crude rose to $28.23 per barrel, crude accounted for 46 percent of the retail price of $1.48 per gallon, taxes were 28 percent, refining costs were 14 percent, and local retail costs were 12 percent.[20]

In many respects, oil resembles other commodities whose prices fluctuate in response to changes in the market. The chief difference is, of course, that the industrialized world depends much more on oil than it does on other commodities. Moreover, prices of basic energy sources, including gasoline, are more volatile than those of other commodities because the consumers are limited in their ability to substitute between fuels. When the price of a food product such as beef rises, for example, consumers can switch to pork or chicken or eliminate meat from their diets entirely. Such alternatives are not available in the field of energy. As with any scarce and precious substance, gasoline prices are influenced by both supply and demand factors. Identifying these factors and weighing their importance are not easy tasks for the nonexpert. Notice the importance of global information flow in many of these factors.

Supply-Side Factors

The Organization of Petroleum Exporting Countries (OPEC). OPEC attempts to manage the price of oil by raising or lowering daily production. OPEC is a consortium of eleven countries that was formed in 1960 to keep world oil prices within a target range by setting an upper production limit for each of its members.[21] OPEC has the capacity to influence world oil prices because its members account for approximately 40 percent of world oil production and possess about two-thirds of estimated world oil reserves.[22] Before 1973 OPEC was unable to influence oil prices very much, and the wellhead price of crude was about $3.00 per barrel (in current dollars). By 1980, a combination of OPEC actions and political and military instability in the Middle East had raised the price to about $29.00 per barrel. Today OPEC attempts to maintain oil prices between $22.00 and $28.00 per barrel by holding collective production at 23.2 million barrels per day.[23] However, even OPEC is not free to set any price it wants. The cartel is constrained by three factors. OPEC member countries may cheat and produce over their quotas; other major oil exporters such as Mexico and Russia are not OPEC members, and they can increase production to gain market share; and high energy prices could cause recession in the wealthy importing countries and thereby reduce demand for all exported oil including that produced by OPEC.

Costs of production, including exploration, drilling, and refining, as well as limits to the capacities of refineries. In some parts of the world, oil is so close to the surface that it requires little drilling to bring it up, while in other places wells must be sunk thousands of feet. Exploration and drilling are usually easier and cheaper on land than in deep water. In the past decade, there have been important technological advances in oil exploration, especially in the use of computer-generated images to improve our ability to "see" what lies far beneath the surface of the Earth.[24] These technologies have reduced the costs of finding, extracting, and producing crude oil outside the Middle East from over $25 per barrel (in 1999 prices) to around $10 per barrel in 1999. Nevertheless, while most Middle East oil still costs barely $2.00 per barrel simply to extract, oil in a challenging location like the North Sea may cost four times that amount. If oil prices reflected simply market forces, virtually all the world's oil would come from the Middle East, particularly from Saudi Arabia, because production costs are so low there. However, oil prices reflect many other factors, including politics and the psychology of scarcity.

Costs of transport of both crude and refined oil, as well as limits to the capacities of pipelines, tanker trucks, and railroad tank cars. The Gulf Coast supplies nearly one-half the gasoline produced in the United States. The farther one goes from the gulf, all other things being equal, the more expensive gasoline is. The difference may amount to as much as 10 to 15 cents per gallon.

Intermediary or brokering costs. Before 1973, crude oil prices were negotiated in long-term sales agreements between the government of the country holding the reserves and the international oil firm extracting and processing the oil. These costs tended to be low and stable. After 1973, costs have been brokered by the New York Mercantile Exchange (NYMEX) for each tanker-load of crude as it is en route. This is known as the "spot" market. These prices are highly volatile. They can rise or fall sharply in a matter of minutes in response to news about important events around the world. Such volatility and sensitivity to global information flows have placed enormous power to shape the world's oil markets in the hands of NYMEX brokers, now known as the "Wall Street Refiners."[25]

Accidents, particularly those affecting tankers and pipelines that create oil spills and leaks. When an oil tanker runs aground and spills its crude into the ocean, it removes this amount of product from the system (a relatively small impact on the larger system). But it also frequently leads to demands for stricter controls on the transport system, which can slow down the movement of crude from wellhead to refinery.

The U.S. Strategic Petroleum Reserve (SPR). After seeing how the nation's economy was hurt by the oil embargo of 1973, the government determined to create the SPR as a buffer against future oil shortages. Before the terrorist attacks of September 11, the reserve consisted of about 570 million barrels of oil stored in underground salt caverns along the Gulf of Mexico coast. Such a reserve amounts to about a sixty-day supply of imports. It can be released by the president when conditions require. Reserves were first released during the Gulf War in 1991 to keep oil plentiful and prices stable. The SPR costs the government about $21 million annually to operate.

Demand-Side Factors

A rapid increase in the consumption of gasoline or other fuels that cannot be matched by an increase in production because of the long time required to find and extract new crude oil reserves. In the United States, oil refineries usually lower production during the spring when they perform maintenance and resume normal production in May when automobile usage begins to rise.

Scarcities, both real and imagined (psychological, anticipated). These latter kind of scarcities can lead to panic buying and hoarding, which in turn tend to produce real shortages.

Special circumstances affecting regional and local markets. For example, in some regions of the country such as California or some cities such as Chicago or Milwaukee, gasoline is required to meet more demanding environmental standards in order to reduce air pollution. Producing this fuel can cause problems in refining, distribution, and storage. Analysts refer to these regions or cities as gasoline-market islands. Each island has peculiar gasoline demands that can be met by only a few refineries. If demand suddenly rises in one of these "islands," the few refineries capable of meeting the demand may experience difficulties in increasing production quickly. Local competition may also affect prices at the pump. Motorists in urban or suburban areas with many competing retail outlets may experience lower prices than do those who live in remote rural areas where there may be only a few service stations.

War, revolution, terrorism, or the threat of these. Events such as the Middle East war in 1973, the Iranian Revolution in 1979, the Iran–Iraq War in 1980, the Gulf War in 1991, and the 2001 terrorist attacks all affected the price of oil. In some cases, the effect was to raise the price of crude by causing motorists great anxiety about the future stability of gasoline supply. In other instances, the effect was to depress prices by triggering an economic recession in the highly industrialized countries. For example, within two weeks after the terrorist attacks on the World Trade Center in New York and the Pentagon, crude oil consumption in the United States dropped by nearly one million barrels a day. Consequently, the price of a barrel of crude oil fell in NYMEX trading by $3.96, or 15 percent, to $22.01. This was the largest one-day drop in the price of crude since the Gulf War in 1991.[26]

Technology and alternative fuels. Earlier we saw that it is not easy for the average consumer to substitute one fuel for another, and certainly it would be difficult to do without fossil fuels entirely. However, suppliers of end-use energy do have alternatives. In particular, the firms that generate and distribute electricity can—and do—switch from petroleum, to natural gas, to coal as market prices and availability vary. Such transfers cannot be done instantaneously, but as new power plants come on line they can take advantage of shifting fuel prices. Advances in gas turbines in the late 1990s, for example, made natural gas much more attractive relative to petroleum.

Seasonal events and regional weather patterns. An unusually cold winter or hot summer can increase the demand for heating oil or for fuel to power electricity-generating plants, and this demand will affect the price of gasoline, with which these other uses compete. The increase in automobile travel and tourism during the summer, especially around the July 4 weekend in the United States, tends to drive up motorist demand and gasoline prices. Demand for gasoline usually rises about 6 percent in the United States during the summer.

General economic patterns, nationally, regionally, or globally. The decline in the price of oil in the late 1990s is usually attributed to the economic crisis that swept across the world beginning in Thailand in 1998 and subsequently affecting the rest of East Asia, Russia, Brazil, and eventually the United States. By the time the world economy had reached its lowest point, oil prices had dropped to about $10 per barrel. Economic prosperity can work in the opposite direction as well. A resurgence of the global economy in 2000 forced the price of oil back up to $37 per barrel.

Environmental concerns. In 1997, representatives of the highly industrialized countries agreed at Kyoto, Japan, to reduce their emissions of greenhouse gases to try to stem the threat of global warming. Even though the United States has officially withdrawn from the accord, the rest of the world's economic powers have reaffirmed their commitment to the Kyoto goals, which will eventually mean a decline in demand for hydrocarbons of all kinds, including oil.

"The oil industry," says one analyst, "is like a ship with its center of gravity above the water line. It can sail smoothly for years, but capsize suddenly in rough seas—and do so quite rapidly."[27] Experts may argue about why this is so: the relative significance of geopolitical factors, global economic cartels, excessive consumption in the rich countries, diminishing supplies, and many others. The Global System Paradigm helps us identify the most important supply and demand factors and assess their probable importance, but the world oil and gasoline industries will remain volatile and potentially destabilizing for many years to come.

NOTES

1. Joseph P. Fried, "High Cost of Oil Seeps Its Way into Everyday Lives, and Pocketbooks," *New York Times,* February 20, 2000. Michael Leahy and Carol Morello, "Some Motorists Fuming over Costly Gas," *Washington Post,* March 18, 2000.

2. Vaclav Smil, *Cycles of Life: Civilization and the Biosphere* (New York: Scientific American Library, 1997).

3. John Peet, *Energy and the Ecological Economics of Sustainability* (Washington, D.C.: Island Press, 1992), 27.

4. Robert P. Clark, *The Global Imperative: An Interpretive History of the Spread of Humankind* (Boulder: Westview Press, 1997), episode 5.

5. Smil, *Cycles of Life,* 53.

6. Smil, *Cycles of Life,* 14–15.

7. For up-to-date data, see the website for the U.S. government's Energy Information Administration, at www.eia.doe.gov.

8. "Oil Reserves," *The Economist,* July 21, 2001: 88.

9. Jonathan Rauch, "The New Old Economy: Oil, Computers, and the Reinvention of the Earth," *The Atlantic Monthly* (January 2001): 35–49. Andrew C. Revkin, "Hunting for Oil: New Precision, Less Pollution," *New York Times,* January 30, 2001.

10. Agis Salpukas, "Oil Companies Drawn to the Deep," *New York Times,* December 7, 1994.

11. Vaclav Smil, *Energy in World History* (Boulder: Westview Press, 1994), 173, figure 5.6.

12. Agis Salpukas, "Shift in Insurance to Cover Oil Ships May Disrupt Flow," *New York Times,* December 12, 1994.

13. Daniel Southerland, "Mobilizing the Fleet," *Washington Post,* June 23, 1996.

14. Neela Banerjee and Andrew Ross Sorkin, "Phillips and Conoco to Form U.S. Gasoline Giant," *New York Times,* November 19, 2001. Neela Banerjee, "Wall Street Sees Possibility of a New Suitor for Conoco," *New York Times,* November 20, 2001. "Minor Majors," *The Economist,* November 24, 2001: 60.

15. Michael Wines, "Spiffing up a Dirty Business: Russia's Oil Barons Say Wildcatter Capitalism Era Is Over," *New York Times,* December 28, 1999.

16. Thomas W. Lippman, "Gasoline Formula Fuels Controversy," *Washington Post,* June 12, 1990.

17. "Cheap Oil: The Next Shock?" *The Economist,* March 6, 1999: 23–25.

18. Mark Potts, "Tortuous Path to the Price at the Pump," *Washington Post,* August 26, 1990.

19. See howstuffworks.lycos.com/gas-price.htm.

20. See www.eia.doe.gov.

21. The eleven member countries are Algeria, Indonesia, Iran, Iraq, Kuwait, Libya, Nigeria, Qatar, Saudi Arabia, the United Arab Emirates, and Venezuela.

22. One reason for the discrepancy between reserves and production is that OPEC governments intervene to keep the price of crude oil higher than it would be under pure market conditions, so oil companies are encouraged to invest in exploration and drilling in what would otherwise be prohibitively expensive areas, such as the North Sea.

23. William Drozdiak, "OPEC Won't Cut Output to Prop up Oil Prices," *Washington Post,* September 27, 2001. Neela Banerjee, "OPEC, Deep in Uncertainty, Leaves Oil Output Steady," *New York Times,* September 28, 2001.

24. Agis Salpukas, "The New Gulf War: Man Your Computers," *New York Times,* June 18, 1995. Allen R. Myerson, "A Wildcatter on the Tame Side: Replacing Roughnecks with Computers," *New York Times,* March 20, 1998. Rauch, "The New Old Economy." Joel Kotkin, "Oil-Patch Epicenter, Embracing the Web," *New York Times,* April 15, 2001.

25. Thomas W. Lippman and Mark Potts, "Oil Traders: Turning on a Dime," *Washington Post,* January 11, 1991. Mark Potts and Thomas W. Lippman, "Is This Any Way to Set Oil Prices?" *Washington Post,* January 12, 1991.

26. Alex Berenson and Jonathan Fuerbringer, "Oil and Gas Prices Tumble, but Stocks Soar Worldwide," *New York Times,* September 25, 2001.

27. Quoted in "Cheap Oil," 23.

4

Changing Systems

KEY IDEAS IN THIS CHAPTER

System dynamics is the science that studies how systems change over time.

Are systems compelled to **grow** and to become more **complex**? The answer for many systems thinkers would appear to be yes.

Entropy and **dissipative structures** are keys to understanding why and how systems grow.

Linear and **nonlinear** growth produce entirely different kinds of system dynamics.

There are **limits to growth.** All systems must stop growing eventually when they reach these limits. Because the involuntary cessation of growth may be disruptive and even at times violent, systems would be better off if they limited their own growth voluntarily, before the environment imposed its limits.

The ways in which systems respond to the limits to growth are described in **four scenarios.** The way system leaders **respond to feedback** is critical.

So far we have considered the system as it exists at a specific moment in time. We must now introduce the notion of system change or the process systems scientists call *system dynamics*. The systems involved in globalization are constantly changing, sometimes in ways that surprise us but almost always in ways that are difficult to see and understand. To achieve a higher level of global awareness, we want to understand how and why systems grow, how system growth is limited, and what systems do when they encounter their limits. In his book on systems thinking, Ervin Laszlo advances four propositions about "natural systems" (systems with an organic component).[1] In one way or another, each of these propositions involves system change.

Proposition 1: Natural Systems Are Wholes with Irreducible Properties

A "whole" is different from a "heap" because the parts of a "heap" do not interact to change each other, whereas the parts of a "whole" do. Adding more parts to a "heap" will simply make the "heap" bigger (we say that the relationship among the parts is additive), whereas adding more parts to a "whole" changes its behavior by their interactions (the relationship is multiplicative). For this reason, systems or "wholes" possess irreducible properties, that is, properties that lie in the system and cannot be found in the parts by themselves. We sometimes refer to these as *emergent properties* because they "emerge" from the interacting behavior of the parts.

Proposition 2: Natural Systems Maintain Themselves in a Changing Environment

If our world were itself unchanging, there would be no need for systems to change to adapt to changes in the environment. On the other hand, if the world changed and systems were unable to adapt, they would not be able to maintain their own internal order in the face of constant environmental pressure toward disorder. The Second Law of Thermodynamics tells us that the world is constantly changing by making energy less available. Energy can be neither created nor destroyed, but it can be changed in form. Such changes produce the fuel that powers all systems and gives them the ability to perform work. But each time there is such a change, some energy is rendered unavailable for future use. As we have seen in chapter 3, this "lost" energy is called *entropy*. If systems had no way to adapt to this dynamic process, then they too would quickly decay. But the reality is that systems *do* maintain themselves in a dynamic environment by engaging in exchanges with that environment: by importing energy and exporting waste (in the form of heat).

Proposition 3: Natural Systems Create Themselves in Response to Self-Creativity in Other Systems

What Laszlo means here is that systems grow and become more complex in response to similar changes going on in other systems with which they share the environment. This proposition is highly controversial. Not all scientists believe that systems have an imperative to grow and to become more complex. We shall discuss this issue in a moment. But Laszlo leaves no doubt where he stands on the matter when he writes: "There is a discernible trend toward differentiation, growth, supra-system formation, and complexity throughout the range of social systems."[2]

Proposition 4: Natural Systems Are Coordinating Interfaces in Nature's "Holarchy"

Holarchy is the term Laszlo uses to describe a "whole" composed of systems arranged hierarchically, that is, with the smaller and less complex systems contained within, and subordinate to, larger and more complex systems. Systems are arranged hierarchically in the world, with smaller and simpler systems integrated into large, complex suprasystems. The term *coordinating interfaces* means that the smaller component systems must interact with the other subsystems with which they share the space of the larger system.

MUST SYSTEMS GROW AND BECOME MORE COMPLEX?

One area of great controversy in systems thinking involves what I call the *dual system imperative: growth and complexity*. By calling these changes an "imperative," I am asserting that systems have no alternative to doing these things, other than self-destruction. If they are to endure, systems must become larger and more complex. Moreover, growth and complexity interact to reinforce each other. That is, as systems grow they tend to become more complex, and as they become more complex they tend to get larger. Thus, these forces interact to create a positive feedback loop.

In my first book on globalization, I argue that our need to become global stems from a need to dissipate the entropy created by the functioning of physical systems.[3] The process of dissipation requires increasingly complex bulk-flow systems of transport and communication. In due course, a positive feedback loop is set in motion. Bulk-flow systems require a concentration of population in cities, and the growth of cities required the support of additional bulk-flow systems. Cities and bulk-flow systems reinforce each other, growing and becoming more complex until they can no longer dissipate their entropy to distant systems. Hence we have the pressure for all human systems to expand, to become more complex, and eventually to become global.

Beneath this process there lies a fundamental assumption: that systems in general confront pressures to grow and to become more complex. There are certainly scholars who see no such imperative in their particular fields or disciplines. At the level of an individual organism, a community of similar organisms called a population, or a class of similar organisms called a species, there is much controversy about this proposition. For example, the biologist Stephen Jay Gould has argued that there is no inherent bias in nature that selects for organisms that are bigger or more complex.[4] Pressures for growth or complexity have not meant the disappearance of the small and the simple. Bacteria are still the most enduring life form on Earth after more than three billion years. Cockroaches and ants have demonstrated the ability to survive and flourish under conditions that would be fatal to larger and more complex creatures. The paleontologist David Jablonski has assembled fossil evidence for a range of mollusks that lived over a span of 16 million years and detects no inherent bias toward bigness.[5] Working with the fossilized vertebrae of various mammals, the paleobiologist Dan McShea has found evidence of trends toward *both* greater complexity *and* greater simplicity over long spans of time.[6] (The response from other biologists was that if creatures are becoming both more simple and more complex over time, the upper limit of complexity is bound to rise, while the lower limit of complexity must eventually be reached.)

On the other hand, many scholars do see evidence of a trend toward both expansion and greater complexity. The physicist and astronomer Eric Chaisson has asserted that there is evolutionary pressure toward increasing complexity at every scale of the Universe, from cellular to galactic. Such pressures stem from the expansion of the Universe itself and the energy gradients (unequal distribution patterns) that result therefrom.[7] The biologist Stuart Kauffman has provided us with a comprehensive statement of his similar vision of such pressures:

> In the beginning, presumably, the universe was simple, homogeneous, featureless, almost isotropic. Now it is vastly complex. In the beginning, the early Earth had a paucity of complex molecules, chemical reactions, linked structures and processes. Now it is vastly complex. The universe as a whole has witnessed the coming into existence of novel structures and processes; so too has the biosphere. Where no difference existed, differences have come into existence. In a general sense, the persistent emergence of different structures and processes is the persistent breaking of the symmetry of the universe.[8]

Many biologists see size and complexity increasing in systems over time. For example, Kauffman asserts that "the species diversity of the biosphere has increased as well as the molecular diversity."[9] John Tyler Bonner agrees that "during the entire course of evolution, from the first appearance of bacteria in primeval mud to the fauna and flora of today, there has been (1) an evolution from small to large, and more importantly (2) an evolution from simple to complex."[10] Bonner contends that the trend toward size increase began when unicellular creatures began to differentiate into multicellular ones.[11] Natural forces selected for multicellular forms for ease of feeding, dispersal in search of food, protection from predators, and developmental ease (it is easier to add to an organism's DNA than to subtract from it). Yet multicellular animals require structural supports (eventually, a skeleton),[12] some means of locomotion, and the ability to coordinate their parts, all of which require considerable resources to create and maintain. The trend toward growth continued largely because of the pressures of natural selection placed on organisms by the environment. Among mammals, large animals defend themselves against predators better than small ones do, and thus the large come to prey on the small. Large animals can also range farther afield in search of nourishment, which is fortunate for them because they require so much food energy.

Large animals, however, also face particularly difficult challenges from their environments. All other things being equal, larger animals need more resources, so an adequate food supply is less abundant and more susceptible to environmental change. Size is inversely related to population density. That is, a given range can support fewer big animals than small ones. Moreover, because large animals require more complex development sequences, they have longer gestation periods and lower reproductive rates. Their populations are therefore more vulnerable to sudden environmental changes than the populations of smaller animals are.

To cope with these challenges, large animals require greater complexity, which Bonner defines as a function of the number of cell types found in an organism.[13] The greater the variety of cell types in an organism, the greater the adaptability of the animal to environmental stresses, so nature selects for diversity or complexity. The ability of an animal to engage in a range of behaviors arises from the complexity of its central nervous system. When a species has become sufficiently complex that it can teach, and learn from, others of its species, then, Bonner says, it is capable of culture, a crucial addition to the fitness of a species.

Some scientists believe that systems become more complex for no other reason than that such a trend is an emergent property of the Universe itself. Kauffman has argued that the Universe has generated, and continues to generate, countless unpredictable systems, never repeating itself exactly. These systems become "frozen accidents" that persist through time, gradually accumulating increasing amounts of diversity. Moreover, diversity is self-reinforcing. By this, Kauffman means that diversity sets in motion a positive feedback loop so that the more diverse a system is today, the more diverse it must become in the future. And this is not just a biological phenomenon. Kauffman sees it at work in the economy as well.[14]

But there are other reasons for thinking that complexity always increases. Some scholars believe that organisms become more complex because they derive significant advantages from doing so. Natural selection will select for the more complex over the less because the more complex is fitter in a Darwinian sense. Complex organisms enjoy certain advantages in competition with more simple creatures, and *up to a point* (difficult to know before the fact) the more complex an organism is, the greater these advantages appear.[15] Some of these advantages show up in the near term, in competition between systems over scarce resources. Complex systems appear to have a long-term advantage as well because they enjoy a greater potential for the appearance of a random characteristic that makes them fitter in the evolutionary sense. John Holland, for example, contends that complexity makes organisms fitter by equipping them with more adaptable procedures for discovering the rules of the ecosystem in which they happen to find themselves.[16] Ian Stewart asserts that chaos and complexity confer advantages on the systems that contain them:

> Chaotic systems can respond to an outside stimulus far more rapidly than non-chaotic ones can. . . . A nervous system that has developed from . . . an underlying sea of chaos could offer definite advantages to an evolving organism. It's reasonable to believe that prey whose nervous systems incorporate chaos are harder for predators to catch. . . . It is advantageous for an eco-system to evolve into a state of high diversity, for a diverse ecology has many more ways to recover from disaster. Everybody knows that a one-crop economy is a mistake, and so is a one-crop ecology.[17]

The advantages enjoyed by complex organisms exact quite a price, however. And the way the organisms pay that price usually involves growth. Large quantities of energy are needed to sustain complex organisms because of their great requirements for motion, coordination, and control. Homeothermic animals (commonly called "warm blooded") can maintain a constant body temperature more or less independent of the temperature of their surroundings. Thus, they enjoy greater adaptability to changing environmental constraints, and greater mobility, than do animals whose body temperatures vary with that of the environment. But homeothermic animals must consume much more energy to pay for their advantages.[18] Because humans cannot ingest many energy sources directly from nature, we must acquire our energy indirectly, at the end of a food chain that processes energy through a series of plants and herbivores until it reaches us. For this reason, the food necessary to supply a growing population could not be achieved until animals were herded and bred systematically. Although higher densities were achieved by pre-agricultural societies near rivers or lakes or on seacoasts, where fishing could supplement hunted and gathered food, in general hunter-gatherer populations achieved no greater densities than 0.1–1.0 person per square kilometer.[19]

The biologist Tyler Volk sees the evolution of complexity as proceeding in two directions. To avoid the implications of superiority and inferiority associated with directional words like *upward* and *downward,* he prefers to describe systems as evolving in an outward or an inward direction. By outward evolution, Volk means that changes in a part of a system influence the appearance of change in the larger whole. Cells had to appear before multicellular organisms could exist. On the other hand, inward evolution occurs when changes in the larger whole influence the appearance of changes in the parts. Once multicellular organisms came into existence, they served as the matrix within which other kinds of cells evolved. As he puts it, "Cells . . . preceded multi-cellular organisms, but multi-cellular organisms as a type preceded particular, specialized kinds of cells. Parts can precede wholes and thus act on the coming into existence of those wholes. Wholes can precede parts and thus act on the coming into existence of those parts."[20] And throughout this process, the resultant organisms are becoming more and more complex.

If biologists debate the tendency for organisms, populations, or species to become larger and more complex, at least there appears to be consensus among social scientists about the imperative for growth and complexity at the level of large social systems. Many systems thinkers do see such an imperative at work, especially in systems that involve human beings exercising their volition and control. For these scholars, growth of a system refers to an increase in the number of its component parts, the space it occupies, and the resources it consumes. Complexity refers to the variety or diversity exhibited by the system's components and the nonlinear nature of the connections between or among them. For example, one leading scholar in this field, Joseph Tainter, writes that complexity is generally understood to refer to such things as the size of a society, the number and distinctiveness of its parts, the variety of specialized social roles that it incorporates, the number of distinct social personalities present, and the variety of mechanisms for organizing these into a coherent, functioning whole. Augmenting any of these dimensions increases the complexity of a society.[21]

Energy is the crucial factor in systems growth. Tainter asserts that acquiring, processing, and maintaining energy are imperatives of all complex systems:

> Human societies and political organizations, like all living systems, are maintained by a continuous flow of energy. . . . Not only is energy flow required to maintain a sociopolitical system, but the amount of energy must be sufficient for the complexity of that system. . . . More complex societies are more costly to maintain than simpler ones, requiring greater support levels per capita. As societies increase in complexity, more networks are created among individuals, more hierarchical controls are created to regulate these networks, more information is processed, there is more centralization of information flow, there is increasing need to support specialists not directly involved in resource production, and the like. . . . The result is that as a society evolves toward greater complexity, the support costs levied on each individual will also rise, so that the population as a whole must allocate increasing portions of its energy budget to maintaining organizational institutions.[22]

Daniel Katz and Robert Kahn see a similar dynamic at work when they assert that an open, living system

> will tend to import more energy than is required for its output. . . . To insure survival, systems will . . . acquire some margin of safety beyond the immediate level of existence. . . . In adapting to their environment, systems will attempt to cope with external forces by ingesting them or acquiring control over them. . . . Social systems will move . . . toward incorporation within their boundaries [of] the external resources essential to survival. Again, the result is an expansion of the original system.[23]

At some point in its expansion, the system changes its character by becoming more complex. As Katz and Kahn put it, "There is a point where quantitative changes produce a qualitative difference in the functioning of a system. . . . Open systems move in the direction of differentiation and elaboration."[24] "Differentiation" and "elaboration" of a system's component parts mean that the system as a whole becomes more complex.

How a complex social system copes with these challenges is critical to its continued survival. Unfortunately, investments in increasing complexity are subject to a law of diminishing returns. Tainter argues that, in many sectors of society,

> continued investment in sociopolitical complexity reaches a point where the benefits for such investment begin to decline, at first gradually, then with accelerated force. Thus, not only must a population allocate greater and greater amounts of resources to maintaining an evolving society, but after a certain point, higher amounts of this investment will yield smaller increments of return.[25]

To meet these challenges, the complex system is frequently forced to grow by expanding its boundaries. The more complex a system becomes, the more it tries to push back the limits to its growth to give itself more time to react to changing circumstances and to avoid the damage of "overshoot."[26] System growth is one of the consequences of such a measure. Complex systems need to acquire additional resources, particularly energy, and access to additional sinks where they can discard waste. These processes lead inescapably to system growth. So the central problem with complexity is this: the more complex a system becomes, the more it is compelled to grow. But the expansion of a complex system can be only a short-term palliative, however, because, as David Ruelle has shown, "the entropy of a system is proportional to its size."[27] For example, all other things being equal, a metropolitan region of, say, 1,000 square miles generates twice as much entropy as the same city when it contained only 500 square miles.

Hence there is the unavoidable dilemma. Systems face pressure to become more complex, but greater complexity leads to system growth. Growth in turn produces proportionately greater entropy, which must be dissipated to other systems, which requires another round of expansion. This sequence continues until the system collapses of its own size and complexity or because it can no longer force or induce other systems to absorb its entropy. Because our social organization and technology have endowed us with the capacity to override (temporarily) the limits to system growth, systems with humans in them eventually become global. Clearly, there are disadvantages in getting big and complex, just as there are limits to the growth and "complexification" of any living system. But so long as we can avoid facing those disadvantages, we will try to keep our system on the positive feedback loop of growth.

ENTROPY AND DISSIPATIVE STRUCTURES

"The one true test of all living systems," writes James Beniger in his book *The Control Revolution,* "is the persistence of [their] organization counter to entropy."[28] But if all living systems tend toward energy loss, decay, and irreversible disorder, how is it possible for life to come into existence in the first place, never mind the much more daunting task of persisting over time against entropic forces? Life began, writes Stuart Kauffman, when "some new union of matter, energy, information, and something more could reach out and manipulate the world on its own behalf."[29] The secret of how a system manipulates the world on its own behalf lies in *dissipative structures,* a term coined by Ilya Prigogine to identify the capacity of a system to transfer its entropic costs to other parts of the Universe.[30] The idea traces its intellectual lineage back to the mid–nineteenth century, when William Thomson, Baron Kelvin, formulated the "law of dissipation of energy."[31] Thomson's law assumes that energy can be graded in quality as well as quantity. High-quality energy, such as the heated boiler of a steam turbine, implies order and predictability. Low-quality energy, such as that stored in a pot of cold water, implies disorder and unpredictability. Though energy is conserved during any process of mechanical, chemical, or physical conversion, it suffers inevitable degradation from high quality to low. High-quality energy, once degraded, cannot be restored to its earlier condition without the expenditure of more energy. The energy contained in the gasoline in one's car's tank is burned to create heat that is then converted to kinetic energy (the movement of the pistons, drive shaft, wheels, and, ultimately, the car itself). But much of the energy is converted to waste and dissipated as heat into the atmosphere, never to be available again to be put to some useful (human) purpose. The value of high-quality energy (what we are calling here available energy or low entropy) lies precisely in its mobility. The fact that we can move energy into, through and around, and out of a system, while at the same time converting it into something useful to the system, is what makes energy crucial to the system's functioning. The property of mobility of energy is captured by Thomson's "law of dissipation," which appears to us today as Prigogine's dissipative structures.

Dissipative structures enable a complex system to achieve and maintain a high level of available energy and order by sending the entropic costs of this exercise to other systems. Some of these systems may be neighbors to the entropy-producing system; others may be on the opposite side of the world. The two systems may exist during the same moment in time, but it is not essential that they do so. The entropic system can spread its costs to systems that existed in the past (for example, the living beings whose fossilized tissue forms the basis of the coal, natural gas, and petroleum we exploit today) or to those that do not yet exist (for example, the muscle power of yet unborn generations). We are aware of, and understand, many dissipative processes and structures, but many others are invisible and enigmatic. Sometimes dissipation takes place with the knowledge and consent of the donor of low entropy, but frequently this is not the case. Dissipation frequently involves deception or coercion, as well as a power inequality between the donor of low entropy and its beneficiary. Erich Jantsch has described how dissipative structures are essential to all self-maintaining systems:

> The metabolism of self-organizing matter systems would soon die down were the exchange processes with the environment left to chance encounters. . . . Entropy would accumulate in the [system] and move [it] toward its equilibrium, at which all processes come to an end. . . . [To prevent this from happening,] the processes within the system as well as its exchange processes with the environment assume a distinct order in space and time, called a *dissipative structure*. It constitutes the dynamic regime through which the system gains autonomy from the environment, maintains itself, and evolves.[32]

There is a tendency among some complexity scientists to assert that the laws of thermodynamics do not apply to systems that are extremely complex, open, non-linear, and adaptive. The very existence of life, they argue, shows that order can emerge spontaneously from disorder, that systems can persist counter to entropy by means of their own complexity. Thus, complex systems can self-organize without outside direction and exhibit order spontaneously.[33] As Stuart Kauffman puts it (in a phrase that has been frequently misinterpreted), the Universe can harbor "order for free."[34] But, Kauffman hastens to add, the phrase "order for free" means that

> such order is natural and spontaneous, it is not "for free" thermodynamically. Rather, in these open systems, the self-squeezing of the system into tiny regions of state space [how Kauffman describes the spontaneous self-organization of a living system] is "paid for" thermodynamically by exporting heat to the environment. No laws of thermodynamics are violated or even contested.[35]

When we identify a given system as "open," we mean that it is connected to other systems in such a way that it can send its entropy *to* others and import available energy (or low entropy) *from* others. Paul Davies and John Gribben have described the process in the following way:

> In open systems, entropy can decrease, but the increase in order in the open system is always paid for by a decrease in order [increase in entropy] somewhere else. . . . All of this [decrease in entropy] is possible because the Earth is an open system, through which energy and entropy flow. The source of almost all the useful energy we use is the Sun, which is a classic example of a system in thermodynamic disequilibrium—a compact ball of hot gas in a relatively low entropy state is irreversibly pouring huge amounts of energy out into the cold vastness of space. . . . [Reversing the flow of entropy has its] origin in our proximity to this great source of energy in the sky, which is like a bucket of negative entropy into which we can dip in order to create ordered systems on Earth.[36]

A dissipative structure is anything—a technology, a social process, a cultural practice, a law, an institutional arrangement—that shifts the entropic costs of a complex system from the system directly benefited to other systems distant in time or space. Such transfers of the costs of growth and complexity occur frequently in social systems. Dissipation of entropy takes place when the leaders of one system (for example, a city or a nation-state) have the will and the ability to cause other systems to absorb the entropy of the former. Some political scientists define *power* as the ability of one person to cause another to do something the latter would not do otherwise. In this instance, the ability of the entropy-producing system to cause another system to absorb its entropy is certainly indicative of the unequal distribution of power between them.

How do these dissipative structures actually work? How can a producer of entropy cause others to absorb the costs of its wealth, prosperity, or power? Several alternative scenarios are suggested below. The reader can supply others. Bear in mind that the dissipation of entropy involves either importing low entropy (such as importing fossil fuel or food) or exporting high entropy (such as transferring entropy-producing manufacturing techniques to a less developed country). The scenarios are as follows:

- By annexation, a city or a nation-state can acquire the territory of a neighbor, to which its entropy (for example, waste) can be transported and deposited.
- By coercion or the repression of resistance by force or threat, the neighboring peoples can be suppressed and forced to accept the entropic costs.
- The costs of dissipation can be concealed by filtering the process through impersonal market mechanisms so that the victims are not aware of what is being done to them or by whom.
- The costs of dissipation can also be concealed through a national accounting system that counts entropy-producing activity as a plus to gross national product while undercounting (or not counting at all) the costs of the entropy produced.
- The producers of entropy may pay neighboring systems for absorbing their entropy. Here, market prices determine the costs of the transaction.

LINEAR AND NONLINEAR GROWTH

Growth is a widely encountered feature of our world. Systems grow by increasing the space they occupy and the number or complexity of their component parts. *How* they grow depends to some degree on the nature of their linearity. *Linear systems* consist of parts that stand in direct causal sequence with each other, and the causal flow runs in only one direction.[37] Thus, change in part a produces change in part b, but change in b has no effect on a. Further, if change in a causes change in b that in turn causes change in c, we can say that change in a brought about change in c (we say the process is "transitive"). In contrast, *nonlinear systems* contain feedback loops that connect their parts in ways that are indirect, and causation flows in more than one direction. Change in part a produces change in part b, but change in b feeds back to cause change in a. Moreover, there may be additional parts (c, d, e, and so forth) that have cause-and-effect linkages to each other.

Thus, growth can occur in two ways. "Heaps" grow by simple addition, aggregation, or summation. That is, a "heap" grows when we simply add more objects to it without connecting them to what was already there. In this case we use the term *linear growth* to describe a pattern of expansion without interruption, forming a straight line on a graph. In contrast, systems or "wholes" grow by multiplication. That is, the newly added matter, energy, or information is arranged in such a way as to interact with what was already there. The system's behavior is changed by the interaction of the new parts with the old. As A. Angyal puts it, "In aggregates it is significant that the parts are added; in a system it is significant that the parts are arranged."[38] When a system grows by multiplication, the pattern of growth tends to be *nonlinear*.[39] Such a pattern produces a curved line on a graph.

These two growth patterns are polar opposites in most respects. Linear growth tends to be slow, easily observable, comprehensible, predictable, and controllable. It is also of relatively limited significance for observers trying to understand global events or trends. Nonlinear growth, on the other hand, is fast (often exponential), often virtually invisible, impossible to understand, unpredictable, and often uncontrollable. However, because nonlinear systems are of the utmost importance to understanding globalization, we must take on the daunting task of mastering them.

To complicate matters, highly complex systems exhibit what systems thinkers call *sensitive dependence on initial conditions*. This idea means that very small (perhaps even invisible) changes in inputs can produce very large (perhaps surprisingly large) changes in outputs. This phenomenon was labeled the "butterfly effect" by meteorologist Edward Lorenz to refer to the now well-known observation that a butterfly fluttering its wings over some distant spot can affect our local weather patterns. Complex systems behave this way because their component parts are frequently connected in ways that no one can see, understand, predict, or control. Policy makers are confounded by such behavior because it leads to what they call "counterintuitive outcomes" or, in other words, the system does not respond to policy changes the way they predicted it would.

In his book *Predictions*,[40] Theodore Modis offers what he believes is a nearly universal model that describes the growth of complex systems. Modis's *Law of Natural Growth* depicts a system whose rate of growth is a function of the amount of growth (a) already achieved or (b) yet to be achieved. If either of these two values is small, the rate of growth is low. That is, at the beginning of a system's "life," when the amount of growth achieved is small, growth is slow. Slow growth is the system's way of responding to the conditions it encounters early in its life. Internally, the system is likely to have only poorly developed capacities for acquiring and processing resources. Externally, the system will face already established competitors into whose space the new system will have to expand. Resources are apt to be scarce and expensive.

After this initial period, the system enters a second stage during which it grows exponentially, that is, by adding a constant (or perhaps even an increasing) percentage to an ever expanding base. Such growth tends to produce a line on a graph that curves upward at a very high and accelerating rate. Indeed, if the system knows no limits (or virtually none within a human's time horizon), then an exponential growth curve will rise literally forever. The system has now acquired the internal capacities to acquire and handle additional resources, and it can now compete with other systems for scarce resources.

Finally, the system enters a third stage during which growth slows once again. Here, growth is a function of the low amount of growth yet to be achieved. The system begins to encounter the limits—both internal and external—to its continued expansion, and it begins to slow down as if in response to a sensing of these limits. As a system grows and becomes more complex, the utility or value of radical experimentation declines.[41] The more complex a system becomes, the fewer are the options for change available to it and the more wasteful it becomes to make large-scale jumps from one alternative to another. Changes consist increasingly of minor adjustments at the margin, a strategy known as incrementalism.[42] In an ideal example of this model, the system exhibits a pattern known as *logistical growth*. Logistical growth produces a line on a graph that we sometimes refer to as a "sigmoid curve" because of its distinctive S-shape.[43] (See figure 4.1.)

In politics as in economics, we are inclined to think of the world of interacting systems as one of equilibrium, in which competing systems keep one another in check. Moreover, the alternating expansion and decline of systems competing for the same space and resources strike us intuitively as not only natural (that is, emulating the balancing acts of ecosystems) but also the most efficient way to allocate resources (as Adam Smith's "invisible hand" coordinates the economy). Thus, there exists only one optimal way to allocate resources,

Figure 4.1. The Natural Growth of Complex Systems

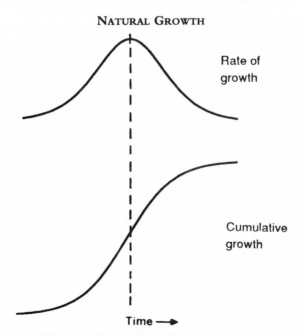

Note: While the rate of growth follows a bell-shaped curve, cumulative growth traces an S-curve.

Source: Theodore Modis, *Predictions: Society's Telltale Signature Reveals the Past and Forecasts the Future* (New York: Simon and Schuster, 1992), 34, figure 1.3. Used by permission.

and that optimum will be found by the never-ending interaction of competing systems as they rise and fall.

This conventional wisdom has been challenged by economists inspired by the paradigm of complex systems. One of the leaders in these studies has been W. Brian Arthur of Stanford University and the Santa Fe Institute.[44] Arthur asserts that there is no one single best way for a complex economy to allocate its resources. There may well exist several alternatives with no clear or obvious way to choose from among them. The market will, of course, make its selection through the countless small production and consumption decisions made daily by uncoordinated agents. But the accumulation of these decisions does not necessarily produce the single optimal outcome. The market "solution" by which firms or technologies succeed and fail may be the most efficient, but it may also be the outcome of random forces or events in the system.

We may never know, however, why a particular system won and others lost the economic competition, for once a particular market solution is reached, it tends to become entrenched through what Arthur calls the *lock-in effect*. The winner is the beneficiary of a positive feedback loop, and exit from a positive feedback loop is expensive. Once the economy allocates resources in a certain configuration (for example, by favoring the internal combustion engine over steam to power individual automobiles), exit becomes difficult because the chosen solution possesses certain advantages over all other possible solutions. These advantages derive from the following characteristics of systems in the presence of positive feedback:

- *Large set-up costs.* Initial investments are high, so the barrier to new entrants in the competition can be insuperable.
- *Learning effects.* Routines become more efficient the more we do them. The early winners in the competition have greater opportunity to learn and to become more efficient.
- *Coordination effects.* There are advantages to cooperating with other agents taking similar actions or operating in similar ways.
- *Adaptive expectations.* The more prevalent a particular firm, product, technology, or so on is, the greater are the expectations that the firm, product, technology, or so on will dominate the market into the future. (Of course, the reverse also tends to work against the less prevalent firms and so forth. That is, firms and so forth that appear to be in decline will fall even further because of declining consumer confidence.)

THE LIMITS TO GROWTH

No system can grow forever. All of the systems in which we are interested exist within a world of limits or constraints. Some constraints exist in the system's environment and may be physical (space, energy, etc.), conceptual (time), or social/organizational (information, decision making). Some constraints may be internal to the system. Stuart Kauffman has argued that the rate of growth of a complex system must eventually slow down because of internal reasons: "The number of conflicting design constraints among the parts increases rapidly."[45] In other words, growth slows down because the supply of superior alternative ways to organize the system begins to dwindle. There may be considerable disagreement about where all these limits are and what will happen if or when they are reached, but no one can doubt their existence.

In 1965, Gordon Moore, one of the founders of the microchip company Intel, predicted that the computing power of the silicon-based chip would double approximately every eighteen months.[46] In 1975, he revised the predicted doubling time to two years to match the observed rate of growth. For more than thirty years "Moore's Law" was an accurate forecast of the chip industry. But by the latter half of the 1990s, even Moore himself was predicting that such growth had to end eventually.

The doubling of chip capacity has to be achieved by the halving of component size, but nothing can be subdivided forever. As the chip manufacturers got closer and closer to components the size of atoms, strange particle behavior began to disrupt the chips' operations. By 1995, transistors on a chip were less than 0.5 millionths of a meter across. The theoretical absolute limit is thought to be 0.18 millionths of a meter. But as the transistor size approached 0.25 millionths of a meter, the distances involved were as small as, or smaller than, the wavelength of the light used to etch the transistor's pattern onto the silicon wafer that would become the chip. A second problem is heat. As small as the chips are, they still give off heat, and when they are packed together in larger arrays this heat begins to impede performance. Aside from packing the array in some kind of cooling medium (which itself would have to dissipate substantial quantities of heat), the only way to reduce heat is to reduce voltage, but there are absolute limits here, not to mention that extremely low voltages behave in an unstable manner. And then there are the financial limits. The expense of building factories and new tools to manufacture chips has risen as fast as the power of the chips, and the industry was finding it harder and harder to locate sufficient capital for investment in this equipment. In the long run, chip manufacturers believed that they would eventually have to abandon silicon and begin to construct computer components from some other material—and thus begin a new round of growth and complexity.

In chapter 3 we learned that the time horizon is a crucial dimension of any large and complex system. Although our choice of a temporal boundary of our system is largely a function of the values of the observers, this does not mean that all time horizons are of equal impact or merit or that we can safely ignore the consequences of the choice we make. Any significant global system will have long-term consequences for future generations and thus imposes real obligations on today's population.

To a degree not generally recognized, the "limits to growth" debate that began in the early 1970s pivoted on one's preferred time horizon.[47] The system models used by the researchers at MIT were such that the limits to growth did not appear within a time horizon of one year or even five–ten years. Indeed, the model needed several hundred years to produce a system collapse, a feature to which many critics pointed to discredit the studies. Economists were quick to point out that econometric models were seldom accurate over a span of months to several years, so how could the MIT model aspire to accuracy over a span of centuries? The counterargument, of course, is that conventional economics harms future generations by discounting their economic worth and interests. The MIT group asserted that sound analyses of very long-term trends were not forthcoming because the market for future intelligence did not value such knowledge highly and no one was willing to pay researchers to produce such studies. But as we came to know more about the behavior of complex adaptive systems, we understood that projecting the behavior of such systems far into the future faces the exponentially growing chances of errors. If the "butterfly effect" means anything, it should warn us of our inability to forecast the behavior of complex systems over the very long term. Thus, these arguments and counterarguments only served to move the debate to a higher level and to a longer time horizon.

Suppose, the critics argued, we really could slow down economic and demographic growth to something approaching a steady state. What then? How great is the moral obligation of the current generation toward future generations, and for how many generations does this obligation prevail? Are we obligated to reduce consumption today to preserve the lifestyle of generations to be born 100 years into the future, or 1,000, or 10,000? Even if we can restrain our consumption today for the sake of N generations, we still leave the $N + 1$ generation unprotected. Lewis Perelman has summed up well the ethical dilemma facing policy makers and planners operating from the systems paradigm:

> Students of system dynamics must recognize that the stipulation of temporal boundaries is not an arbitrary or trivial act. The choice of time horizons is an expression of an intimate, personal image of the future. The choice inevitably raises the dilemma of the individual researcher's relationship and responsibility to future generations. There is no single or simple solution to this dilemma. However, a minimal approach for the purposes of system dynamics would be to establish a set of ethical criteria for defining "reasonable" time constants. . . . At least modelers should make their personal values and judgment of long-term responsibility explicit.[48]

HOW SYSTEMS RESPOND TO THE LIMITS TO GROWTH

Look back at the curve in figure 4.1. You will note that the line bends twice, once when growth accelerates and a second time when growth slows down. It is fairly easy to imagine feedback that brings forth the first bend, but it is less clear how the growing system "senses" that it is nearing its limits and starts to slow down in anticipation of reaching a stable state. In other words, how does a growing system know where it is located on the exponential or fast-growth part of the curve?

Feedback of this kind might include signals from the environment of increasing competition from other systems for scarce resources (matter, energy, information, and so forth). One way the environment sends such signals is through the price mechanism operating in a competitive market. A second kind of feedback might include signals of discontent, disorder, or social pathology. Signals like this are frequently embedded in statistics on crime, political violence such as terrorism, or less dramatic disorders such as a rise in divorce rates or drug abuse. A third kind of feedback comes from "nature" or more precisely from the interaction of "natural disasters" and technology. By causing heavy damage or loss of life, so-called acts of God can send a signal that we have built a city too close to a vulnerable coastline or too near to an earthquake fault. In August 1992, Hurricane Andrew swept across South Florida killing nearly forty, leaving some 200,000 homeless, and causing damage estimated at about $30 billion. Subsequent analyses showed that the damage was increased by inadequate and poorly enforced building codes, overly dense zoning for development, and other economic and political failures. Shortly after the disaster, *Miami Herald* columnist Carl Hiaasen published a "letter to the Deity," which reads in part as follows:

> Okay, God, you got our attention. We've done some dumb things, starting with reckless planning and manic overdevelopment. In our lust to carve up this place and hawk it as a waterfront paradise, we crammed 4 million people along a flat and vulnerable coast. . . . We quintupled the population and idiotically called it progress. Now it's a disaster area.[49]

In calibrating their response to the impending arrival of environmental limits to continued expansion, systems must rely on feedback that is timely, accurate, and comprehensible. In principle, "true" information is never available, but hopefully we can safely disregard a small amount of discrepancy. Unfortunately, too often the feedback we get is flawed to such a degree that it leads us to make erroneous decisions about the system we are managing. Jay Forrester has identified a number of reasons why the information we get about system performance is distorted:

> Information can be delayed. It can be disturbed by a random error. It may be biased so that it consistently indicates a displacement from the "true" value. It can be distorted to produce errors that depend on the time-shape of the information stream itself. And it is subject to "cross talk" whereby the information shifts in apparent definition or source.[50]

If clarity of feedback were all that mattered, we could concentrate on improving the channels of information flow. But there are other reasons why a system might continue to grow despite feedback that signals it to slow down.

One such reason involves the ability of human beings to interpret what they see and hear to match their expectations. The perceptions of the people in the system are extremely important. In the examples above, the clarity of the signal depends as much on the interpretation placed on it by the system's leaders as it does on the signal itself. Political or economic elites have much at stake to maintain their status by keeping the system on the positive feedback loop of growth. Signals from the environment can be suppressed, denied, distorted, or otherwise manipulated to enable the system to stay on the growth track. If a system's elite can force, cajole, deceive, or otherwise encourage others to absorb some of the costs of the continued growth, the signals of impending limits may be muffled and easily discounted or ignored. But, of course, it is not necessary to ascribe malevolent intent to those who misinterpret signals from the environment. We are all plagued by a desire to make the world we observe coincide with our belief systems, so we tend to interpret signals to fit our expectations. In sum, while Modis refers to the process of system growth as "natural," it is, in fact, socially constructed.

With these preliminary remarks in mind, let us consider four scenarios of system behavior as limits to growth are encountered.[51] (See figure 4.2.) Recall the axiom that exit from a positive (growth-producing) feedback loop is expensive, so system leaders almost always try to stay in the growth mode so long as growth remains possible. In the first scenario, the system succeeds in maintaining growth if the limits to growth are far into the distance or if the limiting resource (e.g., energy) is itself growing at a rate at least equal to that of the system. If system elites are unconcerned about the welfare of future generations, they may define the time horizon of the system's limits as more or less equal to their life span. As an alternative, system leaders may take steps to *push back the limits* to growth by, for example, acquiring more land, energy, or some other critical limiting resource.

What is a system to do, however, if the limiting resource cannot be expanded or increased? Scenario 2 offers one possible outcome. (The text in figure 4.2 suggests that this scenario is possible if the system limits itself without needing feedback. For example, human beings grow to a certain height as determined largely by their genes, and they do not continue to grow taller as they age. The systems in which we are interested here, however, lack this kind of internal self-limiting property. They will continue to grow for as long as the environment allows them to do so or until they take measures to limit their own growth.) In this scenario, feedback from the environment is fast (as near to real time as possible) and accurate (it describes more or less what is "really" occurring).[52] Moreover, system leaders understand correctly what the feedback signals mean, and they take measures to respond to those signals by reducing the growth rate of the system. The second scenario produces a line on a graph that we call the sigmoid curve (also called the logistical curve).

Suppose, however, that feedback from the environment is delayed or inaccurate in some way. System leaders are not aware that they are approaching their limits. Or suppose that the signals are fast and accurate, but the leaders either

Figure 4.2. Four Possible Scenarios as a Growing System Nears Its Limits

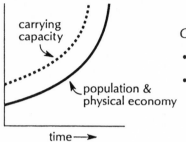

Continuous growth results if

- Physical limits are very far off, *or*
- Physical limits are themselves growing exponentially.

Sigmoid growth results if

- Signals from physical limits to growing economy are instant, accurate, and responded to immediately, *or*
- The population or economy limits itself without needing signals from external limits.

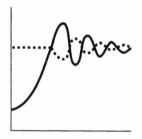

Overshoot and oscillation results if

- Signals or responses are delayed, *and*
- Limits are unerodable or are able to recover quickly from erosion.

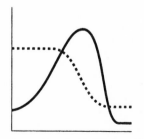

Overshoot and collapse results if

- Signals or responses are delayed, *and*
- Limits are erodable (irreversibly de-graded when exceeded).

Source: Donella H. Meadows, Dennis L. Meadows, and Jørgen Randers, *Beyond the Limits: Confronting Global Collapse, Envisioning a Sustainable Future* (Post Mills, Vt.: Chelsea Green Publishing Co., 1992), 123, figure 4.8. Reprinted with permission; www.chelseagreen.com.

interpret them incorrectly (they lack a correct paradigm) or simply ignore the signals and decide to keep the system in the growth mode and deal with the consequences later. It may be the case that the limiting resources suffer an erosion or degradation that is only temporary. After a period of system decline because of a scarcity of limiting resources, both the resources and the system recover or are restored. In this case, scenario 3 is the result. Here, the system experiences *overshoot* (an exceeding of the limits) and then *oscillation* (during which the system and the limits rise and decline in a synchronized pattern). The worst case is scenario 4. Here overshoot has occurred, but the damage is irreversible. The limiting resources cannot be restored or recovered, and the system goes into decline, leading eventually to total system *collapse*. Such disasters are fortunately very rare.

It is apparent from the foregoing that information flow is the key to achieving system stability and avoiding harmful or even catastrophic growth.[53] Changing the structure of a system means "changing the information links in a system: the content and timeliness of the data that actors . . . have to work with, and the goals, incentives, costs, and feedbacks that motivate or constrain behavior."[54] Transforming the information flow of a complex system does not necessarily mean simply more information (databases, statistics, etc.). It means "information flowing in new ways, to new recipients, carrying new content, and suggesting new rules and goals."[55] In short, it means a new paradigm of system behavior. The problem is that systems (like individual human beings) resist paradigm changes. The identity needs of individuals, like the material interests of the system, dictate that they dedicate considerable energy to the maintenance of the status quo. Changing how we react to feedback about approaching limits is as difficult to achieve as it is crucial to system survival.

NOTES

1. Ervin Laszlo, *The Systems View of the World: A Holistic Vision for Our Time* (Cresskill, N.J.: Hampton Press, 1996), chapter 2.

2. Laszlo, *The Systems View of the World*, 52.

3. Robert Clark, *The Global Imperative: An Interpretive History of the Spread of Humankind* (Boulder: Westview Press, 1997), "Introduction: Why Globalization?" See also John Fenn, *Engines, Energy, and Entropy: A Thermodynamics Primer* (San Francisco: W. H. Freeman, 1982), chapter 12; Herman Daly, "Consumption and the Environment," *Philosophy and Public Policy* 15, no. 4 (fall 1995): 6–7; and Hans Christian Von Bayer, *Maxwell's Demon: Why Warmth Disperses and Time Passes* (New York: Random House, 1998).

4. Stephen Jay Gould, *Full House: The Spread of Excellence from Plato to Darwin* (New York: Harmony Books, 1996).

5. John Noble Wilford, "Horses, Mollusks and the Evolution of Bigness," *New York Times*, January 21, 1997.

6. Carol Kaesuk Yoon, "Biologists Deny Life Gets More Complex," *New York Times*, March 30, 1993.

7. Eric J. Chaisson, *Cosmic Evolution: The Rise of Complexity in Nature* (Cambridge, Mass.: Harvard University Press, 2001).

8. Stuart A. Kauffman, *Investigations* (New York: Oxford University Press, 2000), 93–94.

9. Kauffman, *Investigations,* 48.

10· John Tyler Bonner, *The Evolution of Complexity by Means of Natural Selection* (Princeton: Princeton University Press, 1988), 25.

11. Bonner, *The Evolution of Complexity,* chapter 2, especially 27, figure 5.

12. Donald E. Ingber, "The Architecture of Life," *Scientific American* 278, no. 1 (January 1998): 48–57.

13. Bonner, *The Evolution of Complexity,* chapter 6, especially 120.

14. Kauffman, *Investigations,* chapters 6–7, 225–27.

15. Ian Stewart, "Does Chaos Rule the Cosmos?" *Discover* (November 1992): 56–63. Jack Cohen and Ian Stewart, *The Collapse of Chaos: Discovering Simplicity in a Complex World* (New York: Viking, 1994), chapter 4, especially 104–6, and chapter 5, especially 134–41. Brian Arthur, "Why Do Things Become More Complex?" *Scientific American* (May 1993): 144. Murray Gell-Man, *The Quark and the Jaguar: Adventures in the Simple and the Complex* (New York: Freeman, 1994), 229.

16. John Holland, *Hidden Order: How Adaptation Builds Complexity* (Reading, Mass.: Addison-Wesley, 1995), chapter 2.

17. Stewart, "Does Chaos Rule the Cosmos?" 61–62.

18. Colin Tudge, *The Time before History: 5 Million Years of Human Impact* (New York: Simon and Schuster, 1996), 84–89.

19. Massimo Livi-Bacci, *A Concise History of World Population,* trans. Carl Ipsen (Cambridge, Mass.: Blackwell, 1992), 26.

20. Tyler Volk, *Gaia's Body: Toward a Physiology of Earth* (New York: Springer-Verlag, 1998), 44–50.

21. Joseph Tainter, *The Collapse of Complex Societies* (Cambridge: Cambridge University Press, 1988), 23. There are, of course, other definitions of *complexity.* Complexity theorists differ among themselves as to the preferred definition or even whether a precise definition is possible. See George Johnson, "Researchers on Complexity Ponder What It's All About," *New York Times,* May 6, 1997. The science of complex adaptive systems focuses its attention on the properties of systems that lie somewhere between order and randomness. Thus, Heinz Pagels defines the complexity of a number as the "length of the minimal program required to compute it" (*The Dreams of Reason: The Computer and the Rise of the Sciences of Complexity* [New York: Bantam, 1988], 57). Highly ordered numbers require very short programs; random numbers require programs very nearly as large as the numbers themselves. Complex numbers lie somewhere in between.

22. Tainter, *The Collapse of Complex Societies,* 91–92.

23. Daniel Katz and Robert L. Kahn, "Common Characteristics of Open Systems," in *Systems Thinking: Selected Readings,* ed. F. E. Emery (Baltimore: Penguin, 1971), 97–98.

24. Katz and Kahn, "Common Characteristics of Open Systems," 98–99.

25. Tainter, *The Collapse of Complex Societies,* 92.

26. Donella H. Meadows, Dennis L. Meadows, and Jørgen Randers, *Beyond the Limits: Confronting Global Collapse, Envisioning a Sustainable Future* (Post Mills, Vt.: Chelsea Green Publishing Co., 1992). Theodore Modis, *Predictions: Society's Telltale Signature Reveals the Past and Forecasts the Future* (New York: Simon and Schuster, 1992).

27. David Ruelle, *Chance and Chaos* (Princeton: Princeton University Press, 1991), 102.

28. James R. Beniger, *The Control Revolution: Technological and Economic Origins of the Information Society* (Cambridge, Mass.: Harvard University Press, 1986), 64.

29. Kauffman, *Investigations,* 49.

30. Ilya Prigogine and Isabelle Stengers, *Order out of Chaos: Man's New Dialogue with Nature* (New York: Bantam, 1984). Grégoire Nicolis and Ilya Prigogine, *Exploring Complexity: An Introduction* (New York: W. H. Freeman, 1989), chapters 1–2. Ilya Prigogine, *The End of Certainty: Time, Chaos, and the New Laws of Nature* (New York: Free Press, 1996), chapter 2.

31. Von Bayer, *Maxwell's Demon,* chapter 14.

32. Erich Jantsch, "Autopoiesis: A Central Aspect of Dissipative Self-Organization," in *Autopoiesis: A Theory of Living Organization,* ed. Milen Zelany (New York: North Holland, 1981), 83.

33. Stuart A. Kauffman, *The Origins of Order: Self-Organization and Selection in Evolution* (New York: Oxford University Press, 1993), xiii.

34. Stuart A. Kauffman, *At Home in the Universe: The Search for the Laws of Self-Organization and Complexity* (New York: Oxford University Press, 1995), chapter 4.

35. Kauffman, *At Home in the Universe,* 92.

36. Paul Davies and John Gribben, *The Matter Myth* (New York: Simon and Schuster, 1992), 125–28.

37. Charles Perrow, *Normal Accidents: Living with High-Risk Technologies* (New York: Basic Books, 1984).

38. A. Angyal, "A Logic of Systems," in *Systems Thinking: Selected Readings,* ed. F. E. Emery (Baltimore: Penguin, 1971), 26.

39. Jay W. Forrester, *Principles of Systems* (Cambridge: MIT Press, 1968), 2-21–2-35.

40. Modis, *Predictions.* See also Theodore Modis, *Conquering Uncertainty* (New York: McGraw-Hill, 1998).

41. Kauffman, *The Origins of Order,* 70–74.

42. David Braybrooke and Charles Lindblom, *A Strategy of Decision: Policy Evaluation as a Social Process* (New York: Free Press, 1963).

43. Kauffman, *The Origins of Order,* 183–84.

44. W. Brian Arthur, "Positive Feedbacks in the Economy," *Scientific American* (February 1990): 92–99. See also W. Brian Arthur, "Self-Reinforcing Mechanisms in Economics," in *The Economy as an Evolving Complex System,* ed. Philip W. Anderson, Kenneth J. Arrow, and David Pines (Redwood City, Calif.: Addison-Wesley Publishing Co., 1988), 9–31.

45. Kauffman, *The Origins of Order,* 53.

46. "The End of the Line," *The Economist,* July 15, 1995: 61–62.

47. Lewis J. Perelman, "Time in System Dynamics," in *System Dynamics, Studies in the Management Sciences,* vol. 14, ed. A. A. Legasto Jr., J. W. Forrester, and J. M. Lyneis (Amsterdam: North-Holland Publishing Co., 1980), 75–89, especially 82–88.

48. Perelman, "Time in System Dynamics," 86.

49. Quoted in Neal R. Pierce, "Hurricane's Lesson: Tough Steps Needed," *Washington Post,* September 12, 1992.

50. Forrester, *Principles of Systems,* 9-5.

51. These scenarios are based on the discussion in Meadows, Meadows, and Randers, *Beyond the Limits,* chapter 4.

52. In this case, *real time* means "as it happens."

53. Meadows, Meadows, and Randers, *Beyond the Limits,* 222–23.

54. Meadows, Meadows, and Randers, *Beyond the Limits,* 191.

55. Meadows, Meadows, and Randers, *Beyond the Limits,* 222.

Case Study 4

The Lake Victoria Disaster

KEY IDEAS IN THIS CASE STUDY

East Africa's Lake Victoria, the world's second-largest freshwater lake, and its surrounding region have been the scene of **numerous human interventions** over the last 100 years.

Although the lake's ecosystem appears durable and robust because of its size, in fact the combined effects of these human interventions have brought Lake Victoria perilously close to **ecological, social**, and **economic** disaster.

While the Lake Victoria case is instructive in itself, it also helps us **learn** a number of **valuable lessons** about the nature of global systems and the consequences of their interactions.

Humans did not begin their presence on Earth as a global species. We began as a population numbering barely in the thousands that was confined to a small corner of the planet's surface we know today as the Great Rift of East Africa. Some 150 millennia ago, our distant ancestors began to migrate out of that region, and so began the great adventure we know today as globalization.

In this case study we turn our attention again to East Africa to learn more about one of the great impending ecological, technological, and human catastrophes of our planet. At the center of this disaster sits the magnificent Lake Victoria, the world's largest tropical lake and second-largest freshwater lake (after Lake Superior) with a surface area of nearly 27,000 square miles (larger than the State of West Virginia). About eight million people now live along the lake's shoreline in the three countries that border the lake—Kenya, Tanzania, and Uganda.[1] But the population that depends in one way or another on the resources of the lake now numbers about 30 million.[2]

The disaster to which I refer is actually more than one. It would be more correct to refer to it as a series of interlocking or interconnected systems, each of which is contributing in some way to the larger problem of the general deterioration of the lake and its environs. In this case study we shall learn more about the Lake Victoria crisis, not only about the problem itself but about what it can teach us about the consequences of numerous intersecting and interacting systems. Each system by itself would not be an insurmountable problem. But when a number of these systems come together and interconnect, the results are devastating.

◆ ◆ ◆

Europeans first laid eyes on the body of water the natives called Ukerewe in 1858 when the British explorer John Hanning Speke arrived there in search of the source of the Nile River. Speke named the lake for Britain's Queen Victoria. Although humans had lived near the lake for more than 100 millennia, the heavy hand of human civilization had not yet made itself felt to any great degree. In the next 150 years that would change dramatically—and not for the better. Nancy Chege, an analyst with the Worldwatch Institute, puts it this way:

> The ecological health of Lake Victoria has been affected profoundly as a result of a rapidly growing population, clearance of natural vegetation along the shores, a booming fish-export industry, the disappearance of several fish species native to the lake, prolific growth of algae, and dumping of untreated effluent by several industries. Much of the damage is vast and irreversible. Traditional lifestyles of lakeshore communities have been disrupted and are crumbling. There is a consensus among scientists that if an accelerated push to save the lake is not made soon, this much-needed body of water will cease to sustain life.[3]

The image many of us have of East Africa is dominated by its large carnivores and the massive herds of wildebeests, zebras, and giraffes that roam the region's grasslands and wildlife sanctuaries and on which the carnivores prey. Yet East Africa's most diverse, most fragile, and most endangered ecosystems are not on the grasslands but, rather, under water.

"Civilization" began to intrude into the lake early in the twentieth century. British colonialists sought to exploit the riches of the lake's watershed by clearing surrounding native vegetation, removing large forests, and draining swamps in order to plant cash crops such as tea, coffee, and sugar. Spurred by the booming export markets for these products, the plantations expanded in both number and size. The long-term consequences of this transformation in land use have been enormous and mostly negative. Agricultural chemicals such as fertilizers are washed from the plantations into rivers during the rainy season and drain into the lake where they promote the growth of unwanted algae. The plantations attracted migrant farmworkers to the shores of the lake, and the population began to grow beyond what natural food sources could supply. Traditionally, the lake's fish population had sufficed to sustain a limited human population, but as this population grew, fishing techniques had to change to keep pace. As a consequence, the lake's fish population began to decline, and catch sizes began to drop. To remedy this problem and to provide a fish that would attract sport fishers and tourists, in the late 1950s British colonial officials decided to introduce a new species to the lake: the Nile perch.

Prior to the introduction of the Nile perch, the dominant indigenous vertebrate species in the lake had been the numerous varieties of a small bony fish known generically as cichlids. Evolutionary biologists have been fascinated by the speed with which Lake Victoria's ecosystem spawned such biological diversity. No further back in time than about the beginning of the Neolithic Revolution, what is now a huge freshwater lake was a dry, grassy plain. Yet in only 12,000–14,000 years, some 300–400 different species of cichlids evolved from only five species of ancestors, making Lake Victoria one of the most diverse lake ecosystems in the world.[4] Cichlids feed on different food sources, but the majority of the species prefer detritus, that is, decaying plant matter. Over the course of some ten–fifteen millennia, the cichlid population and variety had evolved in balance with the plant life of the lake.

The people who lived on the lakeshore were an integral part of this system, as they depended on the lake and its fish for much of their protein supply. The species that provided the bulk of the natives' food supply is called the tilapia.[5] For centuries local fishers had depended on a native species of tilapia, and around the mid–twentieth century a second tilapia species, which also thrived, had been introduced. The natives liked the tilapia for its delicious taste but also because they could fish it easily with their traditional nets and preserve it easily by drying the fish in the sun. There was little demand for tilapia outside the local population, however.

The introduction of the Nile perch disrupted this delicate balance. The perch is a large and voracious predator. It can grow to be 6 feet long and weigh 200 pounds, and it eats the smaller fish as its principal food supply. For nearly three decades after the perch was introduced, the lake remained more or less stable biologically. Cichlids still constituted about 80 percent of the lake's biomass. Then the effects of the Nile perch started to be noticed. The 400 species of cichlids dropped in half to 200, and they constituted only 1 percent of the lake's biomass. The Nile perch, on the other hand, were now 80 percent of fish weight. The ecosystem had become so unbalanced that by the late 1980s the Nile perch had begun to feed on their own young.

Although the perch soon came to be seen as an ecological disaster for the lake, from an economic point of view it was a huge success. Foreign demand for the fish inspired business leaders and government officials to encourage the commercial exploitation of the perch. In 1981 only 17,000 tons of perch were exported, but by 1991 this figure had risen to nearly 130,000 tons.[6] By the early 1990s, the booming fish export industry was earning more than $20 million per year. Large commercial fishing boats began to invade the lake to haul tons of the perch from the lake, to be sold to foreign-owned processing plants located near the lake. Here the perch were cleaned, filleted, boxed, frozen, and sent off to markets in the Middle East, Europe, and North America. Over 200,000 tons of fish are exported annually despite the fact that many of the people living around the lake are experiencing malnutrition and protein deficiency.

Meanwhile, without the cichlids to eat the detritus, the mass of decaying organic matter began to increase. As it sank to the lake bottom and decayed, this detritus consumed oxygen, leaving the lowest levels of the lake uninhabitable to the smaller fish species. Before the introduction of the perch, the smaller fish had kept the lake relatively clean by eating algae; but as these smaller fish declined, algae grew thicker in the upper waters. The decaying algae absorbed more and more oxygen as it sank to the bottom, leaving the depths of the lake oxygen starved. Surveys in early 1989 showed the bottom one-third of the lake to be lifeless.[7] In addition, the smaller fish had also fed on snails, whose population now rose rapidly. The growing snail population became a public health hazard because it harbored the parasite that causes schistosomiasis.

The disappearance of the cichlids has also forced the local fishers to change their strategy. The perch live too far from shore to be caught by fishers in small boats using simple nets, so the fishers have had to invest in larger boats and more sophisticated techniques to pull the perch from the water. Processing technologies have undergone a major change as well. Cichlids needed very little drying before they were ready to be eaten, but perch is a very oily species, and they cannot be dried simply by leaving them in the sun. Instead, they must be dried over fires, and the building of so many fires has quickly stripped much of the timber from the shore of the lake. Without this protecting ground cover, the soil on the banks of the lake has become heavily eroded by seasonal rains. As the soil washes down into the lake, it silts up the shallower waters. There is a growing concern, too, about the possibility of overfishing the perch. Because the local population has become dangerously dependent on the perch, if it disappeared there could be mass local starvation.

There have been sociological repercussions as well. In the traditional fishing model, women had a key role to play in the processing of the small cichlids. Now most of the processing of the perch is done by large factories, and the women in the local fishing communities have been reduced to the task of scavenging the remains of the perch and trying to salvage some food value from them.

The intrusion of the Nile perch was only the first of several outside interventions that have brought Lake Victoria to the brink of ruin. In the region surrounding the lake are a number of industrial sites, including sugar factories, leather tanneries, and paper mills, which discharge heavy loads of industrial pollutants into the soil and water. Many of these sites are in Tanzania and Kenya, whose governments do little to regulate this toxic discharge. Even when environmental protection regulations are enforced, the industries find it easier and cheaper to pay the modest fines than to install the necessary equipment. The dumping of untreated sewage bearing human waste stimulates even more algae growth and exposes the surrounding population to all manner of water-borne diseases, including cholera and diarrhea.

Another recently arrived threat is the water hyacinth. This free-floating weed was first noticed on the lake in 1989. The plant is native to South America, and no one knows how it was introduced into the lake. Some observers speculate that it was brought by one of the lake's beachfront hotels, which planted it for decoration, or it may have come aboard a cargo ship operating on the lake.[8] With no local competition or species that uses it as a food supply, the hyacinth spreads amazingly fast. The plant can double in size and volume every five–fifteen days. It thrives in polluted water, has a huge seed capacity, and lives for up to twenty years. It blocks out sunlight, thus harming the organisms below it; it clogs water intake pipes and the engines of motor boats; it harbors populations of disease-bearing snails and dangerous snakes; and it encourages the spread of dysentery, with its stagnant water, and of malaria, by giving mosquitoes an abundant space in which to breed. The plant has so clogged Kenyan ports that about one-quarter of the lake's trade and transportation has been curtailed. The already hard-hit native fishing industry has been hurt by the inability of tens of thousands of fishers to launch their boats through the weed. Many small fishing craft have simply been overwhelmed by the hyacinth. Attempts to destroy the plant by removing it by hand are futile. Mechanical devices such as harvester boats or a barge-grinder nicknamed the Swamp Devil have made little headway through the weed. In 1997, Kenyan officials imported a species of beetle from Australia that is the natural enemy of the hyacinth and spread the bugs across the weed. Some researchers claim that they can see evidence of the impact of the beetle on the hyacinth, but the lake's history should alert us to the dangers of importing an alien species into an ecosystem where it has no known predators.[9]

As if by contagion, the region around Lake Victoria has also been hammered by a number of additional environmental problems that have added to the sense of overall deterioration that afflicts East Africa. Space does not allow a complete discussion, but a list of such problems would include the following:

- Beginning in 1994, lions in the Serengeti National Park in Kenya have been afflicted by a version of canine distemper, commonly known as rabies. Parts of the park actually touch the shoreline of the lake, and the entire territory of the park lies within 100 miles of the lake's shore. In one period of only several months in 1994, about 1,000 lions, about one-third of the entire protected population in the park, were killed by this disease. The rabies virus had made the jump across the species barrier from dogs to lions. The dog population near the park was estimated at more than 30,000, mostly because of the rapid increase in the region's human population, then growing at more than 4 percent per year.[10]
- Only 200 miles from Lake Victoria are two much smaller lakes, Bogoria and Nakuru, which are home to a huge population of Kenya's spectacular bird, the pink flamingo. Although the flamingo flocks may look robust because

of their size (the estimated population is over four million), they are actually quite fragile. The birds spend much of their time standing in the shallow water of these two lakes, which receive runoff from neighboring farms, industrial sites, and medium-sized cities. The lakes are flooded each day with heavy concentrations of pesticides (including the banned chemical DDT), industrial wastes (including mercury, arsenic, cadmium, lead, and chromium), and barely treated waste water dumped by local sewage plants. Within a mile of Lake Nakuru lies a toxic waste dump as well. With so much hazardous material flowing into the water, the lakes have become deadly sanctuaries for the flamingoes. Between July 1999 and March 2000, more than 30,000 of the birds died.[11]

- Several hundred miles to the south in western Uganda is the Queen Elizabeth National Park, a sanctuary for the few remaining elephants in the region. Only three decades ago, the elephant population numbered more than 30,000, but decades of war and poaching of the animals for their tusks have reduced the protected population to only 1,900. About 1,300 of these live in Queen Elizabeth Park. They were joined in early 2001 by about 100 "refugee" elephants escaping the war in the neighboring country of Congo. Unlike the native elephant population, however, the 100 or so "refugees" are much more aggressive toward humans. They have attacked nearby farms, destroying crops and buildings. They have even charged cars of tourists. The speculation is that they have been angered by the violence that has driven them from their native habitat.[12]

- In October 2000, one of the most dreaded of all diseases, the Ebola virus, appeared in the Ugandan town of Gulu, about 200 miles northwest of Lake Victoria. The appearance of Ebola can terrorize a local population for its intensity (90 percent fatal) and the gruesome way in which it kills (by breaking down the body's blood vessels and organs, causing massive bleeding). The Gulu outbreak killed about thirty-five people before it died out more or less naturally. It was the most recent in a series of half a dozen Ebola episodes that have hit villages near the Ebola and Congo Rivers running through Congo, Sudan, Gabon, and Uganda. Health officials speculate that the disease was brought to Gulu by soldiers moving through the region as they returned from fighting in the local rebellion in northeastern Congo, near the Ugandan border.[13]

The many problems confronting Lake Victoria appear overwhelming, but international, national, and local organizations have launched a campaign to save the lake and restore its ecosystem. In 1992, the three countries that border the lake formed the Lake Victoria Organization to coordinate these efforts. Within a year, researchers and fishery experts from the three countries had agreed, in principle, on measures to reduce pollution and overfishing, to monitor the lake's conditions, and to restore some of the native fish species.[14] To implement these measures, in 1994, one of the first steps taken by the three governments was to form the Lake Victoria Fisheries Organization. The organization's principal objectives are to coordinate (or "harmonize") the respective national measures to sustain the living resources of the lake and to adopt regional measures to assure the health of the lake and the sustainability of its resources.[15] Aquariums in the United States and Europe have joined with the World Conservation Union to try to save the cichlids. A Kenyan group of community leaders has formed the Friends of Lake Victoria to protect local fishers, encourage aquaculture, and educate the local populations on how to treat the lake and its surroundings. The Lake Victoria Research Team was formed in the late 1980s to study the lower depths of the lake to see what can be done to restore oxygen levels. Among the outside funding agencies for this research are the U.S. National Science Foundation, the Canadian International Development Research Council, and the Pew Foundation. There is even an organization in Kenya that tries to educate local farmers about the ways the water hyacinth can be turned into useful products, such as woven baskets or landfill.

In a highly interconnected world, systems behave in ways that they might not otherwise and which often surprise us. The Lake Victoria crisis helps us understand this property of systems by teaching us these valuable lessons:

- The long-term consequences of seemingly small and inconsequential decisions cannot be predicted. Small changes in inputs can bring about unexpectedly large changes in system conditions (a phenomenon known as sensitive dependence on initial conditions).
- Negative consequences often result from what were intended to be positive, helpful decisions (counterintuitive outcomes).
- In a highly interconnected world, change often occurs too fast for natural ecosystems to adjust easily (overshoot).
- Often what appears to be a solid and robust equilibrium in a local system (because it has endured so long) is, in fact, very fragile and easily destabilized. Often such ecosystems are preserved by ritualistic or religious restrictions on behavior that may weaken the system, but these restrictions are relaxed or eliminated as modern, rational, industrial ways of thought are introduced.
- When systems break down, there is usually no single cause of the collapse. Rather, the ultimate "cause" is the high degree of interconnectedness among the system's several component parts.
- When a stable ecosystem becomes connected to distant forces by means of the market price mechanism, it can be easily and quickly destabilized. The globalization and commodification of a previously isolated ecosystem subject the members of that system to pressures and incentives that induce

them to make decisions that seem insignificant in the short run but prove to be disastrous in the longer term.

• In a highly interconnected world, colonial relationships between peoples (defined as asymmetric as to power and benefits, distant, and alien) are easier to establish and maintain. Colonialized peoples have difficulty defending themselves against the negative consequences of decisions made at great distances from them.

NOTES

1. About 6 percent of Lake Victoria belongs to Kenya; about 43 percent, to Uganda; and about 51 percent, to Tanzania.

2. Susan Okie, "Lake's Bounty Becomes Its Bane," *Washington Post*, July 7, 1992.

3. Nancy Chege, "Lake Victoria: A Sick Giant," People and the Planet (1995), at www.oneworld.org/patp/pap_victoria.html.

4. Carol Kaesuk Yoon, "Lake Victoria's Lightening-Fast Origin of Species," *New York Times*, August 27, 1996.

5. William Booth, "Lake Victoria's Ecosystem, Vital to Millions, May Be Unraveling," *Washington Post*, June 5, 1989.

6. Susan Okie, "The Race to Save a Dying Lake," *Washington Post*, July 4, 1993.

7. Booth, "Lake Victoria's Ecosystem, Vital to Millions, May Be Unraveling."

8. Ann M. Simmons, "Strangling Africa's Regal Lake," *Los Angeles Times*, October 28, 1997. Marc Lacey, "Amazon Plant Proliferates Again in African Lake, Causing Economic Peril," *New York Times*, November 26, 2001.

9. Karl Vick, "Betting on the Bugs," *Washington Post*, September 22, 1999.

10. John Schwartz, "Scientists Followed 'Viral Footprints' to Serengeti Lion Killer," *Washington Post*, February 1, 1996.

11. Karl Vick, "Kenya's Pink Death," *Washington Post*, March 7, 2000.

12. Ian Fisher, "Grumpy and Big Eaters, Refugees Are Welcomed," *New York Times*, January 2, 2001.

13. Karl Vick, "Where Disease and War Intersect," *Washington Post*, October 17, 2000.

14. Okie, "The Race to Save a Dying Lake."

15. See the Lake Victoria Fisheries Organization's website at www.inweh.unu.edu/lvfo.

5

Global Systems

KEY IDEAS IN THIS CHAPTER

All systems need to be able to move matter, energy, and information from where they exist to where they are needed. This is called the **transport imperative.**

Global systems rely on **bulk flow** to transport resources and wastes. **Central switching points** are critical features of all such systems. Bulk-flow systems need to be firmly located in space and managed by an expert population. **Cities** provide the place where these requirements are met.

For globalization to exist, we had to achieve **global bulk-flow systems for information.** These systems were built on four pillars: **electricity, digitalization, telecommunications,** and **the Internet.**

TRANSPORT AS A SYSTEM IMPERATIVE

When we consider what a system needs in order to maintain itself counter to entropy, the Universe seems like a pretty perverse place. Resources (matter, energy, and information) and wastes are never located where the system needs them to be. Resources must be located and transported *to* the system; wastes must be moved *from* the system to a sink where they can be discarded. This imperative confronts all systems. The human body needs a circulatory system to move glucose, oxygen, and components of its immune system within the body just like America's highly industrialized society needs a global fossil fuel energy system to move crude oil from the Middle East to Houston refineries. The larger and more complex a system becomes, the greater the distance between the origin of resources/wastes and their desired destination. In other words, growing and increasingly complex systems have to go farther and farther away to get what they need and to get rid of what they do not need.

The *transport imperative* of systems derives from one of the fundamental properties of systems: the inescapable and irreversible creation of entropy as they perform work. We have already seen in chapters 3 and 4 that entropy—the energy rendered unavailable when work is performed—is an unavoidable cost of system behavior. According to the Second Law of Thermodynamics, complex systems should be constantly running down, deteriorating, or decaying. But open systems defeat (or, more precisely, defer the consequences of) the Second Law by means of dissipative structures. As we discuss in chapter 4, dissipative structures are the technologies and institutions that a complex system uses to transfer its high entropy to, or (what is functionally the same thing) to import low entropy from, other systems.

Consider the breakfast you ate this morning. In all probability, you consumed some processed sugar that was derived from high fructose corn syrup. A few months before your breakfast, solar energy sweeping over a field of corn in the State of Iowa triggered the process of photosynthesis by which the corn plants created plant tissue containing energy. Over the course of the next several months, the corn was harvested, transported, processed, transported again, added to your breakfast cereal, and transported again to the store. There it was sold to you, consumed by you, and then metabolized by your digestive system to liberate the energy (low entropy) in the sugar. The waste from this process (high entropy) was then dissipated from your body through heat and liquid and solid waste. The heat flowed out into the Universe, while the liquid and solid waste had to be captured by your community's wastewater treatment system, transformed into harmless substances, and transported to a sink such as a nearby body of water or a landfill. To accomplish this tiny example of your body maintaining itself counter to entropy, a system (or more likely several systems) had to shift some of this entropy back to the cornfield, where entropy increased slightly as the corn grew and was harvested. Of course, I do not mean here that entropy itself was transported from your home to Iowa. Rather, I mean that the entropy in and around your home was less than it would have been without this dissipative process, and the entropy of the Iowa cornfield was greater than it would have been. Entropy was also shifted back to the several stops the corn made as it was processed. Then much of the remaining entropy (other than your body heat) had to be shifted forward to waste treatment facilities and sinks. And, of course, the entire network of transport technologies, infrastructure, processing facilities, and retail outlets was highly entropic in itself, without even considering the entropic costs of growing corn and processing waste. Throughout this entire process, dissipative structures were hard at work to move entropy around so you could maintain your body's energy, health, and activity level.

A great city is one of the most complex entities ever created by human beings, one of the crowning achievements of civilization. Yet cities are also prodigious generators of entropy. They must acquire huge quantities of low entropy in the form of critical resources such as industrial and food energy, water, manufactured goods, and information, for which sources must be sought. And they produce huge quantities of high entropy in the form of goods, services, and waste, including heat and garbage, for which markets and sinks must be found.[1] The larger and more complex a system is, the more entropy it generates and the more resources it needs. Thus, as cities grow and become more complex, they find themselves going farther and farther away to acquire inputs and dispose of outputs. As Lester Brown and Jodi Jacobson put it,

> Cities require concentrations of food, water, and fuel on a scale not found in nature. Just as nature cannot concentrate the resources needed to support urban life, neither can it disperse the waste produced in cities. . . . Cities are . . . larger than their municipal boundaries might imply: As urban material needs multiply through the effects of sprawl and mismanagement, they eventually exceed the capacity of the surrounding countryside, exerting pressure on more distant ecosystems to supply resources.[2]

Just how far a city has to go to dissipate its entropy can be illustrated by the concept of the *Ecological Footprint (EF)*.[3] EF refers to the land and water area required to support a defined human population living at a given material standard for a specified period (often assumed to be indefinite). To calculate the EF of a national economy, a city, or an individual, we need estimates for the amount of land needed to absorb the carbon dioxide produced by burning fossil fuel to provide energy for the unit in question. We also need data on the amount of land needed for the buildings, roads, and other structures (the built-up environment); for the wood required for housing and other uses; and for the food needed to sustain the population.

According to data collected by a Swiss bank, the Union Bancaire Privée (UBP), in 1996 every one of the world's 5.7 billion people needed approximately seven acres of land to support his or her consumption (an acre is approximately the size of a football field).[4] At this rate of consumption, the planet's population has an EF about 30 percent greater than the Earth's ecologically productive land. Such consumption is possible only by drawing on the ecological "capital" of the planet, above and beyond the annual production of the biosphere. In other words, we were already in debt ecologically speaking even without additional population (then rising at the rate of nearly 90 million each year) or increased personal consumption. Moreover, the EF of an individual rises sharply as a function of the wealth and productivity of his or her surrounding national or regional economy. Thus, according to UBP, in 1996 each American used about thirty acres to sustain his or her consumption; each Norwegian, about fifteen; each Mexican, about seven; and each Pakistani, about three.

The authors of *Our Ecological Footprint*, Mathis Wackernagel and William Rees, ask the reader to imagine a great city as if it were a closed system, enclosed in a glass hemisphere that lets in light but prevents material things of any kind from entering or leaving.[5] It is obvious, they assert, that such a city would perish within a matter of days. Cut off from its resources and sinks, it would starve and suffocate at the same time. The amount of land needed to sustain the city is its EF and extends far beyond the boundaries of the city or even of its surrounding region. In other words, *"the ecological locations of human settlements no longer coincide with their geographic locations."*[6]

To illustrate their point, Wackernagel and Rees calculate the footprint of Vancouver, Canada, often cited as one of the world's best and most livable cities.[7] Vancouver's surrounding hinterland, the Lower Fraser River Valley, covers approximately 4,000 square kilometers (400,000 hectares [a hectare equals 2.47 acres]) and is home to 1.8 million people. Assuming consumption patterns of typical Canadians, the authors calculate that Vancouver has an EF of 77,000 square kilometers, some nineteen times larger than its home territory.[8] It seems that the EF of a city rises more or less proportionately with its population. Thus, the city of London, with a population about an order of magnitude greater than that of Vancouver, has an EF about 120 times greater than its municipal territory, also about an order of magnitude greater than Vancouver's.

How does a complex global system actually dissipate its entropic costs elsewhere? How can one system force, coax, or otherwise induce another to bear some of the costs of its development or growth? Some dissipative structures are overtly and clearly political. Annexation or colonization by a nation-state of a neighbor provides new territory onto which entropy can be dumped; coercion or the use of force can suppress resistance by the neighboring peoples who object to being used in this fashion. Other processes involve deception to conceal the dissipation from those who must bear the costs. One such technique is to filter the entropic costs through the impersonal market mechanism; another is to adopt a national accounting system that counts entropy-producing activities as a plus to the gross national product. Still other options involve rewarding or paying the neighboring system for agreeing to receive the system's entropy. This process might be called the commodification of entropy.

Occasionally the system can pass the entropic costs back to the past, as when fossil fuel is tapped to provide energy for today's industrial civilization, or forward to the future, by making yet unborn generations absorb the costs of entropy they did not create. Some dissipative structures are so subtle that many people in the entropy-producing system may be unaware of how others are bearing the costs of their standard of living. For example, when ecological disorder or social unrest forces thousands of people to leave their homeland in search of a better life, the receiving society is happy to employ them for lower wages and to do less desirable jobs than the native-born workers would tolerate. There are also instances in which entropy is transported from one system to another by natural carriers, such as wind and moving water that move toxic or hazardous substances or insects that carry diseases.

Regardless of the exact mechanism by which dissipative structures operate, two features of the process are always present. First, whenever the costs of a particular entropy-producing transaction have been passed on to other systems whose members have not been parties to the transaction and did not benefit from it, we say that those costs have been *externalized*. One of the tasks of good public policy in this realm is to internalize the costs of entropy whenever possible. That is, those who benefit from the production of entropy should somehow pay for its dissipation as well.

That this is especially difficult is seen from the second generic feature: the *asymmetry of power* that attends each dissipative transaction. Presumably, no system ever willingly absorbs the entropy of others unless it is compensated or rewarded in some way for doing so. And yet the long-distance spreading of entropic costs goes on all the time, and the receiving party is not always paid for the service rendered to the sending party. That the originating system can secure the cooperation of the receiving system and get it to accept the former's entropic costs is a clear indication of a power imbalance. In other words, dissipation of entropy occurs when one system's elites have the will and the capacity to cause others to bear the costs of their own growth and complexity. This sort of power asymmetry is one of the defining characteristics of colonial systems, which suggests that the absorption of entropic costs is one of the services the colony performs for its metropole.

BULK-FLOW SYSTEMS, CENTRAL SWITCHING POINTS, AND CITIES

In their study of the politics of globalization, Jeffrey Frieden and Ronald Rogowski assert that the growth of international trade and investment is a consequence of a profound drop in the costs, or an equally profound increase in the rewards, of international economic transactions.[9] Frieden and Rogowski identify at least five underlying causes of such a transformation, of which the first two are (1) *declining transport costs,* occasioned by technological innovations in telecommunications, commercial air travel, and containerization, among others; and (2) a more *supportive and reliable infrastructure,* made possible by global telecommunications, which allows for less costly financing of international trade and investment. These two factors are examples of the importance of *bulk-flow* systems in promoting globalization.

Regardless of the exact mechanism by which entropy is dissipated, some kind of transport medium is essential. To dissipate its entropy by exporting waste or importing resources, a complex system must be able to move waste and resources, and there are only two ways to do this: *diffusion* and *bulk flow*. My use of these terms is derived from Steven Vogel's description of the human body's circulatory system.[10] By *diffusion,* Vogel means the random dispersal of molecules from a single source with little directionality other than that provided by downward sloping gradients of heat, pressure, and so forth. Substances spreading by diffusion move from high pressure to low, or from hotter areas to colder, but with little else to guide them. The transport capacity of such a medium is obviously quite low, but this does not matter because the substances to be transported are extremely tiny and the distances to be covered are extremely short.

In contrast, *bulk flow* for Vogel means the movement of oxygen through the blood carried by the red blood cells or corpuscles known as hemoglobin. Oxygen dissolves in hemoglobin much better than it does in blood itself, so the hemoglobin carrier increases the transport capacity of our circulatory system many times over. The fact that blood moves within the boundaries or constraints of the arteries and veins of the circulatory system further increases the system's capacity by focusing or concentrating the oxygen and giving its flow directionality as well. Blood serves us by carrying other things besides oxygen: heat from our body's core to its periphery (the skin) for dispersal to the environment and white blood cells to fight off infections and rid the body of other "aliens."

Blood, hemoglobin, and the circulatory system provide us with a metaphor by which we can illuminate how global systems solve their transport requirements. (See box 5.1.) *Diffusion*—the direct transfer of matter, energy, or information without any intermediary linkages between origin and destination—plays an essential role in human relations, for it is by this medium that all

---

Box 5.1.   Diffusion and Bulk Flow Compared

Diffusion

- Speed: slow
- Distance between origin and destination: proximate, short
- Cost per unit of material moved: high
- Intermediary or linking technologies, processes, and social institutions required: none

Bulk Flow

- Speed: fast
- Distance between origin and destination: long
- Cost per unit of material moved: low
- Intermediary or linking technologies, processes, and social institutions required:
  - Material packed in small containers
  - Small containers loaded onto large container
  - Large container transported to destination
  - Small container unloaded from large container; material unpacked

Source: Based on Steven Vogel, *Vital Circuits: On Pumps, Pipes, and the Workings of Circulatory Systems* (New York: Oxford University Press, 1992), especially chapter 6.

face-to-face communication occurs. Diffusion is adequate if the quantities to be moved are small, distances are short, and time is unimportant. If, however, quantities are large, distances are great, and we are in a hurry, *bulk-flow systems* are required. Globalization could not have been achieved or maintained without bulk-flow systems of enormous capacity.

A bulk-flow system achieves its power and efficiency by interposing intermediary technologies, processes, social structures, and organisms between the origin and the destination. The objects being transported must be packed into a small container, and the small container is then loaded onto a larger, mobile container or conveyance. That large container is then moved to the distant location, where the smaller container is unloaded and unpacked, and the objects are moved to their desired destination. For most of our time on Earth, humans had only their own bodies available to transport things. For about the last 10,000 years, since the Neolithic Revolution, we have been devising bulk-flow systems with increasing capacity, speed, and range. This increase in bulk-flow capacity has been an essential feature of globalization.

Critical components of any bulk-flow systems are its *central switching points*. These components sit at the center of a radiating network of linkages, much like the hub of a wheel sits at the center of the wheel's spokes. Switching points receive shipments of matter, energy, and information coming from many different origins and bound for many different destinations. At the switching point, shipments are unloaded, repackaged according to destination, and then sent out again. Without such central switching points, every point of origin or source would have to be connected directly to every possible destination, and any bulk-flow system would be quickly overloaded by its sheer complexity. Central switching points can be as small as a city's telephone switchboard or as large as an entire city, as Amsterdam was in the seventeenth and eighteenth centuries. Central switching points can be Internet routers moving packets of electronic messages around the world, hub airports such as Chicago's O'Hare Airport moving airplane passengers from one carrier to another, or container ports like Long Beach, California, transferring cargo containers among ships, trucks, and rail cars.

The need for central switching points is not a mere artifact of culture or economics but, rather, is rooted in the fundamental nature of complex systems. Once fairly large numbers of component parts become highly interconnected, they must create linking devices among themselves that channel or route their myriad interactions. Without such linkages, systems can founder in the anarchy of too many fragmented connections or the tyranny of too few that are rigid and overly centralized. Research from disciplines as diverse as communications, organization theory, and mathematics confirms the key role of switching points in complex systems.

In his book on general systems theory, Anatol Rapoport reports on the results of an experiment conducted by Harold Guetzkow and H. A. Simon on the impact of information flow patterns on a group's performance.[11] The subjects were five-person groups given certain tasks to perform. The key variable was a set of rules that set forth who could communicate with whom within the group. In the format known as the All-Channel Network, any member could communicate with any other. In the Wheel Network, one member was placed at the center of the group and given the right to communicate with all others, but all the others could communicate only with the person at the center. In the Circle Network, each member could communicate only with his or her two neighbors. Guetzkow and Simon found that the most efficient network for performing the assigned tasks was the Wheel, thus illustrating the importance of central switching points for facilitating communication and transactions within complex systems.

More recent research by Cornell University mathematician Steven Strogatz and Columbia University social sciences professor Duncan Watts shows that the introduction of switching points, even if done randomly, can facilitate enormously the flow of transactions among members of a complex communications network.[12] For Strogatz and Watts, networks are either "small worlds" or "big worlds." The size of a "world" is a measure not of the number of its components but of the ease with which transactions flow through the network. The "smallness" of a "world," a network, or a system can be expressed mathematically by the number of steps required to get from one element of it to any other. (This number of steps, known as "degrees of separation," can be a reason why important systems become invisible to us. This issue is explored in depth in chapter 6.) "Big worlds" are systems that contain many components that have great difficulty communicating with each other. To make a world "smaller," one only has to introduce a few extra connections or short cuts that immediately link members in unexpected ways. Clusters of interacting members begin to take shape, and the network's capacity is raised accordingly. But the addition of too many linkages can slow the network down again. The system becomes too chaotic to yield small world effects.

For about five millennia after the beginning of the Neolithic Revolution, the bulk-flow transport requirements of human societies were so modest and limited that they did not need such concentrated populations devoted to control and coordination. From about 3000 B.C.E. on, however, the growing complexity and power of bulk-flow systems have both required and made possible the building and maintenance of cities to house the labor force devoted to operating these systems. We can date the emergence of rudimentary global bulk-flow systems from about 1500 C.E., when Europeans established their first lasting contacts with Western Hemisphere native peoples. From 1500 to the mid–nineteenth century, bulk-flow systems serviced the world—but only at speeds and in volumes dictated by natural forces: wind, moving water, and animal and human muscle power. Over the course of the nineteenth century, sailing vessels and animal-drawn wagons were replaced by steam ships and railroads. And after about 1910, the internal combustion engine replaced steam power, and airplanes, trucks, and automobiles became available to provide bulk-flow transport with dramatically increased capacity. Much the same transition occurred with the bulk flow of information. From 1840 to 1940, the principal information technologies were the telegraph, telephone, film, recorded sound, and radio. After 1940, these were all joined by computers, television, fiber-optic cable, telecommunications satellites, and all manner of wireless communication devices.

Central switching points and the other agents operating bulk-flow systems are not distributed randomly across the world. Instead, they are concentrated in cities, the unique places humans have designed to make bulk-flow systems work. The history of globalization can be seen as the deepening interdependent relationship between cities and global bulk-flow systems.[13] Cities and bulk-flow systems form a classic positive feedback loop. (See figure 5.1.)

Cities are not a natural habitat for human beings. For nearly all of our time on the Earth, we lived in groups of 50–150 members. To support populations that now have reached the range of several tens of millions, cities must acquire huge quantities of matter, energy, and information. Then they must process these resources, converting them for the use of the city's residents, and send them out to other systems, including sinks. Cities cannot supply themselves from nearby sources, so they must go farther and farther afield for resources and sinks. And the bigger and more complex a city becomes, the more entropy it generates, so the more it must reply on dissipative structures, which in turn require larger and more complex bulk-flow systems.

But bulk-flow systems need cities as well because as the systems grow they require more specialized operators and designers. At the beginning of the Neolithic Revolution, typical bulk-flow systems (pottery, baskets, canoes, sledges)

Figure 5.1.   A Fundamental Dilemma: A Positive Feedback Loop with No Easy (or Cheap) Exit

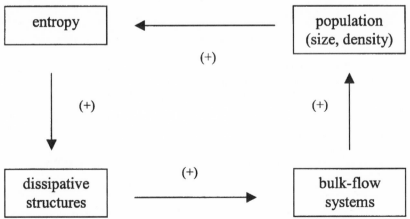

Note: An increase in a system's entropy requires increased dissipative structures to import more high-quality energy (low entropy) and export more waste (high entropy). These dissipative structures require more bulk-flow systems to transport matter and energy. These increased bulk-flow systems require a larger, more complex, more diversified, and more densely concentrated population to design, construct, and maintain them. Cities perform these functions for the larger system. However, because entropy is proportional to mass, as cities get larger they create proportionately more entropy, and the feedback loop continues its spiral.

were sufficiently small and simple that most adults knew enough to be able to make and use them. About five millennia ago, however, bulk-flow systems (amphora jars, sailing vessels, wheeled carts) reached a level of size and complexity at which they required an increasing number of specialized builders and operators who lived in close proximity to each other. And these new bulk-flow workers (carpenters, sail makers, navigators) needed more and more labor devoted to their support, productivity, well-being, and comfort. And as these labor sectors grew, they became more densely concentrated, thereby contributing to even more city growth, more entropy, and so forth. Thus, urbanization increased along with the size of the population generally and the size and complexity of bulk-flow systems. Exit from a positive feedback loop is never easy or cheap, and so it was here as well. The more of us there were, the more urban our habitat became and the more dependent we became on bulk-flow systems for survival.

Thus, one of the important features of the current process of globalization has been the rise of *global cities*. Some scholars would reserve this term to refer solely to the small number of "world cities" or "megacities" such as New York or Tokyo whose role in the contemporary global economy and culture makes them essential to globalization.[14] I prefer a somewhat broader definition: a global city is one whose survival depends on being connected to global systems of matter, energy, and information.

The ability of cities to establish global connections derives from what Donald Janelle calls "space-adjusting technologies."[15] For example, the time required to travel from Boston to New York decreased from 4,700 minutes in 1800 (by stagecoach) to 300 minutes in 1965 (by automobile), which represents a decline of twenty-seven minutes per year for 165 years. In 1838, the steamship *Great Western* crossed the Atlantic in about 380 hours; in 1950, the *United States* achieved the same feat in about eighty hours (and with about fifty times the tonnage, in addition).[16] The time needed to deliver a piece of mail from New York to San Francisco dropped from 600 hours in 1858 to less than twelve hours in 1990. To place a telephone call from New York to San Francisco in the 1920s took fourteen minutes. With direct dialing, the time has been reduced to less than thirty seconds.

ACHIEVING GLOBAL BULK-FLOW SYSTEMS FOR INFORMATION

The history of globalization can be written as the development of bulk-flow systems for matter, energy, and information. We enjoy today's global economy and culture, and we suffer the consequences of global environmental disasters or global diseases, because of our increased capacity to transport all manner of things fast, in large quantities, and over great distances. I cannot review here the entire history of global bulk-flow capacity.[17] Instead, I shall concentrate on the transport of the resource that many see as synonymous with globalization: information.

Many scholars and journalists have written about globalization as a human experience stretching back far into the past. Some writers see global systems emerging as far back as 1492, whereas my own contribution to global history pushes the beginnings of globalization back to the dawn of our species's time on Earth.[18] Other authors find the roots of globalization in the emergence of a global economy between 1880 and World War I.[19] The following quote from *The Economist* is typical of this point of view:

> Despite much loose talk about the "new" global economy, today's international economic integration is not unprecedented. The 50 years before the first world war saw large cross-border flows of goods, capital, and people. That period of globalisation, like the present one, was driven by reductions in trade barriers and by sharp falls in transport costs, thanks to the development of railways and steamships. The present surge of globalisation is in a way a resumption of that previous trend.[20]

Notwithstanding these perspectives, many people continue to think of globalization today as something unprecedented, a phenomenon completely unique to our time. Why do we persist in regarding our age as uniquely global? Why is it so difficult for us to see the deep structural roots of globalization? There are many answers to these questions, but one probable cause lies in the profoundly antiglobal forces that dominated the world in the twentieth century. With the advent of telegraphy and commercial steamship service across both oceans, the world in the 1880s was knitted together ever more tightly by flows of trade, migration, information, and diseases. The door to this stage of globalization was slammed closed by World War I and kept tightly shut by the rest of the traumatic events of the century: the Great Depression, World War II, and the Cold War. Protectionism blocked the flow of commerce, anti-immigrant legislation reduced the flow of people to a trickle, and isolationism ensured that we would remain ignorant of important events taking place elsewhere in the world. Many technological changes (e.g., radio, television, air travel) were occurring beneath the surface with the potential to bind the world's peoples together even more, but the geopolitical and ideological conflicts of the century blinded us to this powerful reality. As a result, when the Berlin Wall fell in 1989, we awoke to what we thought was a "new world order," unaware that global systems were not really so novel. Indeed, they had never really even gone away.

But one thing *had* changed and changed mightily: the increased capacity of global bulk-flow systems.[21] There were increases in the volume of cargo transported and in the distances cargo was moved without being touched, but what really rose dramatically was the speed with which the systems operated. And these increases in speed were due principally to the achievement of global bulk-flow systems for information.

One might think that moving information via global bulk-flow systems would be relatively easy and cheap.[22] After all, information does not weigh anything and does not take up much space, so it should have been easy to devise global bulk-flow systems for information as compared with, say, barrels of crude oil or tons of wheat. Actually, the contrary is the case. Achieving global bulk-flow systems for information proved to be extremely difficult and expensive. Two enormous steps forward, the inventions of writing and of paper, took place millennia ago. But when he became president of the United States, George Washington had at his disposal roughly the same information transmission capacity as did Julius Caesar or Alexander the Great, which is to say, a rider mounted on a fast horse. The four most significant advances in bulk-flow technologies for information were all achieved during the roughly 150-year period between the mid-1840s and the mid-1990s: the generation of electricity, the digitization of information, the invention of the Internet, and the increased capacity of communications.

Electricity

Today information in bulk is carried virtually entirely by devices powered by electricity. Thus, a global bulk-flow capacity for information depends on our ability to generate a reliable supply of electricity on demand and deliver it over long distances to shops, offices, classrooms, and homes at voltage levels that make it feasible for use in small devices such as lightbulbs, radios, or computers. Scientists in the mid–eighteenth century knew that electricity could be produced by friction or by natural processes such as lightening, but because no one knew how to move this power it was referred to as "static electricity." Then, in 1800, a professor of physics at the University of Pavia in Italy, Alessandro Volta, built the first electric battery, known as a voltaic pile.[23] In doing so, Volta had discovered the principle that two different metals separated by nonmetallic materials (for example, cloth soaked in brine) produced electricity that moved—or "electric current." The only obstacle left to overcome was to find a way to produce this "current" in large quantities and move it over great distances. In 1820, the Danish physicist Hans Øersted demonstrated that electric current had the power to deflect a magnetic needle, a discovery that launched the study of electromagnetism. Soon thereafter, the French scientist A. M. Ampère established the relationship between the strength of a magnetic field and that of the electric current that produces it. In 1831, a British scientist, Michael Faraday, discovered the principle of electromagnetic induction. When he passed an electric current through a wire coiled around a magnet, the magnet moved in response to the changing effects of the current. He then discovered that the reverse was true as well: when he moved a permanent magnet near a coiled wire, he could induce an electric current to flow.

Just knowing how to produce electric current in the laboratory was insufficient. A way had to be found to deliver usable electricity to people in their homes and offices. There was steady improvement in batteries through the mid–nineteenth century, and by the 1880s batteries were being used to light railway carriages and propel automobiles. But for electricity to be of much use in homes and offices, a way had to be found to generate large amounts of it on demand (that is, as it was needed), transmit it over great distances, and deliver it to users at low voltages. For these things to happen, the generation and distribution of electric power had to become an industrial enterprise.

In England in 1857, Faraday's discovery of induced electric current led to the demonstration that a steam engine could be used to turn a magnet inside a coil of copper wire to produce a flow of electricity. By the 1870s, steam power was being used widely to generate electricity, and in 1886 the world's first large-scale hydroelectric plant was begun at Niagara Falls, New York. In the United States, electricity was distributed commercially as early as 1879 in San Francisco, but historians date the era of the electricity industry from 1882, when Thomas Edison opened the Pearl Street station in New York City. Edison's station delivered electric power using direct current (DC), but this technology was challenged by a system using alternating current (AC) unveiled at the Chicago World's Fair in 1893.[24] In 1896, AC lines delivered electricity generated by a hydroelectric plant at Niagara Falls to the city of Buffalo, New York, some 20 miles away, thus setting the standard for today's AC-based systems. Meanwhile, between 1878 and 1880, the carbon-filament incandescent lightbulb was invented independently and simultaneously by Thomas Edison and Joseph Swan, although Edison was the one who profited hugely from the invention.

During the twentieth century, the amount of electric power generated worldwide grew by three orders of magnitude, from less than ten trillion watt/hours to more than 10,000 trillion watt/hours. Today, most electric power plants produce electricity by boiling water to produce steam to turn the generators. More than 80 percent of this power is produced by the burning of fossil fuels (coal, petroleum, and natural gas); falling water and nuclear energy each produce about one-tenth.[25] Electricity can be transmitted long distances most efficiently if it is at high voltage levels, so as it nears its destination the current must be fed through distribution substations and field transformers to "step it down" to voltages that are usable by individual customers (usually 120–240 volts).

Today, North America is served by a grid of 700,000 miles of high-tension lines that stretch from one end of the United States to the other and includes most of Canada and part of Mexico. These lines link electric power generators, transmission substations, and distribution substations to provide electric power on demand, that is, in real time as the customer requires it. There is no way to store large quantities of electricity economically; it must be generated and delivered as it is needed. The North American grid is divided into three geographical areas. The Eastern Interconnection services roughly the eastern two-thirds of the United States and Canada. The Western Interconnection services the western one-third of the United States and Canada and portions of northern Mexico. And the Electric Reliability Council of Texas services the Lone Star State. While each division delivers electricity via AC lines, they are all interconnected by DC lines, which are easier to control. So in an emergency, power can be transferred from one division to another, but massive power failures will not spread. Before it reaches homes or offices, electricity travels long distances over circuitous routes, following the path of least resistance. Electricity shipped from Oregon to Los Angeles could very likely flow through Utah; Canadian hydropower destined ultimately for New York City could travel as far south as Virginia.

The growth in the capacity of information technologies (ITs) over the past two decades is sometimes alleged to be the reason for the pressures on the nation's electric power grids, but the evidence is not clear. In late 2000 and early 2001, the crisis in electric power generation in California was blamed by some on the power needs of the IT firms in Silicon Valley in Santa Clara County. According to the California Public Utilities Commission, a typical commercial office building consumes 10–15 watts per square foot, whereas a building that houses Internet networking centers or servers for Web hosts uses 120–200 watts per square foot. A ten-story building filled with Web hosts can consume enough electricity to satisfy the needs of 40,000 homes.[26] On the other hand, data from the U.S. Energy Information Administration place the blame on other home uses. Average household consumption of electricity increased 43 percent between 1978 and 1997, but the principal culprits were refrigerators (which consume 13 percent of household demand), water heating (11 percent), air conditioning (12 percent), space heating (11.4 percent), and other appliances such as electric ovens (42.7 percent combined). Personal computers in contrast used only 1.1 percent of household demand.[27]

Digitalization

The generation and delivery of electric current were crucial to bulk-flow information systems because of the *binary* nature of electricity. The natural media we use to transmit information—the light we see and the sound we hear—exist as continuous waves that exhibit values (of electromagnetic wavelength or air pressure) that vary gradually across an infinite range. These stimuli blend together without any natural boundaries, and their continuous nature makes it virtually impossible to separate or divide them into discrete units without distorting them in some way. Our sensory organs have evolved to capture and process ("make sense of") these waves, and for information transport via diffusion they are extremely powerful media. The seamless quality of continuous waves seems to us to depict reality accurately by portraying variations in light and sound along an infinite range. We use information carried by continuous waves to record the passage of time, to register the movement of images across our field of vision, and to engage in face-to-face conversation with another person.

Unfortunately, it proved to be very difficult to fashion bulk-flow systems to move information embodied in continuous waves. To pack information in some container and then transport that container (the essence of bulk flow), the information first must be disassembled into discrete packages. But information existing in the form of continuous or unbroken waves cannot be easily subdivided and packaged. Writing offers one technology for packaging information, and its invention was certainly a giant leap forward in developing bulk-flow information systems. But the transmission of written material simply transferred the problem to a slightly higher level. For the written documents still had to be entrusted to a person (for example, a Pony Express rider) whose carrying capacity and movement over long distances were still constrained by their dependence on real-time energy (i.e., the natural forces of wind, water, and muscle).

Electric current was the breakthrough needed to overcome this obstacle. Electric current exists in a binary format; that is, in either one of two, and only two, states. Electric current either flows or it does not; it is either "on" or it is "off." This property of electricity made it possible to separate it into packages. The only challenge that remained was to invent a vocabulary to enable sender and receiver to encode information or meaning into the discrete pulses of flowing current as it alternates between its two possible states. The person to whom history gives credit for the invention of the first such vocabulary is Samuel F. B. Morse,[28] and the code still carries his name even though it is no longer used for long-distance information transmission.

The Morse code was the operating protocol of the world's first binary-based communication network: the telegraph. Morse began working on his code in 1832, and by 1844 he had persuaded the U.S. Congress to pay for the construction of a demonstration telegraph line between Washington and Baltimore. The technology of the telegraph was simple: a spring-loaded switch (called a "key") to send messages (by opening and closing an electric circuit), a clicking "sounder" to receive them, and a wire to carry an electric current between the two. By leaving the circuit open for varying periods, the sender could cause the sounder to click for either "dots" or "dashes," and specific combinations of these two clicking sounds were given letter equivalents. Although the code looked dauntingly complex, it soon became clear that some people had a natural facility for learning it, and within a decade Morse's code and telegraph were the accepted communication standard around the world. The Morse code lasted about 150 years as the standard vocabulary of worldwide communications. But the advent of satellites made possible the transmission of enormous quantities of digitized information automatically without the need for skilled operators. The Morse code was replaced in 1999 by the satellite-based Global Maritime Distress and Safety System.[29]

The next advance in communication, the telephone, was an attempt to replicate natural sound waves by means of variations in the voltage of electric current.[30] Transmission of digitally encoded messages along copper wire was an extraordinary achievement, but it proved much more difficult to transmit the human voice through a similar device. Human speech is carried through the air in pressure waves that vary continuously over a wide range, from a low of fifty cycles per second to a high of about 5,000. Moreover, each human voice is made up of a unique and complex combination of frequencies, which we detect and decode to recognize and understand each other as we converse. Fortunately, it proved unnecessary to transmit the entire range of frequencies for a voice to be recognized. A more narrow range of 200–2,000 cycles is adequate.

In June 1875, Alexander Graham Bell discovered the principle on which telephony was based: the *analog* signal. The sender of information speaks into the telephone, sending sound waves into the microphone in the mouthpiece.[31] The microphone is covered by a membrane that vibrates in the same pattern as the sound waves. As the membrane vibrates, it makes a magnet vibrate within an electrified coil of wire. The motion within the coil creates a continuous but varying charge or voltage, which is sent along a copper wire. On the receiving end, the fluctuating charge moves a magnet attached to the diaphragm in the telephone's earpiece. The vibrating membrane in the earpiece converts the electrical pattern back into sound waves. The electrical pattern flowing between the two telephones was called an analog signal because it was analogous to the original sound wave. In other words, the electrical signal and the original sound wave resembled each other in that they both were continuous and fluctuated across an infinite range of values.

As remarkable as the telephone was, there were still obstacles to using analog signals to carry information in bulk. There were limits to volume, speed, and distance with analog; but most significant, each kind of information required its own dedicated medium for transmission. As long as the signal remained analog, separate devices were needed for images, sounds, and numbers. The way around this obstacle lay in converting continuous waves of light or sound into a digital format.

Unlike analog signals, digital information is carried by electric pulses that are discrete (that is, separated rather than continuous) and binary (that is, exhibiting only one of two states rather an infinite range of values). In the case of a telephone call, when the analog signal reaches the telephone company's switching station it is sent through a computer chip.[32] The chip measures each wave of the analog signal at multiple points, sampling several thousand times each second. Each measurement is converted to binary digits, and these are grouped together into bytes. These bytes are transmitted to the destination telephone, but before leaving the telephone company's portion of the network, the digital signal is converted back into analog so that the recipient can hear and understand it.

Digital information has many advantages over analog. Because digital information can be divided into packages, it can be treated as if it were a solid object. It can be packaged, conveyed, and unpacked by means of bulk-flow technologies. Digital information can be handled in much larger volumes than analogs and can be sent over greater distances at greater speeds for lower costs per unit moved. Moreover, regardless of the original form of the information, once it has been digitized it can all be sent at the same time via the same medium.

Binary codes are not new; the ancient Greeks invented a binary message system using fire or torches either covered or uncovered. Francis Bacon invented a binary code for the alphabet in 1605, and as we have seen the Morse code utilizes a binary-based vocabulary as well. But for there to be a global bulk-flow system for information, a technology had to be invented that could receive, process, and transmit enormous strings of zeros and ones: the digital computer. Innovations in computer technology were focused on military applications during World War II, but after the war a flood of advances brought us to the threshold of the Information Age in only one-quarter of a century. In 1947, Bell Laboratories engineers Walter Brattain, William Shockley, and John Bardeen announced the invention of the transistor, the solid-state electronic device that was to replace the vacuum tube. In 1948, Claude Shannon's research provided the theoretical foundation for a binary information code. Texas Instruments engineer Jack Kilby designed the first integrated circuit in 1958, followed in 1959 by the design of a similar device by Robert Noyce of Fairchild Semiconductor. And in 1971, the Intel Corporation unveiled the microprocessor, the first completely programmable computer on a chip of silicon.

The growth of digital capacity can be measured by the number of electronic circuits packed onto a microcomputer chip. Jack Kilby's design in 1958 held one such circuit. By 1970 capacity had risen to about 1,000 circuits per chip; by 1980, it was more than 100,000; and in 1990, capacity passed one million.[33] In 1993, Intel's Pentium processor passed the three million transistor mark, to be followed in 1995 by the Pentium pro with 5.5 million and in 1997 by the Pentium 2 with 7.5 million. Chip capacity exceeded 14 million by the end of the century, and some observers expect capacity to reach 50 million circuits within a decade.

As the capacity of digital systems increased, so did their usefulness, and they began to appear in more and more applications. Telephones were among the first devices to be digitized. In 1990, the Canadian telecommunications firm Northern Telecom reported that its digital lines exceeded its analog services; and by the end of the century there were hardly any analog lines still in use in the highly industrialized countries. Chips were installed in automobiles to monitor engine functions and brakes, in homes to control security systems and appliances, and in countless entertainment devices such as games, films, and music. The average four-wheel-drive vehicle on the road in 2001 carried more computer-processing power than was aboard the Apollo spacecraft that landed on the moon in 1969.[34]

The Internet

Digitalization of information made it possible to separate messages into packages and send them via electric current, but a complete bulk-flow system needs central switching points as well. These were provided by the Internet. The history of the Internet begins with the Cold War competition between the United States and the Soviet Union.[35] Soviet achievements in space technology in the late 1950s prompted the U.S. Department of Defense to create the Advanced Research Projects Agency (ARPA) to promote research in advanced technologies. One of the agency's early priorities was the construction of a command and communications network to link the nation's military computers. The network had to be flexible, to enable incompatible computers to communicate with each other, and it had to be robust, capable of surviving a nuclear war. In late 1967 ARPA awarded a contract to Stanford Research Institute to study the design of such a network, and a year later some 140 research organizations were invited to submit bids on the Net's actual construction. The successful application was that submitted by Bolt, Beranek, and Newman (BBN), an engineering consulting firm founded in the 1950s by faculty members from MIT.

The BBN design established the principles of network architecture that still support the Internet today: packet switching and routing using an Interface Message Processor (IMP). At the point of origin, messages are divided into equal-sized strings of bytes called packets. Each packet is labeled with a "header," which contains the address of the recipient and an identifier code that indicates which message it belongs to and where it fits in the message. The packet is passed from one packet switch (a node in the network) to another until it reaches its destination, where the entire message is reassembled. Packets can travel over different alternative routes before being reassembled at the destination. The exact route for each packet is selected by the switching computer, or router, based on the density of traffic on the various alternative routes at the specific moment of transfer. The IMPs translate each packet's contents from one computer to another and route the message over the most efficient path. The entire process is done so smoothly and at such high speed that the recipient sees or hears only a seamless message, unaware that it has been transported in pieces over different channels.

The first network constructed on these principles, called ARPANET, transmitted its first message on November 21, 1969, between computers at the University of California, Los Angeles, and the Stanford Research Institute at Stanford University, Palo Alto, California. The network expanded slowly, to four computers in December 1969, thirteen in January 1971, twenty-three in April 1972, and sixty-two in June 1974. It took three more years, until 1977, for the number of connected computers to reach 100. The principal obstacle during this early period was the lack of a common protocol that would enable all communications and computing devices to communicate with one another. The network's equivalent of the Morse code was achieved in 1973 when Vinton Cerf and Robert Kahn designed the Transmission Control Protocol/Internet Protocol, which governs the way computers are addressed and packets are transported.

Despite these breakthroughs, during the 1980s the various successor networks to ARPANET remained in the domain of computer specialists and electronics engineers, mostly at research facilities and universities. It is estimated that in 1992 the number of computers connected to the network was slightly more than 23,000, and about 2.5 million people were online to one degree or another. The network, by now called the Internet, was still not accessible to less-than-expert users.

Obstacles to the mass appeal of the Internet were removed by two important developments during the first half of the 1990s. In the late 1980s, the U.S. government's National Science Foundation (NSF) had become a critical sponsor of the Net through its own network, called NSF Net. Although meant to connect a small number of supercomputers at research centers and universities, NSF Net had quickly evolved into a major backbone for the entire Internet. Moreover, the NSF was subsidizing Internet operations financially with about $12 million annually. In the mid-1990s, the government decided to phase out its involvement with NSF Net and turn the network over to private firms. This transfer was largely completed by 1995.

The second major change began in 1989, when Tim Berners-Lee, then an engineer at the European Center for Nuclear Research in Geneva, Switzerland, began work on an in-house communications protocol to assist physicists around the world to collaborate on research projects. By late 1990, the software for his network was completed, and in 1991 he released it to the world over the Internet. By 1992, the protocols and software that created the World Wide Web (WWW) became the property of global cyberspace.[36]

Two features of the Web made it enormously attractive to the average user and thus served to turn it into a commercial venture. One feature is the way the Web combines pictures, sounds, and words to provide a wide range of information. The second, which many believe was the real breakthrough invention, is hypertext, "live" footnotes embedded in the Web page that enable the user to travel from one site to another within the Web simply by clicking a mouse key on the highlighted link.[37] Soon after the WWW was created, a student at the University of Illinois, Marc Andreessen, developed a software program called Mosaic, which makes the hypertext feature user-friendly by pointing the mouse arrow at pictures or underlined text.[38] From that point, the Web became the chief service offered through the Internet, and the network became a central part of global culture (at least for the small percentage of the world's population with access to it).

In December 1995, when interested organizations began surveying Internet users, there were an estimated 16 million persons online. The Internet population crossed the 100 million mark in late spring or early summer 1998, the 200 million mark in summer 1999, and the 300 million mark in late winter or early spring 2000. The latest data available as of this writing are from August 2001: of the somewhat more than 513 million Internet users, 181 million are in North America, 155 million are in Europe, 144 million are in Asia and the Pacific, and about 33 million are in the rest of the (mostly developing) world.[39] As of the end of 2000, there were more than one billion sites on the Web offering every conceivable kind of information to a rapidly growing global audience.

Global Communications

All of the preceding technological advances would have been for naught had it not been for our expanding capacity to communicate electronically around the world. This capacity began its great leap forward in the mid–nineteenth century with the telegraph. On land, telegraph lines expanded along with another great technology of the nineteenth century: the railroad.[40] Telegraph lines were strung on poles erected along the railroads' rights of way, and the telegraph became essential in controlling the movement of trains to increase efficiency and avoid collisions. At sea the same partnership existed between telegraphy and the steamship. The steamship made possible the laying of submarine cable, while wireless telegraphy (now more familiarly known as radio), invented by Guillermo Marconi in 1896, became the link between ships on the high seas and land stations. Telegraph wires connected the two coasts of the United States in 1861, and the first transatlantic submarine cable was successfully laid in 1865 (after several failures). By 1862, the world's telegraph system covered approximately 150,000 miles, including 48,000 in the United States. By 1872, when the mayors of Adelaide, Australia, and London exchanged messages, almost all of the world's principal cities were connected by cable. In 1903, President Theodore Roosevelt sent the first telegraph message around the world. It took just twelve minutes.

Meanwhile, the telephone appeared on the scene eventually to replace the telegraph as the long-distance communication medium of choice during the first half of the twentieth century. Alexander Graham Bell demonstrated his telephone to the world at the centennial exposition in Philadelphia in June 1876. The crucial central switching technology, the central telephone exchange, was unveiled in New Haven, Connecticut, in January 1878. From that point on, the telephone soared in popularity. In 1886, there were 100,000 instruments in the United States; by 1920, the number had risen to 13 million. Local calls grew from one-quarter of a million in 1880 to 50 million in 1920. Because of a number of technological difficulties in sending telephone messages through submarine cable, for many years transatlantic telephony relied on radio waves. Human speech crossed the Atlantic for the first time in a telephone call between Arlington, Virginia, and Paris in October 1915. The first telephone conversation around the world took place in 1935. In 1999, international telephone call volume reached nearly 108 billion minutes. If spread evenly across time, this volume would be equivalent to more than 200,000 international calls being conducted simultaneously every minute for the entire year.[41]

Any time line of globalization in the twentieth century would be dominated by the appearance and rapidly expanding capacity of one communication technology after another.

Radio. The first commercial broadcast in the United States occurred in 1920. By 1930, one-half of all American homes had a radio receiver; by 1950, 90 percent did.

Television. The first television broadcast was of President Franklin Roosevelt's opening speech at the 1939 New York World's Fair. The first simultaneous broadcast of a split-screen image of the Brooklyn Bridge and San Francisco's Golden Gate Bridge was featured on Edward R. Murrow's program, *See It Now,* in November 1951. TV was in 90 percent of American homes by 1960; cable television was generally available by the mid-1960s; and video recording made its appearance in 1956.

Submarine telephone cables. Both before and after World War II, the technology of copper cable construction and installation experienced major improvements that raised communication capacity significantly. Time-Assignment Speech Interpolation took advantage of the silence in a given transmission to send voice signals from a second transmission over the same cable. Transistors were incorporated into submarine cable design in 1970. By 1970, 1,275 voice channels crossed the Atlantic, and 378 crossed the Pacific.

Satellites. In 1961, spurred by Cold War competition with the Soviet Union, the United States made the conquest of space, and the construction of a global satellite communications system, an urgent national priority. In 1962, Congress created the Communications Satellite Corporation to lead the commercial exploitation of space, and AT&T placed its first satellite, *Telstar,* in orbit over the Atlantic Ocean. Images of the funeral of President John Kennedy, in November 1963, were transmitted to Europe, making it the first event in history seen in real time on two continents. *Intelsat I,* the first satellite placed in geosynchronous orbit (to remain over the same spot on Earth), was launched in 1965. As of 2001, there were some 233 functioning commercial communications satellites in orbit around the Earth, as well as an unknown number of classified military satellites.[42]

Fiber-optic cables and lasers. Just as satellites challenged submarine cable as the emerging communication technology, they were in turn challenged by information transmission via light waves. Photons, it was discovered, are a more efficient carrier of information than electrons. This discovery could be exploited by finding a way to concentrate a beam of light sufficiently to transmit it over great distances without losing power and a medium of sufficient purity and transparency to carry the beam. The solution to the first problem was the laser, first constructed in 1960. The solution to the second, the fiber-optic cable, was joined to lasers in 1975 to produce the first generation of light-wave communication systems.

CONSEQUENCES OF THE INFORMATION REVOLUTION

For many people the Information Revolution is synonymous with globalization. The consequences of our transition to the Information Age are truly momentous and cannot be discussed here in depth. However, as a prelude to chapters 6 and 7, we need to understand two important consequences of the Information Revolution.

The first consequence involves the role of information in producing system effects.[43] Sectors of the economy that deal in manufactured products or raw materials tend to be more sensitive to negative feedback signals generated by the market. Thus, as economists would put it, such firms are more influenced by decreasing or diminishing returns and therefore tend to be more stable and grow slowly. Sectors of the economy or firms that deal primarily with information, however, are more sensitive to positive feedback or increasing returns; and so they tend to be more unstable or nonlinear. All of these system properties tend to cluster together: the more global a system becomes, the more it depends on information as its key resource, the more sensitive it is to positive feedback or increasing returns, and the more nonlinear its behavior becomes. These properties make it much more difficult to monitor or track such a system. Where and what the system is at time T are very different from where and what it is at time $T + 1$. As we shall see in chapter 6, system properties like these render global systems invisible.

The second consequence involves the costs of these changes. Our brief review of the history of global information systems makes it clear that the Information Revolution was neither easy nor cheap. On the contrary, the world's information sector represents an enormous investment in technology and knowledge. According to the World Information Technology and Services Alliance, in 1997 the information and communications technology (ICT) market amounted to $1.8 trillion, approximately 6 percent of aggregate global gross domestic product. This sum exceeds the GDP of France and is twice that of California. Moreover, in 1997 spending on ICT was nearly 40 percent larger than in 1992, growing 27 percent faster than overall worldwide GDP. Between 1992 and 1997, ICT investment accounted for a net increase of 90,000 new companies worldwide, 7,200 in the United States alone. ICT employment in the United States increased over 380,000 during this same five-year period.[44] Access to information in general, and to education in particular, came to be the critical difference between personal success and failure. In this way, the Information Revolution contributed to widening the gap between rich and poor, both within countries and worldwide.

With a transformation as enormous as this, with the potential to affect nearly every person on Earth in some way, and with such huge sums of resources at stake, it was inevitable that there would be winners and losers from the process. Every great transformation in the past, from the Neolithic Revolution through the Industrial Revolution, has occasioned the transfer of massive amounts of resources and values between groups and individuals. Indeed, every such transformation brings about a political upheaval precisely because of its potential to create winners (who want to accelerate the process of change) and losers (who wish to retard or even stop it). Globalization is no exception to this rule of human affairs. In chapter 7, we return to this theme as we consider the politics of globalization.

NOTES

1. Abel Wolman, "The Metabolism of Cities," in *Cities* (New York: Alfred A. Knopf, 1966), 156–74. James Trefil, *A Scientist in the City* (New York: Doubleday, 1994), part 1.

2. Lester Brown and Jodi Jacobson, "The Future of Urbanization: Facing Ecological and Economic Constraints," *Worldwatch Paper* 77 (May 1987): 35.

3. Mathis Wackernagel and William Rees, *Our Ecological Footprint: Reducing Human Impact on the Earth* (Gabriola Island, Canada: New Society Publishers, 1996).

4. See the Web site for Redefining Progress, at www.rprogress.org.

5. Wackernagel and Rees, *Our Ecological Footprint,* 9–10.

6. Wackernagel and Rees, *Our Ecological Footprint,* 29.

7. "Quality of Life," *The Economist,* March 3, 2001: 98.

8. Wackernagel and Rees, *Our Ecological Footprint,* 86.

9. Jeffrey Frieden and Ronald Rogowski, "The Impact of the International Economy on National Policies: An Analytical Overview," in *Internationalization and Domestic Politics,* ed. Robert Keohane and Helen Milner (New York: Cambridge University Press, 1996), chapter 2.

10. Steven Vogel, *Vital Circuits: On Pumps, Pipes, and the Workings of Circulatory Systems* (New York: Oxford University Press, 1992), especially chapters 5–6, 9–10.

11. Anatol Rapoport, *General System Theory: Essential Concepts and Applications* (Tunbridge Wells, U.K.: Abacus Press, 1986), 153–56. The research is reported in the original in H. Guetzkow and H. A. Simon, "The Impact of Certain Communication Nets upon Organization Performance in Task-Oriented Groups," in *Some Theories of Organization,* ed. A. H. Rubenstein and C. J. Haberstroh (Homewood, Ill.: Dorsey Press, 1966).

12. Sandra Blakeslee, "Mathematicians Prove That It's a Small World," *New York Times,* June 16, 1998.

13. The British author Geoff Mulgan has pointed out the historical significance of the great struggles between the "edges," such as Venice and Hong Kong, and the "center," such as Rome and Beijing. The edges played the role of central switching points in emerging regional or global bulk-flow systems. Being much more open to external influences than the center, the edges frequently rebelled against the attempts by the center to exert control over them. See Geoff Mulgan, *Connexity: How to Live in a Connected World* (Boston: Harvard Business School Press, 1997), 69–74.

14. Saskia Sassen, *The Global City: New York, London, Tokyo* (Princeton: Princeton University Press, 1991).

15. Donald Janelle, "Global Interdependence and Its Consequences," in *Collapsing Space and Time: Geographic Aspects of Communication and Information,* ed. Stanley Brunn and Thomas Leinbach (London: HarperCollins, 1991), chapter 3.

16. Vaclav Smil, *Energy in World History* (Boulder: Westview Press, 1994), 197, figure 5.18.

17. For more on this, see Robert P. Clark, *The Global Imperative: An Interpretive History of the Spread of Humankind* (Boulder: Westview Press, 1997); and Robert P. Clark, "Bulk Flow Systems and Globalization," in *Space and Transport in the World-System,* ed. Paul S. Ciccantell and Stephen G. Bunker (Westport, Conn.: Greenwood Press, 1998), chapter 10.

18. Alfred Crosby, *The Columbian Exchange: Biological and Cultural Consequences of 1492* (Westport, Conn.: Greenwood Press, 1972). Clark, *The Global Imperative.*

19. Jan Art Scholte, *Globalization: A Critical Introduction* (New York: St. Martin's Press, 2000), part 1. Herman M. Schwartz, *States versus Markets: The Emergence of a Global Economy,* 2d ed. (New York: St. Martin's Press, 2000). Dani Rodrik, *Has Globalization Gone Too Far?* (Washington, D.C.: Institute for International Economics, 1997).

20. "One World?" *The Economist,* October 18, 1997: 79. See also Nicholas D. Kristof, "At This Rate, We'll Be Global in Another Hundred Years," *New York Times,* May 23, 1999; and Keith Bradsher, "Back to the Thrilling Trades of Yesteryear," *New York Times,* March 12, 1995.

21. For a brief listing of other significant differences between the current phase of globalization and that of a century ago, see Rodrik, *Has Globalization Gone Too Far?* 7–9.

22. Malcolm Waters, *Globalization* (London: Routledge, 1995), chapter 1.

23. The following is based on Donald Cardwell, *The Norton History of Technology* (New York: W. W. Norton, 1995), chapters 10, 15.

24. Sally McGrane, "Getting Power to the People: The North American Electricity Grid," *New York Times,* October 21, 1999.

25. Smil, *Energy in World History,* 188, figure 5.16.

26. Chris Gaither, "The Dog Day in June the Lights Went Out," *New York Times,* January 12, 2001.

27. Katie Hafner, "Internet Age Becomes the Dark Age," *New York Times,* February 8, 2001.

28. Maury Klein, "What Hath God Wrought?" *Invention and Technology* (spring 1993): 34–42.

29. Jack Sirica, "Morse Code Operators Becoming Relics of Past," *Washington Post,* November 23, 1984. "(SOS, RIP)," *The Economist,* January 23, 1999: 71–73.

30. Steven Lubar, *InfoCulture: The Smithsonian Book of Information Age Inventions* (Boston: Houghton Mifflin, 1993), 119–46.

31. Tim Race, "What Do They Mean by Digital, Anyhow?" *New York Times,* March 19, 1998.

32. Race, "What Do They Mean by Digital, Anyhow?"

33. Smil, *Energy in World History,* 204, figure 5.22.

34. "Smart Tyres," *The Economist (Technology Quarterly),* March 24, 2001: 14.

35. John Naughton, *A Brief History of the Future: From Radio Days to Internet Years in a Lifetime* (Woodstock, N.Y.: Overlook Press, 2000). "The Accidental Superhighway: A Survey of the Internet," *The Economist,* July 1, 1995. Martin Dodge and Rob Kitchin, *Mapping Cyberspace* (New York: Routledge, 2001), chapter 1.

36. Steve Lohr, "His Goal: Keeping the Web Worldwide," *New York Times,* December 18, 1995. "The Internet: Where's It All Going?" *InformationWeek,* July 17, 1995: 30.

37. Although Berners-Lee gets credit for inventing the World Wide Web, the idea for hypertext is usually credited to two researchers working independently of each other in the late 1960s: Ted Nelson, a social scientist; and Douglas Engelbart, an engineer at Stanford Research Institute. See John Markoff, "Fast-Changing Genie Alters the World," *New York Times,* December 11, 2000.

38. Andreessen went on to found Netscape Communications Corporation, one of the pioneers in making the Internet user friendly and profitable. "The Rise of Netscape," *Fortune,* July 10, 1995: 140–42. Elizabeth Corcoran, "Software's Surf King," *Washington Post,* July 23, 1995. John Markoff, "6 Tips on How to Earn $52 Million by Age 24," *New York Times,* August 14, 1995. "A New Electronic Messiah," *The Economist,* August 5, 1995.

39. See NUA Internet Surveys, at www.nua.ie/surveys/how_many_online/index.html.

40. James Beniger, *The Control Revolution: Technological and Economic Origins of the Information Society* (Cambridge, Mass.: Harvard University Press, 1986), 221–37.

41. *The Economist,* November 4, 2000: 117.

42. For a list of all the commercial satellites still in service, see Ricardo's Geo-Orbit Quick-Look Web site, at www.geo-orbit.org.

43. Robert Jervis, *System Effects: Complexity in Political and Social Life* (Princeton: Princeton University Press, 1997), 158–61.

44. World Information Technology and Services Alliance, *Digital Planet—The Global Information Economy* 1 (October 1998). See also its Web site, at www.witsa.org.

Case Study 5

Global Systems
and September 11, 2001

KEY IDEAS IN THIS CASE STUDY

A measure of the interconnectedness of our world is the way the **consequences of the September 11 terrorist attacks** spread across our consciousness and affected numerous global systems.

For a number of reasons, it is daunting to try to think systematically about all of the consequences of 9-11 or even a substantial proportion of them. **Precise empirical data** about even fundamental aspects of the attacks are virtually impossible to obtain; many of the **systems** involved are **invisible,** some deliberately so; and we lack an **appropriate historical context** through which to view the events. The Global System Paradigm can help us make sense of this enormous tragedy by showing us how to think systematically about its consequences.

An analysis of the consequences of September 11 in all of the dimensions of our lives would be far beyond the scope of this case study, and perhaps such an analysis would be virtually impossible given the range of such effects. This case study simply identifies a select number of **economic consequences** that were severe and far-reaching.

A measure of the interconnectedness of our world is the speed with which the consequences of the terrorist attacks on the World Trade Center in New York and the Pentagon near Washington, D.C., rippled through our consciousness and our systems. Perhaps many hundreds of thousands of people were able to experience at least some of the events more or less as they happened, while tens of millions knew of the events within a few minutes. Within a few hours, hundreds of millions of people were affected, and perhaps three-fourths of the world's population knew about the attacks within a day. The tragedy of the events themselves, combined with the immediacy of global communications, produced one of the most traumatic experiences ever shared by such a large proportion of the world's population in such a brief time. For example, the Web search engine Google, which receives about 150 million queries daily from around the world, reported that in 2001 six of the top ten queries involved the terrorist attacks in some way.[1] A search on December 4, 2001, via Google for websites that dealt in some way with "September 11, 2001" produced 5,280,000 listings (compared with 5,975,737 on another search engine, Lycos). This case study examines some of the ways the events of September 11, 2001, spread across the United States and around the world through global systems to have an impact on people who were very far away from the attacks—and in ways that would have been impossible to predict.

THINKING SYSTEMATICALLY ABOUT SEPTEMBER 11

Thinking globally is not easy. For many of the same reasons, it is not easy to make sense of, or to think meaningfully about, the tragic events of September 11. One consequence of September 11 has been to remind us of how little we actually know about the systems in which we live and how difficult it is to observe and measure their component parts with accuracy. Since 9-11 the media have provided us with many statistics about the attacks and their consequences: the number of people killed in the World Trade Center towers, the number of children who lost a parent in the attacks, the number of anthrax spores required to cause infection, the number of civilians killed by U.S. bombing in Afghanistan, the number of Muslims in the United States, and on and on. Although these numbers are usually cited with great precision, the fact is that no one knows what the real numbers are, nor is there any realistic way for anyone *to* know them.[2] The fact that many of the systems involved are invisible, some intentionally so, further confounds our understanding of the full range of consequences of 9-11. And to make matters even worse, the attacks spawned an enormous number of myths and "urban legends" that will shape how we and future historians interpret what happened that terrible day. Many of these myths were propagated around the world via the Internet in a matter of hours.[3]

The most dramatic example of this statistical ambiguity is the number of people killed in the World Trade Center. Early on in the crisis, in casual conversations and official pronouncements the number of casualties was usually set at between 5,000 and 6,000. Yet, two months after the attack, the official estimate was about 4,700. Within two weeks that figure had dropped to fewer than 3,900; by November 23 it was revised downward to 3,646, and by early December, to about 3,300 dead and missing.[4] By the afternoon of December 14, the number had dropped to 3,018, and by December 19 it had reached 2,992. These changes were attributed to double counting of some individuals with two names or erroneous estimates by foreign embassies of the number of their nationals in the towers at the time of the attack.[5] In addition, there were almost certainly some illegal immigrants killed in the attacks whose identities will never be known because they lived and worked in New York under false names.[6]

Another statistic cited frequently involves the Muslim population in the United States. Muslim organizations provided estimates that ranged between six and seven million, while the American Jewish Committee asserted that the number was no higher than 3.4 million and perhaps as low as 1.5 million. Other estimates, done by social researchers or demographers, put the number at between 1.5 and 4.1 million.[7] Thus, we see the difficulty in thinking systematically about events if we cannot even agree on some common measures of their impact.

One way to think about the meaning of 9-11 is summed up in *Washington Post* writer Joel Garreau's phrase "the hinges of history." Garreau describes these "hinge" events as the "pivots on which our lives move from one world to another." Some "hinge" events are cataclysmic natural disasters like the Lisbon earthquake of 1755, which caused philosophers to doubt that they lived in the "best of all possible worlds," but many, like the Holocaust, are inflicted by human beings on each other. "What changes after a hinge," he writes, "is our stories of ourselves. Who we are, how we got that way, where we're headed, and what makes us tick. . . . [A]ny cultural revolution represents a grand new alignment of great forces. . . . These shape the tales we tell to make sense of our new world."[8] For instance, the destruction of the World Trade Center catapulted new heroes into our popular culture—police, rescue squad members, and firefighters—to replace sports figures and movie celebrities.

The "hinges of history" metaphor is highly suggestive, but it is ultimately limited by our ignorance of the future. To be able to say that 9-11 was a "hinge event," we must know what the "hinge" connects: that is, what is it about the past that changes after the attacks. And to know that, we must be able to extrapolate from immediate trends before we know whether they will persist into the long-term future.

Some trends that appeared to be so important in the immediate aftermath of the attacks faded away within a few months. A significant example was the rise in church attendance.[9] For the last three decades of the twentieth century, the Gallup Poll had found that the percentage of Americans reporting that they attended a weekly religious service fluctuated regularly between 39 and 43 percent. In May 2001, the figure was 41 percent. In the ten days after September 11, it rose to 47 percent, but by early November it had dropped back to 42 percent. Anecdotal evidence from a sampling of churches of different faiths revealed the same trend: a significant increase for several weeks after the attacks followed by a return to "normal" attendance thereafter. Even many of the negative economic effects had been reversed within two months of the attacks. Business at service companies expanded in November, consumer spending rose a record 2.9 percent in October, construction grew unexpectedly, orders to factories for durable goods rose in October more than at any time in nine years, and sales of new houses were the highest in four months. As a senior economist at a New York bank puts it, "Nearly every economic indicator that was adversely affected by the terrorist attacks has recovered much more than the consensus had forecast."[10]

Nevertheless, we persist in our attempts to make sense of the attacks. Some experts in mental functioning have asserted that these efforts stemmed from the hardwiring of our brain. In other words, we looked for "the meaning" of 9-11 because, literally, we cannot avoid doing so.[11] We have evolved with not only the capacity to see patterns and connections in the events that surround us but the compulsion to do so as well. Such a compulsion evolved in our deeply ancestral brain, some experts believe, out of our need to see and comprehend the dangers present in a naturally hazardous world in enough time to be able to avoid them. So strong is this compulsion that we regularly "see" patterns where none exists. Psychologists who use the well-known Rorschach or "ink blot" tests to learn more about their patients' mental functioning are taking advantage of this need we have to project meaning onto otherwise random or meaningless stimuli.

One revealing example of our compulsion to find connections involves our tendency to misunderstand the risks we run of being killed in a terrorist attack as compared with the risks we run in everyday life. Michael Rothschild, an emeritus professor at the University of Wisconsin, has pointed out "the real odds" of suffering from terrorism.[12] According to Rothschild, in any given year the odds that one will die in an automobile accident are about one in 7,000; of dying from cancer, about one in 600; and of dying from heart disease, one in 400. Yet, he asserts, if terrorists totally destroy one shopping mall in the country each week, the odds of dying in one of those attacks for a person who shops at a mall two hours per week are one in 1.5 million. If a terrorist attack results in a crashed airplane once a month, the odds of dying in that attack for a person who travels by air once a month would be one in 540,000. Clearly, we have learned to live with the risks associated with automobile travel and unhealthy lifestyle choices, but terrorism has many of us paralyzed with irrational fears.

Another indicator is the attempt by sociologists and others to identify how the attacks had affected U.S. popular culture.[13] Observers scanned carefully each new film, CD, videogame, and television program for hints as to how 9-11 was going to be incorporated into mass culture. At first, as with church attendance, there were predictions that "nothing would ever be the same again" with pop culture. Comedy programs and cultural forms that relied on irony or sarcasm seemed to recede; earnestness and moderation surged forward. Several months after 9-11, however, cultural objects like films and recorded music seemed to have returned to their previous successful formats. Observers recalled that, after all, the culture business is first and foremost a business, and it responds to consumer preferences, not only in the United States but abroad as well. And, as a professor of media and culture at Syracuse University, Robert Thompson, puts it, "We may be surprised at how capable American popular culture is of dissolving even the most horrible of historical events."[14]

Not surprisingly, our efforts to make sense of 9-11 showed some subtle inconsistencies. Slightly more than three months after the attacks, on December 18 and 19, the *Washington Post–ABC News* poll asked a random selection of Americans to reflect on the impact of September 11 on their country and on themselves.[15] More than 90 percent of those polled believed that the events of September 11 had changed America "in a lasting way." About two-thirds said these changes were for the better, while one-quarter said they were for the worse. Yet only 55 percent said that their personal lives had been changed, and most of these (40 percent) said that the changes had been in "the way you feel about things" as opposed to "the way you live your day-to-day life." In other words, while nine out of ten believed that the country had changed fundamentally, only 15 percent said that the terrorist attacks had altered the way they lived.

In our efforts to understand 9-11, the Global System Paradigm (GSP) can help. First, the use of the systems approach imposes on us a certain discipline in how we think. We are led to organize what we know into the familiar categories of the causes and consequences of change. And this organization forces us to contemplate cause-and-effect relationships, both theoretically and empirically (that is, by direct observation and measurement). This last requirement draws us into a search for confirming evidence. The paradigm cautions us against accepting assertions of causation without the empirical (directly observed) evidence to support them. Clearly, it is easier to say this than to do it; but the systems approach shows us the way to pursue the trails of evidence to identify causes and consequences. Next, the GSP sensitizes us to (makes us aware of) invisible systems, so we can look for these elusive causal connections where others might not see them. As I have just pointed out, however, we must resist the natural human compulsion to find patterns where there is only randomness and a system where there is none. In particular, we must reject any explanation of the terrorist attacks that blames all Muslims for the acts of a very small group of them. Finally, the GSP shows us how to limit the size of the system in question. We know that "everything is connected to everything else," and 9-11 is an example of an event connected to *many* things. However, the paradigm tells us that we must limit our search to those aspects that are realistically pertinent to our inquiry.

SELECTED ECONOMIC CONSEQUENCES OF SEPTEMBER 11

The economic consequences of 9-11 are truly incalculable. About six weeks after the attacks, *Washington Post* writer Steven Pearlstein tried to assess their economic costs. He began with what "seems like a simple question: What is the economic cost of the terrorist attacks . . . ?"[16] He quickly discovered, however, that it was not going to be so easy. One conceptual problem is deciding where to stop counting the costs. How far should one reasonably trace the complex path of consequences? Separating the effects of the terrorist attacks from those of an economy that was already slowing down prior to September 11 is conceptually very difficult. And then there is the problem of the multiplier effect: every dollar lost to, say, the airline industry also represents money lost in tax revenues, income to the oil industry, jobs lost in airports, and on and on. Another challenge comes from the fact that a cost suffered by one sector, firm, or individual usually ends up also being a gain enjoyed by some other sector, firm, or individual. Money that would have been spent on a Caribbean cruise is now to be spent on a holiday closer to home. And finally, the consequences are not confined simply to the United States. Insurance firms in London and Zurich were hard hit by enormous claims; in September alone U.S. firms and individuals received $11 billion in insurance payments by foreign reinsurance companies. On the other hand, German pharmaceutical firms will reap profits from the sale of antibiotics to counter the anthrax scare.

It seems safe to say that nearly everyone reading this book was affected economically in many ways, both positively and negatively, and often via systems that remain invisible. Without question, however, the city of New York and its inhabitants suffered most grievously, as the following examples illustrate:

- New York City's comptroller's office estimated the cost to the city over the next three years at between $90 billion and $105 billion. These estimates include such costs as $42 billion for cleanup and security, $4 billion in lost rent and wages from jobs relocating out of the city, and $82 million in lost parking-violation fees because of street closures.[17] Six office towers totaling 13.5 million square feet were destroyed in the attack, but vacant office space in lower Manhattan still rose 49 percent between September 10 and early November as firms moved their offices to other New York sites or to New Jersey.[18]
- The physical damage done to the World Trade Center and its immediate surroundings inflicted economic costs beyond calculation. The retail stores alone in the Twin Towers constituted the fifth-largest shopping mall in the United States. The Borders Books store on the ground floor was the highest grossing store in the company's chain. Countless hundreds of shops, stores, and services businesses went out of business because of the loss of their chief customers: the financial services firms located in the towers. The single commuter subway from New Jersey into Lower Manhattan is now buried under thousands of tons of rubble, and transportation routes will take years to restore.[19] New York's Chinatown was probably the hardest hit neighborhood outside "ground zero" itself.[20] In particular, the garment industry, which normally employs some 10,000 Chinese immigrants (including many who have entered the country illegally), was practically shut down for weeks because of the disruption in the neighborhood's utilities, telephone service, mass transit, and truck delivery of raw materials.
- One group that was especially hard hit by the attacks was the people employed in low-wage service jobs in New York City. A study issued by the Fiscal Policy Institute forecast that by the end of the year, 80,000 people, the great majority of whom were in personal or routine services, would lose their

jobs. An analysis of the first 22,000 claims for unemployment assistance in New York after the attacks shows that 16 percent worked in bars and restaurants, 14 percent worked at hotels, and 5 percent worked in air transportation. The largest group, 21 percent, worked in business services, mostly temporary workers like clerks and secretaries.[21] Particularly hard hit were those supplying luxury services to New York's wealthy elite: waiters in leading restaurants, bellhops in five-star hotels, and limousine drivers.[22]

- The city's tourism industry, worth more than $17 billion in 2000, was devastated by the terrorist attacks.[23] In particular, international travel to New York was affected negatively by the general perception abroad that the entire city lay buried under tons of rubble. Hotel occupancy rates fell by 12 percent, room rates declined by 13 percent, and attendance at Broadway shows dropped 14 percent. Attendance at museums and zoos fell by similar percentages. Broadway theaters lost between $3 million and $5 million in the week after the attack. Gambling in Atlantic City, New Jersey, casinos dropped 6 percent in September. Several tens of thousands of workers in the tourism industry were laid off as a consequence of these effects. The city's 2,000 arts institutions are facing the gravest economic challenge in more than three decades.[24] New York's famous Guggenheim Museum, for example, was forced to cut its staff by 20 percent to help meet the crisis.

- On the other hand, some New Yorkers reaped economic benefits from the aftermath of 9-11, although in some cases the benefits were slow in coming. In the immediate wake of the attacks, sales in restaurants and bars dropped precipitously, but within weeks they had recovered and even soared beyond pre-attack levels. Sales at luxury restaurants stayed low, but sales at "casual dining" chains like Olive Garden or Red Lobster showed impressive gains. Sales of alcohol rose only slightly in the first week or two after the attacks, but within a month they were showing record gains nationwide but especially in New York. The city's bars were regularly showing gains of 10 percent or more each night as New Yorkers drowned their anxieties in alcohol. Some bars and retailer liquor stores were registering gains of 25 percent over pre-attack levels.[25]

- New York's neighbors also benefited from the devastation. Employment in New Jersey rose by 15,400 jobs in October, mostly in the financial, insurance, and real estate industries that were displaced by the destruction of the World Trade Center and the forced evacuation of adjoining buildings. New Jersey officials attributed these gains to the movement of firms out of Lower Manhattan. While some moved to other parts of the city, many relocated to nearby New Jersey cities. It is too early to say whether these moves will become more or less permanent, but in the near term certainly New York's losses were New Jersey's gains.[26]

Many other American communities were hit hard by 9-11. For example, my home state of Virginia was projected to lose an estimated $1.8 billion in the twelve months following the attacks.[27] Because Reagan National Airport, across the Potomac River from Washington, in Northern Virginia, was closed for several weeks, 18,700 people lost their jobs, and travel spending fell by $247 million, which in turn decreased state and local taxes by $22 million. In the Hampton Roads area of the state, wartime deployments from the region's military bases were projected to reduce consumption by some $338 million, leading to a loss of $15 million in sales taxes. In my home county, Fairfax, one of the richest in the nation, the unemployment rate and initial unemployment insurance claims both doubled in the month after 9-11.[28] On the other hand, post–September 11 spending by the federal government was predicted to pump more than $2 billion into the economy of the Washington metropolitan area. About one-half of this amount was to rebuild the damaged Pentagon, and much of the rest was to pay for increased security, emergency services costs, and so forth.[29]

The nation's economy suffered significantly as well, although here the consequences of 9-11 are especially difficult to see, given that the country was already headed for a recession even before the attacks. In the immediate aftermath of the attacks, the most serious effects were felt in the services sector nationwide.[30] From September to October, some 111,000 service sector jobs were lost, the largest one-month decline in this sector since the Bureau of Labor Statistics began recording trends in the nation's workforce. The airline industry alone laid off more than 100,000 workers between September 11 and early November.[31] Auto services, including car rental agencies, lost 13,000, mostly because of the decline in air travel. Another 81,000 jobs were lost in retail trade, which includes restaurants. Nationwide, but especially in cities dependent on tourism, immigrants were among the most affected. Overall, one worker in eight is an immigrant, but the ratio is one in five in the food service industry and one in four in the cleaning and janitorial services sector.[32]

On the other hand, service employment in detective, security guard, and armored-car companies increased by 8,000 in September and 22,000 in October.[33] Gun sales surged upward 30 percent in California, and a supplier of gas masks in Greenville, Texas, reported sales of 39,000 masks between September 11 and October 1, compared with 250 masks during the same period a year earlier. Take-home sales of foods like White Castle hamburgers rose more than 10 percent, and Penguin Classics printed more paperback translations of the Koran during the first month after the attacks than it sold in all of 2000 (about 20,000).[34] The federal government's newly created Department of Homeland Security asked corporate executives and trade associations to develop new technologies and systems to counter terrorism and prevent mass-destruction attacks and was promptly deluged with thousands of proposals.[35] One example of the private sector's response to 9-11 is from the companies that do background checks on prospective employees. Firms such as HireRight (Irvine, California), Backgroundcheck.com (Irving, Texas), and SureStaffPersonnel (Dallas, Texas) were reporting huge increases in the demand for their services and equally large increases in their revenues.[36] Inventors and entrepreneurs around the world saw 9-11 as a chance to get rich quick with products designed to soothe a nervous world: parachutes for people who live or work in tall buildings, home-use anthrax-testing kits, and bras without metal wires or clasps for women who travel frequently by airplane and wish to avoid setting off airport metal detectors.[37]

The economic consequences of the attacks quickly rippled around the world, showing how tightly the global economy is tied to the U.S. market, U.S.-made products, and American consumers.[38] Global tourism was badly affected by the fears people had about travel. Tourism is the largest source of revenue for Egypt's government and accounts for 10 percent of the country's gross domestic product. Yet tourist activity declined 40–45 percent in October 2001, affecting hotels, restaurants, and local transportation.[39] In Italy, where tourism generates 8 percent of GDP, tourist arrivals dropped 70 percent in the six weeks after the attacks.[40] At the Hyatt resort in Bali, 80 percent of its November reservations were canceled; and the P&O Princess Cruise line in Britain lost 8,000 bookings in the two weeks following 9-11.[41] A decline in tourism meant a decline in air travel, which caused the airlines to cut back on purchases of new airplanes, which reduced the demand for jet engines. This last effect hit the Rolls-Royce Company particularly hard because of its dependence on sales to the commercial airlines. Within six weeks of September 11, Rolls-Royce announced a cut of 11 percent in its worldwide labor force, which meant a loss of 2,000 jobs in the British city of Derby, with serious adverse consequences for the local economy.[42] Shortly after the U.S. bombing campaign began in Afghanistan, leaders of the Muslim community in India called on their faithful (there are some 120 million Muslims in India) to boycott American-made products such as soft drinks and cigarettes. Hundreds of small stores across the country that catered to Muslim tastes felt the impact immediately as sales of Coca-Cola and Pepsi-Cola plummeted. Fortunately for these storeowners, sales picked up again after the Taliban regime fell and Indian Muslims saw television news reports of their co-religionists in Afghanistan celebrating the return of a more open society.[43]

There was a sharp drop in the number of foreigners coming to the United States following 9-11, and this decline was seen in virtually every category of visitor.[44] There was a drop of 11 percent in visas issued to foreign tourists, business travelers, and students between September 11 and October 25 compared with the same period the previous year. The number of illegal immigrants apprehended along the U.S. border with Mexico declined by one-half in October compared with the number caught in 2000, the sharpest decline ever registered by the Immigration and Naturalization Service. The number of refugees from all parts of the world who desire to go to the United States was reduced by at least 10,000 as they faced increasingly stringent security review of their petitions.

One especially important consequence involved the textile industry in Pakistan.[45] The nation's textile and apparel industry employs some 3.5 million people, an overwhelming 60 percent of Pakistan's industrial workforce. In the weeks immediately following the terrorist attacks, retailers such as American

Eagle Outfitters and Tommy Hilfiger, which normally bought tens of millions of dollars of Pakistan-made textiles had cut their purchases to virtually zero. The firms cited the instability of supply as one factor, as well as concern for the safety of their employees and representatives in Pakistan. Within days, 40 percent of Pakistani sales of textiles evaporated (a number that rose to more than 60 percent within two months), and 18,000 textile workers were laid off. Because the United States needed Pakistani support for its war in Afghanistan, Pakistan immediately began to pressure the United States to relax or even eliminate tariffs on textiles from Pakistan, a move that was vigorously opposed by American textile firms. In the eighteen months prior to September 11, the U.S. textile industry had lost 90,000 jobs to foreign suppliers.

Another point of conflict between domestic American interests and foreign policy goals involved the sale of wheat for Afghanistan relief.[46] The U.S. Agency for International Development wanted to use about $50 million of the $320 million in Afghan humanitarian aid funds promised by President Bush to buy wheat in Kazakhstan and Pakistan. Such sales would benefit important economic interests in countries that supported U.S. war efforts in Afghanistan, and in addition the wheat was already close to where it would be needed. The U.S. Office of Management and Budget, however, had held up expenditure of these funds on the grounds that ample supplies of U.S.-grown wheat were available to meet this need and that aid funds should be used first and foremost to purchase U.S. commodities when possible. Trade associations and lobbying organizations representing U.S. wheat farmers criticized the plan to use foreign wheat when U.S. wheat was already available in ample supplies and in nearby stockpiles.

The international trade in commodities like coffee, cocoa, sugar, and cotton was disrupted for several days because the offices of the New York Board of Trade were destroyed by the collapse of the World Trade Center.[47] The trading floor of the New York Coffee Exchange, for example, was located at 4 World Trade Center, a nine-story building at the foot of the Twin Towers. Even though the building was evacuated and there was no loss of life, the trading center was buried under hundreds of tons of debris. Fortunately, the Board of Trade had established a duplicate trading floor in Long Island City following the 1993 bombing of the World Trade Center, and trading opened there only four days after the 9-11 attacks. The cost of keeping that backup system equipped and ready to be occupied, with duplicate files and computer systems, was about $300,000 per year. But the costs of losing the role of brokering the world's coffee sales to competing exchanges like the London Coffee Exchange would have been beyond calculation.

Of course, some sectors of the global economy benefited greatly from the attacks, although their leaders were hesitant to reveal the true dimensions of their gains because they might appear to be opportunistically gaining from other people's tragedy. In New York City, within hours after the towers collapsed, wholesalers had designed souvenirs of the tragedy, such as brooches with images of the Twin Towers or pins with American flags, and had faxed the designs to their suppliers in Korea or China.[48] The manufacturers in Asia retooled their factories and within days were producing these and other souvenirs for the New York market. Although such products are usually shipped via cargo container ship, the huge demand forced the wholesalers to use air freight as soon as the nation's airports opened for business after 9-11. Thus, within a week after the disaster shops and vendors around the city were selling flags, pins, stickers, caps, and other such products to consumers hungry for any sort of symbol of the city's resilience and courage. Especially popular were hats and T-shirts praising the courage and heroism of New York's police and firefighters.

Finally, we must not forget the direct costs of conducting the war in Afghanistan. Very early estimates put the costs at about $1 billion per month, but this level is almost surely too low. Just to deploy 50,000 U.S. troops, three carrier battle groups, and more than 400 aircraft to the region cost $634 million. In the first month and a half of the war, U.S. forces dropped more than 8,000 bombs and missiles on Afghanistan targets. Some of the unguided or "dumb" bombs cost a mere $2,500 apiece, but the precision bombs guided by Global Positioning System satellite technologies cost $25,000 each, and cruise missiles can cost between $1 million and $2 million each. A B-2 "stealth" bomber costs about $13,700 per hour to operate, and some of their sorties that originated in the United States lasted thirty-four hours.[49] One group seriously affected in a very visible way was the 55,000 (at this writing) people called to active duty in their military reserve units (out of 1.8 million reservists). Most of them had to report for active duty literally in a matter of a few days, leaving behind their jobs, families, and financial responsibilities.[50]

A complete and precise count of the lives affected by September 11 would be impossible, as would a precise inventory of the economic costs. But we can be sure that eventually perhaps as many as three-fourths of the world's population will feel the effects in one way or another.

NOTES

1. "Searching the Web, Searching the Mind," *New York Times,* December 23, 2001.

2. John Schwartz, "Numbers Games: Go Figure," *New York Times,* November 11, 2001.

3. John Tierney, "Myth or Not, This Bud's for America," *New York Times,* December 18, 2001. Shankar Vedantam, "Legends of the Fall: Sept. 11 Myths Abound," *Washington Post,* January 4, 2002.

4. These revisions were themselves extremely controversial. Many who had lost loved ones in the attacks complained that the downward revisions threatened to diminish the seriousness of the attacks, while others said it was inappropriate even to be concerned with the exact figures. In the longer term, they said, no one will really care what the precise number is. The toll, as New York Mayor Rudy Guliani has put it, was "unbearable," no matter what the exact numbers turn out to be. George Johnson, "Order of Magnitude: The Toll and the Technology," *New York Times,* September 16, 2001. Eric Lipton, "A New

Count of the Dead, but Little Sense of Relief," *New York Times*, December 2, 2001. Peter Freundlich, "What Counts: The Death Toll Is Far Less Than Feared. Can We Accept That?" *Washington Post*, December 16, 2001.

5. Eric Lipton, "Toll from Attack at Trade Center Is Down Sharply," *New York Times*, November 21, 2001. [Associated Press], "N.Y. Disaster Toll Revised to 3,646," *Washington Post*, November 25, 2001. Michael Powell, "Death Tally Falling as City Sifts Reports and Remains," *Washington Post*, December 15, 2001. "Trade Center Count of Missing and Dead Falls below 3,000," *New York Times*, December 20, 2001.

6. Charlie LeDuff, "For Some, Lives in the Shadows Ended in Attack, Indiscernibly," *New York Times*, December 30, 2001.

7. Bill Broadway, "Number of U.S. Muslims Depends on Who's Counting," *Washington Post*, November 24, 2001.

8. Joel Garreau, "Hinges of Opportunity," *Washington Post*, October 14, 2001.

9. Laurie Goodstein, "As Attacks' Impact Recedes, a Return to Religion as Usual," *New York Times*, November 26, 2001.

10. Quoted in "Slump in the Service Sector Was Reversed in November," *New York Times*, December 6, 2001.

11. Rick Weiss, "You Can't Help It: Our Impulse to Connect the Dots Is Pre-Wired," *Washington Post*, November 25, 2001.

12. Michael L. Rothschild, "Terrorism and You—The Real Odds," *Washington Post*, November 25, 2001.

13. Teresa Wiltz, "Playing in the Shadows," *Washington Post*, November 19, 2001.

14. Quoted in Wiltz, "Playing in the Shadows."

15. Richard Morin and Claudia Deane, "Sept. 11 Changes Were for Better, Poll Majority Says," *Washington Post*, January 1, 2002.

16. Steven Pearlstein, "Confusing Contrasts in the Financial Picture: Attacks' Toll Elusive as Money Shifts from Sector to Sector," *Washington Post*, October 28, 2001.

17. Jayson Blair, "In the Aftermath of Terror, Grab a Calculator and Tally Forth," *New York Times*, November 11, 2001.

18. Charles V. Bagli, "Since Sept. 11, Vacant Offices and Lost Vigor," *New York Times*, November 19, 2001.

19. Michael Powell, "N.Y. Financial Core Wobbles from Attacks' Economic Hit," *Washington Post*, November 26, 2001.

20. Jennifer 8. Lee, "Manhattan's Chinatown Reeling from the Effects of Sept. 11," *New York Times*, November 21, 2001.

21. Leslie Eaton and Edward Wyatt, "Attacks Hit Low-Pay Jobs the Hardest," *New York Times*, November 6, 2001.

22. Steven Greenhouse, "Also Hurt by Sept. 11: A Legion Still Working but Making Much Less," *New York Times*, November 29, 2001.

23. Jayson Blair, "Attacks Called Costly to City Tourism Industry," *New York Times*, December 8, 2001.

24. Robin Pogrebin, "New York Arts Groups Reeling in Wake of Attack," *New York Times*, November 18, 2001.

25. Michelle Leder, "Some Restaurants Thrive in Slowdown," *New York Times*, November 18, 2001. Marian Burros, "In a Stressed City, No Room at the Bar," *New York Times*, December 5, 2001.

26. Iver Peterson, "Wall St. Jobs Are Migrating to New Jersey," *New York Times*, November 17, 2001.

27. Craig Timberg and Katherine Shaver, "$1.8 Billion Va. Loss Estimated from Sept. 11," *Washington Post,* November 3, 2001.

28. Kenneth Bredemeier, "Insulated, but Not Immune," *Washington Post,* November 26, 2001.

29. Spencer S. Hsu, "Terrorism Spending Vitalizes D.C. Area," *Washington Post,* December 2, 2001.

30. Mary Williams Walsh, "A Mainstay of U.S. Job Creation Is Hit Hard by Sept. 11," *New York Times,* November 3, 2001.

31. Blair, "In the Aftermath of Terror, Grab a Calculator and Tally Forth."

32. Mary Beth Sheridan, "Wall Street to Washington, Layoffs Shatter Lives: D.C. Tourism Losses Hit Immigrants Hard," *Washington Post,* October 31, 2001.

33. Walsh, "A Mainstay of U.S. Job Creation Is Hit Hard by Sept. 11."

34. Blair, "In the Aftermath of Terror, Grab a Calculator and Tally Forth."

35. Alison Mitchell, "Security Quest Also Offers Opportunities," *New York Times,* November 25, 2001.

36. Kirstin Downey Grimsley, "Security Concerns Enrich Background-Checking Companies," *Washington Post,* November 24, 2001.

37. Mike Musgrove, "Fear, Mother of Invention," *Washington Post,* October 25, 2001.

38. Joseph Kahn, "The World's Economies Slide Together into Recession," *New York Times,* November 25, 2001. Steven Pearlstein, "Slump Stirs Specter of Worldwide Recession," *Washington Post,* November 4, 2001.

39. Abeer Allam, "Egypt Puts Up Vacancy Signs," *New York Times,* November 28, 2001.

40. "Tourism Industry Seeks Aid in Italy," *New York Times,* November 3, 2001.

41. Alan Cowell, "P&O and Royal Caribbean to Merge into Largest Cruise Line," *New York Times,* November 21, 2001.

42. Alan Cowell, "Caught in Terror's Undertow: Reeling British City Loses More Rolls-Royce Jobs," *New York Times,* October 31, 2001.

43. Saritha Rai, "Long Reach of War in Afghanistan," *New York Times,* January 4, 2002.

44. Mary Beth Sheridan, "International Visitors Staying Away," *Washington Post,* November 20, 2001.

45. Leslie Kaufman, "Companies Cut Textile Orders from Pakistan," *New York Times,* October 31, 2001. Leslie Kaufman, "Pakistanis Urge U.S. to Suspend Textile Tariffs," *New York Times,* November 8, 2001.

46. Dan Morgan, "Source of Wheat for Relief Sparks Debate," *Washington Post,* October 28, 2001.

47. Anthony DePalma, "For Coffee Traders, Disaster Comes in Pairs," *New York Times,* October 28, 2001.

48. Lynette Holloway, "The Rush to Market Souvenirs," *New York Times,* December 8, 2001.

49. James Dao, "The Costs of Enduring Freedom," *New York Times,* November 18, 2001.

50. Christian Davenport, "Reservists' Duty Squeezes Budgets on the Home Front," *Washington Post,* November 13, 2001.

6

Invisible Systems

KEY IDEAS IN THIS CHAPTER

Invisible systems are not "invisible" in the physical sense of that word. Rather, they are invisible because we are not aware of their existence. Thus, we refer to them as **knowledge dependent.**
Systems are invisible because of the following:

- They are **complex** and **nonlinear.**
- Their principal functions involve **information processing.**
- They are **distributed systems** that exemplify the "small world" phenomenon.
- Systems operators **try to hide** them from view.

Invisible systems have a number of consequences, including the following:

- They are difficult for **governments to control.**
- They have **high external costs.**
- They experience **"normal accidents."**
- They are **unaccountable** to citizens and consumers.

There are now a number of organizations whose mission is to **track and monitor** invisible systems in order to make them more accountable to citizens and consumers.

In the weeks following the terrorist attacks of September 11, 2001, a new paradigm of warfare attracted increasing public attention.[1] The paradigm, called "netwar" by its authors, RAND Corporation analysts David Ronfeldt and John Arquilla, had been around since the early 1990s, but the attacks of 9-11 changed dramatically the public context for thinking about such matters. Private citizens and war planners alike suddenly realized that the United States was confronted with a new kind of military challenge for which new weapons and tactics, new concepts, and even a new vocabulary would have to be developed.

The central premise of "netwar" is that groups of people organized as social or organizational networks are capable of launching violent and bloody attacks against the social orders of highly industrialized states. In this usage, social networks are groups of people bound together and coordinated by highly dispersed communications systems in which there is no single, central control point. The technologies of the global information system—telecommunications and the Internet—are joined to a spiderweb of social connections to form a large system consisting of many disparate nodes without a center. Individual nodes or cells of the network may be (and usually are) unaware of each other's existence, but that does not diminish their effectiveness. Indeed, such disconnectedness may actually strengthen the organization in the face of attack.

Actions of the component members of such a network are coordinated by the social relations between and among them (referred to as "social capital") rather than by the command and authority relationships typical of more traditional hierarchical organizations. Organization networks take the paradigm one step beyond social networks by instilling in the network members a sense of common purpose or objective. Such networks resemble complex adaptive systems in that they are much more than the sum of their individual members. What matters are not the component members but the ways they are connected to each other, their network of relationships. As the war against terrorism wore on, it became clear that highly developed states like the United States would have to abandon the traditional paradigm of conventional large-scale land warfare if they were to defeat the "netwar" of Osama bin Laden. In the vocabulary of the new paradigm, "It takes a network to defeat a network."

WHAT ARE INVISIBLE SYSTEMS?

One reason why "netwar" fighters are so resilient is that the systems they inhabit are invisible. Not all global systems are invisible. Many global organizations operate in ways that make them highly visible to outsiders (for example, through organizational charts, accounting procedures, warehouse inventories, and so forth). As important as these visible organizations are, they are only the tip of the iceberg of globalization. My concern here is with the invisible part of the global system, the networks for moving matter, energy, and information that are invisible and unknown to most observers and even to many of the workers whose labor enables them to function. Although the consequences of global systems are highly visible, the systems themselves remain generally undetected or "invisible." This chapter describes the invisibility of many critical global systems, identifies the principal reasons for their invisibility, and assays some of the costs and consequences of their invisibility. I conclude by describing some of the organizations whose job is to identify, monitor, and track invisible global systems and thereby render them more "visible" to consumers, voters, and potential victims.

An "invisible" global system is "knowledge dependent," meaning that an outside observer cannot detect such a system without possessing special knowledge that is not available to the general public (or, indeed, perhaps to anyone). In summer 1999, New York City was invaded by a mysterious illness that for some months could not be identified. Its symptoms included high fever, vomiting and nausea, muscle weakness, and disorientation. At least seventy-seven people became sick from this disease, and at least eleven died. The disease also caused the death of horses, small mammals, and numerous species of birds (especially crows). At first it was believed that the disease was a variant of St. Louis encephalitis, which was remarkable because that disease had never been seen as far north as New York. As more evidence trickled in, however, health officials changed their diagnosis. The cause of the epidemic was even more surprising: West Nile virus, never before seen in the Western Hemisphere. Now, to determine the exact extent of the epidemic, health department workers had to reanalyze blood samples taken from a number of patients who had tested negative for St. Louis. As a spokeswoman for the New York State Department of Health put it then, "Now we know what to look for. We were looking for St. Louis encephalitis, and we weren't finding it. If we know exactly what we are looking for, it's going to be easier to find it."[2] This is what we mean by knowledge dependent.

All global systems contain component parts that are, by themselves, visible in the physical sense of that word. (Of course, there are also many important systems in which some components *are* invisible to the naked eye, such as disease systems in which microbes play the dominant role.) What remain unseen are two things: first, that a given object is a component part of a much larger and more complex assembly of parts that connect to produce a system and, second, the nature of the connections between and among the component parts. To perceive and appreciate these things, one must know that such a system exists, as well as what to look for and where to find it. Such knowledge is not distributed equally across society. One of the merits of the Global System Paradigm is that it alerts observers to the importance of invisible systems by equipping them with "ecolacy," the mastery of connections.[3] This perspective is not innate. It must be acquired.

Language shapes our view of the world around us, including the systems whose transactions are constantly streaming past us. Many such systems are rendered invisible because we lack the language to describe them or to label their component parts. We cannot "see" something that we cannot describe. To make a system visible frequently requires a new narrative or story, with a new vocabulary, that will help us focus our attention on system processes rather than institutional structures. Sometimes words are not enough; we need road signs and maps as well. As the British cybergeographer Martin Dodge puts it, "We need maps not just to navigate but to define and control new territory. Simply having a map allows a new perspective, a new way to orient yourself. Relationships otherwise obscure may be revealed."[4]

In his book *Risk Society,* the German sociologist Ulrich Beck has drawn our attention to the rise in knowledge-dependent problems in postmodern society.[5] While many features of our material world, such as physical possessions, income, and education, can be directly experienced and enjoyed by individuals, many of the risks and hazards of a complex society are, in Beck's words, "mediated on principle through argument."[6] By this he means that many of the features of our world that threaten us completely escape human powers of direct perception. Many of these hazards, such as contaminated food, require the "sensory organs of science" in order to become visible and, thus, to be seen as dangerous. But even science fails us time and again, for opinions within the scientific community frequently are at odds over the true nature of a hazard or a risk, so "the social effect of risk definitions is . . . not dependent on their scientific validity."[7]

Globalization has affected not only culture and commerce but the risks of industrial society as well. As Beck explains, the risks of modernization

> possess an inherent tendency towards globalization. A universalization of hazards accompanies industrial production, independent of the place where they are produced: food chains connect practically everyone on earth to everyone else. . . . The acid content of the air . . . long ago brought about the disintegration of modern customs barriers.[8]

But this very same process of globalization has helped render these processes invisible; as Beck puts it, "Where everything turns into a hazard, somehow nothing is dangerous anymore. Where there is no escape, people ultimately no longer want to think about it."[9]

Perceptions of hazardous or threatening systems depend largely on access to information and education, and such access tends to be distributed unevenly across society, being concentrated disproportionately among well-to-do people. According to Beck, "Risk-consciousness and activism are more likely to occur where the direct pressure to make a living has been relaxed or broken, that is, among the wealthier and more protected groups (and countries)."[10] In an older industrial society, one's material status (such as mode of employment, income, and so forth) determined one's consciousness or class awareness. But in postindustrial society, knowledge or awareness of threat or hazard determines one's notion of solidarity (in other words, with whom do I share my particular affliction?).

The impact of invisible global systems also depends to some degree on the timescale by which we measure such impact. In the immediate term, the better off among us (both individuals and national societies) can detect and anticipate adverse consequences and take appropriate actions to protect or compensate themselves. Because wealth usually translates into education and access to information, the wealthier one is, the more likely he or she is to be aware of knowledge-dependent systems and conditions. Thus, the near-term effect of invisible global systems is to magnify, increase, and harden class divisions, particularly insofar as these divisions are defined by wealth and education. These protections are not absolute or permanent, however, for eventually we must all acknowledge that we are connected to each other through physical, social, and economic ties. In the long term, then, the adverse impact of global hazards will be felt across social classes and across national boundaries.

WHY ARE GLOBAL SYSTEMS INVISIBLE?

Some of the reasons why global systems are invisible, such as complexity and nonlinearity, are inherent in all large systems. Some causes are the inescapable consequences of the design of large systems to perform services that involve information transmission, as is the case with most global systems today. Other causes are the product of the so-called small world phenomenon, in which large and complex systems can be operated and maintained without central direction and coordination or even awareness of system performance. And finally, many global systems are deliberately kept invisible by their operators and managers because they do not want outside observers to be aware of them.

Complexity and Nonlinearity

Global systems are by definition extremely large, encompassing huge numbers of persons and technologies. They are also exceedingly complex. Here, *complexity* is defined as a function of

- the *scope* or *range* of the system (in other words, the distance between the origin and the destination of a product or a waste substance),
- the *number of different kinds of component parts* in the system,
- the *speed* with which the transactions between the parts occur (many now take place in virtually real time), and
- the *degree of interconnectedness* of the components (in other words, the degree to which they are interdependent).[11]

One measure of system complexity is the degree of nonlinearity of the relationships between and among its component parts. It is said that in a complex system, everything is connected to everything else, and this is surely one of the leading attributes or properties of nonlinearity. Global systems are virtually always nonlinear, a property that makes them difficult to detect. The science of complex adaptive systems has demonstrated that nonlinearity is an important property of systems at all levels: from the particles that form the building blocks of matter to the cells that constitute living organisms, the neurons and other parts of the brain that give consciousness to human beings, and the behavior patterns and institutions that make up social systems.[12]

At the most basic level, linearity and nonlinearity refer to a mathematical property of a system. A linear system is one in which the value of the whole is obtained by summing the values of its parts.[13] It is so much easier and simpler to work with systems that exhibit this property that we tend to assume linearity, often an unwarranted assumption. In contrast, nonlinearity means that the value of the whole system emerges from the interaction of the parts rather than from their simple addition. One of the simplest forms of nonlinearity occurs when the value of the whole entails the product of the parts rather than their sum. That is, the system is multiplicative rather than additive. Many such systems contain feedback loops that are unintended and unexpected and are, therefore, unseen (at least until they produce unfortunate consequences). For both mathematical and physical systems, in John Holland's words, "nonlinear interactions almost always make the behavior of the aggregate more complicated than would be predicted by summing or averaging."[14]

Another form of nonlinearity involves the passage of time. A system that changes with time will exhibit nonlinear changes that cannot be described by simply adding the values of the parts at a given moment in the history of the system. One of the chief differences between linear and nonlinear systems has to do with the extreme sensitivity of the latter to the past. Linear systems change little over time, but nonlinear systems are very sensitive to their states at various times. Nonlinear systems have a historical dimension that linear systems lack.[15] Complexity theorists refer to this property as "sensitive dependence on initial conditions," by which they mean that a complex nonlinear system will exhibit great differences in output with very minor differences in input. These differences may be so small as to be invisible to human observers. It is virtually impossible to observe a complex system in repeated trials beginning from exactly the same initial conditions. The variance in initial conditions may be too small for human observers to detect, but even these extremely tiny differences will—with the working of nonlinearity and positive feedback loops—eventually produce great differences in system output or outcome.[16]

In a complex nonlinear system, the component parts (as actors) may frequently engage in actions and responses that seem rational, understandable, and visible from their perspective; but when accumulated via positive feedback mechanisms, these actions at the system level yield patterns of behavior that seem random, counterrational, and unpredictable. Thus, the cognitive link between cause and consequence is broken, and the connection becomes unintelligible and invisible. For example, Bernardo Huberman at Xerox Corporation's Palo Alto Research Center in California has discovered that the Internet displays properties of living ecosystems, a phenomenon he refers to as "Internet ecologies."[17] Because the Internet is a quasi-public good whose users are not charged in proportion to their use, individuals may be greedy in their use while thinking that their actions do not affect others. The reality is, however, that the Internet may become congested, and its performance considerably degraded, as more and more individuals seek to use it.[18]

Another important dimension of complex nonlinear systems involves "emergent properties," the attributes of a system that cannot be inferred from a knowledge of the system's component parts. (See the earlier discussion of emergent properties in chapters 3–4.) These are system properties that can be understood only if we possess a paradigm that helps us know how a system behaves when the parts are interconnected.

Information Processing

Global systems are largely processes rather than things. What matter in these systems are not so much the component parts themselves but the relationships or transactions between and among them. Although the parts that make up the system can usually be seen, the transactions that connect them are invisible. The reason for this is that a growing proportion of the value of a product consists of the information necessary to produce and distribute it.

For some years now, analysts have been telling us that information constitutes a growing proportion of the value added to a product or service by a firm or a government agency.[19] Increasingly, what firms do to add value to a product comes under the heading of information. Indeed, the distinction between "goods" and "services" is rapidly disappearing because the production of even the heaviest and bulkiest of manufactured goods, such as automobiles or jet aircraft, involves large inputs of information-related technologies, such as microprocessors, and services, such as design, marketing, research, product testing, and coordination. Information-based technologies and services become even more critical to the success of a product as the "assembly line" that produces and distributes goods becomes increasingly global in scope.

Because global systems involve high volumes of information flow, much of the labor involved in managing, operating, and maintaining such systems constitutes what Shoshana Zuboff calls "invisible work," that is, work that goes on inside the head of the worker.[20] In an earlier industrial era, the operation of an assembly line or of heavy equipment required physical labor, movement, and, not infrequently, fatigue and exposure to hazardous conditions. In a world of information-based control and coordination systems, the management of complex systems frequently requires sitting passively in a control room watching computer displays and other remote indicators of system performance. Zuboff's concern with these changes has to do with the issues of personnel management under conditions in which most of the work goes on in the head of the worker and thus becomes much more difficult to evaluate and reward appropriately. But the phenomenon of "invisible work" also contributes to the invisibility of the global systems within which such work occurs.

Another way in which information processing contributes to a system's invisibility has to do with the feedback loops to which the system is subject. As the economist Brian Arthur explains,[21] sectors of the economy engaged in mineral extraction or bulk goods manufacture may still be subject to negative feedback loops, which economists call diminishing returns. Such systems tend to be stable, or to change very slowly, because their feedback mechanisms dampen down the forces of change. The sectors of the economy that are knowledge based, however, such as computers, telecommunications, pharmaceuticals, or aerospace equipment, are largely subject to increasing returns or positive feedback loops. Firms that enter a field early have a decided advantage over latecomers, as the dynamic of extended production favors the firms that have the most experience doing it. Thus, the more global and more information-based a firm becomes, the more it is subject to positive feedback loops, making its behavior more unstable, more nonlinear, and less predictable. Systems of this sort are more difficult to track than older industrial firms. Where and what they are at time T tell us little about where and what they will be at time $T + 1$. Systems that change rapidly and unexpectedly are less visible to the outside observer.

The "Small World Phenomenon"

One important dimension of networks is their degree of centralization. *Centralized networks* are those in which all transactions are channeled through a single central switching point. With *decentralized networks,* more switching points are added so that "regions" form within the network. Transactions are processed through regional switching points, and those switching points interact with each other. The ultimate level of decentralization is that exhibited by *distributed networks*. Here, each node is connected to only two or three neighbors, an arrangement that provides for flexibility and redundancy in the larger network.

The Internet was designed intentionally to be a distributed network (see appendix 2),[22] but many global systems possess such a property without having been designed that way intentionally. Global systems tend to be distributed because only such a network can accommodate the operational requirements for coverage, complexity, speed, volume, flexibility, responsiveness, and so forth. Distributed systems like the Internet are likely to be invisible because the route followed by any given transaction is selected virtually in real time—that is, as the transaction is "in transit." No single route is centrally designed, directed, or coordinated. Instead, the network "selects" its own transaction channels by applying a set of rules (called a "protocol" in the Internet) at the moment a transaction requires processing. Not only is no one "in charge" of such a network; no one can even describe what the network is doing from one moment to the next.

We are accustomed to thinking that complex systems require a considerable degree of central coordination provided by hierarchical structures of command and control. More frequently than not, however, global systems of the kind we are examining here have no central coordination. In other words, no one is "in charge."[23] Rather, these systems are examples of the "small world phenomenon" discovered more than thirty years ago by psychologists and communication theorists, including Stanley Milgram and Ithiel de Sola Pool.[24]

Connections between and among people are not distributed randomly but, instead, form patterns of networks such that people within a network are more likely to know and interact with each other than they are to know and interact with people outside the network. The probability that people are connected is a function of several of their characteristics, including social class, economic status, culture (including a common language), behavioral attributes, and the intermediate technologies available to them. The number of intermediaries needed to connect any two randomly selected persons in a large population (for example, that of the United States) is referred to as *degrees of separation*. Milgram's research has demonstrated that in the United States only six degrees of separation exist between any two randomly identified individuals. That is, any two individuals will be connected by, at most, six persons. "Small world" researchers begin with the assumption that each person knows about 300 other people. If so, then the 3,000 or so killed in the World Trade Center attacks could have had as many as 900,000 acquaintances; by extending the reach of this "small world" one more degree of separation we would have described a network that potentially covers the entire American population. Indeed, a survey conducted by the Pew Research Center for the People and the Press has found that 29 percent of all U.S. college graduates had a connection with one of the World Trade Center victims.[25]

However, the kind of system we are considering here is anything but random, for it exists to accomplish a specific mission within the global economy or culture; so one would expect participants in these systems to be connected by even fewer degrees of separation than six. What is true for both random and nonrandom systems is the fact that their members do not need to be aware of each other's existence for the network of connections to function. Typically, any given individual in the chain of transactions will be aware of only the individuals immediately before and after them in the stream, and even these they may not know personally. Because global systems cover so much distance, both socially and physically, the chances are small that the members of a system will know others more than one degree of separation on either side of them. This fact need not (and, indeed, does not) degrade the efficiency with which the system manages its transactions, so long as all system members know what their roles are in the network and carry them out to a minimally satisfactory degree.

Recent research by mathematicians and social scientists now suggests that "big worlds" (that is, relatively uncoordinated populations) can be transformed into "small worlds" (efficiently functioning systems) simply by adding at random several long-distance connections.[26] Such extra connections supply "short cuts" that increase radically the number of individuals with which any one member can interact and, consequently, the speed with which transactions flow throughout the system.

Global systems are not single systems but, rather, dozens (or, in some cases, hundreds) of smaller pieces, or subsystems, each piece oblivious to the larger megasystem more than one or two pieces, or steps, away from itself. The consequence is that global systems consist of interconnected parts not generally known to people in them. A recurring theme in the literature of postindustrialism is the depersonalization of work. People who work in massive complex global systems lose an awareness of how their labor is connected to the labor of others or to the product of the larger system. They come to feel as if they are part of a "pipeline" through which products, energy, and information flow. Perhaps they will see and touch the product as it passes through their hands, but often they will not. The advent of the cargo container, for example, has broken the visual connection between freight workers and the commodities they are moving. Workers know and care about only the node in the system immediately before them, the one immediately after, and what they are to do to move the container from the former to the latter. Whatever else such a development may do to the nature of work, it has certainly made the system invisible, even to those who work within it.

As if all this disjointed system behavior were not enough, many global systems do not even exist as formal organizations with structures, roles, and so forth. Rather, they are collections of component parts bound together by tenuous role expectations and informally understood responsibilities and relationships. Many such systems are not even organizations at all but simply the chaotic (in the sense of chaos theory or the theory of complex adaptive systems) movement of persons and objects through time and space (epidemics, refugee flows, etc.). Such "systems" behave in an unpredictable manner even though we may know quite a bit about the behavior of the individual component parts. For example, we may know quite a bit about how the HIV virus behaves inside the human body; but we are constantly being surprised by the AIDS pandemic as the complex manifestation of the disease at the level of the social system.

Intent to Hide

The operators of many global systems try to keep them hidden from our view. In some cases, a system on which we depend may offend our sensibilities or our sense of aesthetics. Many critical systems are ugly or hazardous, smelly or noisy; so we wish to keep them at arm's length. We spend hundreds of millions of dollars constructing sound barriers on interstate highways passing through suburban areas to avoid angering people who live near the routes. Shopping malls in suburban areas depend almost entirely on large trucks to deliver the consumer goods sold in their shops and stores; but trucks are dangerous and noisy, so the malls are built so that the loading docks are underground or otherwise hidden from the view of the shoppers. Once the trucks take to the open highway, however, they cannot be ignored, and motorists are quick to complain about them and seek to have them regulated or even removed from the interstate system altogether. Virtually the entire eastern seaboard of the United States is dependent on gasoline, diesel fuel, and aviation fuel carried through an enormous network of pipelines that originates near the petroleum refineries between Houston and Beaumont, Texas, and ends near the port of New York. For most of that distance, the pipeline is buried in the ground, and people living directly over it are completely oblivious to its existence—until it ruptures and begins to leak its messy cargo through the ground near expensive suburban homes.

The systems on which we depend may be quite far away from the customers or clients, but the operators do not wish us to know this. They believe that we will feel better about using their services if we believe that the person on the other end of the Internet connection or the telephone is only a few miles away instead of halfway around the world. So they disguise their true locations. One example of such a disguise is found in call centers, which have spread throughout the developing world to handle toll-free telephone calls from the United States. Global corporations like General Electric have established huge telephone banks in a number of cities in India, such as Bangalore. The telephone operators study U.S. television programs to master the nuances of American English pronunciation and slang. They invent false names, families, and lifestyles so they can pass for Americans "just next door" to the caller. Because of its low-wage labor and the English skills of its workers, India is on its way to becoming the back office of the world.[27]

We would like to believe that globalization brings us mostly good things, but the unfortunate fact is that the global system has a dark side as well.[28] Many global systems involve the production and transport of products that are illegal (firearms, narcotics, stolen cars), hazardous or toxic (water pollutants, foodborne microbes), or manufactured by prison or child labor (clothing, shoes, toys). Numerous illegal activities rely on hidden global systems for their successful operation (telephone scams, child pornography, immigrant smuggling, tax evasion, illegal money laundering). Some of these "dark side" systems deal with products or activities that are as old as human civilization itself, whereas others have emerged only in the past decade or so. But they have all taken on a new importance because of the exponential growth of global bulk-flow systems over the past several decades. Such systems include transportation (the rise in air cargo and in the use of containerized shipping to speed the flow of manufactured products around the world) and communications (satellites, fiber-optic cable, the Internet, and the World Wide Web). In addition, the demise of the Cold War international security system, which has occasioned the rise of local instabilities in the Balkans, South Asia, central Africa, and elsewhere, enables drug traffickers and immigrant smugglers to exploit the weaknesses of state law enforcement capabilities.

The illicit global economy is big business. According to Richard Friman and Peter Andreas,[29] trafficking in illegal drugs generates about $0.5 trillion annually, and the illegal transport of toxic waste across national borders is worth some $515 billion each year. The clandestine trade in exotic or endangered animals is estimated at some $10 billion annually, and $0.5 trillion is laundered illegally through the global financial system every year. The smuggling of illegal immigrants has blossomed into a multibillion dollar enterprise, with smugglers charging as much as $50,000 per person for their services. It should come as no surprise, then, that the operators of these and other illicit global systems wish to keep their enterprises hidden from view.

Other global systems are kept hidden not because they are illegal per se but because, if they became widely known, individuals and firms would stand to lose profits from the adverse public reaction. One important example of such systems involves "triangle manufacturing."[30] In such an arrangement, a buyer in the United States places an order with an apparel manufacturer in an emerging industrial country like South Korea or Taiwan. The manufacturer in turn contracts for the actual production to take place in a factory in a third country where wages are apt to be much lower and where workers are not protected against sweatshop abuses. Systems of this sort came into being to enable U.S. retailers to connect with manufacturers with low production costs in areas of the world where they have little experience. In current practice, however, triangle manufacturing enables a U.S. retailer to market products manufactured in sweatshop conditions and yet profess ignorance of such exploitation.

CONSEQUENCES OF INVISIBLE GLOBAL SYSTEMS

Many observers contend that invisible global systems have weakened the nation-state and have made it extremely difficult and costly for the state to regulate such systems or to compensate for their more serious negative consequences. Invisible global systems also generate more external costs, or externalities, than visible systems do. In so doing, invisible systems impose undeserved costs on sectors of society that do not receive any benefits from these systems. Invisible global systems are accident prone, and they may have many other serious unintended consequences. Finally, invisible global systems weaken democracy by subjecting us to forces and conditions that are unaccountable to us.

The "Golden Straitjacket"

Some observers believe that invisible global systems impose "golden straitjackets" on national governments, preventing them from dealing with critical policy issues. By the term *golden straitjacket, New York Times* foreign affairs columnist Thomas Friedman means "all the rules set down by global markets for how a country has to behave economically if it wants to thrive in today's world."[31] Friedman contends that if national governments want their economies to prosper in the context of globalization, they must act within the limits set by global markets in such policy areas as social welfare payments, interest rates, and deficit government spending. In this way, the technologies and economic forces of globalization have reinforced the ideological transformation of national politics that began in the 1980s. This transformation included the policies of Ronald Reagan in the United States and those of Margaret Thatcher in Great Britain, known as neoliberalism, as well as the disappearance of state socialism in formerly communist countries.

Whether or not the state is indeed in retreat before the forces of the global economy (and, if so, whether this is a good thing or not) remains highly controversial. In a 1997 special report on the world economy,[32] *The Economist* argues that the age of big government is not dead, as evidenced by the continued rise in the percent of gross domestic product represented by government spending in virtually every one of the industrialized countries. Never an advocate of big government, the magazine laments the fact that the growth of national political institutions is driven by, among other things, the ambitions of political elites. The pressures of global economics have seemed to have little effect on these ambitions.

On the other hand, even *The Economist* has been forced to recognize the consequences for public policy that flow more or less inescapably from the integration of the world's economies and the growth of electronic commerce.[33] As capital and labor find it easier and easier to escape taxation by emigrating, national governments find that they have only three alternatives. They can either (1) shift their tax bases from corporate and personal income to less mobile sources, such as property or consumption; (2) reduce their spending to match declining revenues; or (3) find ways to increase deficit spending. This last option is really not available, contends Friedman, because the global economy denies to national governments the freedom to engage in inflationary fiscal policies. Any of these solutions will produce pain for some sector of the national body politic; and if governments cannot find creative ways to raise additional revenues, then they will inevitably find themselves under pressure to reduce their spending (and their presence in society) to match their income.

External Costs

For more than a decade, scholars and activists have debated the relative merits of global free market capitalism versus sustainable development and environmental conservation. Although these values appear to be mutually contradictory, in theory, at least, the way to reconcile them is by ensuring that all the costs of a transaction (that is, the sale and purchase of any product or service) are accurately reflected in the market price of that transaction. The cornerstone of corporate environmentalism since the 1990s has been the belief that pricing mechanisms can (and must) correct distortions in the world economy and reflect the environmental costs of doing business.[34]

Unfortunately, in a less than perfect world, market transactions generate external costs or externalities, which are the costs of a transaction not reflected in its price and thus not borne by parties to the transaction. It appears that invisible global systems generate more external costs than more visible systems do. Because the real costs of a transaction carried out by an invisible system cannot be known, it is harder to make the beneficiaries of the transaction pay the costs of system operation.

Why this should be so remains unclear and controversial. Some economists blame consumers who unthinkingly pay any price the market might set; meanwhile, consumer advocates place the blame on producers who employ deceptive marketing devices to beguile consumers into misunderstanding a product's true cost.[35] A more systems-level approach focuses on the impact of rapidly changing technology: making products and services obsolete with great speed, making prices especially volatile, and enabling producers to monitor consumer demand and change prices in nearly real time. But the paradigm of invisible global systems carries this explanation one step further, to focus on the enormous distance between producer and consumer and the complex web of transactions that must be traversed before a product or service reaches its destination. At each step in the process, some small (perhaps even invisible) externality may be generated. By the time the entire process is completed, these externalities have mounted to levels that can exceed the market price; but they remain invisible because they are buried in the network of transactions that connect producer and consumer.[36]

The inequities and inefficiencies inherent in high externalities may cause injustices and individual suffering in the marketplace, but these may not be the most significant consequences. If we are to keep large and complex systems from actions that are harmful to themselves and others, we must devise system feedback mechanisms that are accurate, reliable, and timely. Without accurate information, transmitted in virtually real time, about the consequences of system performance, system operators will likely fail to take corrective measures when things begin to go wrong. The result could well be the condition known as "overshoot" (discussed in chapter 4) whereby a rapidly changing system exceeds its limits and corrective steps are undertaken too late to prevent damage, perhaps of a catastrophic dimension.[37] If the environmental conditions cannot be repaired or restored, the damage may become permanent or virtually so within the time span of an individual's life. Because, in a market economy, the price of a transaction is the most visible indicator of transaction costs, the tendency of invisible systems to generate high external costs weakens the system's feedback mechanisms.

"Normal Accidents" and Other Unintended Consequences

Poor feedback mechanisms and high external costs are two reasons why invisible global systems are highly susceptible to damage. In his book of the same title,[38] Charles Perrow coins the term *normal accidents* to express the idea that highly complex systems will experience costly accidents as a normal part of their functioning or operation. Perrow identifies two reasons why high-risk technologies such as nuclear power reactors or oil tankers experience normal accidents. First, these systems tend to be nonlinear, that is, their component parts are arrayed in such a way that their interconnections produce outcomes that are unintended and unexpected. Second, their component parts are tightly coupled, meaning that when an unintended and unexpected consequence occurs, it is not contained within the boundaries of the system itself but, rather, quickly ripples out into the surrounding environment to cause even greater impact. Invisible global systems exhibit both of these properties.

The notion of "normal accidents" specifically does *not* include those incidents when something "goes wrong" because of the nature of the physical world or because of some sort of "Murphy's Law."[39] These sorts of mishaps were part of our lives long before invisible global systems appeared to bedevil us. Rather, Perrow uses the term to refer to major system failures that occur not because of the failure of any given identifiable component part but because of the high level of interconnectedness, or mutual interdependence, of the parts working as a system. The more widely spread and complex our systems become, the more they are going to fail. And the invisible nature of the connections or interrelationships makes failure that much more likely and costly. For example, many observers believe that the emergence of epidemics of novel diseases (and the reemergence of historic ones, as well) can be traced to a set of interconnected factors, including global urbanization, the spread of high-speed commercial air travel, the rapid mutation of bacteria to develop resistance to antibiotics, the spread of human settlements into areas such as tropical rain forests that had previously not known the hand of civilization, and others.[40]

In addition to normal accidents, invisible global systems produce many other unintended consequences. One consequence involves the way in which undesirable objects are carried along by a system that is apparently doing nothing more than transporting normal consumer goods or perhaps is just a component of a natural ecosystem. Ulrich Beck refers to these objects as "piggyback products," in that they are "inhaled or ingested with other things. They are the stowaways of normal consumption. They travel on the wind and in the water. They can be in anything and everything, and along with the absolute necessities of life . . . they pass through all the otherwise strictly controlled protective areas of modernity."[41]

Epidemics are frequently cited as examples of such unintended transport. A cholera epidemic was unleashed in Peru when a ship's polluted bilge water was discharged in a Peruvian harbor and the pathogens made their way up the food chain through seafood until they reached the plates of Lima's residents. In another example, mosquitoes imported from Asia through the port of Houston in shipments of used tires are known to be the source of a malaria epidemic in the southern United States. The unintended presence of genetically modified seeds or grains in human food supplies is another recent instance of piggyback products. In 2000, Kraft Foods recalled millions of taco shells because they could have contained a variety of corn called StarLink, which has not been approved for human consumption, although it is routinely fed to cattle and other livestock.[42] And in the same year, Europeans learned that some of the canola oil products they had been consuming could have been manufactured from rapeseed grown from bioengineered seeds imported from the United States.[43]

No Accountability

Finally, invisible global systems are irresponsible. In his book *Preparing for the Twenty-first Century,*[44] Paul Kennedy asserts that, because of the unintended consequences of Information Age technology, our lives are increasingly affected by global forces that are beyond our understanding and control and are, therefore, irresponsible and unaccountable. Beck agrees when he observes that, in a complex system,

> there is a general complicity, and the complicity is matched by a general lack of responsibility. Everyone is cause *and* effect, and thus *non*-cause. The causes dribble away into a general amalgam of agents and conditions, reactions and counter-reactions, which brings social certainty and popularity to the concept of system. This reveals in exemplary fashion the ethical significance of the system concept: *one can do something and continue doing it without having to take personal responsibility for it.* It is as if one were acting while being personally absent. One acts physically, without acting morally or politically.[45]

Global systems cannot be held accountable for what they do, or fail to do, for a variety of reasons. For one thing, global systems are market driven, and the impersonal forces of supply and demand will determine much of what they do. In making personal consumption choices, consumers cannot be held responsible for the broad consequences of the aggregated choices of something as impersonal as "the market." (This phenomenon is known as the "tyranny of small decisions.") But if external costs are generated with special ease by global systems, as we have seen, then consumer choices are inevitably going to be made in the context of distorted and highly incomplete information.

Another reason has to do with the long-term consequences of global systems. Much of the social destructiveness of potential hazards is derived from what Beck calls "risk multipliers." Thus, if we do not attend to threats in the near term, they will become aggravated to the point of catastrophe by the time we finally get around to dealing with them.[46] In addition, because many of the consequences of invisible systems are unintended, the consequences become legitimated. Because no one foresaw or wanted bad consequences to ensue from the operations of these systems, no one can be held accountable for them.[47]

Another reason for system irresponsibility has to do with the inadequacy of scientific values or principles in detecting and measuring invisible systemic consequences. Again, to quote Beck: "Where pollution exposures can only be understood and measured within international exchange patterns and the corresponding balances, it is obviously impossible to bring individual producers of individual substances into a direct, causal connection with definite illnesses."[48] Scientists try to make their paradigms applicable to invisible hazards by positing the abstraction of "minimal acceptable levels" of danger from exposure to certain substances. But because these are almost always matters of opinion, such assertions give us little help in identifying the systems that have caused the adverse consequences to appear among us. Even if we accept the scientifically determined minimal acceptable levels of specific toxins or poisons in our world, we would still not have a clear understanding or appreciation of how they work synergistically to cause harm to people, plants, and animals. After all, these substances are not part of coherent institutions at all but, instead, constitute inchoate social forces such as epidemics, refugee flows, and so forth.

While the lack of accountability may be traced to the properties of invisible global systems, it is also the case that many systems cannot be held accountable for the damage they do precisely because their owners or operators keep hidden the real responsibility for these consequences. In their report for Verite, the nonprofit consulting and monitoring service, Heather White and Fredi Munger describe the global assembly line for apparel as a "dizzyingly complex" network of "independently owned businesses connected to one another through a web of brokers and intermediaries."[49] Manufacturers are increasingly occupied solely with the marketing end of the assembly line, contracting out the actual manufacture to factories thousands of miles away, in Asia or Latin America. To avoid the public relations damage that might occur if it were discovered that the factories are run under sweatshop conditions, the manufacturers deliberately operate through brokers or intermediaries who arrange for the outsourcing contracts without divulging the identities of the firms or the locations of the production facilities. That way, the manufacturers cannot be held responsible for the deplorable working conditions under which their shoes, clothing, and so on are produced. Similar arrangements have been used to disguise the adverse environmental effects of rare earth mining or the logging of tropical rain forest hardwoods.[50]

Because they remain unaccountable, invisible systems raise frustration levels among those who are victimized by their operation. The causes of personal and system failures remain unseen and unknown. A loss of knowledge leads to a sense of loss of control, mounting frustration, and a rise in populist or nationalist movements, such as that of Pat Buchanan in the United States, Jean-Marie LePen in France, or Vladimir Zhirinovsky in Russia. The developing world has experienced this phenomenon as well, as evidenced by the rise to power of the Hindu fundamentalist Bharatiya Janata Party in India or of the nationalist ex-army officer, Hugo Chavez, in Venezuela.[51] One consequence of such irresponsibility has been a measurable decline in public confidence in democratic forms of government. Across the highly industrialized world, public opinion polls and voter turnout attest to a decline in the faith citizens have in their states and in their belief that public leaders can be trusted. A second consequence has been the appearance of what Ulrich Beck calls the "scapegoat society."[52] In the risk society, says Beck, social conflicts stemming from invisible system consequences encourage the victims to blame the *visible* "others" (e.g., immigrants, Muslims, communists, and so forth) for the misdeeds of *unseen* "others" to whom we are connected by only the most tenuous of threads. The long-term consequences of these developments for democracy around the world will surely not be trivial.

MAKING INVISIBLE GLOBAL SYSTEMS VISIBLE

If global systems are not only invisible and indispensable but irresponsible as well, how are we to manage and control them and make them accountable for what they do or fail to do? The growing importance of invisible global systems has brought forth new organizations whose mission is to track or monitor these systems and make us aware of their adverse effects. These new organizations are central actors in attempts to get control over the border-crossing (and border-eroding) transactions and flows of global systems. Their mission includes the identification, monitoring, tracking, and control of such systems. For such functions to emerge and be institutionalized, either a government organization or a nongovernmental organization must identify them as part of their public mission or function, or a private sector organization must see that there are profits to be realized by performing such functions.

Tracking and monitoring the behavior of boundary-crossing systems are not new functions. All governments and many international organizations maintain agencies or departments dedicated to identifying global systems for purposes of taxing and regulating them: trade, employment, bank accounts, financial transactions, and so forth. Others are intended to impede the operation of global systems or to interdict them: for example, the Border Patrol (illegal immigration), the World Health Organization (diseases), the Drug Enforcement Administration (narcotics), and Interpol (weapons and terrorists). Still others are dedicated to coordinating complex systems when chaos would cause catastrophic loss of life (air traffic controllers).

The Information Age and the process of globalization have launched a new kind of organization, however. More often than not, these organizations (which now number in the thousands) are in the private or not-for-profit sectors. Their objective is to identify and monitor invisible global systems, to publicize their activities, and to inform the public about the behavior of global organizations or multinational corporations so that consumers can make informed choices in the marketplace and voters can make informed decisions in the voting booth. In some cases, their intent is to protect people from the harmful effects of invisible global systems by making such systems visible. In other instances, their objective is to steer consumers toward products and producers that are safe, protective of the environment, or socially responsible.

"Food crises," reports *The Economist,* "are teaching consumers throughout the world not to trust blindly what they eat. . . . As food fears mount, however, food companies and farmers are at last finding both the means and the motive to track and certify each link in the chain of supply, from farm to table."[53] Fortunately, farmers can now call on a small but growing list of companies to help them track their crops. IdentityPreserved.com, for example, provides a tracking service that identifies for farmers the seed they are using and tells them whether it was genetically modified or not. CropVerifeye.com stores farmers' crop data to provide food processors with the information they need to guarantee seed integrity; and VantagePoint.com offers food processors a system to track grain from seed to sale.

Other organizations focus their attention on the consumption end of the food system. The American Alliance for Honest Labeling is a coalition of trade and agriculture lobbyists, labor unions, frozen produce processors and distributors, farm organizations, and individual growers.[54] The organization was formed in 1997 to secure passage of a proposed U.S. law that would require front-panel labeling of country of origin for all imported frozen produce packaging. The Environmental Working Group is a public interest lobby whose mission is to raise public awareness about pesticides and other toxic chemicals in our food. Its website can provide the reader with the names and amounts of pesticides and other chemicals we consume in our daily diets.[55]

Diseases are the core components of some of the most destructive invisible global systems we confront today. The mission of the APEC Emerging Infections Network, based at the University of Washington in Seattle,[56] is to raise public awareness about new health threats, particularly in the Pacific Basin. Outbreak is an online information service addressing the public's need for up-to-date information about emerging diseases.[57] In addition to providing information about emerging diseases for the interested layperson, it also provides a worldwide collaborative database to gather information about possible disease outbreaks.

The forced relocation of massive populations has become a serious policy area in the past several decades. ReliefNet is a nonprofit organization dedicated to helping humanitarian organizations raise awareness and financial support for their efforts by providing them free websites through which they can receive financial pledges online.[58] One such relief organization is Refugees International, founded in 1979 to assist Cambodian and Vietnamese refugees but now involved in missions around the world.[59] Its objective is to serve as advocate for the unrepresented refugee, those for whom no government speaks.

The global garment and apparel industry is a well-known example of an invisible global system that affects one of the most important aspects of our lives: the clothes we wear. Verite (which stands for Verification in Trade and Export) was founded in 1995 to offer inspection of labor practices, consultant services, and in-house training to U.S. corporations and other organizations concerned with the issues of child labor and sweatshop conditions.[60] A similar organization is Sweatshop Watch, a coalition of labor, community, civil rights, immigrant rights, and women's organizations committed to eliminating the exploitation that occurs in sweatshops.[61]

There are numerous environmental issues connected to the operation of invisible global systems. Ozone Action is a nonprofit public interest organization based in Washington, D.C., concerned with raising public awareness and promoting legislation around two atmospheric threats: global warming and stratospheric ozone depletion.[62] The Environmental Defense Fund is a broad-based environmental action organization whose website, known as Scorecard, "combines vast reservoirs of scientific data with software that makes it available to the layperson as well as the activist."[63] Citizens can get in-depth information about the worst polluters in their neighborhoods and even use the website to send letters to the offending polluters, the Environmental Protection Agency, or their representatives in Congress.

The clearest examples of invisible global systems are those that exist in cyberspace, and organizations have emerged to track and monitor those as well. The Computer Emergency Reaction Team (known as CERT) is based at Carnegie Mellon University in Pittsburgh. Its Coordination Center examines Internet security vulnerabilities, provides incident response services to victims of computer viruses, publishes security alerts, and performs research into security and survivability issues for networked computers.[64] CERT is funded by the U.S. Department of Defense. It is already widely understood that the Internet and the World Wide Web can bring much undesirable information into our homes, so organizations like Cyber Patrol scan the Web twenty-four hours per day in search of pornography, images of violence, hate propaganda, and other objectionable information.[65] They make their services available to parents, schools, and public libraries that wish to keep these kinds of information out of the hands of their computer users.

Finally, we should note the burgeoning "fair trade" movement as an attempt to connect consumers and producers to promote a social, economic, or environmental agenda. Suppose you are a coffee drinker and you want to direct your purchasing power toward those producers who are growing, harvesting, and marketing coffee in a way that protects the environment or provides adequate income for the farmers. But you have no way to know which brands of coffee meet these criteria. "Fair trade coffee" is the answer. The organization TransFair USA monitors closely the production conditions and prices of coffee around the world and is prepared to certify the brands whose production practices meet their criteria. The price to the consumer may be higher than that of other brands, but TransFair is betting that socially or environmentally conscious consumers will be willing to pay the additional price to ensure that their coffee consumption is not harmful to the environment or to the people who live off the coffee's harvest.[66]

Global tracking and monitoring organizations seek to achieve a safer, more secure, more just, and less damaging global order. Despite their best efforts, however, there will still be costs as we move through the process of globalization. How political systems meet the challenge of helping those who lose from globalization is addressed in the book's final chapter.

NOTES

1. The chief source of the "netwar" paradigm is David Ronfeldt and John Arquilla, *Networks and Netwars: The Future of Terror, Crime, and Militancy* (Santa Monica: RAND, 2001). An extended summary of the paradigm is available online at www.firstmonday.org. For contemporary press treatment of the paradigm, see Joel Garreau, "Disconnect the

Dots," *Washington Post,* September 17, 2001; and David Ignatius, "A 'Netwar' Clash," *Washington Post,* October 7, 2001.

2. David Barstow, "With New Diagnosis, Experts Suspect More Died of Encephalitis," *New York Times,* September 27, 1999.

3. Garrett Hardin, *Living within Limits: Ecology, Economics, and Population Taboos* (New York: Oxford University Press, 1993), 14–16.

4. Pamela LiCalizi O'Connell, "Beyond Geography: Mapping Unknowns of Cyberspace," *New York Times,* September 30, 1999.

5. Ulrich Beck, *Risk Society: Towards a New Modernity,* trans. Mark Ritter (London: SAGE, 1992).

6. Beck, *Risk Society,* 27.

7. Beck, *Risk Society,* 32.

8. Beck, *Risk Society,* 36.

9. Beck, *Risk Society,* 36–37.

10. Beck, *Risk Society,* 53.

11. John Tyler Bonner, *The Evolution of Complexity by Means of Natural Selection* (Princeton: Princeton University Press, 1988), chapter 5.

12. Klaus Mainzer, *Thinking in Complexity: The Complex Dynamics of Matter, Mind, and Mankind* (New York: Springer-Verlag, 1994).

13. John Holland, *Hidden Order: How Adaptation Builds Complexity* (Reading, Mass.: Addison-Wesley, 1995), 15–23.

14. Holland, *Hidden Order,* 23.

15. Ilya Prigogine and Isabelle Stengers, *Order out of Chaos: Man's New Dialogue with Nature* (New York: Bantam, 1984), 153–55.

16. Gregoire Nicolis and Ilya Prigogine, *Exploring Complexity: An Introduction* (New York: W. H. Freeman and Co., 1989), 56–61.

17. The reader can get a more complete idea of what "Internet ecologies" entail by visiting Bernardo Huberman's website, at www.parc.xerox.com. See also George Johnson, "Searching for the Essence of the World Wide Web," *New York Times,* April 11, 1999; and John Markoff, "Not a Great Equalizer After All?" *New York Times,* June 21,1999. For other attempts to fashion a suitable metaphor to describe the Internet, see John Markoff, "Illness Becomes Apt Metaphor for Computers," *New York Times,* June 14, 1999; and John Markoff, "In Eden, a Snake. On the Internet, a Worm," *New York Times,* June 20, 1999.

18. Bernardo Huberman and Rajan Lukose, "Social Dilemmas and Internet Congestion," *Science* 277 (July 25, 1997): 535–37.

19. See, for example, Robert Reich, *The Work of Nations: Preparing Ourselves for 21st-Century Capitalism* (New York: Knopf, 1991), chapter 7.

20. Shoshana Zuboff, *In the Age of the Smart Machine: The Future of Work and Power* (New York: Basic Books, 1988), 290–96.

21. W. Brian Arthur, "Positive Feedbacks in the Economy," *Scientific American* (February 1990): 92–99. The system effects of positive feedback loops are discussed in Robert Jervis, *System Effects: Complexity in Political and Social Life* (Princeton: Princeton University Press, 1997), 146–76.

22. John Naughton, *A Brief History of the Future: From Radio Days to Internet Years in a Lifetime* (Woodstock, N.Y.: Overlook Press, 2000), 96–98.

23. Anatol Rapoport, *General System Theory: Essential Concepts and Applications* (Tunbridge Wells, U.K.: Abacus Press, 1986), 140–49. George Johnson, "Mindless Creatures, Acting 'Mindfully,'" *New York Times,* March 23, 1999.

24. Stanley Milgram, "The Small-World Problem," *Psychology Today* (May 1967): 61–67. Manfred Kochen, ed., *The Small World* (Norwood, N.J.: Ablex Publishing Corporation, 1989).

25. Dale Russakoff, "Many Victims Only 'Handshakes Away,'" *Washington Post,* September 29, 2001.

26. For more on the "small world" project conducted at Columbia University by sociologist Duncan Watts, see the project's website, at smallworld.sociology.columbia.edu. For more on the research project carried out by the Santa Fe Institute, see its website, at www.santafe.edu. See also Sandra Blakeslee, "Mathematicians Prove That It's a Small World," *New York Times,* June 16, 1998; and Sarah Milstein, "Using E-Mail to Count Connections," *New York Times,* December 20, 2001.

27. Mark Landler, "Hi, I'm in Bangalore (but I Can't Say So)," *New York Times,* March 21, 2001.

28. H. Richard Friman and Peter Andreas, eds., *The Illicit Global Economy and State Power* (Lanham, Md.: Rowman & Littlefield, 1999). Robert Schaeffer, *Understanding Globalization: The Social Consequences of Political, Economic, and Environmental Change* (Lanham, Md.: Rowman & Littlefield, 1997), chapter 14. Jessica Mathews, "We Live in a Dangerous Neighborhood," *Washington Post,* April 24, 1995. John Kerry, "Organized Crime Goes Global While the U.S. Stays Home," *Washington Post,* May 11, 1997.

29. H. Richard Friman and Peter Andreas, "Introduction: International Relations and the Illicit Global Economy," in *The Illicit Global Economy and State Power,* ed. H. Richard Friman and Peter Andreas (Lanham, Md.: Rowman & Littlefield, 1999), 2.

30. Gary Gereffi, "The Elusive Last Lap in the Quest for Developed-Country Status," in *Globalization: Critical Reflections,* ed. James H. Mittelman (Boulder: Lynne Rienner, 1996), 69–71.

31. Thomas Friedman, "France's New Jacket," *New York Times,* June 5, 1997.

32. Clive Crook, "The Future of the State: A Survey of the World Economy," *The Economist,* September 20, 1997.

33. "Disappearing Taxes: The Tap Runs Dry," *The Economist,* May 31, 1997: 21–23.

34. Joshua Karliner, *The Corporate Planet: Ecology and Politics in the Age of Globalization* (San Francisco: Sierra Club Books, 1997), chapter 2.

35. David Morrow, "Why You Can't Tell What Things Cost," *New York Times,* March 2, 1997. David Barboza, "Farmers Are in Crisis as Hog Prices Collapse," *New York Times,* December 13, 1998. David Barboza, "The Great Pork Gap: Hog Prices Have Plummeted. Why Haven't Store Prices?" *New York Times,* January 6, 1999. John Schwartz, "The Price We Pay: When Everything's Up for Grabs, True Value Is Hard to Find," *Washington Post,* June 27, 1999.

36. Teresa Wyszomierski, "The Threat Abroad in That Bargain Fill Up," *Washington Post,* March 7, 1999. Neil Strauss, "Pennies That Add Up to $16.98: Why CD's Cost So Much," *New York Times,* July 5, 1995. Mark Potts, "Tortuous Path to the Price at the Pump: How a Complex Chain of Events Determines the Cost of Gasoline," *Washington Post,* August 26, 1990.

37. Donella H. Meadows, Dennis L. Meadows, and Jørgen Randers, *Beyond the Limits: Confronting Global Collapse, Envisioning a Sustainable Future* (Post Hills, Vt.: Chelsea Green Publishing Co., 1992), chapter 4.

38. Charles Perrow, *Normal Accidents: Living with High-Risk Technologies* (New York: Basic Books, 1984).

39. Robert Matthews, "The Science of Murphy's Law," *Scientific American* 276, no. 4 (April 1997): 88–91.

40. Laurie Garrett, *The Coming Plague: Newly Emerging Diseases in a World out of Balance* (New York: Farrar, Straus and Giroux, 1994).

41. Beck, *Risk Society,* 40–41.

42. Andrew Pollack, "A Texas-Sized Whodunit," *New York Times,* September 30, 2000.

43. Donald G. McFeil Jr., "Europeans Learn They're Inadvertently Growing Genetically Altered Plants for Canola," *New York Times,* May 19, 2000.

44. Paul Kennedy, *Preparing for the Twenty-first Century* (New York: Random House, 1994), 64.

45. Beck, *Risk Society,* 33.

46. Beck, *Risk Society,* 33.

47. Beck, *Risk Society,* 34.

48. Beck, *Risk Society,* 63.

49. Heather White and Fredi Munger, "Dynamics of the Global Assembly Line." Verite website, at www.verite.org.

50. Karliner, *The Corporate Planet,* chapter 4.

51. Karliner, *The Corporate Planet,* 211–16.

52. Beck, *Risk Society,* 75.

53. "Let Them Eat Data," *The Economist,* April 21, 2001: 58–59.

54. See the website, at www.honestlabeling.org.

55. See the website, at www.foodnews.org.

56. See the website, at apec.org/infectious.

57. See the website, at www.outbreak.org.

58. See the website, at www.reliefnet.org.

59. See the website, at www.refintl.org.

60. See the website, at www.verite.org. For more on Verite, and for information about other organizations involved with this issue, see Heather Hiam-White, "Their Labor, Our Gifts, Your Choices," *Washington Post,* December 20, 1998.

61. See the website, at www.sweatshopwatch.org.

62. See the website, at www.ozone.org.

63. See the website, at www.scorecard.org. See also *The Economist,* April 3, 1999: 28.

64. See the website, at www.cert.org. For an example of CERT at work, see Tim Smart, "'Melissa' Reveals Growing Vulnerability: Virus Able to Spread Easily Over Networks of Computers," *Washington Post,* March 31, 1999.

65. See the website, at www.cyberpatrol.com. John Schwartz, "It's a Dirty Job: Web Childproofers Keep Surfing through the Muck," *Washington Post,* June 23, 1999.

66. John Burgess, "Deal Brews to Give Fairer Deal to Farmers," *Washington Post,* May 13, 2000.

Case Study 6

Mexican Strawberries
and Michigan Schoolchildren

KEY IDEAS IN THIS CASE STUDY

Some of the most **destructive invisible systems** are truly invisible (at least in part) because their principal components (viruses and bacteria) exist at the microscopic level.

Viruses are able to metabolize food sources and reproduce only by **invading the cells of a much larger organism,** such as a human being, and using this host's cells to accomplish the principal tasks of living organisms.

All viruses must have a way to travel from one person to another. Some travel via direct skin-to-skin contact, while others are carried in aerosol form through the air. Still others, however, need a carrier, called a **vector** in medical terminology. Some vectors are living organisms, such as mosquitoes, whereas others involve human inventions (for example, transportation systems). These latter are called **cultural vectors.**

Hepatitis A is an example of a virus that is carried from an infected person to a new host via fecal matter and contaminated food or water.

The **system** that carried the hepatitis A virus from a **Mexican field** to **schoolchildren in Michigan** remained **largely invisible,** even after considerable investigation, in part because the things being transported were so small and in part because several key actors wished for the system to escape public detection.

Invisible systems operate in our world at many levels. Many are invisible only in a conceptual sense. Their component parts are, in fact, visible, and once we know they exist we "see" them in a way we could not before. We say that these systems are knowledge dependent. On the other hand, some of the most destructive invisible systems really are invisible, at least to the unaided eye, because they exist at least in part at the microscopic level. These systems derive their destructive character from component parts that can be seen only under a microscope: bacteria and viruses.

A virus, writes Ann Giudici Fettner, "is essentially a packet of genetic information surrounded by a protein covering."[1] Although viruses are among the most primitive of all organisms, they are today almost the only real biological competitors humans encounter.[2] Some biologists contend that viruses are not even alive because they lack the properties we usually associate with life itself: the ability to metabolize food sources, move about, and reproduce. To accomplish all of these things viruses need to enter the body of a much larger organism, known as the host, invade and seize control of the host's cells, and use their structures and resources to perform the essential functions of life. When such an invasion occurs, it produces physiological changes in the host (for example, coughing, sneezing, or skin lesions) that we interpret as "being sick."

Viruses are able to accomplish their invasive mission because of the molecular markings on their outer envelopes or coverings. Each virus strain exhibits unique external cells that match up with similar markings on the outer coverings of the cells of the host body. When the virus invades a host and encounters the appropriate host cells, the markers on the virus attach themselves to the markers on the host cell, and the virus is thus able to penetrate the host cell and begin to reproduce. There are several ways for viruses to gain entrance to the host's body (for example, inhalation, ingestion, or a wound or other skin opening). And viruses usually have to reach the appropriate organ (for example, lungs, stomach, or liver) before they can find the correct cells to which they can attach themselves and begin to work.

Hepatitis is a general name we give to the class of viruses that use cells in the host's liver for reproduction, thereby causing inflammation of that organ. There are three kinds of hepatitis viruses (known as A, B, and C), which differ in their severity and in the way they are carried into the host's body. Hepatitis B and hepatitis C are highly contagious, potentially deadly, and carried by blood from an infected person to a new host. Both of these varieties can cause cirrhosis, liver cancer, and liver failure. The World Health Organization has asserted that hepatitis B is the second leading cause of cancer worldwide, after cigarettes.[3]

The invisible system in our story involves the third type of hepatitis, the A variety. Hepatitis A is shed in the stool of an infected person two to three weeks before symptoms occur and during the first week of the illness. The disease is spread by food or water that has become contaminated with the infected fecal matter. People most at risk include those traveling in regions where the disease is prevalent and people eating food prepared in institutions such as schools, daycare centers, and nursing homes. Food handlers should wash their hands thoroughly to prevent spreading the disease through food, but they may not even be aware that they are infected for a week or two. The symptoms associated with hepatitis A are similar to those of the flu, but in addition the skin and eyes may become yellow because of the inability of the liver to filter bilirubin from the blood. There is no specific treatment for hepatitis A. The disease usually clears itself from the body in one–two months, and it rarely becomes chronic. There are seldom any serious complications. In the United States, about 25,000 cases of hepatitis A are reported to public health officials each year. But because many cases are unreported or unrecognized, epidemiologists estimate that the real number is between 135,000 and 150,000.

All viruses must have a way to travel from one infected host to another, and yet they are unable to move unaided. Some viruses, such as the common cold, travel via direct skin-to-skin contact, whereas others, such as influenza, are carried in aerosol form through the air. Others need a carrier, called a *vector*. Some vectors are living organisms, such as mosquitoes. Others involve human inventions, such as transportation systems. We call these *cultural vectors*.[4] Hepatitis A is an example of a disease that is moved by a cultural vector, in this case the world's system (or systems) for producing and distributing food.

For most of our history, the United States has relied almost entirely on food produced and distributed within its borders. Indeed, the food for most people was grown locally. It was only in the latter decades of the nineteenth century that the arrival of steam railroads and mechanical refrigeration enabled people in large American cities to enjoy the products of the fields of California, Florida, and other distant sites. Even then, however, food production and distribution remained under the control of U.S. and state-level regulatory authorities and public health officials. Since the mid-1980s, however, food imports have more than doubled, and the incidence of food-borne diseases in the United States has soared accordingly.[5]

During the 1990s, there were outbreaks of food-borne illnesses linked to raspberries from Guatemala; carrots from Peru; strawberries, scallions, and cantaloupes from Mexico; coconut milk from Thailand; canned mushrooms from China; snack food from Israel; and alfalfa sprouts from several countries. It seems that there is an inescapable tension between free trade and an increased flow of food products in global trade, on the one hand, and a desire to preserve food security and safety, on the other. It also bears mentioning that food exports from the United States have also caused illness in the importing countries on occasion, including radish sprouts in Japan and beef containing *E. coli* bacteria in South Korea.

The case of raspberries from Guatemala illustrates the tangled web of causes and consequences that expose the U.S. population to foreign microbes.[6] In 1983, the administration of President Ronald Reagan sought to promote economic growth in Central America through its Caribbean Basin Initiative, which cut tariffs on imports from the region. As part of our effort to defeat left-wing guerrillas in Guatemala, the U.S. Agency for International Development pumped tens of millions of dollars into the country to promote "nontraditional" agriculture. It encouraged Guatemalan peasants to switch from growing corn and beans for themselves to planting exotic crops like raspberries for export to U.S. markets, and it helped finance these shipments. The raspberry trade exploded in the early 1990s, rising from virtually zero in the 1980s to 700,000 pounds in 1996. Much of the raspberry crop is harvested in Guatemala in the spring when there is little competition from domestic fruits. But this is also the time when seasonal rains come to the highlands, and researchers now believe that the raspberry crop brought a parasite called cyclospora to the American market from Guatemala, where it is endemic. Thousands fell ill in 1996 and again in 1997 with the symptoms of this disease: diarrhea, cramps, chills, fever, weight loss, and depression. The Guatemalan government and the farmers themselves angrily denied that they were the source of the outbreak. They contended that raspberry farmers in the United States were exploiting the outbreak to protect the U.S. market from Guatemalan produce. Guatemalan farmers denied inspectors access to some of the suspect farms, so no one was ever able to identify for certain the route by which cyclospora entered the United States.

Scientists at the Centers for Disease Control and Prevention (CDC) have asserted for years that diseases carried by imported foods kill thousands of Americans each year and sicken millions. Almost none of these cases is ever traced back to its cause. Quite simply, the dramatic growth in food trade has outpaced the capacity of America's regulatory system to keep food safe and secure. As an official of the Food and Drug Administration (FDA) has put it, "We built a system back 100 years ago that served us very well for a world within our borders. We didn't build a system for the global marketplace."[7]

That marketplace has come to threaten the public health system of the United States for several reasons. First, there is the complexity of the system. As the director of CDC's food-borne disease branch has put it, "Go to a restaurant and take a look at your supper. How many different continents are on your plate?"[8] For example, the alfalfa sprouts that gave salmonella to hundreds of victims in 1996 and 1997 were grown from seeds that came from Uganda and Pakistan, shipped through the Netherlands, flown into New York, and carried by truck around the country. Because the food is distributed so widely once it is imported, its victims are scattered across the country, and state-level public health authorities often fail to see the epidemic patterns emerge. With some 30 billion tons of food imported into the country each year, inspections at border crossings and ports of entry have dropped to less than 1 percent of all food shipments. U.S. inspectors cannot visit foreign fields to ensure safety at those sites, and the FDA lacks the power to bar shipments from a foreign country just because its agricultural system is suspect. The United States cannot afford to pay to upgrade public health systems worldwide, and the governments in most developing countries lack the funds necessary to pay for such upgrading by themselves. Thus, the United States is forced to concentrate on meeting the outbreaks of food-borne disease when and where they occur.

◆   ◆   ◆

On April 2, 1997, federal health officials in Washington announced that strawberries imported from Mexico and processed in California had caused 153 cases of hepatitis A among schoolchildren and teachers in Michigan.[9] Eventually 185 cases of the infection would be identified. In addition, thousands of school-children in Arizona, California, Georgia, Iowa, and Tennessee were also at risk and were being advised to receive gamma globulin shots to prevent liver disease from the virus. The infected strawberries had been served as part of the school lunch program conducted by the U.S. Department of Agriculture (USDA), which immediately ordered a halt to the serving of strawberries in school lunch programs in fifteen states and the District of Columbia. The USDA prohibits the inclusion of foreign food products in the lunch program. All suppliers of food to the program must certify in writing that the product was grown in the United States, and the three vendors that supplied the berries had such a certification from their supplier. How, then, had these strawberries from Mexico been introduced into the food system in Michigan schools?

Sometime early in 1996 (the exact date is unknown), Mexican farmworkers in the state of Baja California (the exact farm and the exact workers are unknown) harvested a crop of strawberries for shipment to the United States. The strawberries were part of thirteen shipments totaling about one million pounds that were received on April 19 and May 7 and 8, 1996, by a food-processing firm, Andrew & Williamson (A&W) Sales of San Diego, California. About 40 percent of the contaminated berries were shipped to schools, while the remainder was distributed commercially. A substantial but unquantified portion of the commercial berries was used to make jams, jellies, preserves, and fruit juices. Because the fruit would have been heated to make these processed products, the heat would have killed the virus, and the products were not considered dangerous.[10]

A&W is a division of Epitope, Inc., of Beaverton, Oregon. Epitope acquired A&W in November 1996 in a stock swap worth $7.7 million. The parent firm is a biotechnology company founded in 1981 as a paternity-testing company. Subsequently, the firm diversified into such products as AIDS diagnostic tests and genetically engineered grapevines. In its entire history, Epitope had never recorded a profitable year, and stock analysts said that its history of overselling its programs made its stock especially volatile. Epitope's acquisition of A&W, a major fresh fruit and vegetable grower and distributor on the West Coast, was to be the beginning of a joint venture to grow and wholesale new varieties of longer lasting tomatoes.[11]

At the firm's plant, the strawberries were washed, sliced, sorted, packaged with sugar, frozen, and put into cold storage until December, when they were shipped frozen in 30-pound canisters to a number of locations for distribution in school lunches. One of the sites that received the strawberries was Calhoun County, a mostly rural area in south-central Michigan near Battle Creek, where the strawberries were included in strawberry shortcake served on Valentine's Day and in fruit cups served to students in late March 1997.[12] Schools in other Michigan towns, including Battle Creek and Saginaw, also received shipments of infected strawberries and also recorded cases of hepatitis A.

Details of this case became widely known only after officials of the USDA revealed that Andrew & Williamson Sales had falsified documents to make it appear as if the strawberries had come from U.S. farms. Shortly after the infections broke out, the president of Epitope confirmed that

> A&W inaccurately described some of the strawberries associated with the outbreak as having been grown and processed in the U.S. In fact, the berries were grown in Mexico and processed in the U.S. We have notified the USDA of our concern with regard to this matter and have today accepted the resignation of Fred L. Williamson, president and chief executive officer of A&W.[13]

Even after considerable investigation, however, no one knows where or how the hepatitis A virus got into the strawberries. In Mexico, Israel Camacho, the assistant secretary of agriculture for Baja California, said he did not think that irrigation water was the source of the contamination. "It is more likely," he said, "that the strawberries were contaminated, if they were contaminated, during processing and packing rather than during cultivation."[14] A spokesman for Epitope said that A&W had followed federal government regulations covering food processing, and the head of the CDC ruled out food handling at the Michigan school as a possible cause. Two weeks after the infections were made public, it was learned that officials at the USDA had known since January 1997 that A&W was illegally supplying imported strawberries to the school lunch program but had failed to investigate the reports further or take any action to halt the procedure. In testimony before the Education and Workforce Committee of the U.S. House of Representatives, the USDA official in charge of agricultural marketing services said, "I certainly would agree that in hindsight, which is 20-20, I wish we would have followed up more quickly."[15] In June 1997, a federal grand jury in San Diego returned a forty-seven-count indictment against A&W for fraudulently labeling more than 1.7 million pounds of Mexican-grown strawberries as having been grown in the United States. A salesman for the company pleaded guilty to the charges and was free on $100,000 bond pending sentencing.[16] Meanwhile, during the spring and summer, consumption of frozen strawberries declined sharply across the nation, devastating the berry industry in California even though none of the contaminated strawberries came from California fields.

The strawberries had traveled several thousand miles from the field to the Michigan school and had been handled by several dozen persons through a process that contained more than a dozen stages. At almost no point along the way had the strawberries been inspected; indeed, after the fact, no one could even reliably reconstruct the path they had followed to the Michigan school. The strawberries and their virus companions had been harvested, processed, and distributed by an invisible global system.

NOTES

1. Ann Giudici Fettner, *The Science of Viruses* (New York: William Morrow, 1990), 25.

2. Joshua Lederberg, "Viruses and Humankind: Intracellular Symbiosis and Evolutionary Competition," in *Emerging Viruses*, ed. Stephen S. Morse (New York: Oxford University Press, 1993), chapter 1.

3. Fettner, *The Science of Viruses,* chapter 12.

4. Paul Ewald, *Evolution of Infectious Diseases* (Oxford: Oxford University Press, 1994), 68.

5. Jeff Gerth and Tim Weiner, "Imports Swamp U.S. Food-Safety Efforts," *New York Times,* September 29, 1997.

6. The following account is drawn from Gerth and Weiner, "Imports Swamp U.S. Food-Safety Efforts."

7. Quoted in Gerth and Weiner, "Imports Swamp U.S. Food-Safety Efforts."

8. Quoted in Gerth and Weiner, "Imports Swamp U.S. Food-Safety Efforts."

9. Lawrence K. Altman, "153 Hepatitis Cases Are Traced to Imported Frozen Strawberries," *New York Times,* April 3, 1997. Edward Walsh, "Mexican Strawberries Cause U.S. Outbreak of Hepatitis A," *Washington Post,* April 3, 1997.

10. Lawrence K. Altman, "Threat in Tainted Strawberries Has Eased, Officials Say," *New York Times,* April 4, 1997.

11. Lawrence M. Fisher, "A Company Familiar with Controversy," *New York Times,* April 3, 1997.

12. Keith Bradsher, "Strawberry Shortcake Was Culprit," *New York Times,* April 5, 1997.

13. Quoted in Walsh, "Mexican Strawberries Cause U.S. Outbreak of Hepatitis A."

14. Quoted in Altman, "153 Hepatitis Cases Are Traced to Imported Frozen Strawberries."

15. Quoted in Heather Knight, "USDA Heard about Illegal Berries before Outbreak," *Washington Post,* April 18, 1997.

16. William Claiborne, "California Processor Charged in Mislabeling of Bad Fruit," *Washington Post,* June 11, 1997.

7

Globalization and Nation-State Politics

KEY IDEAS IN THIS CHAPTER

Globalization is asymmetrical, meaning that some individuals and groups are able to benefit from it more than others. Like all great social transformations before it, globalization produces large numbers of both **winners** and **losers.**

Has globalization **gone too far?** In answering this question, we examine several sources of tension between global economic integration and domestic social and political stability to illustrate how globalization aggravates conflicts between winners and losers. We shall see, however, that this is not a simple question to answer, and there are counterarguments to consider.

How winners and losers participate in the political process, how they form **interest groups and coalitions** to advance or protect their interests, will do much to shape the nature of politics in both industrial and developing countries.

The impact of globalization on the politics of the nation-state is often hard to identify and understand because the connections between global systems and domestic politics are extremely complex. The Global System Paradigm helps us to identify the political consequences of global changes and thus to understand better the politics of globalization. Globalization is creating new sets of winners and losers and new arrangements of interest groups and coalitions. It often seems as if these new groups cannot be contained easily within the boundaries of the nation-state or its political process. Some observers believe that globalization has "gone too far." By this they mean that global economic integration has done great harm to domestic social stability by threatening the gains achieved by the twentieth-century welfare state model of politics. If so, how can the plight of globalization's losers be remedied?

WINNERS AND LOSERS

Globalization is extremely expensive. Inevitably, this transformation must entail the transfer of great quantities of resources between and among populations, cultures, classes, sectors of production, and nation-states. Some individuals will get more benefits from this transformation than others; some will bear more of the costs.

Consider the case of the great Italian tenor, Luciano Pavarotti. Although he is Italian by birth, still holds Italian citizenship, and owns considerable property in Italy, he resides most of the year in Monte Carlo. Why? Well, among other reasons, to avoid paying taxes in Italy. In 1999, an Italian court held that Pavarotti was liable for more than $2 million in back taxes, but the singer appealed and the case dragged on.[1] The Pavarotti case illustrates several important principles of globalization. First, globalization increases the mobility of the wealthy.[2] Either they themselves move across state boundaries to gain an advantage, or they move their money or property to do so. Second, and much more broadly, Pavarotti shows that the costs and benefits of globalization are not spread evenly across society. Regardless of the categories we select, whether territory or social class, gender or occupation, some groups and some individuals can exploit the benefits of globalization far more than others can. Thus, we say that the *costs and benefits of globalization are asymmetrical.*

An example of such asymmetry involves the distribution of prosperity and poverty. Whatever else globalization has done, it has not made the distribution of the world's wealth more nearly equal. In fact, the opposite has been happening.[3] The gap between the world's richest and poorest populations has been growing. (See figures 7.1 and 7.2.)

One way to measure the degree of inequality in income distribution is to calculate the ratio between the share received by the richest one-fifth of the population and the share received by the poorest one-fifth. In a world of complete equality, the ratio would be one to one, so the higher the ratio, the greater the inequality. In 1989, the richest 20 percent of the world's people received 82.7 percent of the world's gross domestic product, whereas the poorest 20 percent received 1.4 percent, yielding a ratio of fifty-nine to one. And the gap has been growing. Between 1965 and 1990, the share of world income received by the richest one-fifth rose 14 percentage points, from 69 to 83 percent. Thus, the ratio of the richest one-fifth to the poorest one-fifth very nearly doubled in this twenty-five-year period, from 31:1 to 60:1.[4] A more recent study, using the Gini coefficient as a measure of income inequality, reveals a continuation of the trend into the 1990s.[5] Between 1988 and 1993, the Gini coefficient rose from 0.63 to 0.67.[6] The causes of this trend include faster economic growth in the rich countries than in the poor ones; faster population growth in the poor countries than in the rich ones; slow economic growth in rural areas of China, India, and Africa; and a rapidly growing gap between the urban and rural areas of China and India.

Figure 7.1.   Distribution of World Domestic Product, 1989 (Percent of Total to Quintiles of Population Ranked by Income)

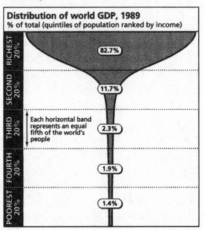

Source: "Why the Poor Don't Catch Up," *The Economist*, April 25, 1992: 48; © 1992, the Economist Newspaper Group, Inc. Reprinted with permission. Further reproduction prohibited.

Figure 7.2.   Distribution of Population by Average Income, per Person, 1993

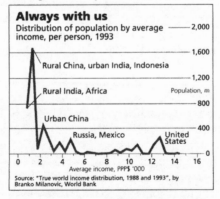

Source: Robert Wade, "Winners and Losers," *The Economist*, April 28, 2001: 73; © 2001, the Economist Newspaper Group, Inc. Reprinted with permission. Further reproduction prohibited.

One clear consequence of globalization (along with a number of other factors, including market deregulation and inflated stock prices) has been what *The Economist* calls "the most exuberant period of wealth creation in human history."[7] The world now has 7.2 million people with assets of at least $1 million. These 7.2 million people now control approximately one-third of the world's wealth, about $27 trillion. About one-third of these millionaires live in North America (the United States alone contains 274 of the world's 425 billionaires), about one-quarter live in Europe, and about one-sixth live in Asia. As the administrator of the U.N. Development Program put it in 1996, "An emerging global elite, mostly urban based and interconnected in a variety of ways, is amassing great wealth and power, while more than half of humanity is left out."[8]

The politics of globalization will be shaped by this asymmetry, the way each issue creates winners and losers, and what these groups do to advance their interests. Like all other great *social transformations* that came before it,[9] globalization transfers large quantities of resources from one group of individuals to another. Because virtually all these resources are scarce in the near term, globalization must inevitably affect the distribution of life chances in a population. *Winners* are those people, social classes, and sectors of production that receive a disproportionately large share of the rewards or benefits from globalization, either because globalization removes or decreases something bad from their lives or because it adds or increases something good. *Losers* are those who bear a disproportionately large share of the costs of globalization, either because globalization adds or increases something bad in their lives or because it removes or decreases something good. Not surprisingly, the winners seek to promote or accelerate the transformation; the losers, to contain, retard, or reverse it. Who these individuals and groups are, and how they struggle to achieve their goals, is our central concern here.

This proposition seems straightforward. But as an empirical matter it turns out to be rather difficult to identify the winners and losers from globalization and to describe how their gains or losses manifest themselves in political action. At the turn of the millennium, the American public seemed to be divided roughly into two-thirds winners (those who favor or support globalization) and one-third losers (those who oppose it). An extensive survey of public opinions about globalization was conducted in 1999 by the University of Maryland's Program on International Policy Attitudes.[10] In response to the question "What should U.S. goals be regarding globalization?" 28 percent selected "actively promote it," 33 percent chose "allow it to continue," 26 percent said "slow it down," and 9 percent answered "stop it or reverse it." Thus, the pro-globalization camp accounted for 61 percent of the respondents, and the anti-globalization group represented 35 percent. Only 4 percent had no response to the question. Roughly these same proportions appeared in a *Washington Post* poll conducted a year later in the context of the U.S. presidential campaign. In this survey, 40 percent were noncommittal about globalization of the economy: 25 percent said it did not make much difference to the United States, 4 percent had not heard of the term, and 11 percent had no opinion. Of the 60 percent who ventured an opinion, however, 63 percent (38 percent of the total surveyed population) said it was "mostly good" for the United States, and 37 percent (22 percent of the total) said it was "mostly bad."[11]

These data are of great interest, but we must be careful to treat them as the ambiguous indicators they really are. Many people (probably most) are *both* winners *and* losers from globalization, but the subtleties and complexities of our conditions are invisible to most of us. The same event or property of globalization (say, the increased importation of a specific manufactured product) can produce winners and losers simultaneously, often in the same community, neighborhood, or even family. Because the huge majority of these transactions and consequences are mediated by the impersonal forces of the market, they remain mostly invisible and unknown.

Such ambiguity becomes highly problematic if we determine that as a policy goal we wish to identify globalization's losers and compensate them for their losses. Who is to pay for such compensation, and how can the funds be levied and collected? Winners and losers are for the most part ignorant of each other's existence. In some cases, losers may know they have lost and be able to blame the appropriate agent, but the more likely case is for them not to understand what has happened to them, or why, or by whose decision. Likewise, winners may not realize how globalization has benefited them. They may ascribe their gains to some merit of their own and resent the state confiscating part of their winnings to repay others of lesser merit. Thus, the only connection between winners and losers is the supply of, and demand for, their resources as expressed in the price the market sets for them. There is no way, other than through collective political action, that the winners can be asked (or required) to compensate the losers for their losses. Claus Offe presents the dilemma this way:

> The great virtue and attraction of market forces and private property consist not in their being the medium of private profit maximization but in their capacity for collective loss minimization. Markets eliminate in a smooth, continuous, and inconspicuous way all those factors of production that fail to perform according to current standards of efficiency. . . . The power that drives this continuous search is more potent than any political authority or planning agency, be it authoritarian or democratic. This is so because the market is an anonymous power that we cannot talk to: it is not to be irritated by election results or any other kind of "voice." The potency of market forces derives from their anonymity and non-intentionality: if factors of production fail in a particular allocation, nobody can be blamed for having caused this event. . . . [A]s "no one else" can be blamed for negative market outcomes, the market invites self-attribution of individual failures.[12]

Many people believe that globalization is all about economics and that economic rationality and market processes explain everything we need to know about the political and social cleavages caused by globalization. I believe that this approach treats inadequately the other sources of conflict arising from globalization, especially those that have a cultural base. If globalization has any meaning for human values, it lies in the way it commodifies virtually everything, including cultural markers (religious beliefs and language), cultural objects (film, music, and food), and access to the carriers of culture (television, the Internet, and immigration). In both industrialized and less developed societies, some people and some sectors have greater access to a globalized culture than others do. And this differential access can spawn just as much political conflict as the unequal distribution of economic costs and benefits can.[13]

Nevertheless, space limitations require that we here treat globalization as primarily a series of economic questions. Even if we restrict our attention solely to economic matters, however, assessment of the politics of globalization is still complex. For example, we are prone to assume the possession of full information as well as considerable rationality on the part of political actors. The fact is, however, that most of us do not know how we are affected by globalization, for good or bad. Thus, when the costs and benefits of globalization conflict, as they usually do, we lack the information necessary to sort out the consequences and choose one policy, one candidate, or one product over others. As we have seen in chapter 6, it is difficult to understand how global systems affect us because many of these systems are invisible. Moreover, globalization is such a vast, complex, and pervasive force in our lives that often a person is *both* a winner *and* a loser at the same time from the same transaction. We lack a paradigm that helps us analyze contemporary issues as cases of the unequal distribution of costs and benefits of globalization.

Consider, for example, the consequences of the trade pact the United States and Vietnam signed in 2000.[14] For many U.S. manufacturers and workers, the pact was bad news because it meant that cheaper Vietnamese apparel, toys, and other consumer goods would soon be entering American markets at lower prices. For the Vietnamese fishing industry, however, the pact was good news because it promised increased demand in the United States for tuna and squid. And that was good news for the U.S. manufacturer of diesel engines, Caterpillar, because most of the new fishing boats being constructed in Vietnam will be powered by Caterpillar-produced engines. And Caterpillar stands to gain in other ways as well: by providing electric power generators for factories (including the Ford Motor Company plant near Hanoi) that cannot be supplied by Vietnam's inadequate public power grid or by providing earth-moving equipment to quarry limestone to make cement for new buildings, bridges, and other infrastructure. Not surprisingly, Caterpillar was among the leaders in urging the U.S. government to end the trade embargo against Vietnam. (It also bears mentioning that when Caterpillar prospers, so do the workers it employs, the owners of shares of its stock and their families, the merchants with whom they do business, the communities where all of these people live, and so on more or less ad infinitum.)

FRAMEWORKS FOR ANALYSIS

Our search for the winners and losers from globalization requires that we first identify an appropriate unit of analysis. Who, or what, are the principal actors or agents in the system? One option would be to focus our attention on the integrated global system. Robert Cox takes this approach when he asserts that the "social structure of the world shaped by globalization takes the form of a three-part hierarchy."[15] At the top of this hierarchy are those who are integrated into the global economy and who enjoy relatively stable and secure employment. This category includes executives, managers, and assembly line workers in global production firms. At the second level are those who serve the global economy in "more precarious employment," such as direct personal services. The bottom level contains "superfluous labor," people excluded from the global economy and who enter it only as a destabilizing force. Because these sectors are distributed globally, we can presumably find examples of all three levels almost anywhere. But obviously some regions of the world will contain more people of one level than of another.

Another way to look at this would be to concentrate on what economists call the "new international division of labor" or "global division of labor."[16] Beginning in the 1960s, much of the world's manufacturing labor and many of its production sites were relocated from the old industrial countries of Western Europe and North America to the newly emerging economies in Asia and Latin America. Rather dramatically, the "core" deindustrialized, and the share of GDP drawn from manufacturing began to rise in countries such as Mexico, Taiwan, and South Korea. This transformation entailed, in the words of James Mittelman, "massive industrial relocation, the subdivision of manufacturing processes into multiple partial operations, major technological innovations, large-scale migratory flows, and the feminization of labor."[17] It also exposed the industrial labor forces of North America and Europe to the stresses and strains of trade liberalization and integration to a far greater degree than they had ever experienced before.

But as Mittelman and others have pointed out, the concept of the "global division of labor" is a blunt instrument with which to analyze the politics of globalization. Much of the writing about the global division of labor sees labor in developing countries as simply a factor of production and ignores the actions of workers as consumers, creators of culture, agents of political change, and so forth. In particular, the role of Third World workers acting through reformist unions to affect their national political economies has been largely unappreciated.[18] Moreover, the new division of labor has affected some parts of the developing world, and some sectors within the global economy, to a greater degree than others. In some parts of Latin America, for example, industrial labor has played a major economic role since the 1930s, and the "new" industrial labor force is more properly seen as coexisting with the old rather than supplanting it. In the highly industrialized economies, some sectors (for example, textiles, shoes, and apparel) have been ravaged by global integration much more than others (for instance, aerospace). Finally, global integration has not been driven blindly by the logic of capitalism and profit; politics matters quite a bit, as well. The state is still a key actor in the process, and international politics still plays an important role in determining who gets what in the global division of labor. For these and other reasons, our inquiry here focuses on the nation-state as the arena within which winners and losers struggle to advance their respective goals regarding globalization.

In a recent book entitled *Has Globalization Gone Too Far?* Dani Rodrik analyzes the key political issue raised by globalization at the nation-state level: the tension between global markets (economic integration, liberalized trade) and domestic social stability.[19] Rodrik identifies three sources of this tension.[20] First, the globalization of markets harms workers by *accentuating the asymmetries,* such as resource endowments and power, between those people who can cross international borders easily (either directly or indirectly via outsourcing, either physically or virtually) and those who cannot. Globalization produces this outcome in three ways:

- through the displacement of low-wage, low-skill labor by importing competitive goods from low-wage countries (these have to be goods, such as shoes or apparel, for which worker productivity is not too important in the production process)
- through closing manufacturing facilities in industrialized countries and moving jobs overseas
- by importing low-cost labor from abroad

Second, globalization *engenders conflict between nations* over domestic norms, values, and the social institutions that embody them.[21] The processes by which this happens include the following:

- Globalization allows exporting firms to engage in production practices not allowed by the importing country (for example, child or prison labor, lack of environmental protection, not allowing free unions, etc.). World Trade Organization rules do not permit importing countries to use criteria like these to raise barriers to trade. These rules do not take into consideration the unequal bargaining power of economic sectors.
- Global economic integration constrains economic policies such as taxation, budget deficits, and social policies.
- Globalization reduces state power to control immigration, especially illegal immigration, leading to the rise of the immigrant-trafficking organizations.

Finally, globalization weakens social stability by *constraining spending on social programs and insurance.*[22] Ever since the 1880–1914 period of globalization, Rodrik contends, there has been a clear and positive relationship between international trade and the welfare state. The more open a state's economy is to foreign goods, the more active a state must be in compensating the losers from this trade. The more open a society is to trade, the more instability it will experience. Welfare state policies are aimed at restoring stability. Yet globalization may now be constraining states' abilities to undertake these policies by weakening their tax bases. This change will mean increased taxes on the factors of production that cannot move easily across national boundaries (labor) and reduced taxes on those factors that can move easily to avoid taxation (capital).

Rodrik's views on the costs of globalization are by no means accepted by all observers or analysts. For the counterargument—that globalization helps far more people than it hurts and its overall effect is overwhelmingly positive—we shall consider a recent survey of globalization published by *The Economist*.[23] The author of the survey, Clive Crook, asserts that globalization in fact helps far more workers in highly industrialized countries than it hurts. There may be some displacement of jobs to poorer countries, but the job-creation effects of increased trade will make available many more jobs to replace those lost. And they will be jobs that pay better and reward skills and education more. Workers in poor countries will also be better off as they move into the jobs once located in the rich countries. The overall economic level of the world generally will be improved by free trade. Consumers will be better off because they will have more money to spend, and there will be more left over after basic needs are met, so governments will be able to reap more in taxes, which they can then spend on education and other essential public goods. If there has been a widening of the gap between the rich and the poor in the world, as data from *The Economist* show (see figures 7.1 and 7.2), the cause has been not globalization but the differential impact of education levels and access to technology.

Crook and *The Economist* also reject the notion that globalization has worked against democracy by weakening national governments and thwarting the wishes of the voters. If one measures the size of governments by the share of the nation's GDP taken in taxes, then, if anything, governments are getting larger, not smaller. With the exception of Japan, the government of virtually every rich country in the world now takes a greater share of the GDP in taxes than it did in 1980. Furthermore, governments in the industrialized countries may profess that they have been forced to make changes in social welfare payments, government budgets, or progressive tax policies in order to meet the demands of the global economy. But these protestations, claims *The Economist,* are usually misleading and even intentionally deceptive. In most cases, the government is usually making some policy change it wished to make anyway and is simply using the global economy and its institutions as the excuse. Voters, says Crook, must be wary of such arguments and must not allow their own government to escape responsibility for its decisions and choices.

Once we have identified the political issues created or aggravated by global economic integration, we have to identify how groups and individuals compete over these issues. One framework for understanding the politics of globaliza-

Figure 7.3. America's "Four-Party System"

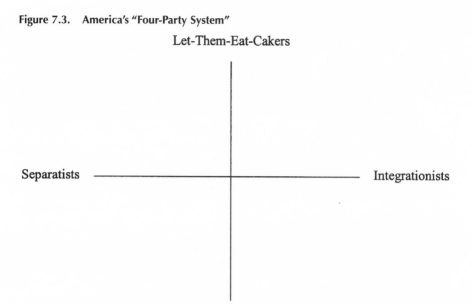

Source: Adapted from Thomas Friedman, "The New American Politics," *New York Times*, November 13, 1997.

tion has been suggested by *New York Times* foreign affairs columnist Thomas Friedman. In a pair of articles that appeared in late 1997, Friedman introduces his four-part matrix formed by two intersecting lines.[24] (See figure 7.3.) The horizontal line represents how a person feels about globalization, which Friedman defines as "the way in which technology and open markets are combining to integrate more and more of the world." At the far right end of the spectrum are the "Integrationists," who believe that global integration is inevitable or good; at the far left are the "Separatists," who feel that integration is neither inevitable nor good and thus must be stopped or even rolled back. Intersecting this line in the middle at right angles is a vertical line that represents the issue of distribution—that is, how the costs and benefits of globalization (and most other changes, for that matter) should be apportioned. At the bottom or "southern" end of this spectrum are the "Social-Safety-Netters," who advocate public policies to help people adjust to the challenges and opportunities of integration, as well as to protect people from the social and environmental damage of free trade. At the top or "northern" end of this line are the "Let-Them-Eat-Cakers," who believe that the free and unrestrained play of market forces is the best way to distribute costs and gains. They would oppose public policies to offset the harm done by global integration.

The two intersecting lines create a matrix of what Friedman calls America's new "four-party system." In the lower left-hand corner are the "Separatist-Social-Safety-Netters," who want to block integration; but if that fails, then they want to remedy its abuses with compensatory public policies. In the lower right-hand corner are the "Integrationist-Social-Safety-Netters," who want to use public policies to move integration ahead by compensating the losers. In the upper right-hand corner are the "Integrationist-Let-Them-Eat-Cakers," who advocate more free trade and no government intervention to distribute the costs and benefits. In the upper left-hand corner are the "Separatist-Let-Them-Eat-Cakers," who want to block integration and also oppose social legislation to achieve any kind of compensatory objective.

Friedman's matrix helps us bring the globalization debate down from its abstractions and focus our attention more concretely on the winners and losers. Its drawbacks are two, however. First, its categories are too blunt and simplistic to help us place specific groups in one cell of the matrix or another; and second, it gives us no guidance or criteria for predicting whether a given group or individual will adopt one position or another within the matrix. Thus, we need to go beyond the Friedman matrix to examine the impact of globalization on domestic politics. We begin this analysis with an understanding that globalization (defined here as increased international economic integration) produces winners and losers in three ways:

- by increasing or decreasing the demand for something of value (for example, one's own labor) that a person owns or controls,
- by increasing or decreasing the supply of something of value that a person wants or needs, and
- by altering the costs of transactions that connect the producers and consumers of things of value.

Winners

Winners from globalization are found all over the world, from the highly industrial countries to those at earlier stages of industrialization. (See boxes 7.1 and 7.2.) We have already seen that globalization has been accompanied by an increase in the gap between the rich and the poor occasioned by an explosion in the numbers

Box 7.1.   Profile of a Winner, I:
Automobile Workers in the American South

One of the most often repeated themes in the story of the globalization of manufacturing involves the relocation of textile and clothing factories in search of cheap labor. In the first half of the twentieth century, mills were moved from New York City and New England to the American South. After 1960, the move south continued, this time to Mexico and even farther offshore, to Southeast Asia. But in the 1980s, manufacturing in the South began to take on a different look. And this time, the owners and firms were primarily from America's leading economic competitors, Germany and Japan.

The transformation began not in the South but close to it. In the early 1980s, Honda opened the first Japanese-owned automobile plant in the United States, in Marysville, Ohio. Then the trek south began in earnest. In 1984, Nissan announced plans to begin manufacturing cars in Smyrna, Tennessee, followed in 1987 by Toyota's plant in Georgetown, Kentucky. In the 1990s, the Germans followed. BMW opened a factory in Greer, South Carolina; and Mercedes-Benz answered with one in Vance, Alabama. By 2001, in all there were seven German or Japanese automobile plants in the South, offering employment to more than 25,000 local workers. Planned expansions promised to raise employment at the plants by some 4,000 by 2003. This is quite a change from the 1930s and 1940s, when poor southerners traveled north to Detroit and other cities to work in American-owned car factories.

The forces converging to attract German and Japanese automobile firms to the American South were local and national as well as global. Like many global corporations, the firms were looking for productive, relatively cheap, and nonunionized labor. Local and state governments willing to offer attractive incentives such as tax breaks and subsidized land were also critical. The South, still lagging behind the rest of the country economically, was eager to provide these things. Then there was the lure of the huge U.S. market, more accessible from within than from outside, and the domestic infrastructure supporting manufacturing. In this last, the interstate highway system proved to be most important. Most of the new factories sprang up near interstate highways, where containerized freight deliveries could speed the movement of car parts from Japan, Europe, or Mexico. And finally, global forces were also at work. Information technologies made it possible to deliver complicated blue prints and car specifications from Europe or Japan in real time. Fax machines and satellite telecommunications connected firm centers with factories, making oversight from a distance easy. And the emergence of global markets for easily recognized automobile brands and designs opened the way for the sale of Nissans, BMWs, and Toyotas in the United States just as if they were American-made cars, which, of course, they are.

Sources: Warren Brown, "Nissan to Build Cars in Tennessee Plant," *Washington Post,* May 12, 1984. Robert Kearns, "Japan's Kentucky Auto Derby," *Washington Post,* March 15, 1992. James Bennet, "Mercedes Selects Alabama Site," *New York Times,* September 30, 1993. Doron Levin, "What BMW Sees in South Carolina," *New York Times,* April 11, 1993. Jane Perlez, "Toyota and Honda Create Global Production System," *New York Times,* March 26, 1993. Allen Myerson, "O Governor, Won't You Buy Me a Mercedes Plant?" *New York Times,* September 1, 1996. Sue Anne Pressley, "The South's New-Car Smell," *Washington Post,* May 11, 2001.

Box 7.2.   Profile of a Winner, II: The Poor of
Latin America and the Globalization of Bulk-Flow Systems

For many of the poor of developing economies, such as those in Latin America, globalization has proven to be of great benefit. The reason is that the arrival of global bulk-flow systems of transport and communication has connected them to the outside world in ways that would have taken centuries using older technologies. The new ways brought by these systems are double-edged swords, however. They can seemingly produce as much pain and conflict as they do joy and benefit. Many of these conflicts stem from the ways the new connecting technologies challenge long-entrenched dominant groups. These struggles have many dimensions: gender, class, and ethnicity and language. Consider these examples:

- In Guyana, on the northeast coast of South America, people of the Repununi region had been isolated from the outside world for centuries. The arrival of the Internet made it possible for indigenous women to sell hand-woven hammocks, some for as much as $1,000 apiece, on the Web to distant buyers. This huge profit immediately brought these women into a clash with the traditional regional leadership, who tried to take control of the weavers' cooperative. The weavers' group fell into disarray as a result of the takeover attempt.
- In the mountainous Cotopoxi region of Ecuador, Quechua-speaking peasants planned to gather crop information from distant agricultural websites, as well as to sell their crafts to distant buyers over the same medium. Before long, it was discovered that some of the men in the villages were using the Web to look at pornography instead. Dismayed, the women began to question the treatment they had been receiving from their husbands, and the subject of wife beating, formerly a strict taboo, was discussed openly. Use of the Internet for these purposes was subsequently curtailed.
- In October 1999, the Internet came to the village of Marankiari Bajo, Peru. Through a joint grant from a Lima-based nonprofit organization, the Canadian government, and the local telephone company, the village received a portable generator, a satellite dish, a computer, and a large-screen monitor for the local school. The result was to empower the Ashaninka Tribe, an ethnic and linguistic minority whose members had frequently been sold into slavery. Tribal leaders received eight weeks of training and designed their own Web site, from which they sell organically grown oranges in Lima, 250 miles away. E-commerce has boosted tribal revenue some 10 percent.

Sources: Simon Romero, "Weavers Go Dot-Com, and Elders Move In," *New York Times,* March 28, 2000.
Simon Romero, "How a Byte of Knowledge Can Be Dangerous, Too," *New York Times,* April 23, 2000.
Anthony Faiola and Stephen Buckley, "Poor in Latin America Embrace Net's Promise," *Washington Post,* July 9, 2000.

of the superrich. Global economic integration was certainly not the only factor working to increase this gap, but it must surely have played a major role.

The impact of all this new wealth rippled out to affect countless other winners who provided the wealthy with luxury mansions, expensive consumer goods, and a wide range of personal services. One *New York Times* article of the period reports on the boom in the construction of supermansions in the Long Island suburb of Southampton. A 12,000-square-foot, $8 million home in the neighborhood boasted "his" and "hers" bathrooms whose showers featured "hand-polished, nickel-plated, thermostatic [water] mixers with overhead shower and hand sprayer on a cradle."[25] They cost $3,000 apiece. But winners are sometimes where we least expect to find them. The construction boom stimulated heavy demand for labor, and much of the demand was met by immigrant workers from Central America. The *Times* article also describes Miguel Velazquez, an immigrant from El Salvador, who worked on the new homes twelve hours a day, seven days a week, earning $23 per hour. His two sons, both in their early twenties, worked with him. One homebuilder is quoted as saying that his firm could not keep up with the demand without the Salvadorans and other immigrants.

Many native-born blue-collar workers were also winners from globalization. For example, the new automobile assembly plants in the American South described in box 7.1 stimulated the construction of numerous neighboring factories to provide components, repairs, and other services. The BMW plant in South Carolina, for example, lead to the opening along Interstate 85 of factories devoted to the manufacture of ball bearings, floor carpet, seat upholstery fabric, tires, oil filters, fuel injectors, pumps, brake systems, shock absorbers, molded plastic parts, steel stampings, and others.[26]

Winners from globalization are found not just in the highly industrialized countries but in developing countries or emerging economies as well. Often the gains of these individuals and sectors stem from their exploitation of new markets for their goods and services that have emerged in industrialized countries and to which they are connected by global telecommunications and transport. However, these winners differ significantly from winners in rich countries in two important ways. First, their newfound prosperity is much more fragile because they are totally dependent on distant and impersonal markets and the invisible networks that connect them. The more distant and more complex these factors are, the more easily something can go seriously wrong. A system failure ("normal accident") or an unexpected economic downturn in the industrialized world can wreak havoc on the newly globalized poor. In addition, globalization and its benefits often force traditional peoples in developing countries to abandon their ancient ways and adopt new values and principles. These cultural changes can frequently be painful.

In the hamlet of Rovieng, Cambodia, for example, most people formerly eked out their livings as subsistence farmers. After the village was connected to the Internet via satellite, a number of village women began to earn money by weaving silk scarves for distant markets.[27] The village's young people are now connected via the Internet to youth all over the world, but they are also exposed to images (film, websites, music, and so forth) that trouble their elders. Furthermore, many workers in developing countries work under harsh sweatshop conditions, but in the La Laguna region of Mexico, 250 miles south of the U.S. border, conditions have improved markedly since the launching of the North American Free Trade Agreement. Workers in one of the numerous jeans factories (the town is known as the jeans capital of the world) have seen their wages triple in two years. They receive free transportation from home to the factory, free lunches, and air conditioning and have Mexican music piped in.[28] But the ultimate cultural affront may have occurred in October 2000, when a Starbucks coffee shop opened within the confines of the Forbidden City in Beijing. While many Chinese were outraged by what they saw as an invasion of one of their most prized cultural landmarks, younger Chinese flocked to the shop in large numbers, eager to embrace Western customs. One young woman customer from Shanghai was quoted as saying, "Coffee is cool now. The Forbidden City can be cool, too."[29]

Losers

Losers from globalization are found everywhere as well. (See boxes 7.3 and 7.4.) In the industrialized world, some of these people were hurt because globalization increased the value of something (for example, a high-paying assembly line job) that was distributed unequally to begin with, and the inequality

---

Box 7.3.   Profile of a Loser, I: Apple Growers in the United States

American agriculture, long the envy of the entire world, has been severely hurt by the globalization of food production, and in some cases the damage has been nearly disastrous. One of the hardest hit sectors has been the nation's 9,000 apple growers, concentrated in the states of Washington and New York. During the 1990s, apple growers were strong supporters of economic globalization because their product was in great demand around the Pacific Rim. Washington State growers exported one-third of their annual production, with one-half of that going to Asia. Partly in response to the Asian demand, apple growers planted thousands of acres of new orchards. Then, in the late 1990s, a number of trends converged to spell trouble for the apple industry:

- China emerged as the world's leading apple-producing nation. Today, China produces one billion 42-pound boxes of apples annually, compared with only 100 million in Washington State. By 2005, it is expected that China will supply about 40 percent of the world's apples. Some of this production is exported as unprocessed fruit to other Asian markets, but much of it is sent to the United States as juice or concentrate to be used for processed fruit drinks.
- A number of other countries began to enter the world apple market. Connected by efficient and fast global systems of trade and distribution, and not required to observe America's costly environmental protection laws, apple growers in such countries as Moldova, New Zealand, Chile, Argentina, and Mexico now regularly supply both fresh apples and juice concentrate to the United States and Europe. The United States now imports juice concentrate equivalent to about one-third of the nation's entire apple crop.
- Demand for apples worldwide began to slow down. In the United States, consumption has leveled off at about 21 pounds per person annually, less than one-half the yearly consumption in most of Europe. Demand in the emerging economies of Asia, which had been rising during the early 1990s, was dragged down by the economic crises in Thailand and other parts of Southeast Asia after 1997. Asian markets consumed 50–85 percent fewer Washington State apples in 1998 than they had the preceding year.
- Production soared at home. The thousands of acres of new apple trees were blessed by ideal weather in the Pacific Northwest, and bumper crops were the result. Canadian producers felt the same weather, and their production expanded as well, offering additional competition to Washington State growers.

The result was a decline in the market price of apples in the United States from more than $8 per bushel to less than $6, less than it costs to grow. The nation's apple growers appealed to the federal government for crop subsidy assistance as well as protection from foreign apple imports at prices below the cost of production.

Sources: Sam Howe Verhovek, "Northwest Farms and Industry Feel Pinch of Asia Fiscal Crisis," *New York Times*, October 1, 1998. William Claiborne, "Global Market Forces Take a Bite Out of Apple Growers' Prospects," *Washington Post*, November 21, 1998. Dan Morgan, "Farm Policy's Blossoming Dilemma," *Washington Post*, May 10, 2001.

Box 7.4.   Profile of a Loser, II: The Chinese and Globalization

Probably the most dramatic examples of winners and losers from globalization can be seen in China as that huge country throws open the door
to its economy and culture and invites the world to enter. China's former
premier, Deng Xiao-ping, launched a tentative opening to the industrialized world in the late 1980s to enable his country to benefit from Western technology and science as well as competition in agriculture and
manufacturing. As China entered into more open trade relations with the
United States and other industrialized countries, and as it prepared to enter the World Trade Organization (WTO) early in the 2000s, there were
many Chinese, both poor and prosperous, who feared the impact of new
competition, both economic and cultural:

- Mr. Wang Tai-ching is a Hong Kong business executive who runs a
  disposable diaper factory in neighboring Guangdong Province. For
  most of the 1990s, Wang's firm owned a significant share of the
  growing Chinese market for disposable diapers, but in 1999 Procter
  & Gamble began selling its product in the country, and a ferocious
  price war ensued. Wang feared that when China became a full partner in the WTO, Procter & Gamble and other Western firms would
  bring their products in duty free, and his firm would be unable to
  compete.
- One of the requirements for joining the WTO will be for China to
  sell off many of its state-owned manufacturing firms to private owners, either Chinese or foreign. In the coastal provinces like Guangdong (neighbor to Hong Kong), many of these enterprises were already competitive and profitable. But in more distant provinces, like
  Shenyang, near the border with North Korea, these enterprises had
  been sheltered from all competition. Privatization and the threat of
  competition from abroad had already caused a sharp rise in the
  province's unemployment rate even before China joined the WTO.
  In at least one instance, the closing of a factory by its new American
  owner provoked the workers to riot and hold the American managers hostage for two days.
- Another WTO requirement is for China to relax its barriers to entry
  of commercial retail outlets such as K-Mart. Large department stores
  and chain stores will now be allowed to establish outlets, threatening to undermine the thousands of small and medium-sized locally
  owned shops and markets.
- Finally, membership in the WTO will cause Chinese tariffs on farm
  products to decline slowly, opening the country's agricultural sector

to foreign competition. Instead of price supports for Chinese corn, now set at about $175 per ton, Chinese farmers will have to compete with imported corn, which costs about $100 per ton. These changes will almost surely increase the already growing economic gap between urban and rural Chinese, with what are likely to be serious political repercussions.

Sources: Mark Landler, "Maverick Chinese Province Fears Opening of Trade," *New York Times,* June 12, 2000. Clay Chandler, "WTO Membership Imperils China's Industrial Dinosaurs," *Washington Post,* March 30, 2000. Elisabeth Rosenthal, "Factory Closings in China Arouse Workers to Fury," *New York Times,* August 31, 2000. Craig Smith, "Chinese See Pain as Well as Profit in New Trade Era," *New York Times,* September 21, 2000. John Pomfret, "China's Poor Fear Cost of Free Trade," *Washington Post,* September 24, 2000. Erik Eckholm, "In China's Heartland, the Fertile Fields Lie Fallow," *New York Times,* December 24, 2000.

remained or grew larger. Some were hurt because globalization took from them something they valued or on which they depended. In many instances, these losses occurred because of a decline in the costs of a certain kind of global transaction. For example, if globalization made it possible for jobs in the United States to be performed by less expensive labor abroad, and as a consequence the jobs were relocated to foreign countries, the resultant job losses by American workers would be counted here.

For example, in 1991 AT&T closed its manufacturing plant in Radford, Virginia, leaving about 1,000 workers without employment.[30] About 100 of the Virginia employees were moved to Mesquite, Texas, where they joined about 650 AT&T workers from Texas in a highly automated facility that absorbed about 90 percent of the work done at Radford. At the same time, AT&T shifted its most labor-intensive operations from Virginia to Matamoros, Mexico, where wages averaged $0.50 per hour, compared with an average of $8.56 at the Radford plant. In June 2000, the Zebco Corporation of Tulsa, Oklahoma, began moving most of its fishing reel production to China, leaving most of its 240 employees out of work.[31] Zebco had resisted moving offshore for years, but when its competitors began selling fishing tackle through such outlets as Wal-Mart at much lower prices, Zebco began to investigate the Chinese market. The company found that it could produce its reels in China for one-third less than it could in Tulsa, and the decision was irresistible.

Some people are hurt because globalization raises the cost of something they value or on which they depend. The rise in fuel prices during 2000 caused considerable hardship to numerous people who lived on fixed or declining incomes and were unable to reduce their consumption of gasoline and heating oil.[32] Included in this category are both urban and rural poor, the former because of the inadequacy of public transportation and the latter because of their need to travel long distances to shop or for medical care. Especially affected were people living on fixed incomes (retirees, persons with disabilities) and the working poor. In September 2000, truckers in France launched a protest against the rising cost of their diesel fuel.[33] Their blockade of fuel-storage depots and service stations thoroughly disrupted the nation's transportation system. The truckers were joined in the protests by farmers, airline workers, bus drivers, taxi drivers, and the operators of sightseeing boats on the Seine. After six days of disorder and serious inconvenience for the country's motorists, the government finally capitulated and agreed to reimburse truckers for some of their increased fuel costs, including a rebate on fuel taxes.

Then there are cases in which people were hurt because globalization decreased the demand for some good they exported or increased the competitive, low-cost supply of that same good from foreign sources. Coal exports from the United States declined sharply from a high of 79 million tons in 1996 to only 58 million tons in 1999.[34] Industry analysts doubt that overseas sales will ever rebound to the high levels of the mid-1990s. The decline in coal exports was caused by a combination of global factors that included the Asian financial crisis that began in 1997, an increase in the export capacity of mines in Australia and South Africa, and the revival of small-scale coal and coke production in China. Especially hard hit were the coal-mining companies of West Virginia, Kentucky, and southwestern Virginia; the railroads that carried their exports to East Coast ports; the coal miners and railroad workers laid off because of the decline; and the mining communities in these states where the economy depends on the income of these workers.

We usually think of agriculture as a sector that produces almost entirely for a domestic market. In fact, much of America's farm produce is destined for foreign markets, and many farmers depend on global markets for their income. This has been the case for a long time; but changes in the federal government's farm price support policy forced many American growers to look abroad for markets in order to sustain their incomes. Farms in central Illinois, for example, are far away from Europe and Asia, but more than one-half of the corn grown here is trucked to the Mississippi River, where it is loaded on barges and sent down to the Gulf of Mexico for shipment around the world. As one Illinois farmer has put it, "Farmers need to think globally, who their customers are, what they want and what our competitors will provide if we don't."[35] In 1998, the local price for wheat in eastern Washington State dropped to $2.24 per bushel, about a dollar below what wheat farmers said they need to turn a profit.[36] The causes for the decline were a complex combination of economic crises in Asia and larger-than-expected wheat crops in Canada and Australia.

Finally, we consider cases in which globalization provides the incentives to attract immigrants from developing countries but then diminishes the quality of their lives (income, employment, family life, health, safety, etc.) by exploiting their minority status in their new homeland. The containerization revolution increased massively the flow of traffic through America's major ports, such as Houston, Long Beach (California), Seattle, and Newark.[37] Key elements in the cargo transport system are the port truckers who haul the 20-ton containers from port to warehouse or railhead and back. In the port of Long Beach, virtually all of the 6,000 port truckers are immigrants from Mexico or Central America. Despite the sixty-hour weeks they are required to work, they earn barely more than poverty-level wages, much of which must go to pay rising fuel, insurance, and maintenance costs for their trucks. In addition, they lack fringe benefits and are faced daily with indignities and abuses from the trucking companies to which they contract their services. Many of these truckers believe that their plight stems from their lack of union representation. Furthermore, in February 2000, Perdue Farms Inc., the nation's third-largest poultry producer, terminated a program that brought hundreds of Korean immigrants to take jobs in its processing plants on Maryland's Eastern Shore.[38] The reason for the termination of the program was a press report that immigrants were made to pay up to $30,000 each to intermediaries in Korea for the right to apply for these jobs and that once in the United States they were subject to abuses by the contractors. Some were made to pay an additional deposit of $5,000, which they would lose if they left the job within a year of arrival. Others had been told that their green cards would be revoked, or their chances for citizenship would be jeopardized, if they quit before the first year. Contractors and agents in Korea, who had made substantial profits from their intermediary services, were furious at Perdue's decision to stop the program.

There are numerous losers in the developing world as well. Some of these losses stem from the highly unequal way in which globalization has penetrated developing countries. One recent *New York Times* report describes the consequences of such inequality. In the city of Hyderabad, India, a glittering office building complex, called Hitec City, symbolizes the city's increasingly important role in the global Information Revolution. In a building known as Cyber Towers, Indian software engineers and designers work in air-conditioned comfort for such U.S. firms as Microsoft and Oracle. At the same time, as the *Times* reporter puts it, "less than 50 miles away, in the poverty-stricken village of Sheri Ram Reddy Guda, the old India is alive and unwell. Illiteracy, sickness, and hunger are the villagers' constant companions. Women and children work in the fields for less than 50 cents a day. The sole telephone . . . almost never works."[39]

Globalization harms people in developing countries by subjecting them to unseen forces in the world economy or by making them live, work, and compete in a global economy that runs according to rules they did not make and over which they have no influence. Foreign institutions, like banks and stock markets, and international organizations, like the International Monetary Fund (IMF) and the World Bank, have enormous power to shape the economic fortunes of the poor of the Third World. Brazil's currency devaluation in 1999 was brought on in large part by the crisis that swept through the world's stock markets from Southeast Asia in 1997, through Korea, Russia, and finally the United States. The country's middle class recovered within a year, but the working poor faced double-digit unemployment and soaring prices for staples such as food and gasoline.[40] The cashew industry of Mozambique was virtually destroyed when the IMF and the World Bank forced the government to get rid of its export tax on the nuts. The tax had been enacted in an effort to ensure a supply of cashews for the domestic processing industry, but the World Bank threatened to withhold critical loans unless the government rescinded it. Without the tax to hold back some of the country's production, the local processing industry practically vanished within a year. Ten of the largest factories shut down, one-half of the industry's labor force became unemployed, and the only winners were the trade brokers who reaped huge profits by arranging transactions between local farmers and foreign processors.[41]

Unlike working-class people in the rich industrialized world, poor people in developing countries have no social or political infrastructure to support them in hard times. In 1997, the working urban poor across Southeast Asia, from Thailand to Indonesia, were devastated by an economic crash that most North Americans and Europeans experienced only by watching news reports or noting changes in their stock portfolios. In November 1997, the 449 workers at the P.A.R. Garment Factory on the outskirts of Bangkok were summarily dismissed and told to go home. But they continued to sleep on the sidewalk by the factory gate because most of them literally had no place to go. There was no work for them in Bangkok, and they could not return to their home villages because there was no work for them there either. Between 1996 and 1998, indicators of social pathology such as suicide rates and the abandonment of children in orphanages soared in Thailand and Indonesia.[42]

Even the discovery of a prized natural resource such as petroleum does not necessarily work to the benefit of the poor in developing countries. In fact, oil may do as much harm as it does good to many of these people. Angola is the seventh-leading oil-producing country in the world, yet government corruption and the effects of a seemingly interminable civil war prevent most of the country's 12 million inhabitants from ever seeing any of the benefits of this resource.[43] The recent discovery of oil off the coast of Equatorial Guinea has brought in new investment (most of which will never be seen by the country's natives). But it has also brought in new Western products such as clothing by Nike and Adidas, which take away the work of local tailors and clothing manufacturers.[44]

INTEREST GROUPS AND COALITIONS

In his 1989 book, *Commerce and Coalitions,* Ronald Rogowski offers a framework for organizing what we know about the impact of trade expansion on domestic political cleavages.[45] He begins with the economic principle that the gains and losses from the expansion (or contraction) of foreign trade are distributed throughout society according to the relative scarcity or abundance of the key factors of production.[46] An *expansion* of trade benefits the owners of the abundant factors of production (relative to the rest of the world) and harms the owners of the scarce factors (again, relative to the rest of the world). A *con-*

traction of trade has the opposite effects: it benefits the owners of the scarce factors and harms the owners of the abundant ones. For example, in a society with abundant labor but scarce capital, trade expansion benefits labor and harms capital. If the factor endowments are different, then so are the social and political consequences of trade expansion.

Rogowski illustrates his framework with four models in the distribution of land, labor, and capital. An increase in trade can be predicted to affect political cleavages in the following ways:

- Model 1, an "advanced economy" (abundant capital) with abundant land and scarce labor: increased trade produces a class cleavage between a land–capital coalition favoring free trade on one side and protectionist labor on the other.
- Model 2, with abundant capital and labor and scarce land: trade expansion produces an urban–rural cleavage between a labor–capital coalition (free trade) on one side and landowners (protectionist) on the other.
- Model 3, a "backward economy" (Rogowski's term) whereby capital and labor are scarce and land is abundant: expanded trade brings forth an urban–rural cleavage between a protectionist labor–capital coalition on one side and landowners favoring free trade on the other.
- Model 4, with scarce capital and land and abundant labor: an increase in trade produces a class cleavage between a protectionist land–capital coalition on one side and labor favoring free trade on the other.

With such diversity involved in the disputes over globalization, it would be surprising indeed if the coalitions that formed in domestic politics were as broad and as undifferentiated as those described in Rogowski's historical analyses.[47] Instead, we are likely to find considerable diversity in the coalitions that compete in the arena of globalization issues. Indeed, each subissue of globalization will feature its own unique policy network. A full understanding of globalization requires that we understand how these subissue policy networks reflect coalitions of winners and losers.

The problem is that many analytical frameworks deal with social aggregates such as "labor" and "capital" as undifferentiated populations and political actors. The Global System Paradigm helps us discover very specific subsectors of the population that experience gains and/or losses from globalization and examine the ways they cope in both personal and public ways with these consequences. The familiar division of the economy into the three factors of production—land, labor, and capital—does not get us very far. We need to subdivide these three sectors and make them more precise, in recognition of the very high level of social and economic differentiation characteristic of highly industrialized societies. We need to understand that the "land" (or, more properly, the product of the land) includes the enormously productive and diverse U.S. agricultural system. "Capital" can no longer be considered a single class when some

60 percent of the households in the United States own shares of stock in private enterprises. And "labor" includes information professionals (the people Robert Reich labels "symbolic analysts"),[48] middle-class professionals, industrial labor in manufacturing enterprises, routine personal service workers, and many other categories. In sum, the search for globalization's winners and losers, and the analysis of their strategic choices in the political realm, is apt to be extremely complex and will require an extremely fine grained approach capable of uncovering the subtle nuances of interest group politics.

With rare exceptions, politics is the business of elites. There are occasions, of course, when, unbidden and uncoordinated, nonelites emerge to take charge of the political agenda, but these moments are few. Indeed, some might regard such events as disruptive indicators that the political system suffers from some serious flaw or inadequacy, a symptom of some pathology. Most of the daily work of politics is done by small groups of elites who frequently (but not always) act in the name of, and on the behalf of, nonelites. Such is the case with globalization politics as well. Affected nonelites rarely appear on the public scene as political actors. Nonelite winners and losers are usually represented by elites who conduct their campaigns in the name of their respective nonelites. In the era of globalization politics the distinction between the roles and status of elites and nonelites is even stronger and clearer. It is worth keeping in mind that the elites who act on behalf of globalization's losers are seldom really losers themselves in any material sense.

Two kinds of interest groups and associations are active in the globalization debate. *National-industrial elites* are groups that originated in the earlier national, industrial era and whose basic agenda derives from the issues of that time. *Global-postindustrial elites* are groups that have emerged more recently to contest the issues created by global integration. Both kinds of groups derive much of their power from the information technologies and transnational flows that are part of globalization itself. Thus, not only are the issues they contest part of globalization; so are the tactics and strategies they use.

National-Industrial Elites

Political scientists divide national-industrial political systems into two kinds: corporatist and pluralist. Corporatism refers to a system in which interest groups are relatively large in size, few in number, and coordinated into a very small number of national peak organizations. Corporatist systems tended in the past to be rather simple, with peak organizations representing agriculture, small businesses, industrial labor and management, and little else. Leaders of these peak organizations, especially those representing labor and management, met and consulted frequently with each other and with government representatives, in a process known as "concertation." The purpose of these meetings was to arrive at comprehensive economic, political, and social agreements that were binding on all participants. The emphasis was on coordination of interest group demands and actions and on compromise between and among all the principal economic actors, including the government.

Through the last decades of the nineteenth century and most of the twentieth, corporatism was the dominant system for many European democracies, especially those in Central Europe and Scandinavia. The growth in the popularity of corporatism was not accidental but, rather, one of the consequences of the expansion of international trade. The more open a nation-state was to international trade, the greater the economic and social dislocations it experienced from that trade were.[49] The smaller European democracies were forced to expand and strengthen welfare state policies to offset the damage done by international trade, and interest groups found the corporatist model the best for protecting their members from such dislocations and instabilities.

The corporatist model of economic policy making began to emerge during the wave of globalization between 1880 and World War I, and it continued to be the dominant European model until the 1980s and early 1990s. Since then, some observers believe, globalization has had the opposite effect on corporatism. By reducing government capacity to intervene in the national economy via macroeconomic policies, globalization has curtailed the ability of the state to steer the economy. If the state is no longer in control of a country's economic system, then private sector groups have little incentive to bargain with it. At the same time, globalization has fragmented the economy into many small and more specialized sectors, each of which demands its own association to represent it.

The pluralist model differs markedly from corporatism. Interest groups tend to be smaller and more narrowly focused, there are many more of them (sometimes in the many tens of thousands), and they seldom are coordinated into peak associations. In pluralist systems, interest groups form ad hoc coalitions around specific issues and disband these coalitions once those issues have been resolved or have otherwise disappeared from the scene. Peak associations do not come together regularly to negotiate broad economic accords, and tripartite agreements binding labor, management, and the state do not figure importantly in economic policy making. Compromise is not highly valued, and a "winner-take-all" mentality tends to dominate economic policy debates. Of greatest importance to this analysis, pluralist interest groups and associations tend to be much more vocal in their criticism of state policy and much more proactive in seeking policies favorable to their members. Thus, if globalization has sharpened political, economic, and social cleavages in all countries, the debate unleashed by this will be louder and more public in pluralist systems than in corporatist ones.

Interest associations in pluralist systems have available to them tactics and strategies that are sometimes public, dramatic, confrontational, and highly visible and at other times private, routine, and relatively invisible to the general public. Both strategies have been used to influence the resolution of globalization issues in recent years.

In 1991, the member states of the European Union negotiated the Maastricht Treaty as the cornerstone of their long-term policy goal of regional political and economic integration. In several ways, the treaty offered the prospect of substantial erosion of national sovereignty. The treaty's Protocol on Social Policy allowed the E.U. to adopt initiatives in social policy by qualified majority vote rather than unanimity, as had been the case. And the adoption of a common currency, the euro, in 1999 threatened to hold member states to rigorous limits in fiscal policy (especially in running government budget deficits and incurring public debt), which would restrain state spending in social policy areas as well. Not surprisingly, in countries where the treaty was subjected to a referendum, the debate was acrimonious and the opposition, vigorous. In France the referendum in September 1992 barely passed, but when the French government began to implement the fiscal and budgetary steps required to join, opposition became even stronger.[50] In mid-1995, the government proposed an austerity plan to raise taxes to pay for health and pension benefits, increase contributions to health care plans, increase the length of government service required to qualify for a pension, and freeze civil service salaries. The result was a series of general strikes in December that involved railway and government workers as well as those in air transport, telecommunications, and trucking. Eventually the government gave in and rescinded most of its proposals.

In Seattle, Washington, in November–December 1999, and again in Washington, D.C., in April 2000, many national-industrial interest groups carried their advocacy campaigns into the streets to engage in direct confrontation with the organizations that manage the global economy (the World Trade Organization [WTO], IMF, and so forth).[51] The American Federation of Labor–Congress of Industrial Organizations, the United Steelworkers of America, and the Teamsters Union were there to protest the dumping of low-cost steel into U.S. markets. The Sierra Club, the National Wildlife Federation, and Friends of the Earth were there urging the WTO to uphold the U.S. ban on the importation of shrimp that had been caught in illegal nets. The Center for Science in the Public Interest, the Consumer Federation of America, and Public Citizen were there to protest the WTO's support of the American export of hormone-treated beef. In Seattle, police and national guard units equipped with riot gear used tear gas and rubber bullets to suppress the demonstrations; in Washington, the confrontation went rather more peacefully. Public, confrontational demonstrations by anti-globalization groups are now expected to occur at meetings of the numerous organizations that manage the global economy.

Globalization politics is not all sound and fury; it has a quieter and more routine dimension as well. National-industrial groups engage in more conventional lobbying activity in courts and before government regulatory agencies. Consider the debate over rules used to assign the "Made in U.S.A." label to a product.[52] In 1995, the New Balance Athletic Shoe Company requested that the Federal Trade Commission (FTC) relax the rules for allowing a manufacturing firm to display the coveted label on its products. The existing rule required that a product had to be made "all or virtually all" in the United States, with the "virtually all" requirement interpreted as meaning that 98 percent of its material had to come from the United States. Because New Balance was manufacturing shoes with outer soles from China, it had been accused of violating the FTC's rule. New Balance responded by proposing that the rule be changed to fit the new global economy. After two years of review, the FTC agreed with New Balance and, in May 1997, issued a proposed change to allow the label to be used if a product was "substantially all" from the United States, which was interpreted as meaning 75 percent. Before publishing the proposed change, the FTC heard testimony from about 150 firms and twenty-six members of Congress, more or less evenly divided over the wisdom of the proposed change. Responses from both proponents and opponents were fairly moderate, and the staff of the FTC's Bureau of Consumer Protection, which wrote the proposed guideline, believed that the issue was going to be settled rather peacefully. Once the proposed change was published, however, a massive backlash of opposition occurred, eventually forcing the FTC to abandon the proposal.

National court systems are also available to help national-industrial groups like labor unions obtain relief from globalization's damage. In November 2000, a judge in the U.S. District Court in Los Angeles issued an injunction preventing the Quadrtech Corporation from dismantling its local factory (which made earrings and ear-piercing machinery) and moving its equipment and operations to Tijuana, Mexico.[53] The firm had made the decision to relocate to Mexico one day after the Communications Workers of America (CWA) had been certified to represent the previously nonunionized workers in the plant. The firm contended that the decision was driven by a desire to reduce labor costs; but the National Labor Relations Board argued that the firm had a history of being anti-union and was using this move to escape having to deal with the CWA. The decision was appealed and would require several years of court hearings for a resolution.

Global-Postindustrial Elites

Elite associations from the national, industrial era have been joined by new elite groups that are much more concerned with the issues on the global, postindustrial agenda. Because many of these issues are "knowledge dependent" (that is, their solution requires information not available to the general public, voters, consumers, or, perhaps, anyone),[54] these interest associations seek to achieve their goals at least in part by acquiring and disseminating that information. In the short run, their goal is to raise awareness among certain audiences of the failure of businesses or governments to comply with international norms in such areas as human rights and environmental protection. In the longer term, they attempt to change the attitudes of key publics toward pressing problems such as AIDS and immigrant smuggling.

Because these groups frequently perform functions involving the public good, they may come to take on some of the attributes of governments. But their status as nonstate actors requires that they be labeled nongovernmental organizations (or NGOs). As one observer describes them,

> NGOs have moved well beyond the nationally based groups of the early 20th century. Increasingly, they are transnational in organization, membership, and objectives. Working as advocacy networks, they shape agendas, publicize events throughout the world, raise public awareness and issue reports on compliance with international standards of behaviour.[55]

Both national and international NGOs have been increasing rapidly over the past two decades.[56] In the United States alone, there are an estimated two million NGOs, 70 percent of which were created since 1970. Citizens' organizations and advocacy groups now number in the tens of thousands in countries such as Indonesia, Slovakia, and the Philippines, where they barely existed at all as recently as the late 1970s or early 1980s. According to data from the Union of International Associations, the number of international NGOs grew from slightly more than 6,000 in 1976 to more than 40,300 in 1997. This figure includes nearly 16,000 "traditional NGOs" (defined as universal membership organizations and internally oriented national organizations) and more than 24,300 "special NGOs" (a category that includes recently reported organizations not yet confirmed and those suspected as being inactive).[57]

National governments and international organizations like the United Nations or the World Health Organization may work closely with these groups. For example, NGOs are now responsible for receiving and disbursing a large share of the world's spending for economic development and emergency relief. It is estimated that NGOs now disburse more money than the World Bank.[58] NGOs are used by national governments to acquire and publish information about events in difficult-to-reach parts of the world, and NGO representatives have even become involved in efforts to settle disputes or establish cease-fires in civil wars.

As Lisa Martin observes, NGOs and advocacy networks are also a special kind of interest group or association. She refers to them as "epistemic communities" because they conduct their lobbying efforts by supplying expert or specialized knowledge—or what she calls "causal knowledge."[59] Their distinctive contribution to the resolution of global issues is to be present at international negotiations and to provide expert knowledge to assist the negotiators. In the field of public health, for example, NGO representatives may know more about the incidence or epidemiology of a particular contagious disease than government representatives do. Environmental protection is another field in which NGOs may provide critical information to help governments solve pollution problems.

NGOs and other citizen associations are engaged in a wide range of activities. Some are "social entrepreneurs" led by people with motivation and vision who seek to channel the resources of the market toward the systemic solution of vexing social problems such as urban poverty and AIDS. In this respect, their emergence parallels the development of private firms in the eighteenth century that gradually took over the tasks of production and distribution that had formerly been performed by the mercantilist state. Other associations are engaged in social, economic, and environmental activism. Their mission is to confront multinational corporations, national governments, and international organizations over a wide range of global issues. Pressing their case via the Internet, global telecommunications, global news media, and occasionally the street, these groups believe that they can achieve the solution of these issues by pressuring governments and corporations to change their policies.[60] For example, at the 2001 meeting of the WTO in Doha, Qatar, intensive lobbying by such groups as Doctors without Borders succeeded in persuading the WTO to issue a declaration affirming the rights of poor countries to override drug patents and obtain inexpensive generic drugs for AIDS victims.[61]

Not all observers see NGOs as unequivocally helpful in resolving political issues stemming from globalization. Fantu Cheru, for example, finds a number of problems that arise from the activism of NGOs in Africa.[62] One such problem is state substitution. Some NGOs build layers of bureaucracy in between themselves and their constituents and begin to resemble states in their distance and unresponsiveness. NGOs also tend to act as though states do not exist, duplicating structures and programs unnecessarily. Finally, NGOs were not elected by anyone and are unaccountable to nonelites, so they cannot be equated with the spread of democracy. In fact, in some cases NGOs actually promote their own version of clientelism, a long-standing barrier to democratization in Africa and some other parts of the Third World.

Jan Aart Scholte asserts that the recent record of the contribution of NGOs to global democracy has been mixed. It is certainly true that globalization has, in Scholte's words, "opened greater space for democratic activity outside public governance institutions."[63] But the news has not been entirely positive. The exercise of economic power, called consumer democracy and shareholder democracy, in fact gives greater voice to those with greater wealth (and thus greater market power). Network democracy (use of global networks of communication), in fact, has excluded the majority of the world's people, who lack access to even the most rudimentary communications technologies. And civic democracy (the use of NGOs to build local activist organizations) still has much to do to promote mass participation, consultation, openness, and public accountability.

NOTES

1. Matthew Bishop, "The Mystery of the Vanishing Taxpayer," *The Economist,* January 29, 2000: 20.

2. Geoff Mulgan, *Connexity: How to Live in a Connected World* (Boston: Harvard Business School Press, 1997), 78–80.

3. Joël de Rosnay, *The Symbiotic Man: A New Understanding of the Organization of Life and a Vision of the Future* (New York: McGraw-Hill, 2000), 147–50.

4. "Why the Poor Don't Catch Up," *The Economist,* April 25, 1992: 48. "Income Distribution," *The Economist,* September 20, 1997: 116.

5. The Gini coefficient measures inequality between 0.00 (perfect equality; all are equal) and 1.00 (perfect inequality; one person possesses everything). Thus, the higher the coefficient is, the greater the inequality.

6. Robert Wade, "Winners and Losers," *The Economist,* April 28, 2001: 72–74.

7. "The New Wealth of Nations: A Survey of the New Rich," *The Economist,* June 16, 2001: 3.

8. Barbara Crossette, "U.N. Survey Finds World Rich–Poor Gap Widening," *New York Times,* July 15, 1996. In 2000 there were 7.2 million people in the world with a net worth of at least $1 million, a figure equal to approximately 0.12 percent of the total population of the world. These 7.2 million people possessed net worth of more than $27 trillion. About 35 percent of these people lived in the United States or Canada. See "Ranks of the Wealthy Grow Worldwide," *New York Times,* May 15, 2001.

9. Stephen K. Sanderson, *Social Transformations: A General Theory of Historical Development* (Cambridge, Mass.: Blackwell, 1995).

10. For a full copy of the Program on International Policy Attitudes report, see www.pipa.org.

11. Richard Morin and Claudia Deane, "U.S. Economy: A 4-Way Contest," *Washington Post,* October 27, 2000.

12. Claus Offe, "Fifty Years after the 'Great Transformation': Reflections on Social Order and Political Agency," in *The Changing Nature of Democracy,* ed. Takashi Inoguchi, Edward Newman, and John Keane (Tokyo: United Nations University Press, 1998), 44.

13. John Tomlinson, *Globalization and Culture* (Chicago: University of Chicago Press, 1999), 130–37.

14. Wayne Arnold, "Clearing the Decks for a Trade Pact's Riches," *New York Times,* August 27, 2000.

15. Robert W. Cox, "A Perspective on Globalization," in *Globalization: Critical Reflections,* ed. James H. Mittelman (Boulder: Lynne Rienner, 1996), 26.

16. James H. Mittelman, "The Dynamics of Globalization," in *Globalization: Critical Reflections,* ed. James H. Mittelman (Boulder: Lynne Rienner, 1996), 3–6.

17. Mittelman, "The Dynamics of Globalization," 4.

18. Glenn Adler, "Global Restructuring and Labor: The Case of the South African Trade Union Movement," in *Globalization: Critical Reflections,* ed. James H. Mittelman (Boulder: Lynne Rienner, 1996), chapter 6.

19. Dani Rodrik, *Has Globalization Gone Too Far?* (Washington, D.C.: International Institute of Economics, 1997).

20. Rodrik, *Has Globalization Gone Too Far?* 4.

21. Rodrik, *Has Globalization Gone Too Far?* 42.

22. Rodrik, *Has Globalization Gone Too Far?* 53, 65.

23. Clive Crook, "Globalisation and Its Critics," *The Economist,* September 29, 2001.

24. Thomas Friedman, "The New American Politics," *New York Times,* November 13, 1997. Thomas Friedman, "Roll Over Hawks and Doves," *New York Times,* December 2, 1997.

25. Blaine Harden, "Wowing Them with Excess in the Hamptons," *New York Times,* July 18, 2000.

26. Doron Levin, "What BMW Sees in South Carolina," *New York Times,* April 11, 1993.

27. Rajiv Chandrasekaran, "Cambodian Village Wired to the Future," *Washington Post,* May 13, 2001.

28. Mary Jordan, "Mexicans Reap NAFTA's Benefits," *Washington Post,* September 17, 2000.

29. John Pomfret, "Tempest Brews over Coffee Shop," *Washington Post,* November 23, 2000.

30. Frank Swoboda and Martha Hamilton, "How Virginia Lost Jobs to Texas, Mexico," *Washington Post,* May 5, 1991.

31. Joseph Kahn, "Playing the China Card," *New York Times,* July 7, 2000.

32. Neela Banerjee, "Fuel Bills Empty Poor Pockets, Unfilled by Boom," *New York Times,* August 9, 2000.

33. Suzanne Daley, "Fuel Shortages Grow as Truckers' Strike Spreads in France," *New York Times,* September 8, 2000. Keith Richburg, "Bitter Fuel Strike Disrupts France," *Washington Post,* September 9, 2000. Jocelyn Gecker, "Truckers in France End Strike," *Washington Post,* September 10, 2000.

34. Don Phillips, "Carrying Coals to Nowhere," *Washington Post,* May 2, 1999.

35. William Claiborne, "Farmers Begin to Think Globally in Price Crisis," *Washington Post,* August 15, 1999.

36. Sam Howe Verhovek, "Northwest Farms and Industry Feel Pinch of Asia Fiscal Crisis," *New York Times,* October 1, 1998.

37. Steven Greenhouse, "On the California Waterfront, Mostly Tough Times for Port Truckers," *New York Times,* April 15, 2000.

38. Peter Pae, "Perdue Ends Program for Korean Immigrants," *Washington Post,* February 25, 2000.

39. Celia Dugger, "India's Unwired Villages Mired in the Distant Past," *New York Times,* March 19, 2000. See also "Indian Poverty and the Numbers Game," *The Economist,* April 29, 2000: 37–38.

40. Stephen Buckley, "Brazil's 'Miserable Class' Finds Recovery Incomplete," *Washington Post,* October 12, 2000.

41. Jon Jeter, "A Less Than Helpful Hand," *Washington Post,* October 18, 2000.

42. Seth Mydans, "Once-Buoyant Hopes Sink in Indonesia's Slump," *New York Times,* December 13, 1997. Seth Mydans, "Thailand Economic Crash Crushes Working Poor," *New York Times,* December 15, 1997. "How Much Did Thailand Suffer?" *The Economist,* January 22, 2000: 41.

43. Jon Jeter, "Angola Paradox: Awash in Oil, Mired in Poverty," *Washington Post,* September 18, 2000. Blaine Harden, "Angolan Paradox: Oil Wealth Only Adds to Misery," *New York Times,* April 9, 2000. Rachel Swarns, "In Oil Bonanza, Frail Visions of a New Angola," *New York Times,* September 24, 2000.

44. Norimitsu Onishi, "Oil Riches and Risks, in Tiny African Nation," *New York Times,* July 23, 2000.

45. Ronald Rogowski, *Commerce and Coalitions: How Trade Affects Domestic Political Alignments* (Princeton: Princeton University Press, 1989).

46. We have seen in an earlier chapter that the expansion or contraction of trade can result from any change in the costs and benefits of an international economic transaction. Recall Jeffrey Frieden and Ronald Rogowski's assertion that trade expansion results from an "exogenous decrease in the costs, or an increase in the rewards," of such transactions ("The Impact of the International Economy on National Policies: An Analytical Overview," in *Internationalization and Domestic Politics,* ed. Robert Keohane and Helen Milner [New

York: Cambridge University Press, 1996], 26). Of course, most of these "exogenous changes" involve precisely what we mean by globalization: that is, changes in the costs and capacities of global bulk-flow systems to move matter, energy, and information.

47. Rogowski, *Commerce and Coalitions,* chapters 2–4.

48. Robert Reich, *The Work of Nations: Preparing Ourselves for 21st-Century Capitalism* (New York: Knopf, 1991).

49. Peter Katzenstein, *Small States in World Markets: Industrial Policy in Europe* (Ithaca: Cornell University Press, 1985). See also Rodrik, *Has Globalization Gone Too Far?* chapter 4.

50. Rodrik, *Has Globalization Gone Too Far?* 41–44.

51. Jonathan Hicks, "National Guard Is Called to Quell Trade-Talk Protests," *New York Times,* December 1, 1999.

52. Eric Schmitt, "How a Fierce Backlash Saved the 'Made in U.S.A.' Label," *New York Times,* December 6, 1997.

53. Anthony DePalma, "Company Is Told to Stay and Face New Union," *New York Times,* November 23, 2000.

54. Ulrich Beck, *Risk Society: Towards a New Modernity,* trans. Mark Ritter (London: SAGE, 1992).

55. Lisa Martin, "The Political Economy of International Cooperation," in *Global Public Goods: International Cooperation in the 21st Century,* ed. Inge Kaul, Isabelle Grunberg, and Marc Stern (New York: Oxford University Press, 1999), 60.

56. David Bornstein, "A Force Now in the World, Citizens Flex Social Muscle," *New York Times,* July 10, 1999. "The Non-governmental Order," *The Economist,* December 11, 1999: 20–21. "Sins of the Secular Missionaries," *The Economist,* January 29, 2000: 25–27.

57. Maryann K. Cusimano, Mark Hensman, and Leslie Rodrigues, "Private-Sector Transsovereign Actors—MNCs and NGOs," in *Beyond Sovereignty: Issues for a Global Agenda,* ed. Maryann K. Cusimano (Boston: Bedford/St. Martin's Press, 2000), chapter 10, 258, table 10-1. For up-to-date figures on international NGOs, consult the Union of International Associations website, at www.uia.org.

58. "Sins of the Secular Missionaries."

59. Martin, "The Political Economy of International Cooperation," 60–62.

60. Alan Cowell, "Advocates Gain Ground in a Globalized Era," *New York Times,* December 18, 2000.

61. Paul Blustein, "Getting WTO's Attention," *Washington Post,* November 16, 2001.

62. Fantu Cheru, "New Social Movements: Democratic Struggles and Human Rights in Africa," in *Globalization: Critical Reflections,* ed. James H. Mittelman (Boulder: Lynne Rienner, 1996), especially 159–60.

63. Jan Aart Scholte, *Globalization: A Critical Introduction* (New York: St. Martin's Press, 2000), chapter 11.

Case Study 7

American Labor Unions and the Cargo Container Revolution

KEY IDEAS IN THIS CASE STUDY

The **cargo container,** invented in the 1950s by Malcom McLean, revolution-ized the global freight system by increasing overall speed and efficiency of the world's bulk-flow systems.

Although most consumers and most freight companies benefited from con-tainerization, **freight workers**—railroaders, truckers, and "longshore" work-ers—**were its victims.**

Nevertheless, the **labor unions** representing these workers were persuaded to **embrace containerization** when they were reassured that jobs would be preserved and the wages and other gains for which they had fought so hard would not be jeopardized. The history of containerization offers us a valuable lesson in how to advance globalization while minimizing harm to its victims.

Globalization is the result of revolutionary changes in the way we move matter, energy, and information around the world, changes that result in declining costs of international transactions.[1] One of the most important factors contributing to such a decline has been a decrease in the costs of building and operating bulk-flow systems.[2] As global bulk-flow capacity and speed have increased expo-nentially, the costs of moving virtually everything have dropped just as sharply (as measured by cost per unit moved). Of the many important bulk-flow system innovations of the twentieth century, one stands out as especially critical to the global systems on which we rely so much today: the cargo container.

The containerization revolution is of critical importance to us not only be-cause of what it did for bulk-flow systems but for what it shows us about how to deal with some of the victims of globalization. A historian of containerization, David DeBoer, has observed that "for an industry [i.e., the freight industry] that took more than three decades to [shift from steam to diesel fuel], the intermodal shift in technology came in the relative blink of an eye."[3] One principal reason why containerization was adopted so quickly is because the major actors in the global freight system embraced it with comparatively little conflict despite the fact that the economic interests of many of these people were threatened by this new technology. How these potential victims of containerization, specifically the members of American labor unions, came to accept such a radical change teaches us an important lesson about how globalization can be advanced without causing unacceptable levels of harm to its victims.

THE CARGO CONTAINER REVOLUTION

As we have seen, bulk-flow systems achieve increased efficiencies and economies by combining social organization with technologies such as containers, conveyances, and central switching points.[4] In all such systems, however, there is considerable handling of the cargo between origin and destination, and any innovation that reduces that handling to a minimum will yield greatly improved efficiencies and reduced costs. The cargo container was such an innovation.

The idea of devising containers so that they could be loaded easily onto, and carried by, more than one kind of conveyance dates from the earliest days of the railroad in Britain and the United States.[5] In the 1830s, the Liverpool & Manchester Railroad used roll-on, roll-off containers to ship coal, and in America P. T. Barnum used end ramps to load and unload circus wagons on and off railroad flatcars as early as 1872. Many of the entrepreneurs who built the freight system in America in the nineteenth century thought of their industry not as isolated single modes of shipping (for example, railroads versus steamships) but as interconnected multimodal systems or networks that delivered a single service: moving freight.[6] Between the end of the Civil War and the beginning of World War I, rail and steamship services expanded jointly to connect at key points on both the East (New York, Philadelphia, Baltimore) and West (Vancouver, Seattle, Tacoma) Coasts.

According to Arthur Donovan, the idea of an integrated freight system was hampered by federal government policies between the 1930s and the 1950s that treated railroads, steamships, trucks, and airplanes as separate modes, each of which needed its own legislative and regulatory regime."[7] Nevertheless, while the legal and corporate structures of freight transport continued to operate from the single-mode paradigm, the technology of shipping was steadily changing.[8] After World War I, freight companies began looking for ways to offset the high labor costs associated with handling less-than-carload (LCL) shipments—that is, small shipments that filled less than one railroad car. As early as 1921, the New York Central Railroad experimented with cargo containers loaded on flatcars. Many of the technological innovations needed to support containerization, such as the containers themselves, the cranes to hoist them, and the devices to secure them to railroad flatcars, appeared during the 1920s and early 1930s. In 1931, however, the Interstate Commerce Commission (ICC, now abolished) ruled that shippers moving freight in containers had to charge rates according to the class of cargo inside instead of the distance each container was moved, as had been the practice. The consequence was to make LCL freight service so expensive that it would no longer be competitive with more traditional service.

Nevertheless, during the Great Depression financially pressed railroads looked for other ways to offer a profitable intermodal service. In 1936, the Chicago Great Western Railroad began moving truck trailers on railroad flatcars between Chicago and Minneapolis, and, in DeBoer's words, "the era of intermodal as we know it began."[9] This approach to shipping relied on ramps or depressed tracks to move the trailers on and off the flatcars, so it did not lend itself to the maritime mode. On the other hand, during these years shippers were learning much about handling and securing cargo, and eventually this experience would pay dividends for ocean-borne shipping as well.[10] By 1959, railroads were moving some 700,000 trailers annually on flatcars, and many of the principal technological problems had been solved with the piggyback system.

The treatment of freight transport as a series of isolated modes began to give way in the 1950s as a result of two developments.[11] One of these, which we will not examine here, was the deregulation of the transport sector beginning in the 1960s. But that development would not have taken place as it did, or perhaps at all, without the second development: containerization. And for that we have to thank principally Malcom McLean.

As the owner of a large East Coast trucking firm, McLean was frustrated by the losses caused by road congestion and delays in port when his trucks were delivering cargoes to be loaded aboard ship. He sought a way to avoid these delays by moving loaded trailers in large lots. His solution was to go one huge step beyond piggybacking and separate the trailer wheels from the cargo box. The box could then be moved from one transport mode to another without the contents being touched.

For years McLean's idea was rejected by the transport industry.[12] The Southern Railway declined to enter into a joint operation, and the established steamship companies on the East Coast all refused to consider adapting their vessels to his containers. So McLean bought the Pan Atlantic Steamship Company, which already had the necessary operating certificates from the ICC, and fitted out an old tanker to carry containers on deck to offer container service to East Coast and Gulf ports. When the ICC ruled that he could operate in only one mode, McLean sold his trucking firm and transformed his renamed shipping company, Sea-Land Services, into a huge success that reshaped the global freight system. On April 26, 1956, Sea-Land's first ship, the *Ideal X,* set out from New York with fifty-eight containers bound for Houston, and, in DeBoer's words, "the transportation world would never again be the same."[13] The container revolution reached the Pacific trade on August 31, 1958, when the Matson Navigation

Company's *Hawaiian Merchant* sailed from San Francisco to Honolulu with twenty containers on deck.[14] Matson also introduced the first all-container ship to the Pacific with the sailing of the *Hawaiian Citizen* in 1960.

The war in Vietnam offered McLean the opportunity to expand Sea-Land operations to the Pacific.[15] The Department of Defense was concerned about the delays experienced in offloading ships carrying war matériel for U.S. forces. McLean proposed to build and operate a complete containerized facility at South Vietnam's natural harbor at Cam Ranh Bay, and the department accepted. The buildup at Cam Ranh began in June 1965. Sea-Land constructed the entire container ship pier in Seattle, Washington, and towed it to Vietnam.[16] To fill empty containers returning from Asia, Sea-Land sought cargo for export to the United States from Hong Kong, Taiwan, and Japan, and the result was the beginning of the massive U.S.–Asia trade that blossomed during the 1970s and 1980s.

During the 1970s and early 1980s, two important developments confirmed the container as the core technology of the future intermodal system. One of these, railroad deregulation, was embodied in the Staggers Rail Act, passed by Congress in 1980, and the implementation order issued by the ICC in March 1981. These actions freed domestic and international intermodal traffic from regulation and allowed much greater flexibility and competitiveness in rate structures. The second was the introduction of the double-stack container train by the Southern Pacific Railroad in 1981.[17]

Up to this point, freight companies had specialized in that portion of the industry that each knew best: railroads supplied cars and engines, truckers supplied the chassis and trucks, the steamship companies supplied movement across water, and terminals and ports provided the connections. Containerization made it inevitable that companies would begin to offer freight service that treated all of the components as simply pieces of a huge "pipeline" through which an endless stream of large steel boxes flowed. In 1979, the American President Lines (APL) inaugurated the first dedicated train service linking port cities with the interior of the United States, followed in 1980 by the introduction of an electronic tracking system to keep track of intermodal shipments. In 1984, by adding double-stack trains to its network, APL began to offer integrated freight service virtually door to door using its own ships, port facilities, containers, flatcars, and terminals. APL contracted only for the railroad engines and crews needed to move the loads across the rail network.[18]

THE IMPACT OF CONTAINERIZATION

Today, the world's commercial fleet consists of about 85,500 ships with a capacity of some 532 million tons (up from slightly more than 100 million tons in 1960 and slightly more than 400 million tons as recently as 1990).[19] About 95 percent of all world cargo moves by ship, and virtually all of that (except bulk commodities like oil) moves via containers.[20] The standard container is 8 feet wide, 8.6 feet tall, and either 20 or 40 feet long. Loaded they typically weigh about 20 tons. Containers are measured in "TEUs," or 20-foot equivalent units. One typical 40-foot container can hold 1,000 cases of bananas, 25,000 blouses, or 16,500 boxes of shoes. A container ship that was state of the art in the mid-1990s was over three football fields long and carried 6,000 TEUs.[21] By the end of the century, a new generation of vessels arrived with twice that capacity. The world's container fleet capacity today amounts to more than four million TEUs. In 1998, the port of Singapore moved more than 15 million TEUs; the port of Hong Kong was a close second with 14.6 million.

The impact of the cargo container has been felt at several different levels. Most fundamentally, containerization transformed the paradigm of freight transport, from "modalism" to "intermodalism." Such a shift meant a change from a transport system in which discrete modes had to be connected to one in which all the modes are integrated into one seamless network or pipeline, which is itself integrated into the production and distribution systems.[22] Such integration has given rise to a new kind of intermediary, the freight "facilitator," whose job it is to stitch into a unified system all the services needed to move the container from production site to retail outlet.

Containerization has also had extraordinary network effects, with consequences for port and railroad operations, trucking companies, labor in the freight industry, and countless other aspects of the world economy. For example, deregulation and containerization together are responsible for the consolidation of America's railroads into a small number of very large companies.[23] In 1980 there were thirty-one railway companies in the United States; by the late 1990s, there were only eight, and four of those accounted for more than 90 percent of the industry's annual income. The increased productivity and efficiency of the railroads have made it possible for them to gain ground on the nation's trucking industry. From the mid-1940s to the late 1970s, the share of domestic freight moved by railroads was cut in half, from 70 to 35 percent. With containerization, however, the railroads' share rose steadily through the mid-1990s to slightly more than 40 percent.[24]

In the shipping industry, on the other hand, the effect has been to spur the proliferation of multinational firms offering container ship services around the world. These new companies, many of them based in Asia, have successfully challenged the control of the industry imposed by cartels known as "liner conferences" that have managed maritime freight movement for more than a century.[25] The leading carrier of containers to and from the United States is still Sea-Land, which moved 688,000 containers in 1998, followed by Evergreen Line (Taiwan) with 649,000, Maersk (Denmark) with 532,000, and Hanjin Shipping (South Korea) with 451,000.[26]

Because of containerization, the freight industry is being restructured to create integrated freight companies that offer customers container service in all modes through their various subsidiaries. For example, Sea-Land is now a subsidiary of CSX Transportation, which in 1996 was the fourth-largest railroad in

the United States. The railroads of North America are being integrated into unified north–south networks that cross the U.S. borders with Mexico and Canada
as if they did not exist. It is already commonplace for an automobile manufactured by Volkswagen near Mexico City to be delivered by a container train without interruption to a rail yard in Toronto.[27]

Containerization has affected the lives and well-being of consumers in the
changes in the volume and value of trade it has made possible. From the mid-
1980s to the mid-1990s, while the world economy grew by about 3 percent per
year, the capacity of the world's container ship fleet tripled from about one million TEUs to more than three million.[28] By the late 1990s, the world's fleet had
reached some four million TEUs, and container traffic was growing by around
10 percent each year.[29] At the same time, the volume of world trade rose by
some 6 percent annually, and the value of trade increased from about $2 trillion
in 1986 to $5.2 trillion in 1996. The composition of trade changed as well, from
heavy and bulky items like coal and wheat to lighter and less bulky manufactured goods like clothing and electronics. Thus, international trade shifted to
goods whose value is relatively unrelated to their weight.

Many of the benefits from containerization have come from huge gains in the
productivity of the freight system. In the 1950s, an average commercial vessel
could carry 10,000 tons of cargo at a speed of 16 knots. The typical container
ship today carries more than 40,000 tons at a speed of 23 knots.[30] But there have
been other significant benefits from containerization that do not show up in
productivity statistics. Before containerization, moving goods over long distances required much handling, and the goods were likely to remain inaccessible (and unprofitable) in warehouses or in transit for long periods. While in
storage or transit, freight was vulnerable to damage or pilferage, and these
losses were an additional barrier to international commerce. Moreover, heavy
wooden crates were required to protect goods other than bulk cargoes like raw
materials or foodstuffs, adding weight and consuming time. Containerization
solved all of these problems by reducing the weight of the cargo, the time in
transit and in storage, and the loss by damage or theft.

For most people, then, the cargo container was unambiguously a blessing,
but there are always some who lose from such innovation, and in this case it
was the workers in the nation's freight transport industries. For the individual
worker, the container changed the rewards and, indeed, the very nature of the
labor associated with freight transport. Before containerization, longshoremen
touched the objects they moved, an arduous and dangerous job but one that
kept them in close contact with their role in the production system and with
each other. Today, freight workers never see or touch the things they move. In
fact, they usually never know what is in the containers they are handling. Such
depersonalization separates the workers from their mission as well as from each
other, and it contributes to making the larger system invisible even to those
whose labor makes the system function properly.[31]

The workers were threatened in a more practical sense as well. For containerization raised the system's productivity so dramatically that it threatened to

reduce the portion of the system's income passed on to workers through their wages and in many instances even threatened to eliminate their jobs altogether. Between the mid-1980s and the mid-1990s, America's twelve largest railroads increased their productivity on average about 7 percent each year. Nevertheless, between 1980 and 1993, employment in these firms plunged from 460,000 to 193,000. Conrail, the corporation created by Congress in a multibillion-dollar bailout of the bankrupt Penn Central Railroad, reduced its workforce from 96,000 to 23,500 in the same period.[32] Investment in track improvements, engines, and rolling stock (in particular, double-stack container trains) was the principal reason behind these two trends.[33] Similar gains in productivity were seen in the shipping industry. Before containerization, five stevedore gangs of eight men each could load or unload about 100 tons per day to or from a cargo vessel. With containerization, fewer workers could load or unload 160 tons per *hour*.[34] It is not surprising, then, that railroad operators, longshore workers, and truckers saw containerization as the enemy that jeopardized their ability to make a living for themselves and their families.

CONTAINERIZATION AND AMERICAN LABOR UNIONS

There is hardly a person in the urbanized half of the world's population whose life has not been touched by containerization. Many have received enormous benefits from containerization; others have been harmed or threatened in some way. American labor confronted the cargo container within a complex web of actors and interests that included freight companies (railroads, trucking companies, steamship companies), banks and other financial institutions, government regulatory agencies, the Department of Defense, and terminals and port authorities on both coasts.

Three sets of labor unions were critical to the success of containerization: railroad operators, truckers, and longshore workers. America's railroads were one of the earliest industries to be unionized. As the railroads grew in power and importance in the nineteenth century, so did the power of their operator unions as well.[35] Railway workers were the first to organize an entire industry, the first to exercise major political power, and the first to benefit from federal social legislation (Railroad Retirement). During World War I, the federal government established the U.S. Railway Administration to manage the railroads, and operating labor benefited from numerous administration decisions regarding wage rates and labor practices.

Until 1968, railroad workers were represented by four different unions. The largest of these, the Brotherhood of Railroad Trainmen, dated from 1883, when its predecessor union was formed to represent railroad brakemen. A second component was the Brotherhood of Locomotive Firemen and Enginemen (BLF&E), founded in 1873. The BLF&E had been instrumental in pressing for an eight-hour day for rail workers and in securing the passage of the Railway Labor Act in 1926. The third was the Switchmen's Union of North America, which traced its heritage back to an association formed in Chicago in 1870. The fourth, the Order of Railway Conductors and Brakemen, was the oldest, having been founded in 1868. These four unions came together in 1968 to found the United Transportation Union (UTU). They were joined in 1970 by the International Association of Railroad Employees and in 1985 by the Railroad Yardmasters of America.

After World War I, wage rates rose, and railroads began to experience competitive pressures from the new player in freight: the truckers. Between 1920 and 1940, intercity trucking increased 400 percent. By World War II, almost five million trucks were in service, moving about 10 percent of intercity freight. The railroads used truckers to move their freight to and from the rail loading site, and the truckers began to see the potential for real gains by competing with the railroads. Trucks enjoyed several advantages in this competition. Their "ways" were built and maintained by the state, whereas the railroads had to build and maintain their "ways" out of their profits. And the ICC protected trucking companies by allowing them to pick and choose the shipments that promised them the greatest return, whereas the railroads, as common carriers, had to haul any shipment that was offered to them and still make a profit.

The International Brotherhood of Teamsters (IBT), known more popularly as the Teamsters Union, was formed in 1903 out of the merger of two unions that represented the drivers of horse-drawn vehicles. Local deliverymen driving teams of horses remained the core of the union's membership until the 1930s, when intercity truck drivers came to dominate. From 40,000 members in 1907, the Teamsters increased to more than one million members by 1950. Already by 1940, it was the nation's largest union. The union's large membership and its potential stranglehold on the shipment of vital commodities gave it great bargaining power, but they also provided great incentives for illegal activity and connections to organized crime. Between 1957 and 1988, three Teamsters presidents were sent to prison, and the union's membership declined in the early 1980s after the deregulation of the trucking industry. This decline was arrested only by the expansion of the Teamsters into fields other than transportation.

For most of the period covered by this study, longshore workers were represented by two unions. On the East Coast, dockworkers were represented by the International Longshoremen's Association (ILA); on the West Coast, by the International Longshore and Warehouse Union (ILWU). The ILA was founded in the nineteenth century and was a member of the American Federation of Labor. The ILA followed the strategy of craft unionism whereby separate unions organized specific jobs within major industries. The ILWU originated as the Pacific Coast District of the ILA, but eventually (in 1937) it separated from its parent union and joined the rival Congress of Industrial Organizations. In part, the separation stemmed from the isolation the West Coast organization felt from its parent, headquartered in New York. But the major issue that drove the West Coast affiliates from the ILA was organizing strategy. The West Coast unions believed strongly in industry-wide organizing and union solidarity, and they believed that craft unionism allowed employers to split union ranks during strike actions and contract bargaining. In any case, by the time the containerization revolution confronted the longshore unions, the split between the two coasts had been consolidated for more than two decades.

Each union confronted its respective industry's owners and managers over different issues related to containerization, and bargaining strategies differed from sector to sector. But the central theme in all three cases was the same.

The Teamsters' acceptance of containerization was obtained as a critical part of a deal that involved the Pennsylvania Railroad (PRR), Bethlehem Steel, and New York Life Insurance Company.[36] In the early 1950s, a transportation innovator named Gene Ryan contracted with the steel company to manufacture 100 75-foot-long flatcars to be delivered to Ryan's new firm, Rail-Trailer Company, which was to provide piggyback service to PRR. The railroad signed a long-term lease, but Ryan needed help from the financial markets to provide funding. When he approached New York Life, the insurance executives wanted assurances that the Teamsters would not fight the innovation.

At his next meeting with New York Life executives, Ryan was joined by the new president of the Teamsters, Jimmy Hoffa, who had earlier chaired an IBT committee to study the effects of piggyback operations on the Teamsters. Ryan had already produced data that showed that Teamsters' jobs would increase because of piggyback. He assured Hoffa's committee of three additional points: (1) Rail-Trailer terminal operations would hire only IBT members as their work grew, (2) Teamster city delivery jobs would increase, and (3) the trucking firms with which Ryan contracted would not lay off any line-haul drivers because of a shift of freight from highway to rail intermodal. Satisfied with these assurances, Hoffa in turn gave his assurances to New York Life that the IBT would not oppose piggyback, and the insurance company agreed to finance the cars.

How railroad operator unions were persuaded to accept containerization is illustrated by an anecdote from the mid-1970s.[37] In late 1974, the Department of Transportation had just completed a feasibility study of the National Intermodal Network, and the Federal Railway Administration (FRA) was looking for a demonstration route that would prove the idea's economic merit. It approached the Illinois Central-Gulf Railroad (ICG) with a proposal to invest some seed money if ICG would initiate intermodal service on a high-volume route. The ICG had already been negotiating with the ICC to establish such a service on the route between Chicago and St. Louis, and it saw the opportunity to advance that project by accepting the FRA offer. The ICG Labor Relations Department asserted, however, that any such arrangement had to be developed with labor input.

As it turned out, the timing was propitious for a containerization agreement that both labor and management could accept. The 1975 recession was ravaging the freight industry. The ICG was losing more money than ever in its history and was desperate to reduce costs and raise revenues. The unions were equally desperate to save jobs; over two-thirds of the railroad workers' jobs had been lost during the preceding half century. On January 14, 1975, the director of labor relations for the ICG, John Lange, met with the general chairman of the UTU, Eugene Abbott, in the coffee shop of a motel in Bloomington, Illinois, and hammered out the work rules for the new service. The ICG proposal was revolutionary: two-man crews, no caboose, three trains per day, no overnight lodging, and four days' pay for six eight-hour days. The union leader replied that he could not sell such a proposal to his membership unless the company was willing to demonstrate its commitment to keeping railroad jobs intact, even if it meant operating the container service at a loss. The railroad accepted the obligation to begin operating container train service immediately between Chicago and St. Louis even if there was no freight and even if the company incurred losses. The two men shook hands on the deal, and railroad history was made.

Containerization became an issue for the longshore workers in the late 1950s. Only a decade earlier, in two separate strikes in 1946 and 1948, the ILWU had successfully faced down not only the association representing the shipping company owners, the Waterfront Employers Association (WEA), but the federal government as well.[38] Out of those confrontations had emerged a new approach to bargaining between the owners and the union, whereby the owners were conciliatory on wages, hiring halls, and working conditions and the union leadership agreed to bring along the rank and file of their unions in support of the agreement.

By 1959, the shipping industry confronted serious problems caused by soaring operating and construction costs. The owners believed that the only way to offset these rising costs was to speed cargo handling and ship turnaround time. Introduction of the cargo container was the inescapable solution to their problem. Union leaders concluded that new methods and machinery would be introduced no matter how great their resistance to change. The result was the landmark 1960 agreement on the West Coast between the WEA and the ILWU known as the Modernization and Mechanization (M&M) agreement.

Negotiated over a span of six months, the 1960 M&M agreement provided that the current longshore workforce could not be laid off. If the cargo container resulted in the loss of work opportunity, the workforce would be reduced from the top, supplemented by a voluntary early retirement program instead of layoffs. If employers determined that they needed to reduce the workforce further, they could invoke compulsory early retirement with higher pension benefits. Moreover, increased profits would be shared with the workers in the form of increased wages and benefits. Although rank-and-file support for the principles of M&M was never unanimous, these principles were accepted in repeated contract negotiations and subsequent membership votes, usually by margins of over 70 percent. Controversies over containerization continued to surface in negotiations between owners and unions in the period between 1971 and 1996, but the fundamental principles laid down in the 1960 contract have never been changed.

On the East Coast, a similar bargain was struck between the shippers and the ILA. By 1959, the ILA leader, Teddy Gleason, had gotten the shippers to absorb a royalty tax per container that went to support union benefits. And two years later, the union and the shippers agreed to what was called the Guaranteed Annual Income agreement. With this accord, union members were assured that they would not experience a decline in income as the docks became automated.[39]

CONCLUSIONS

The logic of collective rational economic behavior suggests that America's transport workers' unions would have fought containerization to the bitter end. They were, after all, among the country's oldest, largest, and most militant unions, with strong, charismatic leaders and a reputation for the tough defense of the interests of their members. They had just emerged from several decades of bitter labor struggles through the Great Depression and World War II, when the interests of workers were expected to be subordinated to the greater need to support the war effort. Moreover, these three sets of unions occupied some of the most critical and strategic nodes in the country's economic system. There was little doubt that the nation's railroads, ports, and highways were the chokepoints of the national economy, and intransigent strikes or other work interruptions by these unions would have dealt a severe blow to the nation. Finally, it was abundantly clear that the advent of the cargo container threatened to take away the jobs of tens of thousands of their members.

Why, then, did the unions acquiesce so readily to containerization? Some observers might see their acceptance as the product of the economic depression in their respective industries, and this was certainly a factor in the case of the railroad operators in the 1970s. Others might argue that many union leaders, particularly in the ILWU, saw containerization as inevitable and knew that their only real option was to bargain for the best deal they could get before the container was forced on them. And, of course, many workers saw the positive side to containerization because it promised to make their jobs safer and less arduous.

But there was much more to the story than that. First, in all three cases the groups representing management, employers, and interested government agencies accepted readily and from the beginning the need to involve labor in their plans to integrate the cargo container into their operations. In all cases, labor leaders were at the table as full participants at the earliest stages of discussion. Second, business leaders and negotiators were prepared to offer the unions contracts with explicit guarantees that the increased productivity that resulted from containerization would not be used as an excuse to reduce the workforce or hours worked or to lower wages. In fact, the shipping and transport firms saw that containerization would increase the volume of their business so much that, if anything, there would be more jobs available, not fewer. In this sense, then, the huge increase in productivity that the container offered made it easier for the transport companies to share some of their profits with labor. Most importantly, once they received the guarantee of no reduction in jobs, wages, or hours worked, union negotiators were ready to commit their memberships to embracing containerization. This leadership was not achieved without a price. Even the charismatic ILWU leader Harry Bridges was booed by union members at meetings where he urged them to vote for the agreement. But so long as the workers knew that their jobs and income levels were safe, they would not block the cargo container revolution.

The cargo container revolution teaches us a commonsense lesson: that the benefits of globalization can be felt broadly and relatively quickly if the potential victims are allowed to participate in the transformation and if they know that they will not be unduly harmed by the changes. As globalization continues to sweep across the world's economies, leaving considerable damage in its wake, it would be wise to learn and apply this simple lesson to other potential victims. In the long term, we will all be the beneficiaries.

NOTES

1. Jeffrey A. Frieden and Ronald Rogowski, "The Impact of the International Economy on National Policies: An Analytical Overview," in *Internationalization and Domestic Politics,* ed. Robert O. Keohane and Helen Milner (New York: Cambridge University Press, 1996), chapter 2.

2. Robert P. Clark, "Bulk Flow Systems and Globalization," in *Space and Transport in the World-System,* ed. Paul S. Ciccantell and Stephen G. Bunker (Westport, Conn.: Greenwood Press, 1998), chapter 10.

3. David J. DeBoer, *Piggyback and Containers: A History of Rail Intermodal on America's Steel Highway* (San Marino, Calif.: Golden West Books, 1992), 165.

4. Robert P. Clark, *The Global Imperative: An Interpretive History of the Spread of Humankind* (Boulder: Westview Press, 1997), 17.

5. Much of the following history is drawn from DeBoer, *Piggyback and Containers,* especially 10–11.

6. Examples of such entrepreneurs would include J. Edgar Thaompson and other leaders of the Pennsylvania Railroad, which they connected to Europe via the American Steamship Company at Philadelphia, and James J. Hill, who connected his Great Northern Railway Company to Asia via his Great Northern Steamship Company at Seattle. See Arthur Donovan, "Intermodal Transportation in Historical Perspective," in *Intermodal Transportation: The New Millennium,* ed. Joseph S. Szyliowics (forthcoming), 16–20.

7. Donovan, "Intermodal Transportation in Historical Perspective," 20–47.

8. DeBoer, *Piggyback and Containers,* chapters 1–4.

9. DeBoer, *Piggyback and Containers,* 22.

10. DeBoer, *Piggyback and Containers,* chapter 3.

11. According to DeBoer, the regulatory climate began to change with the ICC's so-called 20 Questions declaratory order handed down in late 1953 in response to a request for clarification filed by the New York, New Haven & Hartford R.R. The order stipulated, among many other things, that the movement of truck trailers on flatcars did not constitute travel over a public highway, so the railroads could operate a piggyback service using its own trailers leased to the customer without a license to engage in interstate truck-

ing. The result was, as DeBoer puts it, that "piggyback literally exploded" (*Piggyback and Containers,* 37–39). See also Donovan, "Intermodal Transportation in Historical Perspective," 39–42.

12. DeBoer, *Piggyback and Containers,* 56–58.

13. DeBoer, *Piggyback and Containers,* 57.

14. See the Matson Navigation Company website, at www.matson.com.

15. Stewart Taggart, "The 20-Ton Packet," *Wired* (October 1999), at www.wirednews.com.

16. Edward Doyle and Samuel Lipsman, *The Vietnam Experience: America Takes Over, 1965–67* (Boston: Boston Publishing Co., 1982), 24–27. Edward Doyle and Stephen Weiss, *The Vietnam Experience: A Collision of Cultures* (Boston: Boston Publishing Co., 1984), 68.

17. DeBoer, *Piggyback and Containers,* 138–41.

18. See the American President Lines website, at www.apl.com.

19. Russell Working, "Flags of Inconvenience," *New York Times,* May 22, 1999.

20. Taggart, "The 20-Ton Packet," 1–2.

21. See the American President Lines website, at www.apl.com.

22. Donovan, "Intermodal Transportation in Historical Perspective," 3–4.

23. "American Railways: Steaming," *The Economist,* October 19, 1996: 66–71.

24. Barnaby Feder, "How Conrail Became a Hot Ticket," *New York Times,* November 1, 1996.

25. "Sinking the Container Cartels," *The Economist,* November 2, 1996: 64.

26. Andrew Pollack, "High Seas, Higher Costs," *New York Times,* April 21, 1999.

27. Anthony DePalma, "All Aboard for a Big Rail Deal?" *New York Times,* February 22, 2000.

28. "Delivering the Goods," *The Economist,* November 15, 1997: 85–86.

29. "Sinking the Container Cartels."

30. See the Matson Navigation Company website, at www.matson.com.

31. Ulrich Beck, *Risk Society: Towards a New Modernity,* trans. Mark Ritter (London: SAGE, 1992), chapter 1.

32. Feder, "How Conrail Became a Hot Ticket."

33. "Casey Jones Had Better Watch His Speed," *The Economist,* September 17, 1994: 68.

34. *Fighting the Tide,* a video documentary on the impact of the container, produced by Portfolio Project (Producer: Manuel Santos-Millan) and broadcast on PBS stations in 2000.

35. DeBoer, *Piggyback and Containers,* chapter 1.

36. DeBoer, *Piggyback and Containers,* chapter 3.

37. The anecdote is told in a letter from George Stern, an executive of the Illinois-Central Gulf Railroad, in DeBoer, *Piggyback and Containers,* 123–24.

38. The following account is drawn from the ILWU website, at www.ilwu.org.

39. *Fighting the Tide.*

Appendix 1

A Glossary of Selected Terms

analog literally, a model of a real world object that resembles that object in every important particular; in communications, an electrical signal that resembles the original message, which means in practice that the signal varies smoothly and continuously over time; contrasts with *digital* (John Naughton, *A Brief History of the Future: From Radio Days to Internet Years in a Lifetime* [Woodstock, N.Y.: Overlook Press, 2000], 303).

ARPANET the first electronic communication system using packet switching; the forerunner of the Internet.

autopoesis literally, "self-creation"; the process by which a complex system can create or generate itself without instructions from the environment; thought to be an important quality of living systems.

binary a numbering system using a base of two (0, 1); variables expressed in this format can exist in one of only two states or exhibit one of only two values (e.g., "on" and "off," "yes" and "no," "positive" and "negative," and so forth); such a format enables the transformation of analog information into discrete units, which can then be transported by bulk-flow systems.

bit literally, the abbreviation of *binary* and *digit*; the smallest unit of information in computer applications; in information theory, the fundamental unit of information.

bulk-flow systems transport systems that employ intermediary technologies and social systems to connect sender and receiver; essential when things to be moved are large, distances to be covered are great, and speed is important; contrasts with *diffusion*.

byte (usually) eight *bits*; the basic unit of information on which packets are based.

central switching unit   an essential feature of all bulk-flow systems; the site(s) in the system where incoming shipments are unpacked, repacked according to a common destination, and sent out again to that destination.

chaos   the behavior of a complex system in which known and understood causes can produce multiple, unpredicted, and only partially understood outcomes; a property of a complex system that causes its behavior to be unpredictable even though the system's components are understood and predictable.

closed system   a system able to exchange energy, but not matter, with its surrounding environment (e.g., the Earth).

complexity   a system property of having many interacting components; in operational terms, the amount of information needed to describe a system's structure or "the rate of energy flowing through a system of given mass" (Eric J. Chaisson, *Cosmic Evolution: The Rise of Complexity in Nature* [Cambridge, Mass.: Harvard University Press, 2001], 230). This property is a function of the number and variety of the system's component parts, the degree of nonlinearity of their relationships, and the tightness or looseness of their connections.

conversion processes   the component of a system that disassembles received matter, energy, and information and reassembles them; highly energy intensive.

cybernetics   the science of the control or guidance of complex systems, based primarily on the idea of *feedback*; term coined by Norbert Wiener from the Greek word for navigate (see *cyberspace*).

cyberspace   from the Greek word *kyber,* meaning "to navigate, to guide, or to steer"; literally, "navigable space." Refers to the virtual space created electronically by networked computers. Such space does not exist in a physical sense but, rather, as conceptual space where computer users communicate with each other without ever necessarily coming into direct contact (Martin Dodge and Rob Kitchen, *Mapping Cyberspace* [New York: Routledge, 2001], chapter 1).

diffusion   transport system that employs no intermediaries between sender and receiver; feasible only when things to be transmitted are small, distances to be covered are short, and time is unimportant; contrasts with *bulk flow.*

digital   format that treats information in discrete, separable units that can be transmitted by electronic pulses; enables the expression of information in a format that can be packaged and moved via bulk-flow systems; contrasts with *analog.*

dissipative structure   a system feature that enables the system to spread entropy to other systems. This property enables complex systems to flourish despite the Second Law of Thermodynamics.

ecology   the study of the interconnectedness of system components and of a system with its environment.

emergent properties   the properties of a system that appear as a consequence of the interaction of its parts; not knowable or predictable from knowledge of the components. These properties cannot be observed in the isolated components but only come into existence when enough components have been accumulated to change the nature of the whole. Thus, system behavior is not just the summation of its parts but, rather, results from their interactions.

energy   the property of matter that enables that matter to perform work or to produce change.

entropy   energy rendered unavailable when a system performs work; also a measure of randomness or disorder in a system, reaching a maximum under thermodynamic equilibrium.

environment   that which is not part of the system; the conditions that form the context within which the system resides.

exponential growth   growth by a constant (or increasing) percentage of the growing quantity over time; may be characterized by very short doubling times.

feedback   (usually) information about past and current system performance that affects future system performance; *positive feedback* signals the system to continue or increase current actions and thus tends to be associated with system growth or decline; *negative feedback* signals the system to discontinue or reduce current actions and thus tends to be associated with system stability (usually within some parameters).

free energy   that energy available to do work; contrasts with *entropy*.

global awareness   an awareness of or an ability to experience the world as a single place; contains four elements: a perception of the world as a single place, an understanding of how the component parts interact, a focus on the system as the unit of action and analysis, and the internalization of these ideas so well that they become tacit knowledge.

global network(s)   a network (or networks) whose scope is global or near global (i.e., transcends the limits of a single continent); similar to *global system(s)* except that the term *networks* is reserved for those systems constructed by human beings (e.g., telecommunications). As human activity intrudes into more and more natural systems, however, the distinction between a *global network* and a *global system* becomes less and less meaningful.

global system(s)   a system (or systems) of interconnected parts whose scope is global or near global (i.e., transcends the limits of a single continent).

Global System Paradigm   a *paradigm* that helps us experience the world as a single place by providing us with the mental tools necessary to think systematically about that world.

global systematique   a set of global systems that are interconnected; also an inventory that we can use to organize information about system properties and structures.

globalization   the process by which people acquire global awareness.

holism   the principle that a system in its entirety has properties that are greater than the sum of its parts.

information   literally, from the Latin *informare*, meaning "to give form to"; the property of matter that enables us to know and understand it; a sequence of data that gives meaning to a process; contrasted with "noise," which is random and therefore "meaningless" (Ray Kurzweil, *The Age of Spiritual Machines* [New York: Viking, 1999], 304).

inputs   matter, energy, and information received by a system.

Internet, the   the global network that connects computer networks; currently connects about 400 million individual computer users worldwide.

linear   a relationship in which one component affects (causes change in) a second but the second does not affect the first. The graphic depiction of such a relationship is a straight line. Contrasts with *nonlinear.*

nonlinear   a relationship in which system components affect each other through *feedback* loops; a relationship in which the cause produces a disproportional effect or consequence; a relationship in which the interaction of two factors produces a multiplied outcome, as opposed to linear relationships, in which the cause and effect are proportional to each other (Donella H. Meadows, Dennis L. Meadows, and Jørgen Randers, *Beyond the Limits: Confronting Global Collapse, Envisioning a Sustainable Future* [Post Mills, Vt.: Chelsea Green Publishing Co., 1992], 277).

open system   a system able to exchange matter, energy, and information with its environment.

outputs   matter, energy, and information that are produced by a system from the disassembled and reassembled inputs.

overshoot   system growth that exceeds the environment's sustainable carrying capacity; caused by flaws in the feedback mechanism that erode the system's ability to control itself; may also be a function of the speed or nonlinearity of change *(exponential growth)* (Meadows, Meadows, and Randers, *Beyond the Limits,* 277).

packet   a format for handling information for computer communications; *bytes* of information are packaged together with labels, called headers, which specify where they should be sent and how they should be reassembled at their destination.

packet switching   the *central switching technology* for information; enables messages to be sent via the *Internet* in small packages called *packets* through the most efficient routes available without keeping open a dedicated channel for the entire message (Naughton, *A Brief History of the Future,* 310).

paradigm   narrowly, used to denote a culturally sanctioned theoretical framework that guides a given scientific community in its research; more broadly, a worldview or established way of thinking that helps an individual make sense of his or her world by explaining cause and effect, individual identity, and other aspects of our surroundings.

sensitive dependence on initial conditions   the property of complex systems that causes the output of the system to be extremely sensitive to input changes so small as to be virtually invisible to outside observers.

social transformations   changes in the fundamental bases of an existing social order. These bases may be economic (the modes of production or of capital accumulation), political (the locus of ultimate political authority), cultural (the values or ultimate beliefs of a population), or technological (the sources of energy). There have been relatively few such transformations in history (for example, the Neolithic Revolution). Globalization is treated here as one such event. Such transformations inescapably involve the transfer of large quantities of resources and thus produce significant populations of winners and losers (see Stephen K. Sanderson, *Social Transformations: A General Theory of Historical Development* [Cambridge, Mass.: Blackwell, 1995]).

system a set of highly interconnected component parts; interconnection in this case means that change in one part causes change in another and that this change brings about change in the first part; "an interconnected set of elements that is coherently organized around some purpose" (Meadows, Meadows, and Randers, *Beyond the Limits,* 278).

thermodynamics the study of the changes in the energy in a system.

Thermodynamics, First Law of energy in the Universe can be neither created nor destroyed but only transformed from one state to another.

Thermodynamics, Second Law of the entropy of the Universe increases irreversibly to a maximum; also energy flows naturally from hotter to colder systems and never the reverse. The efficiency of any process is always less than 100 percent (Kurzweil, *The Age of Spiritual Machines,* 305).

World Wide Web "a highly distributed (not centralized) communications network allowing individuals and organizations around the world to communicate with one another" (Kurzweil, *The Age of Spiritual Machines,* 314); one of the most important services carried by the *Internet*; a system of more than one billion sites that carry data, text, images, video, and sound in a single integrated package; made possible by the invention of hyperlinks, which enable users to explore *cyberspace* electronically and in real time.

Appendix 2

Global Systems and the Structure of Cyberspace

KEY IDEAS IN THIS APPENDIX

Cyberspace is composed of numerous technologies, institutions, conventions, and practices. Some of these are visible to us, but others are not. The decentralized nature of the Internet makes it difficult to know **how much it costs** and **who pays for it.**

It is frequently said that the Internet functions without government controls, but in fact there are a number of important **regulatory institutions and rules** that govern the operation of cyberspace.

To grasp the enormous size and complexity of cyberspace, we have to use metaphors drawn from other disciplines, including biology and complexity theory. These latter approaches are referred to as **Internet ecologies.**

THE STRUCTURE OF CYBERSPACE

The word *cyberspace* means literally "navigable space."[1] It is derived from the Greek word *kyber,* meaning "to navigate, to guide, or to steer." The term belongs to the group of words with the *cyber-* prefix that were coined following Norbert Weiner's book, *Cybernetics,* published in 1948. According to Martin Dodge and Rob Kitchin, the original source of *cyberspace* is William Gibson's 1984 novel, *Neuromancer. Cyberspace* refers to the electronic space created by networked computers. Such space does not exist in a physical sense but, rather, as conceptual space in which computer users interact with each other without ever necessarily coming into direct contact. Some writers refer to cyberspace as "virtual space" because it is where people interact as if they were in each other's physical presence. In fact, the interacting parties may be tens of thousands of miles away from each other. Moreover, they may not know each other's physical location or even identity; and they may not care. Indeed, some forms of interaction in cyberspace depend on this very anonymity or shared ignorance.

Describing the structure of cyberspace stretches our imagination and vocabulary to their limits. Some parts of cyberspace are visible, such as the personal computer on which I prepared the manuscript for this book. Other parts are invisible to the casual observer even though they occupy physical space; for example, the telephone lines I lease from our local telephone service provider over which my computer connects me to the Internet. Some parts of cyberspace exist only as electrons or photons traveling along copper wire or fiber-optic cable, so they should be considered part of the interactivity of the "cyberworld." And finally, a considerable proportion of cyberspace has no physical referent at all; that is, although we say that it exists, it does not exist in any way that is detectable or measurable by our senses. This latter realm of cyberspace exists solely in our imagination (which does not, of course, mean that it is "unreal"). With due regard, then, for the ambiguities and complexities that lie ahead, let us sketch out the principal components of cyberspace.

Individual Users: The "Residents" of Cyberspace

The firm Nua Internet Surveys admits that "the art of estimating how many [people] are on line throughout the world is an inexact one at best."[2] Its best estimate as of August 2001 was 513 million. If this "cybernation" were a nation-state, it would be the third most heavily populated, after China and India. The largest group was in North America: 181 million. There were 155 million online in Europe and 144 million in Asia and the Pacific. In the developing countries of Africa, the Middle East, and Latin America there were somewhat more than 33 million. In the United States, 54 million households (about 51 percent of the total) had at least one computer, and 44 million households (42 percent) were connected to the Internet.[3] The average American user spent nineteen hours per month online in 2000.[4]

One of the principal ways in which these "cybercitizens" communicate is through e-mail messages sent through the Internet. The e-mail protocol was developed by Ray Tomlinson in late 1971. He is credited with having invented the now familiar "@" sign and for sending the first e-mail message (to himself, via two computers only 15 feet apart). Today, there are an estimated nearly 900 million "electronic mailboxes" worldwide whose users each day generate about 9.8 billion electronic messages to each other.[5]

Packets

One of the core operating principles of the Internet is the packaging of electronic digital signals in groups of bytes called packets (see chapter 5). When one places a telephone call, the message is routed through a network that is "circuit switched," meaning that one's call has a line dedicated to it alone.[6] Nothing else can travel over that line while one is talking on it. This procedure is extremely expensive. The Internet uses "packet switching," meaning that each packet of one's transmission is sent along with hundreds or even thousands of other packets from other transmissions, all mixed together on the same line. Each message is divided into packets according to the rule established by the Transmission Control Protocol (TCP), which also numbers the packets for reassembly at their destination. Following the "end-to-end" operating principle, the Internet does just one thing: it sends packets from one node to another, treating all packets equally and not tampering with the contents. The machines at each end of the connection are not involved in the actual transmission, and neither sender nor receiver really cares much about how their interaction is transmitted, so long as it is handled quickly and efficiently.

Host Computers, Servers, and Other Connecting Devices

Individual users are connected to the Internet by computers that may be personally or institutionally owned. Some of these computers may have one or two users; others, such as those at universities, may have hundreds. One estimate of Internet users in January 1995 assumed an average of five users for each host computer. At that early stage of the Internet's development, about 24 million users were online via slightly fewer than five million host computers. Two years later, the number of hosts had risen to 16 million.[7] Although the personal computer remains the principal way users connect to cyberspace, a number of other smaller devices, referred to as "digital appliances," evolved during the Web's first decade. These devices, small enough to carry in one's pocket, enable users to interact in cyberspace from virtually any location. Many observers of Internet development believe that mobile connecting devices will outnumber stationary computers within a few years.[8]

Internet Protocol Address

When a device connects to the Internet, it is assigned an Internet Protocol (IP) address, a string of thirty-two binary digits, or bits, which allows for some four billion possible combinations. Packets are labeled with the IP address of the sending and receiving devices, and the two machines communicate by sending packets with the appropriate addresses back and forth. The IP address also tells each router how to handle the packets.

Connecting Media and Technologies

The first users of cyberspace were connected to it by means of the same copper wire or fiber-optic cable over which telephone service was provided. In addition, these users were tethered to a fixed spot by their need to connect to a source of electricity. By the end of the 1990s, however, hand-held devices enabled users to connect to cyberspace via wireless connections, and battery power freed users completely from any need to remain in one place. Most computers are connected to the Internet over a phone line by means of a dial-up connection to a telephone number operated by the Internet Service Provider (see below). In the late 1990s, this mode of connection was challenged by much faster alternatives: fiber-optic cable (frequently offered by the same company that brings cable television into the home), a compressed electronic signal that travels along telephone lines but at a much faster rate, or wireless service via satellites.[9]

Internet Service Providers

Internet Service Providers (ISPs) are the companies that provide the connections between our computers and the Internet. The ISPs use computers to receive transmissions from users and forward them to the network.[10] As of 1999, there were about 4,500 ISPs offering services in the United States alone.[11] By far the largest of these was America Online (AOL), which accounted for nearly 40 percent of all home accounts in the United States. The approximately 17 million subscribers to AOL constituted a group larger than the combined daily circulation of the nation's twenty largest newspapers. Other larger servers, such as AT&T and Earthlink, collectively accounted for about 15 percent of the market, whereas small ISPs (each of which had less than 2 percent) collectively accounted for 41 percent.

Exchanges and Network Providers

Once an ISP has connected my computer to the Internet, exchanges and network providers carry my electronic traffic around the world by handing off the individual packets from one to another, much as a relay racer passes the baton to the next runner. The largest of these, known as "backbone providers," include such telecommunications firms as Verizon and Sprint. The computers that perform the switching function are called "routers." Routers have a rough idea of where things are on the Internet, and they transmit packets in the correct general direction using the best path available at the moment. The actual path selected may bear little relation to physical distance and direction.

VisualRoute is an Internet mapping service that provides customers with a list of all the network connections (called "nodes") between any two Internet addresses.[12] To demonstrate how their service operates, they provide a sample. By sending a single signal (called a "ping") between one of their host servers in, say, Warsaw, Poland, and my computer, VisualRoute can show the route of the ping and the exchanges that handled it: two separate network providers in Poland, the second of which carried the signal to Amsterdam; from there through Brussels and London to New York by a third network; and from New York through Washington, D.C., to Northern Virginia by a fourth network, where the signal was finally handed off to my ISP, which carried it the rest of the way.

World Wide Web Sites

The World Wide Web (WWW) is a collection of multimedia sites to which users can connect via the Internet. The Web is given credit for making cyberspace not only user friendly and attractive but commercially profitable as well. The most important feature of the Web is hypertext or hyperlinks. These are electronic footnotes embedded in the text of the site that enable the user to connect electronically and more or less instantaneously to many different sites. These links enable each Web user to create his or her own customized information world. There were as of January 2000 an estimated one billion websites in existence—or one for every six people on Earth. Some experts estimate that this number doubles approximately every eight months. In October 2000, the most popular site on the Web, AOL Network, received 61.5 million visitors.

Search Engines

Search engines use software to do two things that cannot be done by individual users on a large scale.[13] First, they find and index sites almost as soon as they appear, and second, they can match sites with keywords typed by the user in the engine's search box. As of June 2000, there were some 3,200 search engines available to online users. About 150 million searches are conducted each day.

Data Centers

All these networks appear to the average user to be invisible, but they have a spatial dimension just like any technology.[14] Web sites, ISPs, and network exchanges all use computers as servers or routers, and these computers must be housed in special places called data centers or sometimes "server farms."[15] These centers must offer their occupants large amounts of open space, extremely reliable electric power supplies (power interruptions would be catastrophic), and security against terrorists, hackers, and natural disasters. The floors of these buildings must be able to withstand at least 200 pounds of weight per square foot, twice the capacity of floors found in ordinary buildings. Moreover, their electric power needs are enormous, perhaps an order of magnitude greater than an ordinary office building of the same size: 50–200 watts per square foot versus 5–10 watts.

WHO (OR WHAT) OWNS CYBERSPACE . . .
AND WHO (OR WHAT) GOVERNS IT?

Who pays for all this? Because of the decentralization and invisibility of cyberspace, it is difficult to discern how much all of this technology costs, who pays for it, and through what medium or market transactions are channeled.[16] According to Metcalfe's Law (named after Bob Metcalfe, the inventor of the Ethernet local area networking system), the value of an electronic network increases as the square of the number of computers connected to it.[17] We have seen in chapter 5 that if cyberspace were a separate economy, it would be worth $1.8 trillion, larger than the economy of France. In 2000, consumers spent more than $36 billion in online purchases. Advertising on the Web brings in about $600 million per month, primarily for the placement of banner ads on Web pages.[18]

Presumably, some small percentage of these sums is channeled to each of the component parts of the network on which cyberspace is based. The ISPs and the exchange networks (backbone providers) lease the transmission lines from telephone companies; advertisers pay websites for banner space; users pay ISPs for their connections to the Net. Not-for-profit organizations, charitable or philanthropic organizations, and nongovernmental organizations make contributions to websites to advance their causes. Once a user has paid his or her monthly fee to an ISP, the Internet appears to be a free service, at least for each increment of usage. The one millionth email I send costs nothing additional beyond what I paid for the first. In truth that one millionth email does cost something because it occupies an extremely tiny bit of cyberspace for an extremely brief moment. But the ISPs have no way of billing for such a small amount, so they average their costs among all their customers, and as long as the average does not get too far out of line with each user's consumption of cyberspace, the system works tolerably well. But this property makes cyberspace appear to be a free good, sort of an "electronic commons," and some observers worry that this condition will lead to congestion of the Internet by what are essentially "free riders."[19] By early 2001, the collapse of many "dot-com" firms had caused many websites to stop delivering their information for free and to begin charging for their many and varied services.[20]

The governance of cyberspace is as difficult to grasp as the economics of the Internet are. Unlike many other kinds of space, cyberspace has no visible central government authority. At times, it seems as if the Internet had been designed intentionally to thwart attempts to regulate or control it. Or, as one of the founders of the Electronic Frontier Foundation, John Gilmore, puts it, "The net interprets censorship as damage, and routes around it."[21] Because the Internet was designed initially to be able to withstand the devastation of a nuclear attack, it should also be able to avoid any sort of centralized political control—or so it is said. Moreover, it seems that whenever a national government tries to block access to certain sites, groups of users invent software products such as SafeWeb and SilentSurf that can circumvent the barriers.[22]

There have been attempts by national governments to regulate the Internet's content or to tax the commercial transactions carried out through cyberspace, and there will doubtless be many more such efforts in the years to come. In the United States, as one analysis has put it, "The Net has become a First Amendment battleground."[23] In the coming decade, courts will be asked to determine how far the Constitution can be stretched to protect offensive transmissions on the Net. National legislation has aimed at curbing the transmission of information that could be of use to terrorists or ordinary criminals, such as instructions on how to make a bomb out of chemicals available in fertilizer. States have attempted via legislation to prevent the Internet from being used to stalk victims or harass people in the cyberspace version of an obscene telephone call.[24]

Pornography transmitted on the Net has been of great concern to parents, but constitutional protection of free speech in the United States has prevented governments at national and state levels from blocking it. Congress passed the Communications Decency Act in 1995 to outlaw the transmission of indecent material to minors, but the Supreme Court declared the law unconstitutional. National governments are also much concerned with how the Internet promotes certain crimes (such as the theft of copyright-protected intellectual or creative material like recorded music) and shields criminals from detection and surveillance.

Another contentious issue is the degree of liability of the firms that operate the networks for material they carry. Firms such as ISPs contend that they are nothing more than a carrier of dangerous or obscene material, and they bear no greater liability for the damage done by such transmissions than do telephone companies for carrying conversations that are dangerous or offensive. If there is liability, it rests, they contend, solely on the individuals who originate such material. But these users may live where such material is not illegal, or they may even be anonymous. In either case, they may be beyond the reach of national governments.

The United States is certainly not alone in facing these issues. In 2000, a French judge ordered the Yahoo! website to block the access of French users to transmissions advertising the sale of Nazi memorabilia.[25] From the perspective of Yahoo! these advertisements were just another electronic transmission, beyond its power to control or its interest in doing so. But French law forbids the display of Nazi images, and the judge was determined to uphold French law on French soil. As of this writing (January 2002), the case is being appealed in a U.S. District Court. In a similar case, German courts held an Austrian website publisher liable for publishing comments that denied the existence of the Holocaust, a violation of German law. The government of Singapore blocks access to pornographic sites, most Middle East governments ban anti-Islamic and gay sites, and China prohibits many Western publications and the sites of human rights organizations.

Bringing some order out of all this anarchy is the goal of a recently drafted treaty called the Hague Convention on Jurisdiction and Foreign Judgments. In mid-2001, negotiators from some fifty countries began meeting at The Hague to try to achieve more uniformity on national laws governing transborder lawsuits. At stake would be the right of an injured party in Country A to bring suit in his or her nation's court against an alleged offender in Country B, even though the alleged offense might not be considered criminal in Country B. Clearly, the ability of one person to injure another in a distant country has been magnified by the power and reach of cyberspace, and the existing international legal regimes will have to be adapted to meet this challenge.[26]

The arrival of the Internet has raised a number of very thorny problems for regulatory agencies like the U.S. Federal Communications Commission (FCC).[27] Ideally, the FCC would have preferred not to regulate the Internet at all, but this option faded because the Internet uses connecting technologies (telephone lines or cable television) that are themselves regulated. Consider, for example, the problems that arise by the Internet's use of telephone lines. Typically, the transmission travels from a user's personal computer to his or her ISP over local telephone lines. The ISP routes the packets to their destination over telephone lines as well. The Internet part of the transmission is carried by long-distance providers like AT&T, which lease the use of the lines from local phone companies. AT&T must pay the local companies for the use of their lines as if the transmission were a long-distance telephone call, but the ISP pays the long-distance provider an access fee as if it were a local call. The FCC ruled in 1998 that ISPs would be exempt from the requirement to pay long-distance fees. Were it otherwise, users would have to pay the ISPs per-minute rates as if they were making a long-distance call, which would make the Internet extremely expensive to the average user.

Just because national governments have had little success in regulating the Internet does not mean that anarchy prevails. Part of the mystique of the Internet is that it is anarchic, but in fact some very important instruments of self-governance have evolved in cyberspace.[28] Websites and other components of the WWW have developed mechanisms for regulating themselves in the interest of making their services more attractive commercially. Many ISPs now offer services to enable parents to block websites that are violent, pornographic, or considered offensive in other ways. Other Web-based services identify offensive material and offer customers software that they can download that will filter out such material. Most important, the Internet itself has evolved a set of institutions, conventions, and practices that some say are the beginnings of a global government of cyberspace.[29] Here are some of the most significant elements of such a "government":[30]

- A *constitution* is a set of fundamental decision rules that set forth how a political system will operate. In the case of the Internet, the constitution is in the TCP/IP. All the participants in the Internet have agreed that they will abide by the rules set down in this protocol, which specifies that transmitted signals will be divided into packets headed by labels that specify where each packet should go. The participants also agree to transmit each packet along the network without concern for its origin, its ultimate destination, or its content.
- The *World Wide Web Consortium (W3C)* was created by the founder of the Web, Tim Berners-Lee, after he moved from CERN (the French acronym for the European Centre for Nuclear Research) in Geneva to the Massachusetts Institute of Technology in September 1994.[31] The consortium's members number more than 400 and include all the major corpo-

rate participants in the Internet. Firms must pay a fee of $50,000 annually for membership. The consortium's job is to set and maintain technical standards that govern the Web's operations. Working groups and committees are formed to make recommendations about Web standards, but ultimately it is Berners-Lee who decides. Berners-Lee's commitment to an open Web accessible to all via a single operating system has been a critical component of the way the Web functions, but there is no guarantee that openness and accessibility will be protected and defended by the next generation of Web governors.[32] As the W3C becomes even more powerful, its decisions start to take on some of the characteristics of public policy, so critics have argued that it should start operating more openly and with broader representation of the public's interests.

- The *Internet Engineering Task Force (IETF)* develops agreed-on technical standards, such as communications protocols that govern network operations. It is characterized by a high degree of openness instilled by the small group of graduate students who built the Net in the 1960s and 1970s. Any individual can become a member just by signing up to the mailing list of a working group. Anyone can attend the meetings the task force holds three times each year; and anyone can propose a standard to the task force, which will study the proposal and forward it to its steering group (see below) for approval. Decisions are taken by "rough consensus," meaning more than a majority but not unanimity, and formal votes are never taken. The *Internet Engineering Steering Group* receives recommendations from the IETF and approves them.

- The *Internet Corporation for Assigned Names and Numbers (ICANN)* oversees the assignment of domain names, such as ".com" and ".org." This task sounds quite technical and even boring, but in fact it lies at the heart of cyberspace operations. Domain names enable the network servers to direct transmissions to their correct locations. Control over these markers gives an institution control over the network as well. Moreover, many of these domain names have become widely recognized as trademarks or even as part of popular culture (for example, the phrase "dot-com millionaires"). Originally, domain names were awarded by a private firm, Network Solutions, of Herndon, Virginia, under contract to the National Science Foundation, which had been designated to perform this function by the U.S. Department of Commerce.[33] In 1998, the Department of Commerce shifted this important authority to ICANN, a private international firm with headquarters in Marina del Rey, California. ICANN's decision-making body is an eighteen-member Board of Directors. Nine of the board's members are elected by representatives of the corporation's three constituent interest groups: companies that register domain names, ISPs, and the groups that set technical standards for the Web. The other nine are elected by the "at-large membership," which in practice means any person older than sixteen with verifiable email and physical addresses who wishes to register as an ICANN member. The at-large board members are distributed geographically to ensure that the entire world is represented. The first round of elections for these "public" representatives took place in 2000–2001, with votes cast via email. Some 158,000 online users registered to vote, but only about 34,000 actually cast ballots. Still, cyberspace enthusiasts professed to see in this election the beginnings of global electronic democracy.[34] The sovereign authority of ICANN is still in question, however, because it still reports to the Department of Commerce and is ultimately responsible to the U.S. Congress.[35]

The maintenance of *law and order* is an essential attribute of all states, and this task is especially critical in the case of the Internet, which has rapidly grown from a toy for academics to an electronic utility on which we depend nearly as much as we do on electricity itself. Here the very openness of cyberspace makes the policing of it especially challenging. To date, the job of protecting the Internet's security has been performed by national governments. Perhaps, however, a cyber–police force is beginning to take shape at Carnegie Mellon University in Pittsburgh, where the Computer Emergency Response Team acts as a clearinghouse for information about security problems on the Net.

It would appear that the only attribute of a state lacking in cyberspace is, well, space. That is, the only thing that states have that cyberspace does not have is a territorial base. Even today such a statement overgeneralizes things,[36] for most Web domain names outside the United States end with a country designator, such as ".uk" for the United Kingdom. But there have been proposals to organize the Web according to a much narrower geographical base. In 2001, SRI International in Menlo Park, California, proposed to ICANN the adoption of a new top-level domain called ".geo."[37] In SRI's proposed system, the world would be divided into cells, each represented by one or more local Internet servers, called "georegistries." Cells would vary in size depending on how much Internet traffic there is into and out of the cell. The entire "dot-geo" system would overlay the existing Web structure like a template. Then when a site registered with the Web, it could also register with the georegistry and provide its location by latitude and longitude. The georegistry would provide search engines with Web sites organized by location to sharpen and speed up Web searches. ICANN rejected SRI's proposal as too radical, saying it needed more time to study the technical implications. But SRI continued to test and refine its system and will no doubt return to ICANN for a possible favorable ruling at a later date.

So far the regulatory system of cyberspace has worked remarkably well considering its lack of mechanisms for resolving conflict in a democratic and representative manner. The smooth operation of these institutions appears to derive from several quite unusual features of the cyberspace community: homogeneity of values, accepted technical criteria for favoring one proposal over another, open and fast communication, a decision-making process that is difficult to manipulate for narrow advantage, and easy exit from the system for those who have grievances. It remains to be seen how these institutions behave when they are confronted with political, economic, and social issues that governments have to grapple with all the time. For example, in 2000 IETF members were sharply divided over whether their organization should help law enforcement agencies conduct surveillance of Internet transmissions. The task force dealt with this issue by deciding not to discuss it, but such tactics may not suffice very much longer.

INTERNET ECOLOGIES

Thinking systematically about the world meets its greatest challenge when we try to understand cyberspace or, more specifically, the electronic information networks that constitute the Internet. Confronted with such an enormous, complex, invisible, and nonlinear system, we have to resort to metaphors drawn from other fields to make sense of such an entity. In the early 1990s, for example, we heard a lot about the "information superhighway," but people soon came to realize that the Internet is much more complex and nonlinear than a highway system and much less visible as well. Increasingly, people saw increased "traffic" on the Web causing "traffic jams" and eventually "gridlock."[38] As the WWW grew larger, more complex, and more difficult to navigate, search engines had to expand their capacity to find and retrieve information. The improved search processes were said to be able to "mine the 'deep Web' with sharper shovels."[39] In the early days of e-commerce, online merchants described the Web as an "interconnected global bazaar of ideas and products." But later research showed that the complexity of the one billion websites made it "more like the vast bureaucracy in Kafka's 'Castle': a mountain of disconnected information, lost files and frustrating dead ends."[40]

Biological metaphors and images have always been popular with writers about cyberspace. Computer scientists and engineers have used biological metaphors almost from the beginning of the Information Age. When a computer program failed, for example, we were told that it suffered from a "bug" and that its program had to be "debugged." In the 1980s, Fred Cohen, a scientist now with Sandia National Laboratories, described for the first time, and gave the name "virus" to, the short strings of computer code that can destroy a computer's operating system. Today, we still use the vocabulary of epidemiology to describe such events: "viruses" are seen to "infect" computers and then create "epidemics" through entire networks before finally "dying out."[41] Whereas "viruses" spread by connecting themselves to other documents, "worms" propel themselves through the Internet on their own messages.[42] Computers catch the "cyberflu," and the whole process must obey some sort of electronic version of the "Darwinian imperative," whereby competition filters out weaker "viruses" so that only the "fittest" survive. Computer security experts study immunology in hopes of getting ideas about how to protect their systems from "infection" by creating "digital immune systems."[43]

Today, many observers see the boundary blurring between living organisms and electronic devices. Ray Kurzweil cites the inexorable increases in computer capacity yet to come and foresees the day when machines will have acquired humanlike capabilities.[44] The French scientist Joël de Rosnay uses the science of complex systems to envision the emergence of a new life form, a symbiosis of humankind, other organisms, and informatics.[45] Experts in artificial intelligence have produced software that can emulate human thought and language patterns. These "computer robots," or simply "bots," inhabit cyberspace, intervening in chat rooms in ways that make it impossible for most correspondents to differentiate them from real people.[46] It is thought that eventually these "bots" will be able to guide us through cyberspace much more efficiently than we could manage unaided. Search engines attempt to keep pace with the explosive growth of Web pages by enlisting human judgments in the process of scanning the Web. They have become, in the words of one recent news article, "more like cyborgs, part human, part machine."[47]

Insightful uses of biological metaphors go beyond these examples to show how the inhabitants of cyberspace obey the same rules as living organisms. For example, citing the research of George Dyson, John Naughton asserts that the

> networked computers which now surround us by the million constitute, collectively, a form of intelligent life, . . . a globally networked, electronic, sentient being. . . . [F]ragments of software replicating across the Internet are analogous to strings of DNA replicating in living cells. As in biology, evolutionary pressure provides the drive: what works survives; what doesn't gets deleted.[48]

Some researchers have gone beyond biology to find illustrative metaphors in the science of complex adaptive systems. Some use complexity science to study websites that are "self-organizing" (that is, they use interactive software that allows visitors to the site to build the site).[49] Others see the Web as some sort of gigantic quasi-organism that is organizing itself according to the same rules that govern the self-organization of any large, complex system.[50]

One of the leading groups engaged in this kind of research is located at the Xerox Corporation's Palo Alto Research Center (known as PARC) in California. Led by Bernardo Huberman, this group's research focuses on "Internet ecologies," which are described on its website as "the relation between the local actions and the global behavior of large distributed systems, both social and computational."[51] Using techniques drawn from complexity theory, the PARC group studies the behavior of large, nonlinear systems whose "overall dynamics . . . is determined by the collective interactions of many autonomous agents." Huberman's writings involve rich and suggestive metaphors that liken the Internet to

> a beautiful garden . . . that grows on its own like an ecosystem. . . . The sheer reach and structural complexity of the Web makes [sic] it an ecology of knowledge, with relationships, information "food chains," and dynamic interactions that could soon become as rich as, if not richer than, many natural ecosystems.[52]

In one recent article, PARC researchers conclude that because the Internet is a public good and its users are not charged in proportion to their use, it appears rational for individual users to "consume" it greedily, thinking that their actions can have little consequence for the Net as a whole. If each user reasons this way, the Internet's overall capacity can be degraded considerably, with adverse consequences for all users.[53] Readers from the social sciences will recognize this analysis as the cyberspace version of the tragedy of the commons.

NOTES

1. Martin Dodge and Rob Kitchin, *Mapping Cyberspace* (New York: Routledge, 2001), chapter 1. For more on cybergeography, see Pamela Licalzi O'Connell, "Beyond Geography: Mapping Unknowns of Cyberspace," *New York Times,* September 30, 1999. See also the Internet Mapping Project website, at www.cs.bell-labs.com/who/ches/map/index.html.

2. See the Nua Internet Survey website, at www.nua.ie/surveys.

3. "Report Counts Computers in Majority of U.S. Homes," *New York Times,* September 7, 2001.

4. John Markoff, "Fast-Changing Genie Alters the World," *New York Times,* December 11, 2000.

5. Katie Hafner, "Billions Served Daily, and Counting," *New York Times,* December 6, 2001.

6. John Schwartz, "How the Internet Takes You There," *Washington Post,* October 14, 1998. Glenn Fleishman, "To Sail Data across the Web, Computers Seek the Best Routes," *New York Times,* December 31, 1998.

7. *The Economist,* April 15, 1995: 98. *The Economist,* February 15, 1997: 98.

8. "Upgrading the Internet," *The Economist (Technology Quarterly),* March 24, 2001: 32–36.

9. Peter Wayner, "Plugging in to the Internet: Many Paths, Many Speeds," *New York Times,* July 2, 1998. See also the series of "technology briefs" in *The Economist* on high-speed connecting technologies: July 6, 1996: 72; July 13, 1996: 88; July 20, 1996: 69; and July 27, 1996: 70.

10. Peter Wayner, "How Servers Find Needle in Haystack of the Net," *New York Times,* May 21, 1998.

11. Peter H. Lewis, "The New Internet Gatekeepers," *New York Times,* November 13, 1995. Tina Kelley, "A World of Choices to Plug in to the Net," *New York Times,* May 20, 1999.

12. For more on this service, see the website, at visualroute.visualware.com.

13. Lisa Guernsey, "The Search Engine as Cyborg," *New York Times,* June 29, 2000.

14. "Special Report: Geography and the Net," *The Economist,* August 11, 2001: 18–20.

15. Steve Lohr and John Markoff, "Computing Centers Become the Keeper of Web's Future," *New York Times,* May 19, 1999. Harriet King, "Data Centers Are Springing Up in Seattle," *New York Times,* March 25, 2001. Kenneth Bredemeier and Sarah Schafer, "Data Bunkers Protect Off-Site Sites," *Washington Post,* November 9, 1999.

16. "America's Information Highway: A Hitch-Hiker's Guide," *The Economist,* December 25, 1993–January 7, 1994: 35–38. "The Economics of the Internet: Too Cheap to Meter?" *The Economist,* October 19, 1996: 23–27.

17. John Naughton, *A Brief History of the Future: From Radio Days to Internet Years in a Lifetime* (Woodstock, N.Y.: Overlook Press, 2000), 37. Christopher Anderson, "The Accidental Superhighway: A Survey of the Internet," *The Economist,* July 1, 1995: 4.

18. Markoff, "Fast-Changing Genie Alters the World."

19. "The Economics of the Internet," 23.

20. Saul Hansell, "Free Rides Are Now Passé on Information Highway," *New York Times,* May 1, 2001.

21. Anderson, "The Accidental Superhighway," 15.

22. Jennifer 8. Lee, "Punching Holes in Internet Walls," *New York Times,* April 26, 2001.

23. Edwin Diamond and Stephen Bates, "Law and Order Comes to Cyberspace," *Technology Review* (October 1995): 22–33. Joan Biskupic, "In Shaping of Internet Law, First Amendment Is Winning," *Washington Post,* September 12, 1999.

24. Jonathan Rabinovitz, "In Connecticut, Harassment by Computer Is Now a Crime," *New York Times,* June 13, 1995.

25. Lisa Guernsey, "Welcome to the Web. Passport, Please?" *New York Times,* March 15, 2001.

26. "Regulating the Internet: Tied Up in Knots," *The Economist,* June 9, 2001: 67.

27. Seth Schiesel, "The F.C.C. Faces Internet Regulation," *New York Times,* November 2, 1998.

28. Katie Hafner, "The Internet's Invisible Hand," *New York Times,* January 10, 2002.

29. "Regulating the Internet: The Consensus Machine," *The Economist,* June 10, 2000: 73–79.

30. For a complete description, complete with organizational diagram, of how the Internet is managed, see the website "The Living Internet," at livinginternet.com.

31. Steve Lohr, "His Goal: Keeping the Web Worldwide," *New York Times,* December 18, 1995.

32. In theory, another operating system could emerge to challenge the Web, but the practical obstacles to one doing so are enormous. The task would be analogous to a firm trying to convince world markets to adopt a lightbulb that screws in counterclockwise.

33. The Commerce Department enjoyed this authority because the U.S. Constitution gives Congress the power to regulate interstate commerce, and Congress had delegated it to the Department of Commerce.

34. Jeri Clausing, "Democracy Tugs at Internet Agency," *New York Times,* August 30, 1999. "Internet Governance: Election Time," *The Economist,* September 30, 2000: 64–65. Susan Stellin, "Internet Domain Administrator Holds Its First Public Election," *New York Times,* October 12, 2000. Susan Stellin, "Internet Groups Urge Public Participation," *New York Times,* September 1, 2001.

35. Ariana Eunjung Cha, "Losers, Lawmakers Worked Up over Internet Suffixes," *Washington Post,* February 9, 2001.

36. "Special Report," 18.

37. Catherine Greenman, "New Rules for Net Searches: Location, Location, Location," *New York Times,* April 5, 2001.

38. Sara Robinson, "Multimedia Transmissions Are Driving Internet toward Gridlock," *New York Times,* August 23, 1999.

39. Lisa Guernsey, "Mining the 'Deep Web' with Sharper Shovels," *New York Times,* January 25, 2001.

40. Ian Austen, "Study Reveals Web as Loosely Woven," *New York Times,* May 18, 2000.

41. John Markoff, "Illness Becomes Apt Metaphor for Computers," *New York Times,* June 14, 1999. Curt Suplee, "Anatomy of a 'Love Bug,'" *Washington Post,* May 21, 2000.

42. John Markoff, "In Eden, a Snake. On the Internet, a Worm," *New York Times,* June 20, 1999. John Markoff, "Even a Worm Needs Love," *New York Times,* June 4, 2000.

43. "A Thousand Ills Require a Thousand Cures," *The Economist,* January 8, 2000: 77–78.

44. Ray Kurzweil, *The Age of Spiritual Machines* (New York: Viking, 1999).

45. Joël de Rosnay, *The Symbiotic Man* (New York: McGraw-Hill, 2000).

46. Ariana Eunjung Cha, "Lost in Cyberspace? Try a 'Bot,'" *Washington Post,* December 26, 2000.

47. Guernsey, "The Search Engine as Cyborg."

48. Naughton, *A Brief History of the Future,* 37–38.

49. Katie Hafner, "Web Sites Begin to Get Organized, on Their Own," *New York Times,* January 18, 2001.

50. George Johnson, "First Cells, Then Species, Now the Web," *New York Times,* December 26, 2000.

51. See the "Internet Ecologies Area" of the PARC website, at www.parc.xerox.com. For an early statement of Huberman's paradigm, see Bernardo A. Huberman, "An Ecology of Machines," *The Sciences* (July–August 1989): 38–44.

52. George Johnson, "Searching for the Essence of the World Wide Web," *New York Times,* April 11, 1999.

53. Bernardo A. Huberman and Rajan M. Lukose, "Social Dilemmas and Internet Congestion," *Science* 277 (July 25, 1997): 535–37.

Index

Italic type indicates a page reference to a box or figure.

Abbott, Eugene, 244
access to information, 177
accounting schemes, 16
acquired immunodeficiency syndrome.
    See AIDS
Adler, William, 19–20
Advanced Research Projects Agency
    (ARPA), 153–54
Africa: AIDS in, 27–29; population
    growth, 24
agriculture, and global markets, 222
Ah-Mei, 68
AIDS (acquired immunodeficiency
    syndrome), 23–34; biographical
    perspective, 33–34; biological
    perspective, 29–30; drugs for, 27–29;
    economic perspective, 26–29; factors
    contributing to, 24–25; futurism
    perspective, 32–33; historical
    perspective, 30–31; sociological
    perspective, 25–26
air travel, and AIDS, 24
alternative futures, 17
America Online (AOL), 258
American Alliance for Honest Labeling,
    192
American Federation of Labor, 242

American Federation of Labor-Congress
    of Industrial Organizations (AFL-CIO),
    228. *See also* Congress of Industrial
    Organizations
American President Lines (APL), 238
Ampère, A. M., 148
analog signal, 152, 153
analogy: in historical interpretation,
    12–13; organismic, 15. *See also*
    metaphors, for cyberspace
Andreas, Peter, 184
Andreessen, Marc, 155, 160
Andrew and Williamson (A&W) Sales,
    201–2
animals: AIDS and export of, 24;
    competition with humans of, 66–68;
    growth and complexity in, 110–11
antiglobal forces: anti-immigrant
    legislation, 147; isolationism, 147;
    protectionism, 147
anti-globalization groups, 228
anti-immigrant legislation, 147
AOL. *See* America Online
APEC Emerging Infections Network, 192
APL. *See* American President Lines
apple growers, 218–19
Arctic Climate System Study, 48

Aristotle, 71
ARPA. *See* Advanced Research Projects
  Agency
ARPANET, 154
Arquilla, John, 174
Arthur, W. Brian, 120, 181
artificial intelligence: global
  consciousness and, 17–18; human
  nature and, 17–18; and human
  simulation, 266
Asia, world system role of, 14
Atlantic Richfield, 97
AT&T, 221, 258
automobile industry, 214–15, 217

Bacon, Francis, 152
Bardeen, John, 153
Barnet, Richard J., 8–9, 36
Barnum, P. T., 236
Beck, Ulrich, 177, 188, 189, 190
Bell, Alexander Graham, 152, 156
Bell Telephone Laboratories, 73
Beniger, James, 114
Berlin Wall, 147
Berners-Lee, Tim, 155, 160n37, 262–63
Bertalanffy, Ludwig von, 13, 71, 74, 78,
  80, 86
Beyond the Limits, 46
Bharatiya Janata Party, 190
binary condition: and digitalization, 152;
  of electric current, 151; of information,
  73; Morse code and, 151
bin Laden, Osama, 175
bioengineering, 188
biographical writing, 18–20; AIDS
  perspective of, 33–34
biology, 9–12; AIDS perspective of,
  29–30; computer/cyberspace
  metaphors from, 265–66; ecology (*see*
  ecology); growth and complexity in,
  109–10; systems thinking and, 74–75
biosphere, 52
bits, 73
Boehringer Ingelheim, 27
Bolt, Beranek, and Newman (BBN), 154
Bonner, John Tyler, 110, 111
Border Patrol, 191
bots, 266

Boulding, Kenneth, 74
boundaries, 79
boycotts, 169
Brattain, Walter, 153
Bridges, Harry, 246
Bright, Charles, 36–37
Bristol-Meyers Squibb, 27
British Petroleum-Amoco, 97
Brown, Gordon, 72
Brown, Guy, 84
Brown, Lester, 139
Buchanan, Pat, 190
bulk-flow information systems, 146–57;
  costs of, 147–48; digitalization, 150–53;
  electricity, 148–50; global
  communications, 155–57; Internet,
  153–55
bulk-flow systems, 109, 141–57; cargo
  containers and, 235; central switching
  points in, 143–44; cities and, 145–46;
  description of, 143; diffusion
  compared with, 142; globalization
  and, 143, 145; in human history,
  144–45; for information (*see* bulk-flow
  information systems); intermodal, 236,
  237, 238, 239
Bush, Vannevar, 72
bytes, 73

call centers, as invisible system, 184
capital emigration, 186
Caribbean Basin Initiative, 199
carrying capacity, 11–12
Caterpillar, 209
cause and effect, systems and, 77
Cavanagh, John, 8–9, 36
cellular processes, 84–85
censorship, of Internet, 260–61
Center for Science in the Public Interest,
  228
Centers for Disease Control and
  Prevention (CDC), 24, 200, 202
central control, 81
central switching points: in bulk-flow
  systems, 143; in complex systems,
  143–44; in emerging systems, 159n13;
  examples of, 143; in information flow,
  143–44; Internet as, 153

Cerf, Vinton, 154
CERT. *See* Computer Emergency
  Response Team
Chaisson, Eric, 110
chance, 76
chaos theory. *See* complexity theory
Chase-Dunn, Christopher, 13
Chavez, Hugo, 190
Cheru, Fantu, 231
Chevron-Texaco, 97
cities: bulk-flow systems and, 145–46;
  ecological footprint of, 139–40; global,
  146; as system, 138–40; transport and
  entropy in, 138–40
clientelism, 231
climate change: Kyoto accord, 105;
  scientific cooperation on, 48;
  understanding of, 37
closed system, 79; Earth as, 94; entropy
  in, 87
Club of Rome, 45–46, 47
coal, 222
coalitions, 224–31
coevolution, 10–11
Cohen, Fred, 265
Cold War: as anti-global force, 147;
  Internet development and, 153
collective thinking, 17
colonialism: and dissipative structures,
  140, 141; in highly interconnected
  world, 136
Columbus, Christopher, 40
commodification of culture, 209
common properties, in systems, 53, 61;
  universal, 54
commons, Internet as electronic, 260, 267
communications, global, 155–57
Communications Workers of America
  (CWA), 229
competing needs, and AIDS pandemic,
  28
complex adaptive systems paradigm,
  76–77
complexity: advantages of, 111; of
  animals, 110–11; and central switching
  points, 143; computer models and,
  89n3; controversy about, 109-10;
  culture and, 111; definitions of, 113,

127n21; as emergent property, 111;
  energy consumption and, 112;
  evolution and, 110, 111; and growth of
  systems, 108–14; and information, 87;
  of Internet, 266; and invisibility of
  systems, 178–180. *See also* diversity
complexity, self-organizing, 75, 266
complexity theory: deterministic chaos in,
  76; and Internet, 266; sensitive
  dependence on initial conditions in,
  76, 118, 135, 179; and systems theory,
  75–77; unified theory and, 75–76
Computer Emergency Response Team
  (CERT), 193, 264
computer models, 47, 89n3
computers: capacity growth of, 121;
  complexity and, 89n3; invention of, 72
computer viruses, 64, 193, 265
Congress of Industrial Organizations, 242
connections, in systems: and boundaries,
  79; ignorance of, 53; between
  individual and world, 56–58; invisible
  system detection and, 176; among
  unrelated events, 61–68
ConocoPhillips, 97
Conrail, 241
consensus techniques, 17
consent, 56–57
Consumer Federation of America, 228
containerization, 235–46; and bulk-flow
  systems, 235, 236; consumer effects of,
  240; freight workers and, 240–41; and
  immigration increase, 222–23; impact of,
  238–41; invention of cargo containers,
  235, 237; labor unions and, 241–45; and
  revolution in freight industry, 236–38;
  U.S.-Asia trade and, 238
continental drift, 40
conversion processes, 82
Cook, James, 40
corporatism, in national-industrial elite,
  226–27
Cox, Robert, 210
Crook, Clive, 212
CropVerifeye.com, 191
CSX Transportation, 239–40
culture: commodification of, 209;
  comparative study of, 5; complexity

and, 111; definitions of, 4–5; global, 5–6
cybernetics: development of, 72; feedback in, 72; systems thinking and, 71–73
Cyber Patrol, 193
cyberspace, 255–67; "cybernation" in, 256; economics of, 259–69; government of, 260–65; metaphors for, 265–66; self-government of, 262–64; structure of, 255–59; word origin, 255. *See also* Internet
cybiont, 18

Davies, Paul, 116
DeBoer, David, 235, 237
decentralized networks, 181
degrees of separation, 182
Delphi technique, 17
democracy, effect of globalization on, 190, 212, 231
Department of Commerce, 263, 264
Department of Defense, 238, 239
Department of Transportation, 243
depersonalization of work, and distributed networks, 183
deregulation, railroad, 238, 239
De Rosnay, Joël, 18, 266
deterministic chaos, 76
diffusion: bulk flow compared with, 142; and entropy, 141; in human relations, 142–43
digitalization, 150–153; versus analog signal, 152, 153; binary condition and, 151, 152; versus continuous waves, 150; and digital computers, 152–53
diseases, tracking of, 192. *See also* epidemiology
dissipative structures, 109, 114–17; and cost externalization, 140–41; in open systems, 87, 115–16; political aspects of, 140–41; and power asymmetry, 141; processes of, 116–17; and self-maintaining systems, 115; in social systems, 116; unnoticed, 115, 140
distributed networks, 181
diversity: reduction of, 62–63; as self-reinforcing, 111

Doctors without Borders, 231
Dodge, Martin, 177, 255
domain names, Internet, 263–64
domestic interests, and foreign policy, 169–70
Donovan, Arthur, 236
Drug Enforcement Administration, 191
drugs, pharmaceutical: for AIDS, 27–29, 231; generic, 27–29, 231
Dyson, George, 266

Earthlink, 258
Eckert, J. Presper, 72
ecolacy, 10, 45, 176
ecological footprint (EF): of cities, 139–40; definition of, 139; versus ecologically productive land, 139; per individual, 139; of London, 140; of Vancouver, 140
ecology: carrying capacity, 11–12; coevolution, 10–11; definition of, 9–10; energy flow, 11; on human role, 42, 44; of Internet, 266–67. *See also* ecosystems
economics, 6–9; AIDS perspective of, 26–29; international political economy, 7–8; multinational corporations (MNC), 8–9; system components, 6–7
ecosystems: fragility of, 10; imbalance, case study of, 129–36; scale of, 10; self-regulation of, 10
ectropy, 86
Edison, Thomas, 149
EDVAC (Electronic Discrete Variable Automatic Computer), 72–73
EF. *See* ecological footprint
Einstein, Albert, 57, 88
electricity, 148–50; history of, 148–49; information technologies and, 150
electronic commerce, 186
Electronic Frontier Foundation, 260
El Niño, 48
e-mail, 256
emergent properties: complexity of universe and, 111; and futurism, 16; in self-organizing systems, 75; in systems, 78–79, 108
emerging paradigm, 43–44

endangered species, 62
energy: complexity and, 112; definition of, 94; flow of, 11, 95; in open systems, 113; real-time, 95; stocks of (*see* stored energy); in systems, 86, 113. *See also* global energy system
Engelbart, Douglas, 160n37
ENIAC (Electronic Numerical Integrator and Computer), 72
Enlightenment thought, 41-42
entertainment, 68
entropy: and body functions, 138; and cities, 138–39; in closed systems, 87; commodification of, 140; definition of, 86, 108; dissipative structures and, 87, 109, 114–17; information and, 86; in open systems, 86; in physical systems, 109; and size of system, 114; and transport imperative of systems, 138
Environmental Defense Fund, 192
environmentalism: global capitalism and, 186–87; on human role, 42, 44; and invisible global systems, 192–93
Environmental Working Group, 192
epidemiology, 32–33, 188, 197–202. *See also* diseases, tracking of
Epitope, 201–2
equilibrium: complex systems and, 119–20; feedback and, 83; market, 90n15; as system goal, 75
euro, 228
European Union, 228
Evergreen Line (Taiwan), 239
evolution, 74; complexity and, 110, 111; growth and, 110
Ewald, Paul, 32
existing paradigm, 43–44
Exxon-Mobil, 97
extinction: language, 62–63; species, 62

fair trade movement, 193
Faraday, Michael, 148
Federal Communications Commission (FCC), 262
Federal Railway Administration (FRA), 243
Federal Trade Commission (FTC), 228–29

feedback, 45; as element of generic system, 82–84; flawed, 123; and growth limits, 122–26; theory development, 72
feedback loops: as basic system unit, 83; of cities and bulk-flow systems, 145; and invisible systems, 181; and lock-in effect, 120; negative, 83–84; with no exit, 145–46; positive, 83–84, 145–46, 181
Fettner, Ann Giudici, 198
fiber-optic cables, 157, 258
Financial Action Task Force, 63
First Amendment, 260–61
food-borne illnesses, 199–202
Ford Foundation, 45; Center for Advanced Study in the Behavioral Sciences, 74
forecasts, 16; after September 11, 2001, terrorist attacks, 163–64
foreign policy, and domestic interests, 169–70
Forrester, Jay, 37, 45, 46, 72, 83, 123
FRA. *See* Federal Railway Administration
Frank, Andre Gunder, 14–15
freedom, individual, 56
freight industry: and containerization, 235–46; as intermodal system, 236, 237, 238, 239; workers, 240–41
Frieden, Jeffrey, 141
Friedman, Thomas, 185, 186, 212–14
Friends of the Earth, 228
Friman, Richard, 184
frustration, global system unaccountability and, 190
FTC. *See* Federal Trade Commission
fuel prices. *See* gasoline prices
fundamentalism, 190
futurism, 15–18; AIDS perspective of, 32–33; emergent properties, 16; information technology, 17–18; organismic analogy, 15; prediction techniques, 16–17

Gaia, 10
Gao Yaojie, 1–2
garment and apparel industry, 185, 190, 192

Garreau, Joel, 163
Garson, Barbara, 19
gasoline prices, 93–94, 100–105; demand-side factors in, 103–5; impact of, 94, 221–22; supply-side factors in, 102–3; system of, 101
Gates Foundation, Bill and Melinda, 29
gay culture, and AIDS, 24
genetically modified organisms, 188
georegistry, Internet, 264
Gerard, Ralph, 74
Geyer, Michael, 36
Gibson, William, 255
Gilmore, John, 260
Glaxo Wellcome, 27
Gleason, Teddy, 244–45
global awareness, 36, 40–58; benefits of, 36; elements of, 44–45; obstacles to, 41, 53; scientific method and, 41–42
global cities, 146
global division of labor, 210–11
global energy system, 93–100; natural foundations of, 95–96; oil production in, 96
global history versus world history, 15
global integration, 210–11, 213
globalization: and antiglobal forces, 147; anti-globalization groups and, 228; asymmetry of, 205-24; benefits of, 212; and city/bulk-flow system interdependence, 145; and commodification of culture, 209; costs of, 211–12; definition of, 1, 3; effect on isolated systems of, 135–36; nation-state politics and, 204–31; public opinion on, 207–8; rise of cities and, 146; roots of, 147
Global Maritime Distress and Safety System, 151
global-postindustrial elites, and politics of globalization, 229–31; activism, 231; expert knowledge, 230; information dissemination, 229; social problem solution, 230; state substitution, 231
Global Systematique, 48–50; systems of, 49
global system dynamics, 46

Global System Paradigm (GSP), 44–58; and analysis, 225–26; benefits of, 36, 55; elements of, 44–45; history of, 45–48; and invisible systems, 176; moral aspect of, 55–57; and politics, 204, 225–26; versus scientific method, 55; and September 11, 2001, terrorist attacks, 165; tools of, 48–52
global warming. *See* climate change
golden straitjacket, 185–86
Gould, Stephen Jay, 109
Great Depression, 147
Gribben, John, 116
Group of 7 (G-7), 63
growth: of animals, 110–11; and complexity of systems, 108–14; controversy about, 109–10; evolution and, 110; limits to, 120–26; linear versus nonlinear (*see* linear versus nonlinear systems); Modis's model of, 118–19, 124; as socially constructed, 124; time horizon and, 121–22
GSP. *See* Global System Paradigm
Guetzkow, Harold, 143–44
Gulf War: gasoline prices and, 101, 104; U.S. petroleum reserves and, 103

Haeckel, Ernst, 10, 45
Hague Convention on Jurisdiction and Foreign Judgments, 261
Hall, Thomas, 13
Hanjin Shipping (South Korea), 239
Hardin, Garret, 45
Hawking, Stephen, 88
Hazen, Harold, 72
hepatitis A, 197–202
Hiassen, Carl, 123
hierarchy, 80, *81*
historical interpretation, 12–13
history, 12–15; AIDS perspective of, 30–31; analogy and, 13; global history vs. world history, 15; interpretation of history, 12–13; laws of history, 12; world systems, 13–14
HIV. *See* AIDS
Hoffa, Jimmy, 243
holarchy, 108–9

holism: definition of, 55; versus mechanism, 55–56; versus scientific method, 71
Holland, John, 111, 179
homogenization, promotion of, 62–63
Huberman, Bernardo, 179, 266
human competition with animals, 66–68
Human Dimension of Global Environmental Change Program, 48
humanism, 41–42
hypertext, 155, 160n37, 259

ICANN. *See* Internet Corporation for Assigned Names and Numbers
ICC. *See* Interstate Commerce Commission
IdentityPreserved.com, 191
IETF. *See* Internet Engineering Task Force
IGBP. *See* International Geosphere Biosphere Program
ILA. *See* International Longshoremen's Association
illicit business, as invisible system, 184–85
Illinois Central-Gulf Railroad (ICG), 243–44
ILWU. *See* International Longshore and Warehouse Union
immigration: and exploitation, 222–23; illegal, 63, 184–85; labor demand and, 217; tuberculosis and, 65
income distribution, 205, 206
incrementalism, 17
individual, and global system, 56–58
industrial dynamics, 45
industrial-mechanical worldview, 55–56
information: access to, 177; bulk-flow systems for (*see* bulk-flow information systems); complexity and, 87; costs of, 158; entropy and, 86; and invisible systems, 180; noise, 87; and system effects, 158; in systems, 87
information flow: and central switching points, 143–44; and system performance, 123–26
information gap, 158
information revolution, and system effects, 157–58

information technology: and boundary extension, 17–18; and demands on electric power, 150
information theory: binary condition in, 73; bits in, 73; systems thinking and, 73–74
initial conditions, sensitive dependence on, 76, 118, 135, 179
input, as element of generic system, 82
Institute of Medicine of the National Academy of Sciences, 65
Intel Corporation, 153
interest groups, 224–31
intermodal systems, 236, 237, 238, 239
international agreements, 8
International Biological Project, 48
International Geophysical Year Project, 48
International Geosphere Biosphere Program (IGBP), 48
International Institute for Applied Systems Analysis, 47
International Longshore and Warehouse Union (ILWU), 242, 244, 245, 246
International Longshoremen's Association (ILA), 242, 244–45
International Monetary Fund (IMF), 223, 228
international political economy (IPE), 7–8; liberal view, 7, 21n18; Marxist view, 8; realist view, 7–8
International Social Science Council, 48
Internet, 50, 179–80; censorship of, 260–61; as distributed network, 181; ecologies, 266–67; as electronic commons, 260, 267; georegistry for, 264; globalization effects of, 216; history of, 153–55; metaphors for, 265–66; security issues on, 193, 264; self-government of, 262–64. *See also* cyberspace
Internet Corporation for Assigned Names and Numbers (ICANN), 263–64
Internet Engineering Task Force (IETF), 263, 265
Internet Protocol (IP), 154, 257, 262
Internet Service Providers (ISPs), 258, 262
Interpol, 191
interpretation, historical, 12–13

interspecies competition, 66–68
Interstate Commerce Commission (ICC), 237, 242, 243
invariances, in systems. *See* common properties, in systems
"invisible hand," 119
invisible global systems: consequences of, 185–90; economics and government restraints in, 185–86; external costs of, 186–87; making visible of, 191–93; unaccountability of, 189–90; unintended consequences, 187–88
invisible systems, 174–93; access to information and, 177; complexity and, 178–80; distributed networks and, 181–83; information processing and, 180–81; intentional hiding and, 183–85; knowledge dependence of, 176–78; nonlinearity and, 178–80; and September 11, 2001, terrorist attacks, 165; social class division and, 178. *See also* invisible global systems
IPE. *See* international political economy
Iraheta, Vilma, vii
Iranian Revolution, and gasoline prices, 104
Iran-Iraq War, and gasoline prices, 104
isolationism, 147
ISPs. *See* Internet Service Providers

Jablonski, David, 109
Jacobson, Jodi, 139
Janelle, Donald, 146
Jantsch, Erich, 115
Jefferson, Thomas, 56
Jervis, Robert, 41

Kahn, Robert, 113, 154
Katz, Daniel, 113
Kauffman, Stuart, 74, 75, 78, 80, 110, 111, 114, 121
Kennedy, Paul, 189
Kilby, Jack, 153
Kitchin, Rob, 255
knowledge dependence, 176–78
Kuhn, Thomas, 38–39
Kurzweill, Ray, 17–18, 266
Kyoto accord on global warming, 105

labor, global division of, 210–11
labor unions, and containerization, 241–45
Lange, John, 244
language, for describing systems, 176–77
language extinction, 62–63
lasers, 157
Laszlo, Ervin, 55, 80, 107–9
Leibniz, Gottfried Wilhelm, 71
LePen, Jean-Marie, 190
Limits to Growth, The, 46, 47
linear versus nonlinear systems, 77, 117–20, 179; aggregation, 117; multiplication, 117–18
Liverpool & Manchester Railroad, 236
lock-in effect, 120
logistical growth, 118–19, 124, 125
London, ecological footprint of, 140
Lorenz, Edward, 76, 118

M & M agreement. *See* Modernization & Mechanization agreement
Maastricht Treaty, 228
macrohistory, 14
"Made in U.S.A." label, 228–29
Maersk (Denmark), 239
Manhattan Project, 72
Mankind at the Turning Point, 46
Marconi, Guillermo, 156
Martin, Lisa, 230
Massachusetts Institute of Technology (MIT), 45, 46, 47, 121
Matson Navigation Company, 237–38
Mauchly, John H., 72
Maxwell, James Clerk, 72, 85
McLean, Malcom, 235, 237
McShea, Dan, 109
Meadows, Dennis, 46, 72
mechanistic thinking, 55–56
medicine, 27
Melko, Matthew, 5
mercantilism. *See* international political economy: realist view
Merck, 27, 28, 29
metaphors, for cyberspace, 265–66. *See also* analogy
Metcalfe's Law, 259–60
meteorology, and complexity theory, 76

Middle East war, gasoline prices and, 104
Milgram, Stanley, 181, 182
MIT. *See* Massachusetts Institute of Technology
Mittelman, James, 210
MNCs. *See* multinational corporations
models, computer, 47, 89n3; *see also* paradigms
Modernization & Mechanization (M & M) agreement, 244
Modis, Theodore, 118–19, 124
money laundering, 63–64
Moore, Gordon, 121
Moore's Law, 121
morality: and global awareness, 55–57; temporal horizons of system and, 88–89, 122
Morse, Samuel F. B., 151
Mulgan, Geoff, 56–57, 159n13
multinational corporations (MNCs), 8–9; benefits of, 9; containerization and, 239; impact on economy of, 8; power of, 8–9; and state power decline, 8
Munger, Fredi, 190
Murphy's Law, versus normal accidents, 188

NAFTA. *See* North American Free Trade Agreement
national-industrial elites, and politics of globalization, 226–29; corporatism, 226–27; court system use, 229; lobbying, 228–29; pluralism, 227
National Intermodal Network, 243
nationalism, 42, 190
national policy, and global economics, 185–86
National Science Foundation (NSF), 154–55, 263
National Wildlife Federation, 228
nation-state politics, and globalization, 211–31; elites versus non-elites, 226; foreign trade effects, 224–25; "four-party system," 213–14; global market-domestic social stability tension, 211–12; global-postindustrial elites, 229–31; national-industrial elites, 226–29; power decline, 8, 185–86

natural systems: coordination of, 108–9; growth and complexity of, 108–14; maintenance of, 108; wholeness of, 108
Naughton, John, 266
Nelson, Ted, 160n37
neoliberalism, 186
Netscape Communications Corporation, 160
"netwar," 174–75
Network Solutions, 263
Neumann, John von, 72
New Balance Athletic Shoe Company, 228–29
Newcomen, Thomas, 86
"new world order," 147
New York City, 166–67, 170–71, 176
New York Mercantile Exchange (NYMEX), 103, 104
New York Times, 62–64, 65–66, 68
noise, in information, 87
nongovernmental organizations (NGOs), 229–31
nonlinear systems: invisibility of, 178–80; versus linear, 77, 179
normal accidents, in complex systems, 187–88; versus Murphy's Law, 188; reasons for, 187–88
normal science, 38–39
North American Free Trade Agreement (NAFTA), 8, 218
Noyce, Robert, 153
NSF Net, 155
NYMEX. *See* New York Mercantile Exchange

Øersted, Hans, 148
Offe, Claus, 208
oil: deposits of, 96; extraction of, 97; production of, 96, 102; transportation of, 97–100, 102–3
Omukuba, Paul, 33–34
O'Neill, John, 25–26
OPEC (Organization of Petroleum Exporting Countries), 102
open system, 79–80; dissipative structures in, 87, 115–16; energy in, 113; entropy in, 86

operational code, 16
organismic analogy: in futurism, 15; in history, 13
oscillation, of growth, 125, 126
Outbreak, 192
output, as element of generic systems, 82
overriding problem, 16
overshoot, 114, 125, 135, 187
Ozone Action, 192

packet switching, 154, 256–57
Pagels, Heinz, 127n21
Palo Alto Research Center (PARC), 179, 266
Pan Atlantic Steamship Company, 237. *See also* Sea-Land Services
paradigms, 37–44; definition of, 38; emerging, 43–44; existing, 43–44; of globalization, 40–44; purpose of, 37–38; in social interaction, 38–39; in thought processes, 38
paradigm shift: Columbus and, 40; continental drift and, 40; definition of, 38; process of, 39; resistance to, 39–40
Pavarotti, Luciano, 205
Peccei, Aurelio, 45
Peet, John, 94
Perdue Farms, 223
Perelman, Lewis, 89, 122
Perrow, Charles, 187–88
Pfizer, 27
pharmaceutical firms: and AIDS pandemic, 27–29; and anthrax scare, 166; and generic drugs, 27–29
pipelines, gasoline, 98–99; as invisible system, 183–84
plague, bubonic, 30–31
pluralism, in national-industrial elite, 227
Poincaré, Jules Henri, 76
Polanyi, Michael, 45
policy, national, 185–86
politics. *See* nation-state politics, and globalization
population: change in, 51; tracking relocations in, 192
populism, 190
postmodernism, 42
Prigogine, Ilya, 114, 115

projections, and complex systems, 122. *See also* forecasts
Project on the Predicament of Mankind, 46
protectionism, 147
Public Citizen, 228

Quadrtech Corporation, 229

radio, 156
Rail-Trailer Company, 243
Rapoport, Anatol, 54, 55, 74, 78, 143
rational humanism. *See* secular humanism
Reagan, Ronald, 185–86, 199
real-time energy, 95
reciprocity, 57
recognition, pattern, 56, 164
Rees, William, 139–40
Refugees International, 192
ReliefNet, 192
risk assessment, 164
Robertson, Roland, 3–4, 40–41, 44
Roche, 27, 28–29
Rodrik, Dani, 211–12
Rogowski, Ronald, 141, 224–25
Romanticism, 42
Ronfeldt, David, 174
Rothschild, Michael, 164
routing, of Internet messages, 154, 258
Royal Dutch/Shell, 97
Ruelle, David, 76, 87, 114
Ryan, Gene, 243

SafeWeb, 260
Santa Fe Institute, 75, 120
satellites, 157
Scholte, Jan Aart, 231
science fiction, 17
scientific method: global awareness and, 41–42; versus Global System Paradigm, 55; versus holism, 71; social replication of, 42
Scorecard, 192
Sea-Land Services, 237–38, 239
search engines, 259
secular humanism, 41–42
self-organizing complexity, 75, 266

sensitive dependence on initial conditions, 76, 118, 135, 179
September 11, 2001, terrorist attacks: economic consequences of, 165–71; gasoline prices and, 104; "netwar" and, 174–75; statistical ambiguity and, 162–63; systematic thinking about, 162–65
sequential development, 16
Servomechanisms Laboratory, 72
sexuality, 67–68
Shannon, Claude, 73, 86, 87, 153
Sheridan, Mary Beth, vii
Shockley, William, 153
Sierra Club, 228
sigmoid curve. *See* logistical growth
SilentSurf, 260
Simon, H. A., 143–44
Singh, Ram Lakhan, 66
size: of animals, 110–11; of systems, 114
small world phenomenon, 181–83; and invisibility, 182
Smil, Vaclav, 11
Smith, Adam, 119
social physics, 16
Society for General Systems Research, 74
sociology, 4–6; AIDS perspective of, 25–26; civilization comparisons, 5; cultural identities and differences, 4–5; global culture, 5–6
Sola Pool, Ithiel de, 181
South, American, 214–15, 217
Southern Pacific Railroad, 238
Southern Railway, 237
species introduction, 130–33
Speke, John Hanning, 130
SPR. *See* Strategic Petroleum Reserve, U.S.
Sprint, 258
SRI International, 264
Stanford Research Institute, 154
Starbucks, 218
state socialism, 186
steady state, 79
Stewart, Ian, 111
stored energy, 95–96
Strategic Petroleum Reserve, U.S. (SPR), 103
Strogatz, Steven, 144

structural certainties, 16
structural requisites, 16
sustainable development versus global capitalism, 186–87
Swan, Joseph, 149
sweatshop conditions, 185, 190, 192
Sweatshop Watch, 192
system dynamics, 107–26
systems, 71–89; cause-and-effect and, 77; closed (*see* closed system); common properties of, 53; dynamics of (*see* system dynamics); energy in, 86, 113; entropy in, 85–86, 108, 114; generic, 82; holism and, 55; information in, 87, 123–26; laws of, 53; natural (*see* natural systems); open (*see* open system); processes of, 84; structure and functioning of, 77–84; time and, 88–89. *See also* natural systems
systems thinking: advantages of, 53–54; cybernetics and, 71–73; in everyday life, 70; versus industrial/mechanical worldview, 55–56; information theory and, 73–74; metaphors and, 265; obstacles to acceptance of, 70–71; versus scientific method, 71

tacit knowledge, 45
Tainter, Joseph, 112–13
TCP/IP, 154, 257, 262
Teamsters Union, 228
telegraph, 155–56
teleological fallacy, 78
telephony, 151–52, 156; submarine telephone cables, 157
television, 156
terrorist attacks. *See* September 11, 2001, terrorist attacks
Thatcher, Margaret, 185–86
thermodynamics, 85–86; laws of, 86, 108, 115–16, 138
Thomas, William (Baron Kelvin), 114–15
Thompson, Robert, 164
time: evolutionary conception of, 88; growth and, 121–22; nonlinear systems and, 179; scientific conception of, 88; systems and, 88–89

Tomlinson, John, 4–5, 53
Tomlinson, Ray, 256
Total-FinaElf, 97
tourism, 167, 169
tracking invisible systems, 191–93; in
    agriculture, 191–92; in cyberspace,
    193; of disease, 192; in environment,
    192–93; of population, 192
Trade Related Aspects of Intellectual
    Property Rights (TRIPS), 28
TransFair USA, 193
Transmission Control Protocol/Internet
    Protocol (TCP/IP), 154, 257, 262
transport, transportation: in circulatory
    system, 141–42; containerization and,
    235–41; intermodal systems and, 236,
    237, 238, 239; labor unions in,
    241–45; of oil, 97–100; as system
    imperative, 137–41; and unintended
    consequences, 188; vectors and, 199
trends, 16; after September 11, 2001,
    terrorist attacks, 163–64
triangle manufacturing, as invisible
    system, 185
TRIPS. *See* Trade Related Aspects of
    Intellectual Property Rights
tuberculosis, 65
Tukey, J. W., 73

uncertainty, 87
United Nations, 230; U.N. Development
    Program, 207; U.N. Economic and
    Social Council, 48; U.N. Environment
    Program, 48
United Steelworkers of America, 228
United Transportation Union (UTU), 242,
    244
U.S. Public Health Service, 23

vaccination, and AIDS, 24
values, globalization and traditional, 216,
    217–18
Vancouver, ecological footprint of, 140
VantagePoint.com, 192
vectors, 199
Velazquez, Miguel, 217
Verite, 190, 192
Verizon, 258

Victoria, Lake (East Africa), 129–36;
    ecosystem imbalances of, 130–36; fish
    population of, 130–32; industry and
    pollution, 132–33; plant introduction,
    133
viruses: biological, 197–202; computer,
    64, 193, 265
VisualRoute, 258
Vogel, Steven, 141
Volk, Tyler, 10, 112
Volkswagen Foundation, 46
Volta, Alessandro, 148

Wackernagel, Mathis, 139–40
Wang Tai-ching, 220
Warner-Lambert, 27
Washington Post, 64–68
Waterfront Employers Association, 244
Watt, James, 86
Watts, Duncan, 144
waves, continuous, 150
weather forecasting, and complexity
    theory, 76
Wegener, Alfred, 40
Weinberg, Gerald, 70
welfare state, 211–12
West Nile virus, 176
White, Heather, 190
Wiener, Norbert, 72, 87, 255
winners and losers in globalization,
    205–24; in China, 220–21; loser
    participation in process, 246; losers,
    218–24; winners, 214–18
World Bank, 223–24, 230
World Climate Research Program, 48
World Conservation Union (WCU), 62, 135
world domestic product, distribution of,
    206
World Health Organization, 28, 191, 198,
    230
world history: versus global history, 15;
    and globalization, 37
World Meteorological Organization, 48
World Ocean Circulation Experiment, 48
world problematique, 45–46
world systems, 13–14; Afro-Eurasian, 14
World Trade Organization (WTO), 28, 29,
    211, 220, 228, 231

World War I, 147
World War II, 147
World Wide Web, 155, 259; as self-organizing system, 266; World Wide Web Consortium (W3C), 262–63

Yahoo!, 261

Zebco Corporation, 221
Zhirinovsky, Vladimir, 190
Zuboff, Shoshana, 180

About the Author

Robert P. Clark is professor of government in the Department of Public and International Affairs and director of the Honors Program in General Education at George Mason University in Fairfax, Virginia. For more than a decade he was coordinator of the interdisciplinary program in global systems and taught courses in global systems at George Mason. His most recent books on globalization are *Global Life Systems: Population, Food, and Disease in the Process of Globalization* (2001) and *The Global Imperative: An Interpretive History of the Spread of Humankind* (1997).